Reparation
in World Politics

Reparation in World Politics

France and European Economic Diplomacy, 1916–1923

Marc Trachtenberg

Columbia University Press
New York
1980

The author and publisher gratefully acknowledge the generous support given them by the National Endowment for the Humanities. Research leading to this book was funded by a Summer Stipend, and publication has been assisted by a further grant from the Endowment.

Library of Congress Cataloging in Publication Data

Trachtenberg, Marc, 1946–
  Reparation in world politics.

  Bibliography: p.
  Includes index.
  1. European War, 1914–1918—Reparations. 2. France
—Foreign economic relations. 3. European War, 1914–
1918—Germany. I. Title.
D648.T72   940.3′1422   79-26898
ISBN 0-231-04786-X

Columbia University Press
New York   Guildford, Surrey

Contents

Preface

AFTER THE FIRST World War, the Allies tried to make Germany compensate them for some of the damages they had suffered; this attempt to extract reparation dominated European politics during the critical period immediately following the conclusion of peace. It was in fact the conflict over reparation in the early 1920s, climaxing in the Ruhr occupation of 1923, that in large measure determined the structure of power in Europe. The outcome of this struggle sealed the fate of the system of restraints on German power imposed at Versailles, and thus paved the way for the resurgence of Germany as the dominant force on the European continent.

Is there any point to taking a fresh look at reparation? One might suppose that the definitive verdict of history has already been rendered and that little of any consequence remains to be said on the subject. Although the specialized literature has always been reserved and moderate, it is not too much of an exaggeration to say that the historical profession as a whole has long held rather strong views on the subject. Judging from the textbooks and general accounts, it seems that a wide range of scholars still holds to what might be called the orthodox interpretation: that it was economically impossible for Germany to pay reparation on anything like the scale prescribed in the Treaty of Versailles; that for this "preposterous" demand, the "vengeful" policy of France was primarily responsible; that the French hoped to use reparation to "debilitate" Germany in order to assure their own security, and that for this reason the French government refused to compromise on reparation in the immediate postwar period, insisting instead on the strict application of the treaty. The more detailed studies are generally more measured in tone; the analysis, particularly in recent years, has become more scientific in nature. But much of the spirit of the traditional interpretation still persists, even in the best recent works; and the orthodox approach has never been subject to systematic analysis.

This interpretation will, however, be examined here. The focus will be on French policy, and in this area the analysis, I think, substantially discredits traditional views. The French government, it will be shown, did not intend to "crush" Germany under an enormous reparation burden, but rather hoped during and immediately after the war to solve France's economic problems primarily through what it called Allied economic cooperation. America's refusal to go along with these schemes led the French government to threaten huge reparations as a way of inducing the Americans to change their minds. When this did not work, it stated its real demands; French reparation policy then more or less converged with that of the United States, and it was British insistence on higher figures at the peace conference that blocked agreement on what was then considered a reasonable fixed sum of 30 billion dollars. Moreover, beginning at this time—that is, in the middle of the peace conference—the French began to make overtures to Germany for a reasonable settlement of economic issues, including reparation. These efforts climaxed in the Seydoux Plan negotiations at the end of 1920. While certainly not the whole story, this striving for "economic collaboration" with Germany was an important and in some respects dominant strain in French policy and deserves to be taken seriously.

But these efforts were ultimately to fail—and this failure was in large measure responsible for the deterioration of the international situation in the early postwar years. Was a settlement along lines acceptable to both France and Germany simply out of the question? Some of the most important German leaders were eager to "seize the outstretched hand" as one of them put it, and work out an arrangement with the French. But their efforts were in the final analysis blocked by the opposition of the great Ruhr industrialists and their allies within the government; overall, Germany made little effort to comply with the reparation provisions of the treaty.

The crisis this normally would have led to was put off for years because the British government, which had been converted to a very moderate position by the beginning of 1920, successfully prevented French action against Germany. Far from being a period of "French predominance in Europe," the very early 1920s were marked by French dependence on, and virtual subordination to, Great Britain. Even Poincaré's coming to power at the beginning of 1922 did little at first to change the situation. There was no headlong rush to coercive tactics; indeed the way Poincaré backed into the occupation of the Ruhr, and hardly knew what he wanted to do once he got there, is one of the most striking aspects of the story.

This study concentrates on Allied, and especially on French, reparation policy; on the whole, other issues are examined only to the extent that they bear directly on this subject. Thus there is not much discussion of domestic politics because I became convinced, and in fact try to demonstrate, that the impact of domestic politics was not nearly as great as many historians had supposed. And similarly the attention given to a foreign policy issue like the problem of the Soviet Union or the Upper Silesian question corresponds not to its inherent importance, but rather to its direct bearing on the diplomacy of reparation.

Is there a need to defend this kind of approach? Perhaps some sense of the larger picture, and of those things which might have had an indirect influence on policy, has been lost. But if the argument was not to go off in all directions, if it was to be developed rigorously and brought into focus, then, it seemed to me, the parameters of the study had to be rather strictly respected. It was in the final analysis a question of personal style. My one regret was that I was not really able to do more than scratch the surface of the German side of the issue. But the German sources are exceptionally rich; and the German issues, closely oriented toward domestic politics and fiscal and economic policy, are to a large degree logically distinct from the problems dealt with here. A full-length study of the reparation question from the German side should certainly be written—and given the current interest in the field, probably will be undertaken in the near future. In any case no one should try to do everything: the principle of the division of labor applies as much to scholarship as to other areas of economic life.

I have been working on this subject for about ten years. If I had been working in a vacuum, I doubt whether anything worthwhile would have ever been produced. So I am deeply grateful for the interest, advice and criticism of a number of people. Richard Kuisel, who directed the dissertation on which this is based, Gerald Feldman, Bruce Kuklick, Charles Maier, Robert Paxton, Jacques Bariéty, Georges Soutou, David Landes, Richard Dunn and especially Vartan Gregorian—I would like to thank all of them for their support, for their having reacted, in their various ways, to the substance of my work. It is difficult to put into words how much all this has meant to me. I wish also to thank the National Endowment for the Humanities and the American Philosophical Society for supporting some of the research on which this book is based. But above all I want to express my gratitude to two people: my wife Susan, and the late Raymond Sontag, who taught me what it is to be an historian.

One final note on the system of references: I have tried to keep the baggage of source citation light, so abbreviated forms have been used extensively. In keeping with accepted procedure, a full reference is given the first time an abbreviated source is cited. But to spare the interested reader a tedious search for the first footnote, abbreviations are explained and listed at the end of the volume.

Reparation
in World Politics

A New Chapter One
Economic Order

AS THE First World War drew suddenly to a close in the fall of 1918, it was clear in France that victory would not in itself solve all the nation's problems. The economic situation was particularly disturbing. The devastation in the north of France had been so enormous, and the economic and financial side effects of the war had been so wide-ranging, that the country would inevitably face a severe and complex problem of reconstruction. What kind of solution did the French government have in mind?

Traditional historiography had a simple answer: German reparations, it was hoped, would solve the whole problem. But in fact French leaders looked not to Germany but to their allies for a solution. Allied cooperation would enable France to overcome her economic problems, and to secure it became a central aim of French policy during and immediately after the war.

Within the government, it was the Ministry of Commerce that was most active in formulating policy on postwar economic matters. This ministry worked out a definite economic program for the postwar period, and its plans in fact came to represent the policy of the government as a whole. It was the Minister of Commerce, Etienne

Some of the material in this chapter was first published in the Fall 1977 issue of *French Historical Studies* and is reprinted by permission of the editor.

Clémentel, who represented the French government in vital negotiations with the Allies on these postwar questions and it was his policy in these matters that was presented to the Parliament in February 1918 as official government policy. More important, a lengthy exposition of his views on postwar economic problems was formally accepted by Prime Minister Georges Clemenceau in September 1918 as the official basis of postwar economic policy, and French policy after the armistice actually proceeded along these lines.[1]

Clémentel had been made Minister of Commerce in the government of Aristide Briand that took office in October 1915. He remained in this post in various cabinets until shortly after his defeat in the elections of November 1919. During his long tenure as minister he developed a sure sense of his own ability and importance. He had, moreover, something of an artist's temperament—as a young man he had studied to be a painter—and a taste for grandiose and imaginative ideas was the most striking characteristic of his policy. He wanted nothing less than a radical restructuring of both the French and the international economy—a shift to a system where the state would assume primary responsibility for the control of economic life. He felt he had found in the suppression of the free market the solution to the principal short- and long-term economic problems that France, and indeed the world, would face. In Clémentel's mind, "organization," both on the national and the international level, was a magic word. An ordered economy, based on cooperation rather than competition, had to replace the "anarchy" of the free market. The policy he pursued took this set of assumptions as its point of departure.[2]

Clémentel's vision of a "new economic order" was generally shared by his collaborators at the Ministry of Commerce. His most intimate associate—his "alter ego," according to the well-informed economist Léon Polier—was Henri Hauser, the eminent historian of early modern Europe.[3] The young Jean Monnet, the Ministry of Commerce representative in London, actively participated in the execution of Clémentel's policy. The presence of Monnet suggests a certain link with important post-1945 developments—economic planning in France and European economic integration—and thus gives the discussion here a particular interest.[4]

What the Ministry of Commerce as a whole ultimately aspired to was a permanent, universal system where world resources would be pooled and allocated at fixed prices on the basis of "need."[5] Germany, its officials contended, would eventually receive her fair share of these resources, if she restrained her ambitions and accepted the place offered her in the new economic and political order. For the period of transition right after the war, the system would be modified somewhat to favor France and Belgium. Because of the scarcity of raw materials, Germany at this time would be allocated less than the share to which she would normally be entitled. Times would then be hard for the Germans, but never was it proposed that their economy be crushed. Indeed, Clémentel and his collaborators repeatedly insisted that there would eventually be room for a reformed Germany to participate fully in the new system.[6]

The important thing, however, was to moderate German ambitions and bring German industrial activity into harmony with the rest of the world economy. For the Germans, seen as peculiarly industrious, efficient and economically aggressive, were viewed with mixed feelings of fear and admiration. The best measure of this attitude toward Germany is that in the midst of the slaughter, Ministry of Commerce planners sought consciously to emulate German methods.[7] Germany, it was commonly believed, had discovered the "secret of organization." This was held largely responsible for her impressive and dangerous commercial success before 1914. Artificial restraints were necessary lest Germany again threaten to overwhelm her neighbors economically, and reestablish her economic hegemony in Europe.

But how could such a system of controls be brought into being? Clémentel felt that the creation of an Allied economic bloc was of central importance in this regard. Wartime feelings of comradeship and solidarity provided an optimal environment for the formation of such a bloc; once it came into being, the Allied organization would be the core of a larger international system. The idea of a permanent Allied economic union had in fact been mooted about in the press virtually since the beginning of the war. Public discussion focused on the possibility of creating preferential tariffs among the Allied nations. Clémentel, on the other hand, stressed the importance of establishing an inter-Allied control of raw materials: the Allied governments, acting together, would directly ration out, at prices set by them, the vast supplies of raw materials they controlled. Such an arrangement would be the key feature of the Allied-led economic bloc he hoped to see emerge in some form from the war. The control of raw materials, to be sure, would be supplemented by other forms of cooperation—especially by preferential tariffs within the bloc and by accords on financial and currency questions—but in the final analysis these features were of secondary importance.[8]

The creation of such a bloc, in Clémentel's mind, had both economic and political functions. By providing a steady supply of raw materials at fair prices, and also by helping to secure export markets by means of favorable tariff arrangements, the proposed system would help France overcome the severe postwar economic problems that she would otherwise face. The new structure, moveover, would provide a permanent basis for an orderly expansion of trade, and defend against what were viewed as violent policies of commercial "aggression," such as the Germans were supposed to have practiced before the war. Allied economic power could also be mobilized for political ends. By threatening to cut off Germany's supply of vital raw materials, her ruling caste could be brought to renounce what Clémentel and his associates assumed to be its ambition to dominate the world. Moreover, they felt that removing conflicts over raw materials by instituting a system for the distribution of these commodities on the basis of "need" would in itself be an important step toward world peace.

The "organization" of French industry completed the Ministry of Commerce plan. Under the guidance of the state, firms within an industry would cooperate with one another, sharing technical knowledge, dividing markets, each perhaps specializing in the manufacture of particular products. Destructive competition would be avoided, and price stability assured. More generally, in guiding the development of production, the state would preserve economic balance, ensuring a measured and secure growth in output.[9]

Schemes to organize French industry and plans to organize world trade were thus both animated by the same spirit. Moreover, the two sides of Clémentel's policy complemented each other. Industrial organization at home, for example, was needed to provide the means of distributing raw materials allocated to France by international bodies. It was only through such measures of centralization that needs could be determined and rations justified. And in fact during the war the two forms of organization developed together, reaching their fullest development in 1918.

Clémentel had begun much earlier to lay the basis for the implementation of his plans. At the end of 1915, soon after he became minister, he took the initiative in calling for an inter-Allied meeting to discuss the matter.[10] This attempt was successful, and an Allied Economic Conference was convened in Paris in June 1916. There were delegations from Britain, France and Italy, Belgium and Portugal, Russia, Serbia and Japan. (The United States had not yet entered the war.) Wartime measures were discussed, but the principal accomplishment of the conference was the adoption of a program of postwar economic collaboration.[11]

At the conference, Clémentel stressed the importance of instituting an inter-Allied control of raw materials. No raw material under Allied control, he felt, should be released for sale to the rest of the world before the needs of all the Allied nations for that commodity had been met. If only the Allies would organize themselves in this way, he said, they could be the "masters of the future."[12] He therefore urged that each ally prepare an inventory of its natural resources and raw materials—inventories that would be compared with requirements to determine which raw materials had to be produced in greater quantity: "We are at the beginning of a new economic era, one which permits the application of new methods, founded on control, on collaboration, on everything that can introduce some order into the process of production. If the Allies know how to put these ideas into practice, they will have founded a new order of things which will mark one of the great turning points in the economic history of the world."[13]

The British delegation at the conference, led by the Colonial Secretary and Tory leader Andrew Bonar Law, seemed to support Clémentel completely on this and other points; Italy and Russia were more reticent. For that reason, the resolutions of the conference, which were not binding in any case, did not go as far as Clémentel would have liked. The control of raw material was accepted, but only for the period of economic restoration; and instead of actually setting up a system of preferential tariffs within the Allied bloc, the Paris program merely called upon each ally not to waive its right to discriminate against Germany commercially—Germany, that is, would not automaticlly be treated as a "most favored nation" for tariff purposes.

Limited though they were, the resolutions of the conference were still not taken too literally by many of the Allied leaders. The

Paris program, with what appeared to some its call for an economic "war after the war," seems, for example, to have repelled many in Britain, and it is hard to know whether it meant anything more to the British government than a threat useful in possible peace negotiations with Germany. But to Clémentel and his associates, the Paris program was of great significance, for in it they saw the charter of the new economic order that they hoped to see emerge from the war.

Were these hopes inevitably doomed to disillusion? One decisive development in the last year of the war convinced Clémentel that there was a real possibility of putting his ideas into effect. An Allied economic organization, similar in scope and structure to the kind of organization to which he aspired, was brought into being at this time to deal with the critical problems then confronting the Alliance. Thus, it would no longer be a question of creating something vastly new to solve postwar problems, but of simply extending and developing the system that already existed. It was precisely this that Clémentel and other French officials had in mind when they spoke of Allied economic "cooperation": postwar "cooperation" came to mean the continuation beyond the armistice of the wartime system of controls exercised by inter-Allied bodies.[14]

To a large degree, the new system grew out of the specific economic and military situation of 1917. By the middle of the year the Allied governments had become painfully aware of the inadequacy of existing systems of supply. The submarine war was cutting deeply into the normal amount of available shipping, while at the same time the need to transport the American army—especially urgent after the collapse of Russia—created large new demands for tonnage. It was no longer possible to allocate ships and supplies in response to the urgent pleadings of prime ministers. A more rational procedure had to be substituted for what was called the "system of competitive panics."[15]

The emergence of the inter-Allied regime was, however, more than just an ad hoc response to the pressing needs of the moment. Clémentel played a leading role in the gradual shaping of the new system: he was consciously seeking to put into effect the kind of policy that he had outlined at the Paris Economic Conference a year earlier.[16] In August 1917 he went to London to win the British over to his ideas. The system he hoped to see take shape during the war, he explained, would be retained to solve the economic problems of the postwar period; a permanent inter-Allied system for the control of world supplies of raw material would be "the practical way of preventing wars in the future." The British received these ideas sympathetically, but they held back from a full and formal acceptance of the French point of view, both in these discussions, and in new talks with Clémentel in October.[17]

Clémentel wanted a system whereby Allied resources would be pooled and allocated by inter-Allied bodies in accordance with need.[18] Because of the scarcity of tonnage, a joint control of shipping was the key to the establishment of a common import program. Anglo-French negotiations therefore focused on this point. But the British wanted to bring the Americans in before they committed themselves wholeheartedly, even for the duration of the war, to a full-fledged inter-Allied system.[19]

American support came more quickly than anyone had anticipated. A high-level American delegation headed by President Wilson's close advisor Colonel Edward House came to Paris in December 1917 to take part in an important Allied conference. Jean Monnet, with the help of J. Arthur Salter, the British Director of Ship Requisitioning, worked out in detail a plan for inter-Allied economic cooperation which was accepted by the Americans and adopted at the conference.[20]

In accordance with this plan a number of inter-Allied committees, called "programme committees" or "executives," were soon created to set import programs for particular classes of commodities. The members of these committees were specialists from corresponding branches of each national administration, so that committee decisions automatically became the policy of each national government. The supply programs elaborated by the programme committees were submitted to the body that allocated shipping space, the Allied Maritime Transport Council (AMTC). Since there was not enough tonnage to carry out the full supply programs, the AMTC had to decide which programs to cut or postpone; in so doing, it set the aggregate supply program of the European Allies. Once this program was set, the War Purchase and Finance Council automatically took care of the financial side of the transaction; American credits were extended to cover these purchases.[21]

The AMTC thus dominated the whole system. Its day-to-day

work was done by its executive (composed of civil servants like Salter and Monnet) while the council itself, staffed by ministers, met occasionally to decide questions of principle. Working together, the members of the executive were able to adjust potentially conflicting national policies as they were being formed—a procedure obviously more efficient than the traditional one of coordinating policies through diplomatic channels only after they had taken final shape. The officials closest to the inter-Allied system were enthusiastic about its possibilities. Here, they felt, was the model of what true international cooperation might be. Salter, writing in 1920, expressed hopes and aspirations that many of his colleagues on the inter-Allied bodies had shared in late 1918. War conditions had "created a kind of hothouse in which international cooperation, normally a delicate plant of slow and precarious growth, developed in a few months to a completeness of form and structure which it must otherwise have taken many years to achieve." In it he could "see something of the probable and desirable development of the future."[22] Gradually, within the context of the League of Nations, governments, he felt, might learn to coordinate their economic policies to the long-term benefit of all.

The hope of extending the inter-Allied economic system beyond the war—a hope shared by most of those directly connected with the new bodies—thus became intertwined with the idea of the League of Nations.[23] The organs of economic cooperation might be made an integral part of the League. In the exercise of international decision making in these areas, a new supranational spirit would be cultivated, and new institutions would gather a strength of their own; this was an important way in which the noble idea of an association of nations could be transformed into something real and truly important in world affairs.

The new system bore a striking resemblance to the scheme Clémentel had long sought to bring into being, and the emergence of the inter-Allied economic regime and the attitude of the Allied officials connected with it clearly encouraged him. He was optimistic in early 1918 that the postwar economic system would grow naturally and easily out of the wartime organization—the essential features of the system that had proved its value during the war would be retained to solve the problems of peace.[24]

This applied not just to the international regime, but also to the system that had taken shape within France for the control of the national economic effort. In 1918, to a large degree as a result of pressure from Britain and the United States,[25] much of French industry was organized into "consortiums." Each consortium purchased and allocated supplies of a particular group of raw materials. The consortiums were supervised by the government—most by the Ministry of Commerce, although the Ministry of Armament, responsible for the sector of the economy most directly related to military needs, controlled some of them—and it was this organization that enabled the state to control imports, regulate many prices, and thereby direct the industrial effort.[26]

The consortiums came into being at about the same time as the inter-Allied system, and the link between the two is unmistakable. The inter-Allied bodies had to know what specific supplies were required and had to be able to satisfy themselves that the contingents assigned would be distributed efficiently and used for proper purposes; only a state-controlled system of industrial organization could fulfill these conditions. On the other hand, an inter-Allied system was the necessary connective tissue tying the various national systems together. The logic of the situation was quite clear: the suppression of the free market on the international level implied its suppression on the national level as well, and vice versa; with the market suppressed, the demand for rationalization and aversion to an ad hoc, arbitrary regime led to the gradual emergence of an increasingly complete system of planning, on the national and on the international levels.

Clémentel hoped that the organization of French industry in one form or another would outlive the war, and it seems that the government as a whole by the end of 1918 had come to share this aspiration—Clemenceau's letter of November 27 outlining the functions of the new Ministry of Industrial Reconstitution actually foresaw a kind of state economic planning.[27] But it was this new ministry, an outgrowth of the wartime Ministry of Armament, and not the Ministry of Commerce, that was to play the leading role in directing the economy—a development that clearly indicates just how much Clémentel's position had been eroded in the course of 1918. He had in fact overplayed his hand, only half-concealing his hope that the consortium regime could be perpetuated in one form or another. Business interests, whose preoccupations were reflected in the *Journée Industrielle,* and others, like the influential economist Léon Polier, had no trouble grasping Clémentel's real intent, and throughout

1918 and into 1919 a lively campaign against the commerce minister's policy was conducted in the press and in Parliament.[28]

As far as Clémentel could see in 1918, there was only one way
of overcoming this opposition: if the inter-Allied system could be
maintained, then a system of economic centralization in France
would also have to be preserved. The consortiums or their equivalent
would still be necessary to determine needs, distribute commodities
received through the inter-Allied bodies, and assure that these imports were used effectively and for proper purposes. The retention of
the inter-Allied economic system was thus of central importance,
valuable not only in itself, but also as a means of perpetuating the
system of state control and industrial organization within France.

The inter-Allied regime could be continued beyond the war's
end only if the British and American governments consented to its
continuation; yet Great Britain and the United States, unlike France,
had little or no direct material interest in the retention of the system.
Was there any reason, therefore, to suppose that the major Allies
would go along with these French ideas? To Clémentel, there seemed
an excellent chance that they would readily "cooperate." In reality
the attitude of both governments was more complex than he knew.

The British were deeply divided on the question of postwar economic policy, and so British policy constantly vacillated and in fact
remained unclear to the end.[29] The British government "approved"
the Paris resolutions, but in Parliament government spokesmen
stressed their vagueness and avoided definite commitments on postwar economic policy.[30] Privately, high officials in the new government which had come to power in December 1916, headed by the dy-
namic and mercurial David Lloyd George, opposed the Paris
program. In April 1917, a discussion of the Paris resolutions took
place in the War Cabinet during which "considerable doubts were
expressed in regard to their expediency." A cabinet committee under
Lord Milner was set up to look into the question of postwar economic
policy. The Milner Committee was hostile to the proposed system,
Lloyd George himself opposed the Paris resolutions, and even Bonar
Law, Chancellor of the Exchequer in the new government, had by
mid-1917 lost his earlier enthusiasm for the Paris program.[31]

Toward the end of 1917, following Clémentel's discussions with
British statesmen in August and October, British policy appeared to

change again. At the suggestion of Sir Edward Carson, like Milner one of the five members of the War Cabinet, an "Economic Offensive Committee" was created to look into the question of postwar economic policy.[32] Carson was made chairman, and his committee framed proposals for the postwar control of raw materials similar in thrust and motivation to the kind of controls advocated by Clémentel.[33] The report was sympathetic to the plight of the continental Allies, and urged a defense against a carefully prepared and highly organized German economic offensive after the war. It stressed the importance of Allied economic organization in bargaining with Germany. The War Cabinet, emphasizing the need to secure American cooperation, approved this report on November 27.[34]

It is nevertheless clear that British leaders continued to be divided on these basic questions. While there was general agreement that the organization of Allied economic might would be a potent force for inducing the Germans to consider peace terms acceptable to the Allies, British leaders did not agree on what actual policy in the postwar period should be. For example, the War Cabinet discussed another Carson Committee report on January 3, 1918. Lord Robert Cecil, Minister of Blockade, favored real postwar cooperation with the Allies. Britain, he believed, should honor her commitments to her associates in the war.[35] But other members of the government disagreed with Cecil. Winston Churchill, then Minister of Munitions, opposed the Carson Committee's recommendations, except insofar as they were merely war measures, necessary "for the wearing down of the enemy."[36] The Carson Committee report was finally approved, but with the proviso that no one's views were compromised, "the measures proposed being accepted as essential as a war measure for bargaining in the peace negotiations and for the rationing of materials in the transitional period at the close of the war."[37] Divided within itself, the government put off further commitment to any particular line of policy. In 1918, Carson continually complained, both inside and outside the government, about its failure to define its policy clearly and in public.[38]

After Carson left the government, a new War Cabinet Committee on "Economic Defence and Development" was set up in mid-1918 headed by Austen Chamberlain, a new member of the War Cabinet. The Chamberlain committee sought to work out a policy statement that could be formally adopted by the government. On September 10, Cecil presented it with a suggested outline for economic policy. He wanted the wartime system of controls to be "completed and continued" during the period of reconstruction, both to protect British interests and to carry out "the obligations which we have repeatedly acknowledged to come to the economic assistance of those of our allies who have suffered most severely from the ravages of war."[39] The idealistic Cecil was still the most ardent advocate of Allied economic collaboration in top-level British circles. He seems to have taken the principle of "equality of sacrifice" seriously, seeing in it a moral imperative transcending immediate national interest.

Again, other elements of the British government did not share Cecil's ardor. His scheme was opposed, for instance, by Sir J. Maclay, the influential Shipping Controller.[40] And John Maynard Keynes, then an important Treasury official, objected even to a thorough-going system of wartime "cooperation." He wrote to Chamberlain in April 1918 to oppose the Italian expert Attolico's advocacy of an inter-Allied regime. He said,

It is not right, for example, that an Inter-Ally body should sit in judgment on the international distribution of British Empire supplies of wool or jute or tin or rubber. The French, on the other hand, mainly with an eye, in our opinion, on postbellum developments have made strong efforts to establish Inter-Allied Executives in just such cases as those I have cited above. I am therefore a little afraid lest Professor Attolico's proposals may play into their hands and allow control of British Empire supplies to pass out of our hands.[41]

Inter-Allied controls would be acceptable, in his view, only if the United States agreed to finance European needs.

The attitude of the Foreign Office is harder to characterize. A long Foreign Office memorandum, circulated to the Chamberlain Committee in late October, called for the continuation of controls during the armistice period—that is, between the ending of hostilities and the conclusion of peace.[42] Indeed, during this period some controls would be strengthened and extended to cover neutral and former enemy nations. But following the peace only a minimal framework for economic cooperation would be retained. The tone of the full document is perhaps as important as its substance. Grudgingly the Foreign Office memorandum admitted Britain's commitment to assist her allies, but at the same time insisted on minimizing the burden this would entail: during the armistice period, "the British Empire should aim at relieving itself, as soon as it can honourably do so, of its most onerous obligations toward the Allies in regard to finance, shipping and raw materials." "The whole basis of the present organization," the memorandum further insisted, "tends to breed irresponsibility in the French and Italian governments mainly at the expense of the British government." Therefore, "the needs of our Allies on the basis of pre-war imports, with additions for the purposes of reconstruction, must to some extent even at first, and after that progressively, be modified by their ability to carry and pay for such imports."[43]

A version of this document (with these possibly offensive passages deleted) was circulated "semiofficially" to Allied and American representatives after the War Cabinet had on November 13 finally adopted a relatively weak plan for continued economic cooperation.[44] Salter explained to them that the revised Foreign Office memorandum "may be taken as indicating generally the considerations influencing" the War Cabinet when it decided to support the continuation of the inter-Allied economic regime.[45] But to the extent that the full document was a true expression of British policy, British eagerness for real cooperation—the kind that would involve British and not just American sacrifice—is open to question.

Yet a month before the War Cabinet formally adopted a policy on November 13, the British Embassy in Washington had presented to the American government a far-reaching plan for postwar economic cooperation. "The Associated Government," this note declared, "are under a moral obligation . . . to carry on during the period of reconstruction that cooperation in the economic sphere which is being developed as a result of war conditions."[46] Thus the British government, though itself reluctant, appeared to the Americans as the champion of the inter-Allied system. The reason for this seems evident: with the United States as a partner, European needs would overwhelmingly be a charge on American rather than British resources. The British could then appear as far-sighted, profoundly concerned with the economic future of Europe, while American rather than British taxpayers would be obliged to bear the lion's share of the bill. Thus the British attitude toward cooperation came to be a function of the American attitude: the British would cooperate if and only if the Americans would.[47]

Everything therefore turned on the attitude of the American government. The Americans had at first strongly opposed the Paris resolutions. Secretary of State Lansing, for example, condemned them in a letter to Wilson in late June 1916, principally because he feared that the program would injure American trade.[48] But after entering the war, the American attitude appeared to change. President Wilson's vision of a "steadfast concert for peace" developed into plans for a League of Nations. Clémentel saw in this his chance to win the American government over to his ideas. In letters to President Wilson in late 1917, he set out his views linking the League with the "economic weapon" that would be created by instituting a permanent control of raw materials.[49]

Clémentel was encouraged by what appeared to be the American response. Colonel House, Wilson's closest adviser, was particularly sympathetic to the French point of view. He supported the idea of legislation that would lay the basis for a postwar control of raw materials, and suggested in January 1918 that France and Britain pass similar legislation.[50] Wilson himself, in a December 1917 speech, alluded to the possibility of postwar restraints on trade with Germany—Clémentel frequently cited this as proof that American policy was evolving in a favorable direction.[51] In fact, when Wilson laid down some basic principles for a restructuring of international affairs in his Fourteen Points speech in January 1918, he was careful to leave the door open to postwar economic discrimination against those nations not fully committed to the peace: his third point called for "the removal, so far as possible, of all economic barriers and the establishment of an equality of trade conditions" but only "among all the nations consenting to the peace and associating themselves for its maintenance."[52]

Thus in early 1918 Clémentel was optimistic about the possibility of putting his plans into effect. The time had come to outline these ideas in public. In articles and speeches, the most important of which was his speech to the Senate in February, Clémentel and his associates sought to inspire confidence that postwar economic problems would be readily resolved.[53] Indeed they stressed that in the Allied economic machinery that had recently come into being, the solution was already at hand. That the wartime regime would be carried over into the period of reconstruction was taken for granted; the more interesting question was whether a permanent economic organization could be instituted.

It was a bold plan for a sweeping and permanent reorganization of the world economy that was now revealed to the French people, but the public reaction was surprisingly tepid. Clémentel's remarks to the Senate were for the most part ignored by the press. The moderate left-wing journal *L'Europe nouvelle,* just about the only important organ to stress the significance of Clémentel's remarks in the Senate, condemned in an editorial "la tacite et unanime entente de la presse française pour n'en point parler, ou presque."[54] What comment there was was generally favorable. *L'Europe nouvelle* fully endorsed Clémentel's views.[55] A number of newspaper articles also supported the concept of an Allied economic association, often linked to the idea of the League of Nations. The head of the Fédération des Industriels et Commerçants Français, André Lebon, supported Clémentel's policy, and the main labor organization, the Confédération Général du Travail, also—but in all likelihood independently—supported the idea of a postwar system of international and national economic controls.[56]

While Clémentel on the whole failed to excite the public imagination, he could console himself with the thought that his policy had not met with any sharp resistance either. With no strong opposition to contend with, he felt he could press on, and in mid-1918 the Ministry of Commerce began to elaborate detailed plans for a new postwar economic order. Hauser played a leading role in this: his memoranda served as the foundation for Clémentel's important letter of September 19, 1918, the clearest and most complete expression of Clémentel's policy on these matters. Indeed, it seems clear that Hauser drafted this document.[57]

The September 19 letter was accepted by Clemenceau as the basis of French policy about a week later. It thus epitomizes French economic policy on the eve of the armistice, and therefore merits careful examination. The letter echoed all the characteristic themes of Clémentel's policy. Allied "cooperation" would see France through the period of reconstruction, but it was a permanent economic bloc and not just a temporary continuation of the wartime regime that was needed. The aim was not to crush Germany, but rather to provide a framework for the ultimate reintegration of Germany into the international economic system: the system itself would restrain German ambitions—both policial and economic—up to the point where they no longer posed a threat to other nations.[58] German power could be counterbalanced and contained only by Allied power—a permanent economic organization was needed if Allied power was to be a reality. This was particularly true in mid-1918: after the peace settlements the Germans had imposed in the east earlier in the year, their dream of a powerful Central European economic bloc seemed well on the way to becoming a reality.

Clémentel's analysis thus focused on the specter of a German-led Mitteleuropa, now (after the Treaty of Brest-Litovsk) extended to include Russia. "It is banal to repeat," Hauser wrote in one of the preliminary memoranda, that the Bolshevik government "is economically in the hands of the Germans." But no Russian government, he argued, could pull the country out of the German economic orbit. Close economic relations between Germany and Russia, he believed, corresponded to a "permanent necessity," and there was little the French could do about it.[59] The September 19 letter itself took a slightly less pessimistic line. "Of course," Clémentel wrote, "France must not abandon all hope of reconquering the Russian market. With her allies she is already doing her best to accomplish this. But it will be a long and difficult task."[60]

In order to avoid being overwhelmed by the now-enlarged Mitteleuropa, Clémentel urged in the letter that an Allied economic union be formed. This would then be the core of an "economic union of free peoples."[61] An inter-Allied control of raw materials would be the heart of this new economic bloc. There would also be a system of preferential tariffs within the block—a return to the old system of commercial equality was still anathema to the Ministry of Commerce officials.

To gain a free hand with which to build the new tariff system, Clémentel continued, the French government had denounced all its old commercial treaties. But it was necessary to act swiftly in laying the foundations of the new system lest France find herself isolated. The British were planning a system of Imperial Preference—that is, of preferential tariffs within the Empire; there was even talk of an Anglo-American commercial entente. It would be deplorable if France were to be admitted to such a British or Anglo-Saxon bloc only as a second-class member.[62] But in the economic union Clémentel and Hauser envisaged, France would play a leading role. It was therefore urgent that the Allies be brought to accept his plans while the memory of France's extraordinary war effort and disproportionate suffering was still fresh in their minds.[63]

Clémentel's concept of an "economic union of free peoples" could easily be tied to the idea of a League of Nations, and in this letter he stressed this connection. This was of more than purely theoretical significance: the American commitment to the League, Clémentel felt, would lead the United States to support his plans. For this reason, he felt confident that the Americans could be brought to accept the French point of view. President Wilson, he wrote, had opposed the specter of a permanent economic bloc raised by the Paris resolutions, but was now "bit by bit coming around to the points of view set out by us in June 1916." As proof of this, he again cited Wilson's December 1917 speech.[64]

It was out of the question, the September 19 letter continued, that the American government would accept the Paris resolutions. The Americans, however, would support the essential features of the French program if it were put in terms of Wilson's own ideals: "With the magnificent ideal, which is his, inspiring us, and making this ideal a defense against the possible return of certain forms of national selfishness, the time has come to invite the American government to examine, in concert with us and our principal allies, the means of dealing with a new situation."[65] Clémentel therefore concluded his letter with a call for an Allied conference "to reach an agreement on the basis of the principles already accepted by France, England and Belgium in 1916, but extended and adapted to the present situation."[66]

A meeting was held on September 28 to discuss the project. Clemenceau and Clémentel were joined by the Foreign Minister, Stephen Pichon, and by André Tardieu, the brilliant Commissioner-General for Franco-American Affairs. Everyone agreed that the suggestions outlined in the September 19 letter should be accepted as the basis of French policy. Clemenceau in particular "declared that the document M. Clémentel had sent him was of the greatest interest and that he judged it proper, as soon as events permitted, to begin to discuss with our allies a preliminary accord along the lines suggested by the Minister of Commerce."[67]

The American attitude, they agreed, would be decisive. In negotiating with the United States, extreme caution was necessary. Tardieu emphasized that no mention must be made to President Wilson and his government of the Paris resolutions. Instead, he said, Clémentel's proposals should be placed "under the aegis of President Wilson's principles." In this way, he believed "it would be possible to win the support of the American government."[68] Clemenceau then asked Tardieu, who would be in America shortly, to discuss these proposals with Wilson, House and Lansing "in such a way as to obtain their preliminary adherence to all the points if possible, or at least to certain of them, and their opinion on those which they did not find acceptable."[69]

Allied cooperation was thus the essential aim—the heart of the French plan for reconstruction and economic resurgence. Reparation from Germany, on the other hand, was to play only a subordinate role. The claim for reparation could be used to force Germany to deliver needed supplies of raw material, especially coal. Beyond that, a nominal demand for vast payments was the instrument by which vague "concessions" could be extracted from Germany, and by which recalcitrant allies might be induced to favor the idea of a "world fund" to finance the rebuilding of the devastated areas. But it was not supposed that Germany in fact could or should be made to pay enormous reparations.

"In strict justice," Clémentel wrote in the September 19 letter, it was Germany who should pay for the rebuilding of the devastated areas. "To this elementary truism" was contrasted the "material impossibility for Germany to rebuild so many ruins." Furthermore, the Minister of Commerce noted, it was argued that to hold Germany financially liable for all war damages "would completely crush her and reduce her to a state of economic bondage which would strip away from humanity all hope of a lasting peace. Thus was born the idea of a kind of world fund for the reparation of war damages, a fund which would be one of the first organs of the League of Nations."[70]

Clémentel was therefore not eager to have Germany pay enormous sums in reparation, and Hauser in fact explicitly argued that huge reparation payments would be detrimental to France. Large money payments, he wrote on December 28, 1918, were undesirable. Such payment would cause in France "an enormous monetary inflation, a disorderly rise in prices," and would in no way satisfy French industrial needs. "By virtue of their size," he wrote, these money payments "would transform France into a country rich in mere cash, a buyer of products and incapable of working, like Spain in the Sixteenth Century"—a striking illustration of the "relevance" of historical study. Furthermore, to force Germany to pay in this way would cause a decline in the exchange rate of the mark. For those German industries that did not have to import raw materials, this fall would be "an incentive to exportation against which no customs duty can defend us."[71]

How then could Germany pay? German property in Alsace-Lorraine and in the rest of France could be liquidated; German assets in neutral countries could be turned over; even title to certain enterprises within Germany, such as the Saar coal mines, could be transferred. Germany could pay in kind, principally by furnishing raw materials like coal. There was no reason why Germany could not deliver finished goods "during the period of reconstruction," Hauser thought, but only during this period, lest "our own industries" be deprived of any business.

Should the product of certain German taxes be turned over to France? The money could be used to purchase German goods that could then be imported into France. Hauser was, however, remarkably hostile to this idea, "an inadmissible interference by us in the fiscal life, and consequently in the political life of Germany." Customs duties, however, and especially export duties, were acceptable. Export duties would help defend France against an invasion of German merchandise resulting from a decline in the German exchange rate. It would also compensate France for a detrimental revival of German foreign trade: the faster German exports expanded, the faster the debt could be paid. Customs receipts could be collected in foreign currency, but what could be done with the proceeds of internal taxes? Hauser believed that any marks acquired by the French should be applied only to the purchase of raw materials: "Let us not, under the pretext of getting Germany to pay, ruin our own manufacturing industries."

To Clémental as well, the protection of French industry against an "invasion" of German goods was of paramount importance. He wanted raw materials from Germany, not finished goods. It seems likely, therefore, that it was in large part on the basis of this kind of reasoning that he was attracted to the idea of a limited German liability supplemented by a world reparation fund. In his September 19 letter, he in fact endorsed this kind of scheme. He felt, however, that it would be foolish for France to propose it. At the peace conference, the French delegation should instead insist that Germany be presented with the whole bill. Then privately, among allies, the question of alternative ways of doing what Germany was unable to do could be discussed; "but it would be naive and dangerous" to let this become known to the Germans.[72]

Clémentel of course believed that there was a certain amount Germany could and should pay, and he indicated in his letter the same kinds of payment that Hauser was to outline in his note of December 28: the transfer of foreign assets supplemented by reparation in kind. The amount Germany could pay in these ways would nevertheless fall far short of the full reparation bill. Recognizing this, he said, the Allies would revive the idea of a world fund for the reparation of war damages—but it would now be put forward as a concession to Germany, "a concession which could be paid for with equivalent concessions."[73] (Neither Clémentel's letter, nor the related passages in Hauser's memoranda, give any indication of the kind of concession that Germany was expected to make in this way.[74]) The entire September 19 letter was adopted as government policy, and these views on reparation and financial questions should therefore be considered as representing the official French point of view. French policy at the peace conference did in fact proceed along these lines.

Clémentel was apparently convinced that the Allies would cooperate with this policy of substituting a world fund, tied to the League, for an exclusively German reparation liability. "Our new ally, the United States," he wrote in the September 19 letter, "will certainly come around to this way of thinking and will agree that the complete reconstruction of the North of France and of Belgium is in essence everyone's business, the primordial task of the economic league of free peoples."[75]

Alas, Clémentel's whole policy was based on a grave misconception. The Americans were reluctant to cooperate, either financially or economically. Those who idealized "cooperation" misunderstood what American policy had been during the war. Although eager to see the Europeans coordinate their economic programs (thereby limiting the strain on the American economy and on American financial resources), the United States consistently remained somewhat aloof and never really accepted the ideal of "equality of sacrifice." The Americans approved of the inter-Allied economic machinery because it enabled them to satisfy themselves that the Europeans, whom they distrusted, were already doing all that could be expected of them, and that such assistance as was granted was really needed in the war effort and would not be used for other purposes.[76]

Assistance was given to secure the common goal of German defeat, but somewhat anomalously America expected to be paid back: the heavy sacrifice of life and treasure by the European Allies did not have as its counterpart the relatively light contribution of freely granted American material aid. Even on the central question of shipping, American willingness to cooperate fully is open to question.[77] For the war the United States was waging was not precisely the same as the war of the European Allies. How scrupulously Wilson distinguished between the European "Allies" and their American "Associate"! In the name of justice, of "equality of sacrifice," the French expected full American cooperation as a matter of right. The Americans did not concede this right and would not support French plans for a continuation of economic controls, which is what "cooperation" had come to mean.

Tardieu, the French High Commissioner in the United States, had sensed this American attitude. Since the beginning of 1918 Clémentel had been trying to get him to press energetically for an American commitment on postwar cooperation. But Tardieu did not want to rush things ("je ne veux pas brusquer") and insisted on the "need for a certain prudence" in these negotiations.[78] Clémentel, however, now with the support of the Foreign Minister Stephen Pichon, continued to press the issue. The two ministers repeatedly demanded that Tardieu propose a conference on postwar economic matters to the Americans. Tardieu wrote back that Wilson was sympathetic, but given the opposition of some Republicans to measures of this sort, the President was reluctant to deal with the matter at that point. Irritated and frustrated, Clémentel and Pichon replied on May 19: "Whatever repugnance the Americans feel right now about examining, at an inter-Allied meeting, a policy for the control of raw materials during the peace negotiations and in the post-war period, the usefulness and the urgency of such a meeting are, however, not to be denied, and it is therefore important that the question be put to them repeatedly (par des démarches répétées).''[79]

Clémentel and Pichon thus knew in mid-1918 that full American cooperation was not a foregone conclusion. But it was only toward the end of September that they began to gauge the real depth of American opposition to their plans. Pichon had learned from the Italians that Robert Lansing, the American Secretary of State, was opposed to the whole idea of an inter-Allied economic policy, and in particular to the idea of a conference of experts to study the question of an inter-Allied control of raw materials. If this were true, Pichon wrote Tardieu's deputy Edouard de Billy on September 26, it would be a "real disappointment"—could Billy find out just what the American attitude was? Wilson's speech of September 27, Billy replied, gave Pichon his answer: the President ruled out any "special, selfish economic combinations within the League" and opposed "any form of economic boycott or exclusion," except insofar as the League might impose economic penalties "as a means of discipline and control." War, he added, was to a large degree rooted in "economic rivalries and hostilities," and "it would be an insincere as well as an insecure peace that did not exclude them in definite and binding terms."[80]

There was still a certain amount of ambiguity in Wilson's position—a system for the international control of raw materials was not in theory inconsistent with his point of view—but the thrust and tone of American policy could no longer be ignored. The Americans wanted a return to the prewar structure of free markets and commercial equality. Even Wilson's commitment to the League could not be used as a lever for moving him closer to the French point of view. Economic sanctions, in Wilson's view, were to be held in reserve as a means of disciplining aggressors, but a system of controls was not to be made an integral part of the peacekeeping apparatus. Political and economic questions were to be kept largely separate, and Wilson was relatively indifferent to the use of economic power for political ends. Thus no form of economic cooperation was ever a vital feature of Wilson's plans for a "new world order"—an omission for which he is sharply criticized even by his great admirer Ray Stannard Baker.[81]

French policy in 1918 was thus based on certain misconcep-

tions concerning the American attitude. This was possible only because American statesmen had avoided a firm stand throughout; their
attitude had been generally ambiguous and at times even sympathetic
to the French approach. It was really not until the eve of the armistice
that the United States government—which had known about French
intentions at least since mid-August—finally made its policy clear.[82]
After conferring with the President, Herbert Hoover, United States
Food Administrator and Wilson's chief economic advisor at this time,
cabled his representative in London that the American government
"will not agree to any programme that even looks like inter-Allied
control of our economic resources after peace."[83] It was not that
Hoover rejected the system of controls out of doctrinaire laissez-faire
liberalism. In the last weeks of the war, he in fact called for "some
systematic arrangement" to determine how American surpluses "are
to be divided amongst the various nations," and he felt that the arrangement should cover both food and raw materials.[84] But the
United States government had to do the controlling itself: America
alone was unselfish, he believed, and only if she preserved her independence in these matters could she use her resources in a way that
would "maintain justice all around."[85]

To allow foreigners, through their control of the inter-Allied
councils, to dictate how the United States would dispose of its surpluses was, Hoover wrote, "wholly inconceivable."[86] He and his
colleagues were particularly wary of plans for continued "cooperation" because they felt that the British controlled the inter-Allied
bodies. Hoover, for example, on November 11 sharply rejected "arrangements which the English may set up in London for provisioning
the world with our foodstuffs and on our credit."[87]

The degree to which American policy was shaped by such anti-
British considerations is somewhat surprising, and should be stressed
at this point. Anglo-American rivalry was commonly accepted by
high American officials as a fact of life. Thus when at the end of
1918 the American representatives on the Allied Maritime Transport
Council met in Paris with Wilson, Hoover and the head of the United
States Shipping Board, "They found considerable distrust toward the
British in the minds of all three. The President, it seems, has been
surrounded by anti-British advisers, who have said that the British
Ministry of Shipping was slyly diverting tonnage to trade. . . ."[88]
This attitude by no means died away: throughout the peace confer-

ence period there was an increasingly strong undercurrent of Anglo-American rivalry and even hostility. By the end of the conference, matters had deteriorated to the point that House, referring above all to the naval question, was able to write Wilson that relations between the two countries were beginning to look like Anglo-German relations before 1914.[89]

American suspicion of British economic policy at the time of the armistice was not entirely baseless. The wealthy and influential member of Parliament, Waldorf Astor, Parliamentary Secretary to the Ministry of Food and an associate of Lloyd George, stressed in a note to the prime minister at about this time that British leadership in international economic matters was menaced by the prospect of an independent American policy. "It was, he suggested, urgently necessary that Britain's own policy should be quickly formulated and some 'leading British personality' made responsible for its execution. His own suggestion for this role was Lord Reading."[90] Reading, the Lord Chief Justice and a brilliant advocate, had represented Britain in negotiations with the United States on related questions during the war. Astor enclosed a copy of his note to Lloyd George in mid-November in a letter to another close associate of the prime minister. He was disturbed that Lloyd George had "practically stopped our representatives" from attending a meeting in Paris of inter-Allied shipping and food organizations, because the meeting had been called by Clemenceau, and Lloyd George apparently

did not want Clemenceau to take this lead. As the work would probably have been done subsequently in London by our mainly British organization he may have probably lost the substance while grasping for the shadows . . . I cannot but think it is vital and urgent that we should get someone of outstanding position, like Reading, to collar the existing Allied machinery before it breaks, so that when Hoover and Woodrow arrive they can each be more or less quietly placed into the niches which ought to be ready for them.[91]

Clearly the American government would not tolerate British efforts at manipulation; it would refuse the "niches" being offered. It seems that it was in part for this reason that the Americans came to oppose plans for the continuation of the inter-Allied economic system.

Would the United States, however, offer alternative forms of assistance to those Allies, like France or Belgium, who had suffered so much? A member of the French High Commission had discussed the matter at length in September with Robert Leffingwell and Albert Rathbone, both influential Assistant Secretaries of the Treasury, and it was his impression that the United States would "lend to France all the aid she really needed, now and after the war."[92] And in fact in late October William McAdoo, Secretary of the Treasury in Wilson's Cabinet and a politician of national stature in his own right, wrote the President that America should help France reconstruct; he asked only that Britain share the burden—otherwise Britain would get the jump on the United States and "secure an undue share of the cash markets of the world."[93]

McAdoo enclosed a memorandum by Rathbone which argued in similar terms for a relatively generous policy. Rathbone wrote,

The financial problems involved in the reconstruction of France are most serious and merit the sympathetic consideration of the Treasury. The United States cannot look without apprehension upon a termination of the war that will leave France without the funds or credits essential to re-establish its industrial life in the devastated districts. The future peace of the world may depend on the financial and commercial prosperity of the United States, France, and Great Britain, and the adoption by them of broad and equitable financial policies.

The United States should assist France, but Rathbone stressed that it should insist on something in return from the European Allies: the British should supply the ships needed for the swift repatriation of the American army, and the French should supply the francs needed until repatriation. A "single negotiation" linking reconstruction aid to a satisfactory settlement of these questions was desirable. He therefore called for the three governments to reach a "temporary working arrangement," adding that a "final settlement" could probably not "be determined until the peace conference." Again, it is clear that his sense of urgency was rooted in the suspicion that the British, if not brought into line through a binding agreement, might unfairly exploit American generosity: "The United States cannot afford to establish large credits to be used by France for reconstruction purposes if while the United States is thus selling on credit, the British Empire is to be free to sell for cash and provided with shipping to make deliveries and thus to obtain a preponadering position in other markets."[94]

The Treasury was, however, sympathetic to France, and when

Tardieu arrived in America in November to discuss economic matters he found the Americans receptive. Billy had advised him to focus on reconstruction, and Tardieu in any case was inclined to ignore his instructions and avoid bringing up Clémentel's grandiose project: to present to the Americans even a theory of financial solidarity, he wrote later, "would have been enough to have sustained a reverse whose consequences would have been disastrous."[95] He was, however, able to reach an informal agreement with Leffingwell that the United States would help France during the period of reconstruction. Everyone understood that all this depended on specific Congressional authorization, since, as McAdoo noted, under present law the Treasury had "no authority to make advances for reconstruction."[96]

Here indeed was the rub: the Congress refused to grant even the limited authority to lend for postwar purposes that McAdoo had requested.[97] Was it therefore a case of a simple conflict between a tight-fisted Congress and a relatively generous administration? The differences within the American government should not be overdrawn. The executive branch was itself divided on this question, and even the Treasury's commitment to European reconstruction lacked real depth. High administration officials were inclined to underestimate the size of the problem—Hoover wrote in October 1918 that the damage in northern France was not large enough to be an "international question" and Assistant Secretary of the Treasury Crosby thought that the dollars France received in exchange for the francs needed by the American army would "easily cover for several years" French needs in America. Many in the administration were coming to feel that Europeans should be obliged to rely primarily on their own resources for a solution to their problems.[98]

The Treasury itself was evidently not immune to the prevailing atmosphere and its attitude began to harden right after the armistice. Whereas previously the informal American commitment on reconstruction was more or less open-ended, by November 21 McAdoo was arguing in favor of a policy of "retrenchment" and limiting assistance to "extraordinary replacements." Private channels of finance were to be stressed, in part because a large-scale intergovernmental loan program would strengthen the hand of those who wanted a continuation of the wartime system of international economic controls.[99] In any case, he wrote House on December 11, all loans for postwar purposes should come out of the unexpended existing appropriation;

anything more was to be avoided if that were at all possible.[100] By this time, McAdoo had changed his mind about discussing and settling the whole financial question at the peace conference: any negotiations would have to take place in Washington.[101] What this meant was that the possibility of a broad settlement for the financial liquidation of the war was being ruled out. Now the different problems—the inter-Allied war debt, reconstruction, reparation—were to be handled in isolation, with the Europeans coming as supplicants to Washington.

To the French, the thrust of American policy was clear by December: it seemed that the United States was refusing to cooperate on all fronts. This refusal was something that the French government in general, and Clémentel in particular, could not readily accept. All of Clémentel's plans had been based on the assumption of American support. The French government, therefore, did all it could to induce the Americans to reconsider their position and accept some kind of continued cooperation, for the period of reconstruction at least.

It is in this light that the economic policy pursued by the French delegation at the peace conference must be understood. The positions it was to take on relief and especially on reparation were designed to impress upon the Americans the necessity of formulating an economic policy that took French requirements into account.

Chapter Two
Reparation at the Peace Conference

UNLIKE WILSON and Lloyd George, Clemenceau elaborated no public peace program during the war and refused even to engage in public discussion of peace terms. "When you ask me about my war aims," he told the Chamber a few days after he took office, "I answer you: my aim is to win." [1] Words, he thought, were empty; discussion was essentially futile. "I promise you nothing," he told a cheering Chamber; the deputies would simply have to trust him. [2] By an overwhelming vote of 418 to 65 the Chamber placed its confidence in the new government.

The end of the war did little to alter Clemenceau's attitude. In his extraordinary speech to the Chamber of December 29, 1918, he spoke of peacemaking only in the most basic terms. What would be the guiding principles of the peace? People spoke of a peace of justice. Make this kind of peace, they said, and the problem of security would be easily resolved. Clemenceau was skeptical: in a world shaped not by heavenly decree but by centuries of struggle, justice was not so readily defined. Every people had its own idea of justice, just as every people would inevitably defend its own interests. There would necessarily be bargaining. And because the need to preserve

Part of this chapter appeared originally in the March 1979 issue of the *Journal of Modern History*.

the Alliance was paramount, the French government would have to be flexible: "My guiding thought . . . is that nothing must happen which might in the future separate the four powers who came together in the war. To preserve this entente, I will make any sacrifice."[3] Clemenceau therefore refused to outline the claims that France would make at the peace conference. His "main preoccupation," he said, "was not to give rise to too many hopes for fear of ultimately causing too much disappointment. I do not believe it is good policy to promise too much, because, whatever happens, it will always be found that not enough is given."[4] Again he insisted that France would make concessions at the peace conference. Why did he refuse to discuss French demands just then? "Because some of them I may and perhaps will have to sacrifice in a higher interest."[5] The Chamber was not, therefore, offered a specific program to justify its continued support. Clemenceau again demanded that it would simply have to trust the government. Did anyone doubt that he had the interests of France deeply at heart?

Clemenceau prided himself on his realism and did not believe lofty phrases and high ideals could conjure away real problems. He was a pessimist, a skeptic, and his skepticism carried with it more than a touch of contempt for those who did not share it—for those both on the right and on the Wilsonian left who expected too much from the peace. Negotiations with Britain and America, he knew, would be long and difficult. The Anglo-Saxon powers clearly did not see things the same way the French did. France was more exposed, more vulnerable, and thus more preoccupied with the problem of security; America and even Britain were more remote, more protected, and it was natural that their interests and concerns should diverge from those of France. And the problem was by no means purely theoretical: to Clemenceau, as to many Frenchmen, the problem of security was intimately bound up with the question of a continued French—or preferably inter-Allied—presence on the Rhine.[6] To what degree would the Anglo-Saxons, invoking the principle of self-determination, prevent France from pursuing a Rhenish policy? Ideally an effort at mutual understanding was the key to a solution: the Allied statesmen soon to assemble at Paris would have to make a sincere attempt to see things through each others' eyes, and in any case to avoid playing politics with the peace. An unsigned memorandum of Nov. 26, 1918, on "French opinion and President Wilson," argued against exploiting the recent success of the Republicans in the American congressional elections as a way of "making the President more manageable"; Clemenceau wrote in the margin: "No one is considering it." As to the rumor that France and Britain were getting together to reach agreement before Wilson even arrived, Clemenceau wrote that this was "absurd." [7] He did go over to London a few days later for preliminary talks with Lloyd George, but he was careful to insist there that no decisions could be reached without the United States. [8] On December 3, for example, Lloyd George bitterly condemned American economic and naval policy. Hoover, he said, was trying to create an "economic dictatorship" which would give the United States "immense political power." Wilson was enthusiastic about the idea of a League of Nations except when America herself would have to make a sacrifice. Wilson spoke of disarmament, but had just had Congress appropriate money to double the size of the American navy. Clemenceau listened, but said nothing. [9] He was not prepared at this point to indulge the kind of feeling that could poison the atmosphere of the peace conference. If it was at all possible, he preferred to see the Allied governments as collaborators rather than as antagonists.

But what if the Allies could not be brought to see things through French eyes? If conflict could not be avoided, Clemenceau wanted to be able to make the best bargain he could—to preserve the Alliance while not completely sacrificing all prospect of a Rhenish policy— and to do this he felt he had to keep his hands free by remaining silent.

How did French reparation policy relate to all this? Policy in economic matters was much more closely tied to the aim of preserving the Alliance than it was to the idea of a Rhenish policy. Allied cooperation was seen as the key to the solution of France's economic problems; at this time, "cooperation" meant the continuation of the system of economic controls that had evolved during the war. But the Allies were to refuse to "cooperate," and this refusal was to lead the French government—as in other areas of the peace negotiations—to use the very tactics of pressure that Clemenceau had hoped at the outset to avoid. As for the relation between the demand for reparation and French ambitions in the Rhineland, it is surprising how little connection there was between these two aspects of French policy. It is true that the final peace treaty established a certain linkage between the payment of reparation and the duration of the occupation, but there is no evidence that reparation demands were framed with the idea of providing a pretext for an indefinite occupation. Indeed, the linkage can be interpreted in exactly the opposite sense, as providing the Allies with a weapon that would be needed to assure German compliance with the reparation provisions of the treaty. Moreover, if it were true that the main function of French reparation policy was to provide a pretext for an extended occupation, then one would expect that French demands would be on the high side: that is, the more "impossible" the burden, the better, from this point of view. But French demands (as will be shown) were surprisingly moderate in 1919; this in itself tends to discredit the idea that reparation policy was to any large extent a function of France's Rhenish ambitions. There is more direct evidence as well. For example, Clemenceau was to approve an important French concession on the size of the reparation debt while at the very same time expressing his fury that Lloyd George was blocking French aims in the Rhineland.[10] If reparation demands had as their primary purpose the furtherance of France's Rhenish policy, one would expect a much harder line on reparation at this point—if Clemenceau was not being given what he wanted in the Rhineland directly, he would try to get it indirectly via a harsh reparation policy, one that would virtually guarantee a German default. The fact that this was not the case points to a certain disjunction between these two areas of policy—indeed to a certain incoherence, or at least uncertainty, in French policy as a whole. But what this means for our present purposes is that because reparation policy had a life of its own, it can be analyzed fundamentally in terms of its own internal logic; other factors, such as Rhenish policy, will only be discussed to the degree that they relate directly to the diplomacy of reparation. By limiting the analysis in this way, it will be possible to keep the discussion on track, to bring things into clear focus and thus to make sense of how the reparation issue developed in this period.

America's refusal to "cooperate" economically had become evident by December 1918. "The moment we knew the armistice to have been signed," Wilson told the Congress on December 2, "we took the harness off."[11] The War Industries Board was dismantled—that is, controls on raw materials and on industrial production were removed. Without these national controls, the wartime system of program committees and inter-Allied councils could not be continued.

From the French point of view, the abrupt and permanent collapse of the wartime system of economic cooperation would be disastrous. Etienne Clémentel, Minister of Commerce and still the chief maker of French economic policy, was distressed by the American attitude. All his plans had been predicated on the assumption that the United States would cooperate, at least during the period of reconstruction. He and his colleagues in the French government had been convinced that they could win American support for their plans.

The hope of continued cooperation died hard. Clémentel still sought to bring the Americans around. French needs during the period of reconstruction would be enormous; the means of payment available to a country as yet substantially unable to export would be severely limited. Would the United States government do what was necessary to see that France received her fair share of raw materials, and that these commodities were provided at a fair price? Or would the Americans simply abandon France, and indeed all of Europe, to economic chaos, or worse? Once aware of the facts, the generous and high-minded Americans, it was felt, would certainly be won over to the French point of view.

The American government was eager to organize the relief of Europe, and in December 1918, its representatives negotiated with European officials on relief schemes. Clémentel saw in this an opportunity to press the United States to accept the French economic plan. It was not just emergency food that was required, but more far-reaching measures designed to put Europe back on its feet economically. In discussions with Hoover and other officials, Clémentel urged the "drafting of a complete plan for the control of all foodstuffs, raw material, and shipping for a lengthy period subsequent even to peace."[12]

It seemed to Hoover that the French intended "to force the grafting of this issue on to any plans of the President, and use our desires on relief as a point of pressure."[13] He firmly rejected Clémentel's proposals. The American people, he felt, would never accept foreign control of American resources. If any controls over the American economy were retained, they would have to be operated exclusively by American officials. In the face of this resistance, Hoover wrote, Clémentel for the moment abandoned the idea of a "complete economic Council controlling all raw material, finance, transportation and food."[14]

The Minister of Commerce, however, only provisionally renounced his effort to secure American cooperation. He intended to renew the attempt at the peace conference, but in December he already knew that the American government would resist his proposals. At the end of the month he forwarded to Clemenceau an "Avant-project des clauses économiques des préliminaires de paix," a project put together by the high officials in the Ministry of Commerce, and in whose preparation his collaborator Henri Hauser played a leading role.[15] This project was apparently approved by Clemenceau; and according to the deputy Louis Puech in his report to the Chamber on the economic clauses of the peace treaty, the Ministry of Commerce project as a whole "represented as exactly as possible the position taken by the French government at the start of the conference."[16]

In the letter to Clemenceau covering this project, Clémentel reviewed the economic problems that France would face and again urged the need for continued Allied "cooperation." But now his proposals were limited to the period of reconstruction. Knowing that the Americans would oppose even these modest plans, he outlined a strategy designed to overcome their resistance. The French should stress that the kind of peace "imposed" on Germany would be a function of the arrangements the Allies made among themselves. If the Allies and the Americans abandoned the wartime policy of mutual assistance and economic solidarity, then France would insist on a harsh peace. The "associated states" gathered at Paris to make peace would then be presented with a choice: "They must decide if they will institute, by means of measures based on common agreement, an economic organization designed to assure the world a secure recovery in the aftermath of the upheaval, or if the only guarantee of this security that they envisage is a peace of reprisals and punishments."[17]

What kind of severe claim would the French present to their allies? The "Note introductive" to the Ministry of Commerce project, drafted by Hauser, left little doubt that an enormous demand for reparation would figure prominently in the bargaining. "Full reparation," Hauser wrote, "does not merely include the restoration of Belgium and of the invaded areas of the North and East of France, Italian territories and others directly touched by the war." It also included compensation for "inability to produce," both in the occupied areas and in the rest of France. If it were admitted at the peace conference that such reparation was beyond Germany's capacity to pay, then "it will be up to the Allied and Associated governments to study alternative schemes to assure the nations who have suffered most from the war the full reparation of their losses." [18]

At the peace conference, French policy did proceed along the broad lines sketched in the Ministry of Commerce project. The Supreme Council (of heads of government, sometimes assisted by other officials, also known first as the Council of Ten and then as the Council of Four), on January 27, acting on Clemenceau's proposal, set up an Economic Drafting Committee to propose the economic questions that the conference should study. [19] It seemed that the Americans were now willing to consider a kind of limited cooperation on economic questions. It was Wilson's suggestion that the committee propose questions relating to "privileges that should be granted to the devastated regions for their revictualling in raw materials and for the sale of their manufactured products." The "revictualling and re-starting of industries in devastated regions," he said, "would call for co-operation between the Allied and Associated Powers in respect to shipping, priority of supply, etc." [20]

When the Economic Drafting Committee, which was chaired by Clémentel, first met on February 5, it had before it a memorandum expounding the French point of view. This document stated explicitly that French approval of a moderate peace would depend on the continuation of Allied cooperation. If the Allies refused to cooperate, the French would insist on a harsh peace. [21] In this way Clémentel hoped to induce the American government, eager for a "Wilsonian" settlement, to accept the French economic program. The French memorandum left no doubt as to what Clémentel meant by "cooperation." As usual, Allied control of world supplies of raw material was the key feature of the French plan, and there would also be "cooperation" on the questions of shipping and exchange rates. [22]

British and American memoranda at the next meeting of the committee basically agreed that the proposed Economic Commission of the peace conference should study these questions. Clémentel was elated by the American memorandum—his pleasure penetrates even the *Procès-verbal:* "The American project has his full approval, he considers it as being very wide in scope, and is ready to reduce the French project to the American text." [23]

In the discussion that followed, the American delegate Bernard Baruch took the same position that Wilson had taken on the Supreme

Council. The key problem calling for exceptional measures was the restoration of the devastated areas; the Americans evidently would cooperate in the solution of this narrowly circumscribed question. Clémentel, however, pressed for a much broader system of "cooperation." France in its entirety, he said, had in effect been devastated by the war. The reconstruction of the French economy as a whole depended on Allied cooperation. Reparation alone would not be enough:

But everyone agrees in recognizing that there is a limit to possible enemy reparations. France does not want to go beyond this limit and execute her own debtor. Without, however, intending to transfer to her allies the debt of her enemy, she is certain that she can find, in a system of understanding and cooperation, the means of coming to the aid of the countries who have suffered most from the war.[24]

Baruch did not at this time care to present the full American point of view. It was not the function of the committee, he said, to settle policy, but merely to agree on what topics should be discussed at the conference. To make the point absolutely clear, he had the minutes note that the decision to discuss in no way bound the American government to take a particular position.[25]

The drafting committee submitted to the Supreme Council a list of questions that the proposed Economic Commission should be authorized to deal with. In particular, it suggested that the proposed Commission consider economic measures to be taken in common for the supply of Europe, and special reference was made to the problem of the restoration of the devastated areas.[26] This document was considered by the Supreme Council on February 21. These "transitory measures," it decided, should be considered by a newly created Supreme Economic Council (SEC).[27] The Economic Commission, on the other hand, would discuss problems more directly related to the peace treaty with Germany—permanent commercial relations, "dumping," liquidation of enemy property, prewar commercial debts, and so on.

The SEC had been set up by the Supreme Council on February 8, on Wilson's suggestion, to deal with such questions as "finance, food, blockade control, shipping and raw materials" during the period prior to the signing of the peace treaty.[28] The creation of this body perhaps encouraged Clémentel—the inter-Allied economic system that had proved so effective in the last months of the war now might be revived under a different name. Indeed, the wartime bodies were to be absorbed into the new council, the Allied Maritime Transport Council, for example, becoming the Transport Section of the SEC.[29]

The creation of an institutional framework for cooperation, however, meant little in itself. What was crucial was the policy each nation pursued within that framework. The Americans continued to resist sweeping plans for inter-Allied control of raw material, shipping and finance, and their earlier position seemed even to harden. Until early February, American spokesmen had evidently favored a system of "cooperation" limited to the reconstruction of the devastated areas. For the rest of the conference, however, they were hostile to all schemes of "cooperation" involving the American government.

The SEC discussed questions of relief and blockade, but because of American resistance, the problem of French reconstruction, and in particular the question of raw material, was barely touched. Clémentel was keenly aware that the American attitude was responsible for the final frustration of his schemes. "The very sharp opposition of the American delegation," he wrote in November 1919, "prevented the SEC from carrying out . . . the task that had been entrusted to it."[30]

Any assistance, the American leaders came to believe, would have to come through private channnels. "It is perhaps unfortunate, but nevertheless true, that public sentiment in this country is in no mood to tolerate the assumption by government of further financial burdens in aid of Europe," the Assistant Secretary of the Treasury, R. C. Leffingwell, cabled Norman Davis from Washington in May 1919. (Davis was the Treasury representative in Paris.) During the war, Leffingwell wrote, government intervention was the panacea. "It is hard for business men," he continued, "even in this country, to realize that the time has come for reliance upon individual initiative. I realize how hard it must be, therefore, for business men in the countries which have been devastated by the war to begin again. That is, however, what must be done if sound and permanent relief is to be given." Through the War Finance Corporation, he said, the United

States government would help finance American exports through private channels; but this was as far as the American government could go.[31]

American hostility to economic controls sharpened as the conference continued, culminating in the striking "Memorandum on the Economic Situation of Europe" that Hoover wrote in early July.[32] Hoover, who had earlier sympathized with the argument for controls (providing that it was the American government that exercised them) now disputed the very basis of this argument. It was production, not distribution, that was the central problem; a return to free markets was essential if Europe was to get back to work and production was to be stimulated. To control prices would destroy initiative, thereby limiting output, and the supposed beneficiaries would be the greatest sufferers:

. . . all attempts at international control of price, with view to benefiting the population in Europe at the cost of the producer elsewhere, will inevitably produce retrogression in production abroad, the impact of which will be felt in Europe more than elsewhere. A decrease of 20 per cent of Western Hemisphere wheat would not starve the West; it would starve Europe.[33]

It was toward this kind of opposition to economic controls in principle that the American attitude as a whole had evolved during the peace conference.

French policy had to adjust to the new situation. As the failure of Clémentel's policy of direct inter-Allied control of vital world resources became evident, French representatives pressed for alternative solutions to their economic problems. Financial questions in particular assumed prime importance. While in this regard French policy became more flexible, much of the original spirit persisted—notably the strategy of using large reparation demands as a lever for eliciting Allied aid.

The progressive failure of Clémentel's policy—clearly an integral part of the strong postwar movement toward rapid decontrol which pervaded the entire industrialized world[34]—had a number of important consequences. In particular, with the failure of economic "cooperation," Clémentel's grandiose plans for industrial organization were also doomed. The Americans were no longer insisting on a highly centralized economy under government control. Instead, they constantly urged the prompt restoration of free market conditions, and seemed to suggest that this would be a condition of further aid.[35]

The American government was particularly hostile to the consortium system. The U.S. War Trade Board's chief representative in Europe, George McFadden, began attacking the consortiums even before the armistice; on November 27 he asked the Treasury to put pressure on the French to end the system, which he feared might otherwise become permanent.[36] As with Lansing's opposition to the Paris program of 1916 and Hoover's hostility to the inter-Allied system at the time of the Armistice, McFadden's argument stressed American interest in the narrow sense—in this case, the interest of those Americans who wanted to export to France—and showed no sign of being rooted in an ideological commitment to the free market as an end in itself. High American officials in December and early January in fact made their opposition to the consortium regime very clear to the French.[37] By mid-January hasty steps had already been taken to disband the system—an article in the *Journée Industrielle*, which on the whole did not sympathize with Clémentel's policy, had even spoken of a "premature liquidation"—and by February 14, when Louis Loucheur, the Minister of Industrial Reconstitution, formally heralded the "complete suppression of the consortiums," only three of them were still in operation.[38]

Soon the whole system was gone, but Clémentel had already begun to look around for an alternative way of salvaging something from the situation. He now called for the voluntary organization of industry on a regional basis. Business was skeptical—was this just an "ingenious attempt" to achieve his aims through the back door?—but it went along with the plan in a halfhearted manner.[39] This attempt, a faint echo of a dead dream, never amounted to much. Employers were organized into a national body, the Confédération Générale de la Production Française, but this artificially created group never developed much cohesion or power.[40] As Lucien Romier pointed out in a perceptive report on the consortiums for the Association Nationale d'Expansion Economique, real centralization could not be imposed on a reluctant industry from without; if it were to exist at all it would have to develop organically from within: "Il ne peut y avoir de concentration réelle des industries qu'autant qu'il y a concentration, hierarchie et dépendance des capitaux qui alimentent chacune de ces industries. . . . La concentration interne doit précéder la concentration externe par voie administratif.''[41]

Thus all of Clémentel's hopes had been frustrated, and by early January 1919 the Minister of Commerce was no longer playing a prominent part in either international or national economic affairs. It was Louis Loucheur who replaced Clémentel as the real maker of French economic policy. A graduate of the elite Ecole Polytechnique and a successful businessman, Loucheur's technical skills had been put to use during the war. Eventually, in December 1916, he was appointed Under-Secretary of State for War Manufactures under the Socialist Minister of Armament, Albert Thomas. When Thomas left the government for political reasons in September 1917, Loucheur succeeded him, becoming Minister of Armament in the short-lived Painlevé cabinet. Clemenceau retained him in his position when he came to power two months later: with the expertise conferred by two years of experience, Loucheur was the obvious man to put in charge of this highly technical ministry. By virtue of his position, Loucheur worked intimately with Clemenceau, who in addition to being Prime Minister was also Minister of War. Clemenceau came to appreciate Loucheur's ability and to respect his keen and supple intellect. When the Ministry of Armament was converted into the Ministry of Industrial Reconstitution shortly after the armistice, Loucheur as minister was assured a leading role in the postwar economic life of France.[42]

At the peace conference, Loucheur became Clemenceau's chief—virtually his only—adviser on economic questions. It was Loucheur in particular who represented France in the really important negotiations on reparation. In 1918, the reparation question had been a subordinate issue; but now, at the beginning of the peace conference, with the American government stubbornly resisting Clémentel's plans for a direct solution to economic problems through rationing world supplies, all financial questions took on much greater importance: unable to continue to get needed supplies through inter-Allied bodies, it was essential that France be able to finance the purchase of these supplies on newly freed markets.

Financial assistance, if it came at all, would come from America, and the French reparation claim was of central importance in the attempt to secure this assistance. At first, a large theoretical reparation claim was put forward by the French, hoping that in return for concessions on this question, the Americans would agree to assist France financially. When this policy failed, French policy shifted to favor the American idea of putting a moderate fixed sum in the treaty. The hope was then that such a limited reparation debt could be readily "mobilized," that is, converted into German bonds that would be sold in America, a large part of the cash proceeds going directly into the French treasury. Primarily because of British policy, attempts to set Germany's reparation liability at a fixed sum also failed.

In spite of the increased importance of financial questions, the Minister of Finance, L. L. Klotz, continued to play only a subordinate role in the formulation of French policy. Klotz was more a spokesman than an actual maker of policy. In the reparation negotiations, he presented the formal French demands, while Loucheur, in more private arenas, pursued a relatively moderate policy based on real French aims. The two levels of policy of course fit together well; high formal demands strengthened Loucheur's hand in these private dealings: in making great concessions, the French could call upon their Allies to make corresponding sacrifices. But it is evident that it was Loucheur and not Klotz who played the leading role, and that the line taken by Loucheur expressed real French aims in the reparation question.

What is known of the personal relations of the French leaders confirms this view of the relative importance of Loucheur as opposed to Klotz. Clemenceau seems to have respected Loucheur and to have trusted his judgment. But his contempt for Klotz is well-known— "the only Jew I ever met who had no capacity whatever for finance," he allegedly called him, a remark that greatly amused the English and American delegates in late February.[43] A month later, Lloyd George told his friend Lord Riddell "the latest Clemenceau story." Some deputies had asked Clemenceau to dismiss Klotz. "He said it was impossible, and explained the reasons, adding 'May I remind you that Rome was not saved by eagles?' "[44]

Historians have hardly been kinder to Klotz. He has gone down as the naive fool who said "L'Allemagne paiera"—"Germany will pay." By this, it is commonly alleged, he meant that the German indemnity would take care of all of France's financial problems. Not only does the evidence strongly indicate that he never used this expression, but it is actually a gross distortion to reduce Klotz's position to this formula.[45] It is simply untrue that he maintained that there would be no financial problem facing the French government because huge German reparation payments would completely cover the deficit. In fact, when asked what his budgetary policy was, Klotz consistently responded that it was first necessary to see how much Germany would in reality pay; only after that was decided could the French consider how much to tax themselves.[46] He explicitly declared that German reparations would not cover the entire French budgetary deficit, and that the French taxpayer would eventually be asked to make a "fiscal effort."

"You must not think," he urged the Senate in December 1918, "that making the enemy pay off his entire debt to our beloved country will be enough to relieve the French taxpayer of any future concern. Great duties are being held for him in reserve. What is necessary, in my opinion, is that we turn to the French taxpayer only after he is convinced that every effort had been made by the government of the Republic to demand from the enemy reparation for all his crimes."[47] He reiterated the point in an important speech to the Chamber on financial policy in March 1919: the French taxpayer should not be under the illusion that reparation payments would in themselves solve the budgetary problem. The country had made a great fiscal effort during the war, but "it is necessary to claim no longer that that is the limit of the sacrifice that we can ask the taxpayer to make."[48] (He had in fact proposed a vague tax on capital, which had been received with great hostility by the press.)

If it were necessary, therefore, to sum up Klotz's policy in a slogan, it would not be "l'Allemagne paiera," but rather "que l'Allemagne paie d'abord"—"let Germany pay first." The hope of German reparations was not the basis of his financial policy; rather, the unsettled status of the reparation question was the excuse he gave for evading the budgetary problem.[49] Is there no basis then for the common belief that it was French policy to "make Germany pay"? Of course everyone agreed that Germany should pay something, but the phrase was highly ambiguous—make Germany pay what? There was a widespread demand for "réparation intégrale des dommages"—for "full reparation of damages"—but the meaning of this phrase was left vague. Perhaps this was in part deliberate. Pressing it to a precise definition would arouse differences of opinion, while the country could unite around a vague formula.[50] Clearly the phrase included the restoration of the devastated areas. Even the Socialist spokesman Vincent Auriol agreed that "full reparation for these devastations must be made by the enemy."[51] This seemed but elementary justice, especially in view of the fact that German territory had been spared the ravages of war. Feelings were sharpened by the publication, in translation, of a study prepared by the German Quartermaster General's Office in 1916, *Die Industrie in besetzten Frankreich,* which confirmed the suspicion that much of the destruction had been for economic rather than military purposes. The aim had been to destroy French competition while creating a postwar market for German exports—German firms, for example, could sell some of the machinery needed to reequip the pillaged factories.[52] Furthermore, the destruction of the most important French coal mines during the German retreat of 1918 was deeply resented by many in France. It seemed that the German aim, even as defeat impended, was to cripple France economically, for the destruction of the mines had no direct military purpose.

The French thus generally believed that Germany should fully compensate France for the material devastation. But beyond that, what if anything did the demand for full reparation include? In particular, did it include war costs? Here the evidence is mixed. Generally, the common usage was to distinguish between "full reparation" and "war costs" as two separate claims, or to treat reparation as just one category of war costs, but not vice versa.[53] "Reparation" was the more restricted term; when people used it, they thought above all of the restoration of the devastated areas. (This was similar to the original British usage, which used "reparation" in the narrow sense, reserving the term "indemnity" for the total payment, including the reimbursement of war costs, that many hoped Germany would be obliged to make.) It follows that when any government spokesman publicly called for full reparation, he was not necessarily calling for anything that went beyond the reparation that Germany had already agreed to make.

For as a condition of the armistice, Germany had agreed to make compensation "for all damage done to the civilian population of the Allies and their property by the aggression of Germany by land, by sea and from the air." This was an elaboration, proposed by the

European Allies and accepted by President Wilson, of those parts of the Wilsonian program that called for a restoration of the invaded territories. By accepting these terms, Germany obliged herself to make reparation within these limits: this "pre-armistice agreement" established a "contractual" basis for reparation, recognized as legitimate by the German government.[54]

A campaign on the theme "Germany will pay" was nevertheless pursued by the press, but there is no evidence that it was directly inspired by the government. Pierre Miquel's recent study argues to the contrary that the campaign was directed against the government, and is best understood in terms of internal politics. Though immensely popular in the country, Clemenceau had many enemies in political circles. Because of his prestige, he could only be attacked obliquely. The occasion for the attack came in mid-February when Klotz proposed a tax on capital. Until then, the press had not been much concerned with reparation, but from mid-February on, many newspapers, led by the important antigovernment journal *Le Matin*, played up the theme "Germany will pay." It was above all an attack on Klotz's project of a capital levy: seize Germany's wealth before touching France! This campaign, Miquel concludes, should be viewed as "a kind of general conspiracy against a Minister of Finance whose position had become weak, rather than as a *mise en question* of the government's policy in the reparation negotiations; the campaign 'Le Boche paiera' was thus apparently destined for internal consumption."[55]

It is not to be assumed, therefore, that French opinion seriously, and with virtual unanimity, insisted on a huge indemnity from Germany. Leading economists like Charles Rist and Charles Gide sharply attacked the idea of enormous reparations, and André Lebon, head of one of the most important business organizations, the Fédération des Industriels et Commerçants Français, throughout the period of the peace conference conducted what amounted to a campaign against demanding vast sums from Germany.[56] Whether Lebon's views were in any sense representative of the attitude of French business as a whole is difficult to know; but a speech he gave in May 1919 attacking those who had aroused the hope of enormous payments was "warmly applauded" by the businessmen and merchants who belonged to his organization.[57]

The argments made by these critics of a large indemnity and the solutions they proposed recall the views set out by Clémentel and Hauser in late 1918. The link between a money payment and the movement of real wealth was recognized and used to discredit the notion of large reparations: vast payments meant a tremendous influx of German goods into France, and the crippling of the French export trade. As an alternative, people like Gide and Lebon opted for an "international solution": the cost of the war, or at least the cost of the reconstruction of the devastated areas, was to be equitably distributed and borne by the international community, rather than by Germany alone.

Such relatively moderate views had an obvious appeal. The left as a whole had long advocated such a solution—the Confédération Générale in Travail in February 1918 for example had called for an "international fund controlled by an international commission"—but such ideas were by no means limited to the Socialists and the trade unions.[58] Many newspapers, Miquel demonstrated, particularly in the center of the political spectrum, emphasized the difficulties of making large payments, and independently of the government urged instead schemes for a "Financial League of Nations."[59] Here they followed the lead of the moderate deputy Jacques Stern, who had called for such an organization in December 1918. The principal idea was to pool war costs among the Allies, and this had wide support in Parliament. Blissfully unaware of the American attitude, Raoul Péret, the influential president of the Chamber's Budget Commission, for example, urged the government "to use the authority at its disposal at the conference to lead all the peoples taking part in the peace congress to transform into reality the idea of the Financial League of Nations."[60]

In the speeches and articles that looked to this as a panacea, there is hardly a recognition of gap between idea and reality. Naively optimistic, many observers assumed that all that was needed was for the French government to adopt the idea as its own. There was little recognition of the possibility, let alone the likelihood, of American resistance. Clemenceau undoubtedly saw all this as justifying his contempt for Parliament and public opinion. Here was yet another instance of Parliament, ignorant of the facts, being seduced by a pretty phrase. "It is all very nice to put down formulae on a piece of paper," he patiently explained to Péret, "but one must find people to accept them."[61]

The whole affair of the Financial League of Nations is a good measure of the ignorance in which Clemenceau kept even the leaders of Parliament, not only of what was going on at the peace conference, but also of what the policy of the French delegation was. Men like Stern and Péret were completely unaware that the government essentially shared their views, and in fact had done all it could to secure their acceptance.

The first step in the French plan was to put forward a claim for a large indemnity. Then when it was recognized that such a claim, which in justice should be paid, went far beyond what Germany in fact could pay, the Allies would agree that the part of the burden not charged to Germany would be supported by them in common. This was of course the basic idea of the Financial League of Nations. It seemed but elementary justice that the burden of a joint struggle should be shared equitably. If the principle of "equality and community of sacrifice" meant anything at all, it meant this. Therefore at the outset of the peace conference the French delegation supported the British position, resolutely opposed by the Americans, that war costs should be included in the bill.

Throughout the period of the peace conference, Great Britain was to pursue a reparation policy more demanding and more intransigent than the policy of any other Allied Power. Yet at the same time Lloyd George and other British leaders would, from time to time, argue forcefully for a moderate peace, a peace of reconciliation with Germany. How then is British policy, or more precisely Lloyd George's policy, to be understood?

It is possible to argue that Lloyd George favored a moderate settlement, but was forced for political reasons to pursue a much harsher policy than he personally would have preferred. The chronology alone strongly suggests this interpretation: at the beginning of November 1918, Lloyd George, and the British government as a whole, favored a moderate reparation settlement, insisting only on compensation for civilian damages (chiefly shipping). But then the issue of the German indemnity became heated as the general election campaign gathered momentum, and in the latter part of the month, the public utterances of Lloyd George and others in his government changed dramatically and fell in line with the popular desire for enormous reparations.[62]

Lloyd George nevertheless continued to be skeptical about Germany's ability to pay, and worried in particular about the effect of large German payments on British trade. "They must pay to the uttermost farthing," he told his friend Lord Riddell at the end of November 1918.

But the question is how they can be made to pay beyond a certain point. They can pay only by means of gold or goods. We do not mean to take their goods, because that would prejudice our trade. For instance, if we insisted on their supplying so many million pounds' worth of aniline dyes every year, that would not suit our people, as we should thus be ruining our manufacture of dyes. I said to Hughes [Australian Prime Minister and arch-advocate of a huge indemnity] the other day, "Shall you take their goods? We shan't!" He did not know what to reply.[63]

And in his public speeches at the time, he similarly stressed the dangers to British industry of a large German indemnity. Thus even at the height of the agitation for punitive reparations, Lloyd George was careful to provide himself with something of an escape clause.[64]

Evidence from diplomatic sources provides additional support for the view that political pressure for a large indemnity ran counter to Lloyd George's personal inclinations, and that he sought to accommodate and yet ultimately to circumvent that pressure. When Clemenceau visited him in London at the beginning of December, he suggested to his French colleague that an Interallied Financial Commission should be set up, to calculate how much and to decide in what manner Germany could pay. "The findings of a commission of this sort," he said, "will allow us to respond to a public opinion whose demands might go beyond what is reasonable."[65] The same kind of concern is apparent in a conversation he had with Colonel House in March 1919. "He admitted," House wrote in his diary, "that he knew Germany could not pay anything like the indemnity which the British and French demanded. He said that my ideas and his were not different as to the actual sum she should pay, but he wanted the amount named to be large, even if Germany could never pay it, or even if it had to be reduced later. He said it was a political matter in which the English were greatly interested and he did not want to let the Conservatives 'throw him' on a question of such popular concern."[66]

Thus there is a good deal of evidence that indicates that Lloyd George basically wanted a moderate peace, but was prevented by political conditions from pursuing a conciliatory policy of this sort. This interpretation is clearly plausible, especially in the light of Lloyd George's career prior to 1914 and as prime minister from 1920 to 1922. Moreover, his Parliamentary position was precarious—he was not the leader, nor even a member, of the majority Unionist Party— and this circumstance obviously suggests a certain dependence on the "hard-faced men" elected to Parliament in December 1918.

Nevertheless, there are basic problems with this interpretation. Lloyd George's beliefs and attitudes were simply not as clear-cut as this point of view would have it. In 1918, in private and before political pressures for a harsh settlement really came into play, Lloyd George repeatedly argued for a punitive peace. "Germany had committed a great crime," he told the Imperial War Cabinet in August 1918, "and it was necessary to make it impossible that anyone should be tempted to repeat that offence. The Terms of Peace must be tantamount to some penalty for the offence."[67] As the armistice approached, he seemed furious that hostilities would end before the war touched Germany:

> The Prime Minister said that industrial France had been devastated and Germany had escaped. At the first moment when we were in a position to put the lash on Germany's back she said, "I give up." The question arose whether we ought not to continue lashing her as she had lashed France.
> Mr. Chamberlain said that vengeance was too expensive these days.
> The Prime Minister said it was not vengeance but justice.[68]

Later, in early March 1919, he explained to the War Cabinet why British reparation demands were so much greater than those of the other Allies:

> The Prime Minister said that, as regards the possibility of Germany raising and maintaining a large conscript army, he thought our best safeguard lay in the imposition of a huge indemnity which would prevent the Germans spending money on an army. In regard to this indemnity, however, he understood that the French and the Americans had now agreed it should be no more than £8,000,000,000 [160 milliard gold marks]. As we had been the chief financiers of the war, it was intelligible that the French and Italians would not be so greatly concerned about the size of the indemnity as ourselves.[69]

In this, and in related documents, there is no hint that he was pressing British demands reluctantly, solely in response to inescapable political pressure.

It is important to recognize this strong admixture of punitive sentiment in Lloyd George's approach to peacemaking, whatever sympathy he might have felt for the notion of a peace of reconciliation. Political pressure alone simply does not adequately account for the reparation policy Great Britain pursued after the armistice and at the peace conference. Lloyd George did not have to commit himself, a few days before the elections of December 1918, to demanding the whole cost of the war from Germany. He did not have to appoint Hughes and Lord Cunliffe, both of whom he knew to be strong advocates of a huge indemnity, to key positions on the commission set up by the peace conference to deal with the reparation question.[70] He did not have to hold out so stubbornly for figures for the German debt which—as will be shown later—were substantially higher than those the Americans and the French were ready to accept. He was no slave to Parliament—in Britain, unlike France, the government can threaten dissolution—and his relations with Unionist leaders, and especially with Bonar Law, were excellent. There was at no time any prospect of a Parliamentary conspiracy which had a serious chance of overthrowing his government. If Lloyd George opted for a relatively harsh reparation policy, it was to some extent, therefore, because such a policy had a real appeal for him. This was no quirk of his personal temperament: the idea of a punitive peace was organically related to the whole moralistic approach to international politics characteristic of the moderate left.

This general approach revolved around a few key propositions. The natural order was peaceful; war, therefore, was the deliberate product of perverse human will. If war could only be caused by aggression, the deterrence of aggression through the introduction of the rule of law into the international sphere would be an adequate guarantee of peace. But the rule of law had substance only if lawbreakers were punished. To establish the rule of law and to vindicate principles of justice, those responsible for the war—the German government backed by the German people—would have to be forced to make amends for their crime. It was only after the German people had demonstrated its ability to control its own government and its willingness to accept the new international order based on principles of justice—an order symbolized by the League of Nations—that Germany could be reintegrated into the international system.[71]

In the latter part of the war, Woodrow Wilson, in particular, tended to approach the problem of peacemaking from this point of view. This of course has been overlooked by many historians and others, inclined because of their sympathy with Wilson to project their own image of "Wilsonianism" back on American policy in 1918 and 1919. But the evidence abundantly indicates that Wilson was at this time no advocate of a compromise peace, or of a peace of accommodation with Germany. His public speeches alone show how completely the notion of "peace without victory" had disappeared following the declaration of American belligerency in 1917. In his view, the issue of the war was clear-cut: "The whole world is at war because the whole world is in the grip of that power [Germany] and is trying out the great battle which shall determine whether it is to be brought under its mastery or fling itself free."[72] If the war was a struggle of good with evil, it followed that absolute victory was essential, and that the forces of evil must be destroyed: "This intolerable Thing of which the masters of Germany have shown us the ugly face, this menace of combined intrigue and force which we now see so clearly as the German power, a Thing without conscience or honor or capacity for convenanted peace, must be crushed and, if it be not utterly brought to an end, at least shut out from the friendly intercourse of the nations."[73]

With such aims, a compromise peace was unlikely: the rulers of Germany would hardly consent voluntarily to their own destruction. But Wilson had no desire in any case for a compromise peace: his speeches bristle with contempt for the very notion of a compromise settlement. Principles of justice, and not the accommodation of interests, should dictate the terms of the settlement; the rule of law, and not the balance of power, would assure the stability of the peace.[74] Anyone who thought otherwise, and was willing to explore the proposals for a compromise peace that emanated from Berlin, was a dupe of the German government—or worse.[75]

Wilson's approach to peacemaking certainly had punitive overtones. "We are at the beginning of an age," he declared in April 1917, "in which it will be insisted that the same standards of conduct and of responsibility for wrong done shall be observed among nations and their governments that are observed among the individual citizens of civilized states."[76] This seems to imply that Germany's rulers would be held responsible for their crimes: clearly Wilson viewed them as conspirators against the peace and freedom of the world. But his views about the responsibility of the German people are less clear. He often publicly absolved them of responsibility for the crimes of their rulers, insisting that they were victims and would in fact be liberated by an Allied victory.[77] To what extent this was propaganda designed to split the German people from their government is difficult to say. Wilson, in any event, was clearly aware that the German government had not developed its plans in isolation from its own people: it was following the policy that German professors and publicists had long been expounding openly.[78] Moreover, he insisted that the German people "agree to a settlement based on justice and the reparation of the wrongs their rulers have done."[79] But if they were completely guiltless, why should they be obliged to bear any special burden at all? Certainly Wilson was later to defend the treaty by arguing that it was just to punish the German people for their crimes:

I hear [he said in a speech on September 18, 1919] that this treaty is very hard on Germany. When an individual has committed a criminal act, the punishment is hard, but the punishment is not unjust. The nation permitted itself, through unscrupulous governors, to commit a criminal act against mankind, and it is to undergo the punishment . . . it must pay for the wrong it has done.[80]

He had in fact made much the same argument privately at the end of the peace conference.[81]

This is not to say, of course, that the ideal of reconciliation played no role whatsoever in Wilson's thinking; reconciliation was of course desirable as an end in itself. It seems, however, that in early 1919 liberals like Wilson and Lloyd George thought—or very much wanted to think—that there was no conflict between the ideal of justice, with all its punitive overtones, and the notion of reconciliation with Germany.[82] Germany, it was assumed, would accept the Allies' judgement, make penance, and undergo a period of probation to make sure that her conversion to democratic and peaceful ways had been genuine. Then she would be formally "redeemed" and rehabilitated as an equal member of the community of civilized nations.[83]

The very fact that a period of probation was thought necessary shows that the peacemakers of 1919 were to some extent aware that things might not be so simple. Indeed it is clear that Wilson had grounds to suspect the sincerity of the German Revolution of November 1918. He knew the dominant role that American insistence on the end of the imperial regime had played in its demise. Was it not possible that the ''revolution'' had been largely cosmetic, designed to appeal to the democratic prejudices of the West and thus get the best possible peace settlement? Wilson probably had his suspicions. In any case, the turmoil of the revolutionary period was a serious cause for concern: how much could the Allies rely on a regime whose hold on power was so tenuous?[84] And just after the armistice Wilson took a definite position on a point that he had previously left somewhat vague: Germany would have to undergo a period of probation before she could be admitted to the League.[85]

But if it was somehow understood that the liberal scenario might not work—that there might be a conflict between the ideals of justice and reconciliation—this was a problem that liberal peacemakers preferred to push aside. As a result, both American and British policies were built on a weak conceptual base—weak, because both were rooted in ideas that were to prove inconsistent. This was to be a basic cause for the instability of American and British policy in the post-conference period: the great speed with which the policy of both powers was to shift at the end of 1919 cannot be understood without taking these conceptual weaknesses into account. For Germany was not to accept the Anglo-Saxon notion of justice, and so a choice had to be made: Reconciliation or Justice? Revision of the treaty or its enforcement? The fact that reparation had by this time become the central issue in Germany's relations with the West had a lot to do—as will be seen—with the tendency of Anglo-Saxon opinion to opt for the first alternative.

How did French policy fit into this? Clemenceau understood the weaknesses of the Anglo-Saxon approach. To him it was obvious that every nation had a different idea of justice, that the hope of Germany accepting the Allies' notion of justice was chimerical, and that a peace based on that notion therefore needed force to uphold it. He worked to uphold the Alliance, because he understood that superior force had to be put behind the treaty if the postwar system was to endure. But he also feared the disruption of the Alliance, for how long would America and Britain, countries whose position and whose interests differed fundamentally from those of France, be willing to commit their military power to the maintenance of the peace settlement? For to liberals, it was clear, peace meant that force no longer had a legitimate role in international politics. It was therefore important to keep other options open; the Rhenish policy was one result. But it was not the only one, for Clemenceau (it will be clear) was also willing to probe the possibilities for an arrangement which at the very least contained the seeds of a future Franco-German alignment.

Insofar as reparation is concerned, what all this implies is that contrary to the traditional interpretation, there was no great conflict of principle between the Americans, say, and the French. If the Americans had had as their overriding goal a peace of reconciliation with Germany, and if the French had sought primarily to crush Germany, there would have been such a conflict of principle. But with Wilson convinced that Germany had committed a great crime and should pay, and with Clemenceau to a certain degree sharing this view, and eager in any case to compromise with the Americans, great disagreement in this area simply did not exist.

Given all this, it should not be surprising that French and American reparation policies were later to converge. But at the start of the conference the French, for tactical reasons, supported British claims to a huge indemnity, including war costs. The Americans in the Commission for the Reparation of Damages (CRD), on the other hand, scrupulously adhering to the terms of the "pre-armistice agreement," opposed the inclusion of war costs.[86] But there was an important difference between the British and French positions. The French wanted priority for reparation, strictly defined. The British opposed this demand, for given the limitations on Germany's capacity to pay, allowing reparation of damages as a preferred claim would mean that the rest of the bill would probably never be paid. Since the British share of war costs was quite high, while her share of direct civilian damages was quite low, the actual amount the British Empire would receive, if priority were admitted, would be unacceptably small.

On February 19 Lloyd George informed the War Cabinet that "he had sent a note to Mr. Hughes, urging that reparation must include indemnity, and had added that, in his judgment, reparation should not come first; if it did, Great Britain would recover nothing at all." He was alarmed by apparently premature reports that the French "were restricting their claims to claims for war damage, and would not press for indemnity." The British, he said, "were standing alone in this matter."[87]

If priority for reparation in its strict sense were not accepted, it would perhaps be unwise for the French to insist on the inclusion of war costs. Their total share of German payments would be much smaller, for example, than that allotted to the British. Moreover, the French attempt to use large reparation claims as a lever for inducing the United States to provide financial aid through accepting an "equitable" redistribution of costs arising from the war was proving fruitless. The idea of pooling war costs had earlier been adopted as French policy when proposed by Clémentel, and at the conference French delegates continued to pursue this policy. While formally presenting large claims, they hinted broadly that they would moderate their reparation demands if their associates agreed to come to their assistance and share part of the burden that would not be placed on Germany. Thus in the Financial Commission on February 20, Klotz insisted on the link between reparation and the settlement of inter-Allied financial questions. "The attitude of the Minister of Finance," he said, "will depend to a certain extent on the way inter-Allied questions are solved." If French reparation claims were not adequately satisfied, "it will then be necessary for my friends to come to my assistance."[88]

In private conversations, French representatives were more specific. They made it clear to the Americans that they wanted to pool war costs and reapportion the inter-Allied debt, each nation paying according to its ability.[89] President Wilson and his advisers were extremely hostile to these plans and would not even discuss them. Norman Davis, Wilson's principal financial counselor in Paris, wrote the President on February 2 to inform him of the "concerted movement, which is on foot, to obtain an interlocking of the United States with the continental governments in the whole financial situation." Wilson assured Davis on February 5 that he was already aware of it and "on my guard against it."[90]

The American position was starkly laid down in early March. In a letter of March 8, Albert Rathbone, an Assistant Secretary of the Treasury, declared his displeasure at reports that Klotz favored the reapportionment of war debts. "I have, however, to state most emphatically," he wrote, "that the Treasury . . . will not assent to any discussion at the peace conference, or elsewhere, of any plan or arrangement for the release, consolidation or reapportionment of the obligations of foreign governments held by the United States. The

Treasury would discontinue advances to any government that supported such schemes."[91] And on March 9, Davis "very frankly" stated to Klotz

. . . that his efforts to bring pressure to bear from one direction for the increase of American advances to France, and from other direction to bring up the matter of reapportioning war debts, etc., was very ill advised, because no one can do anything or give any consideration to the latter, but should there be any further attempt to bring it up for discussion, it would have to be insisted by us that the discussion be had with the Secretary of the Treasury and that we would feel obliged, pending such discussion, to make the suggestion to the Secretary of the Treasury that it would not be advisable to continue to accept further obligations.[92]

From the American point of view, this harsh medicine brought the French back to their senses. His declarations to Klotz, Davis wrote, "apparently had the desired effect and it was stated by Klotz that he would not again bring the matter forward." A few days later, Davis expressed satisfaction that the French were "not difficult to do business with now that the intrigue has been rounded out of the situation."[93]

Thus the French effort to manipulate the United States had ended in utter failure. That the effort was made at all is in itself remarkable, for it was based on a profound and surprising misunderstanding of American attitudes and policy. By the beginning of March, there was no use in playing the game any longer, and from then on, the French delegation delicately pursued an essentially moderate reparation policy, going so far as to approach the Germans directly, as will be discussed later in this chapter. The new French policy was not as forthright as it might have been, evidently for fear of publicly appearing more moderate than the British.[94] As a result, the image that had formed in liberal American and British circles of a vindictive France, eager for crushing indemnities, remained intact.

Many Americans, including some of the delegates at the peace conference, were disposed to think in these terms anyway. In their highly moralistic but somewhat provincial view, the peace conference was basically a struggle between America, moderate and conciliatory, "the disinterested nation," in Wilson's phrase, and France, eager for crushing indemnities, incurably addicted to the old devious ways of diplomacy that the war had discredited and that Wilson intended to overthrow.

In reality, French policy was more moderate than many of these Americans supposed. Raw materials were what the French officials really wanted from Germany by way of reparation; above all they wanted to secure a substantial supply of coal. In general, they were not interested in finished goods. Loucheur and Clémentel made this point explicitly in a note of April 1: to pay reparation, "Germany must increase her exports, not in manufactured products, but in raw materials and in products demanded by the Allied and Associated nations."[95]

Aware that their real demands on the German economy were relatively modest, the French representatives were willing to see the German debt set at a comparatively modest figure. Moreover, they wanted a fixed sum of this sort in order to be able to "mobilize" the debt. The French government needed the money immediately, not spread over a large number of years. Only a moderate, fixed debt could be readily "mobilized"; if the debt were too large or too indefinite, the American investors would simply not risk buying the reparation bonds. Thus the French government hoped to derive two basic advantages from the reparation settlement: deliveries in kind, and indirectly, American credits.

The essential moderation of French reparation policy in 1919 is best demonstrated through an examination of French policy on the fixed sum. Here Loucheur, with Clemenceau's support, fundamentally sided with the Americans in the negotiations on a figure, while the British consistently took a more intransigent position.

By early March, the attempt to include war costs in the bill had been abandoned. All that remained was a proclamation of German responsibility for the war. This had evolved out of an American attempt to break the deadlock over war costs. John Foster Dulles, then a leading American representative on the CRD, suggested that Germany could be held theoretically liable for all costs growing out of the war; in practice, because of her limited capacity, her real liability would be limited to the list of damages acceptable to the Americans. In subsequent drafts, the Americans sought to avoid any recognition of the right of the Allies to be reimbursed for war costs. Instead, they preferred the more indirect form of an affirmation of German responsibility. To avoid any implication of legal responsibility, Norman Davis preferred that the treaty text imply that Germany was morally responsible: "It can be said that Germany was morally responsible for the war and all the consequences thereof, and legally that she is responsible in accordance with the formula adopted for damage to property and to persons.''[96] It was in this way that Article 231, the famous "war-guilt clause," was drafted into the Treaty of Versailles.

Even before the war costs debate faded away, French tactics on reparation had changed. Obliquely at first, then more directly, they broke their front with the British and began to side with the Americans on the key issue of a relatively moderate fixed sum. This shift first became evident in the second subcommission of the CRD, which had been charged with studying Germany's capacity to pay. The British delegate Lord Cunliffe was chairman of this subcommission. As Governor of the Bank of England during the war, Cunliffe had defied the authority of the government, and had been forced to resign in 1917.[97] But he was on good terms with Lloyd George personally, and had been appointed to the Committee on Indemnity in 1918. In this body, he had claimed that Germany could pay the costs of the war, and he seemed to defend this point on February 21 in a remarkable speech to the subcommission.

Cunliffe refused in this speech to engage in anything approaching a systematic study of Germany's economic capacity. Instead, he emphasized the role of credit, conceived of as a semimystical endowment, as the true determinant of Germany's ability to pay.

In the future even more than in the past, the world will be guided by credit even more than by capital or liquid money. Credit is more important than money, capital or wealth. Credit pays no income tax, it pays no tax at all. It can be extended, it can be enlarged. In a word, it is much more extensible than money, capital or wealth.

By never losing sight of this fact, we will most certainly be able to set enemy capacity to pay at a satisfactory figure. In the world of finance, to which I belong, the credit of a nation is estimated by taking account of its industry, its wealth, its spirit of economy, its laboring spirit, and its discipline. . . . Nobody will deny that the Germans very precisely fit the description of a credit-worthy nation.[98]

The difficulty here lies in Cunliffe's failure to distinguish between credit in the sense of an extension of money, generated by the banking system, and credit in the sense of ability to borrow, which is determined ultimately by ability to pay through earnings made by real economic transfers. Cunliffe inverted this connection: credit, he implied, was a determinant rather than a function of capacity to pay. By confusing the two meanings of credit, he gave the impression that Germany's ability to borrow, and hence capacity to pay, was virtually unlimited. Indeed, the point of his speech was that the subcommission need not worry about the problem of capacity at all. "I repeat," he said, "we must expect that many will find the figures that we will demand monstrous. We will answer their criticisms by saying that we have only made an estimate; and if they ask us to prove that our figures are exact, we will reply by asking them to prove their inexactitude. However, it is impossible to make this proof."[99] Although Cunliffe had at first warned the subcommission against concerning itself with war costs, he clearly implied that Germany could pay such costs, remarking that Lloyd George had estimated these at 480 milliard gold marks.[100]

Loucheur was probably amazed by this speech. After all, the subcommission had been specifically charged with investigating the question of German capacity, and now Cunliffe, in his muddled way, was suggesting that the problem did not exist. Loucheur began an indirect attack on Cunliffe's position. First, he stated that if war costs were included, the bill would come to about 800 milliard gold marks, but for the sake of argument he would take the British figure of 480 milliard. He estimated that Germany could make an immediate payment of about 20 milliards, principally in gold, ships, and foreign assets and securities. The balance had to be amortized at 5 percent over a fifty-year period. This amounted to an annual payment of about 24 to 28 milliard gold marks. Reparation in kind—coal, wood and potash principally—could account for 3 to 4 milliards annually. The balance of the annuity amounted to 22 milliards.[101] "Is this an impossible figure?" Loucheur asked. "I do not think so."[102] But far from being an expression of support for Cunliffe's position, this statement was merely the first step in a *reductio ad absurdum* designed to demolish the idea that such a large figure was within reason.

Loucheur surveyed some possible means of payment. A tax on German exports? "That is one way" that the Germans might be made to pay. "But I fear," he said, "that the use of this means of payment might hurt us more than it would help us, for it threatens to put Germany in such a state of inferiority in export markets that she will no longer export at all." He concluded that for the balance of the annuity beyond what Germany could pay in kind, "I declare myself unable to indicate the means of payment. I would be very happy if any of our colleagues can bring up any new ideas which might open up horizons that I am presently unable to see."[103]

The next day he took the argument to its conclusion that enormous payments were impossible. The American delegate on the subcommission, Thomas Lamont, had suggested a bill of 120 milliard gold marks. This was equivalent to an annuity of about 6.4 milliards. But was even this relatively modest figure within Germany's capacity? "I have listened with great care to all that has been said here," Loucheur declared, "and I am obliged to state that all the means of payment that we have succeeded in finding can only cover an annuity of 4 to 5 milliards [of francs, equivalent to about 3 to 4 milliard gold marks]. If the Commission adopts the figure of 1000 milliards [800 milliard gold marks—equivalent to an annuity of over 40 milliard gold marks], what new means of payment will we propose? I see only one, seizing the fortune of the enemy countries in the enemy countries themselves. I am not suggesting that we adopt this method. Only if we demand that much this is what we will have to do."[104]

He then posed the question more sharply. Should the Allies become the owners of German forests, mines, houses and factories? Perhaps ownership of the forests was possible. But as for the mines, "I confess that I would not want them at any price, because the mine without the miners, and the miners without political control is impossible."[105] Should the Allies seize Germany's industrial fortune, say half of her corporate wealth? Loucheur doubted whether the Allies were willing to take this kind of measure. If this was out of the question, he said, "our labors are just about over. We have only to sum up and conclude first, that we can get an immediate payment of 25 milliards [20 milliard gold marks], and second, that they will pay us an annuity of 8 milliards [6.4 milliard gold marks, corresponding to Lamont's 120 milliard figure for the debt], or 33 milliards [26.4 milliard gold marks, corresponding to Cunliffe's 480 milliard figure], that we can just about see how the payment of the 8 milliards can be made, but as for the payment of the 33 milliards, *we leave to the poets of the future the task of finding solutions.*"[106]

By this analysis, Loucheur completely discredited Cunliffe's baseless estimates. He was thereby laying the groundwork for a relatively modest settlement. At this meeting of February 22, Loucheur, Cunliffe, and Lamont were appointed a special committee to draft the subcommission's report. These three delegates used the occasion to negotiate privately on the size of the German liability. "To Lamont, Loucheur appeared very conciliatory, for he agreed rapidly to make a great concession, to come down to 160 milliard marks. After this, Cunliffe promised to consider a figure of 190 milliard marks. As Lamont has said, 'This was progress'; but then Cunliffe and Sumner 'put their heads together, went off the deep end, and refused to compromise at all.' According to Lamont, Loucheur had been brought substantially to accepting the American view, but Cunliffe proved the chief obstacle to complete agreement."[107]

This evidence of French moderation disturbed both the British and the American delegations. Cunliffe suspected foul play. He wrote Lloyd George on March 2 that the American and French delegates on his subcommission had "come to some arrangement" whereby the latter had reduced his reparation figure from 600 down to 160 milliard gold marks. "I cannot say what the bargain is," Cunliffe added, "but the result is that we shall be practically left out in the cold." He urged Lloyd George to "settle" the matter directly with Colonel House.[108]

House himself was concerned about the situation. According to his intimate Sir William Wiseman, he informally indicated to the British that he was "very anxious to avoid an open collision of view between the British and the Americans with the French supporting the Americans against us."[109] In outlining the situation to the Cabinet on March 4, Lloyd George did not take an accommodating tone; he merely noted that since the British "had been the chief financiers of the war, it was intelligible that the French and the Italians would not be so greatly concerned about the size of the indemnity as ourselves."[110] Nevertheless, he did cooperate with a new effort initiated by House to reach agreement on a figure: "after some hesitation and largely on my advice," according to House, Lloyd George appointed Edwin Montagu, the Secretary of State for India, to a three-man committee charged with working out a fixed sum.[111] Loucheur represented France on the committee, and Norman Davis was the American delegate.

The Committee of Three reported to the heads of government on March 15. It recommended a reparation debt of 120 milliard gold marks, payable half in gold and half in German currency. According to Davis, Lloyd George at first protested this figure, but then was persuaded by Davis's argument to agree to its inclusion. Loucheur recorded that at this meeting Lloyd George "cried out against the smallness of this figure," but does not record his eventual agreement. Loucheur, incidentally, noted that Clemenceau had approved the concessions he had made.[112]

Three days later, on March 18, Sumner had replaced Montagu as the British representative on the Committee of Three, and Lloyd George denied that any figure had been accepted.[113] The pretext for Montagu's replacement was that he had to return to Britain because of his mother's death. But he was able to return to Paris shortly, and the substitution of Sumner, who took a much harsher line, must be seen as a political move.[114]

It is sometimes argued, however, that soon afterwards Lloyd George made a serious effort to pilot British policy into more moderate channels. This attempt, it is said, was frustrated because of the "intrusion" of domestic politics.[115] It is correct that Lloyd George, in the famous Fountainebleau Memorandum written toward the end of March, in principle advocated a moderate settlement out of the fear that harsh peace terms might drive Germany to Bolshevism. But this document marked no change in actual British reparation policy, and in fact there is no evidence that the upswell of political pressure in early April had any substantive effect on British policy at all: Lloyd George at no point opted for a moderate stand on reparation, let alone drew back from this position as a result of a parliamentary rebellion at home.

The Fontainebleau Memorandum was circulated to Lloyd George's colleagues on the Council of Four on March 25. In it he declared that "we ought to endeavour to draw up a peace settlement as if we were impartial arbiters, forgetful of the passions of the war."[116] It seems, however, that Lloyd George was talking mainly about the territorial settlement, not the reparation clauses. When the Council of Four discussed the memorandum on March 27, he rhetorically asked: "What did France resent more, the loss of Alsace-Lorraine or the obligation to pay an indemnity of 5 milliards? I know your answer in advance. What impressed me the first time I went to Paris most was the statue of Strasbourg in mourning." Germans must not be placed under Polish rule. Anything else, he declared, the Germans would accept, "including a very heavy indemnity."[117]

The memorandum itself seemed to continue the call for a heavy burden: "Our terms may be severe, they may be stern and even ruthless, but at the same time they can be so just that the country on which they are imposed will feel in its heart it has no right to complain."[118] Lloyd George evidently supposed that the German people would share his conception of justice, that they would feel "in their hearts" Germany's guilt and their consequent obligation to pay an indemnity. The treaty, declared the Fontainebleau Memorandum, must take "into account Germany's responsibility for the origin of the war, and for the way in which it was fought."[119]

The more explicit references to reparation were remarkably vague. "If possible," he hedged, the reparation burden should disappear "with the generation that made the war"—a statement no one would disagree with. In the attached "Outline of Peace Terms," the section on reparation began with the statement that Germany was "to undertake to pay full reparation to the allies." But since this was greatly in excess of Germany's capacity, "it is therefore suggested that Germany should pay an annual sum for a stated number of years."[120] But this, in effect, was what the American and French delegates had already agreed to in the negotiations on a fixed sum, only to be blocked by British intransigence in holding out for higher figures. And the Fontainebleau Memorandum marked absolutely no change in the British position on this question, as will be demonstrated presently.

Finally, without even explicitly endorsing it himself, Lloyd George declared that "it has been suggested" that a commission be set up to allow postponement of payments and cancellation of interest on these payments, but only "during the first few years." The one precise suggestion he made referred to the allotment of German payments. He proposed that they be distributed according to the formula 50 : 30 : 20—50 percent for France, 30 percent for the British Empire, 20 percent for everyone else. In view of the fact that the British Empire had not been directly touched by the war in its home territories, this suggestion was neither very generous nor very enlightened. It contradicted Lloyd George's principle that the Allies should limit their claims to those the Germans would regard as just, for an indemnity to Britain would be viewed by the Germans as a clear violation of the prearmistice agreement.

It is important to note, moreover, that the Fontainebleau Memorandum and even Lloyd George's harsh criticism of a proposed reparation scheme in the Council of Four led to no change in the substance of British policy.[121] On March 22, Lloyd George had told Davis and Lamont that 100 milliard marks would be "quite acceptable to him" if they could get Sumner and Cunliffe to agree, "which he would like to have them do for his own protection and justification."[122] Lloyd George had thus given a veto over a reparation figure to a man who he realized was very far removed from the spirit of the Fontainebleau Memorandum: on March 26, the day after the memorandum was circulated, Lloyd George told his colleagues on the Council of Four, "when I spoke to Lord Sumner . . . of the danger of Bolshevism in Germany if we went too far in our demands, he answered, 'in that case the Germans would be cutting their own throats, I could not hope for anything better.' "[123]

Indeed, the same day that the memorandum was circulated the reparation figure proposed by Sumner was considerably higher than those proposed by the French and American representatives. The British suggested 220 milliard marks, the French a minimum of 124 and a maximum of 188, and the Americans a minimum of 100 and a maximum of 140 (in the French and American schemes, a commission would each year fix the annuity between the minimum and maximum levels).[124] Thus the noble generalities of the Fontainebleau Memorandum had little to do with actual British reparation policy.

It was British policy, especially British intransigence on figures, that was ultimately responsible for the failure of the treaty to include a fixed sum. The French and American delegates evidently wanted a figure. The latter repeatedly argued that the uncertain atmosphere that would prevail if the treaty failed to name a fixed sum would be disastrous to all concerned, to Germany as well as the West. In particular, a restoration of the international credit system was dependent on a fixed sum. No one would lend Germany anything, it was argued, if the amount due for reparation were not limited, for the money which would otherwise be used to repay such loans might have to go into paying reparation. But unable to borrow, Germany would be unable to procure "working capital," and the reparation annuities could not begin to be paid, let alone "mobilized" through the sale of reparation bonds abroad.

The French delegates could not fail to be impressed by these arguments. They needed the money immediately, and besides, "mobilization" would relieve them of the worry of enforcing payment.

This would become the problem of the bondholders. The French insisted, however, that their share of the reparation receipts cover the direct material damages they had suffered in the war: the French share of Loucheur's "minimum" figure of 124 milliard gold marks would "just about cover," he told the Council of Four on March 26, "the reparation of material damages."[125]

At this meeting, Clemenceau supported the plan outlined by Loucheur: the treaty would set minimum and maximum figures, and within these limits a commission would each year set the German annuity, taking account of German capacity. The American and French delegates had agreed on the principle of the plan, differing somewhat (by about 25 percent) on the figures. Clemenceau further declared that the governments could reserve the right to make further cuts in these figures, and could "even suppress the minimum," if it became clear this was more than Germany could pay; he even was willing to discuss the question with the Germans themselves, a point later reiterated by Loucheur: "there remains the possibility of not definitively setting our figure before discussing it with the Germans at Versailles."[126] In the discussion that followed, and in spite of the conciliatory language of the Fontainebleau Memorandum circulated the previous day, Lloyd George completely ignored this French suggestion.

In early April, Clemenceau and his closest advisors continued to favor some kind of fixed sum. He told Loucheur that it was "necessary to put a figure in the treaty," and asked him to "calm down Klotz, who now wants the moon."[127] Tardieu at this time proposed a plan which would have amounted to a debt of 120 milliard gold marks—the same figure Loucheur had previously agreed to with the Americans.[128] How moderate a figure would Clemenceau and Loucheur accept? They were willing to go quite far—indeed all the way back to the Fourteen Points and the pre-armistice agreement. In the afternoon meeting of the Council of Four on March 26, Loucheur presented the French claim for material damages—80 milliard francs, or approximately 64 milliard gold marks. Lloyd George vehemently attacked these figures as exaggerated and then demanded that British pensions be reimbursed at the higher British rate—he opposed Loucheur's proposal for a uniform scale based on the lower French rate.[129]

To avoid these unseemly battles over what amounted to apportionment, Norman Davis proposed the setting of percentages through direct negotiation. Loucheur and Lloyd George agreed; the heads of government left, and the experts began to negotiate. Loucheur gave a history of the previous bargaining on apportionment. By accepting direct bargaining on percentages at all, he said, France was abandoning the principle of an absolute priority for direct material damages, and so was making a great concession. He had at first proposed a proportion of 72 : 18, while the British suggested 50 : 33. "In a conversation with Mr. Montagu," he continued, "I went down to 58 : 25. Mr. Montagu suggested 56 : 28, which would have given England half of what France was to receive. I did not accept this suggestion, which in addition was not a firm proposition; from this Mr. Montagu concluded that no accord was possible."[130]

John Maynard Keynes, representing the British Treasury, asked Loucheur if he still proposed 58 : 25. Although Clemenceau had not authorized him to go that far, he replied, he was willing to endorse this proportion; "as a proof of good faith," he would even recommend the proportion 55 : 25.[131] Since the negotiations with Montagu in early March, however, the British had hardened their positon. While Montagu had been willing to accept 56 : 28, Lloyd George and now Sumner insisted on 50 : 30, considerably less from the French point of view than the Montagu ratio. Loucheur declared this unacceptable.

He then made an extraordinary declaration. He was willing, he said, to accept the literal definition of the word "reparation," "even if it excludes pensions." "I would prefer," he said, "the pure and simple application of the Fourteen Points to what is proposed." Limiting reparation to direct material damages would mean alloting France 70 percent of the payments. (Since he had estimated French direct material damages at 64 milliard gold marks, a strict application of the Fourteen Points would have meant a total German Liability of only 91 milliard gold marks.) But France had "made a concession to England taking into account her political situation." The French government, however, could go no further.[132]

Davis's response was equally remarkable. "If we Americans had followed our instincts," he said, "we would have kept to a strict interpretation of the Fourteen Points, which could not have yielded more than 25 milliard dollars [100 milliard gold marks]. We do what we can to interpret this definition in a broad sense, in order to find what is necessary to cover the pensions.''[133] The French were now more ''Wilsonian'' than the Americans! Davis refused the opportunity to form a common front with the French on a really moderate reparation settlement, firmly based on the prearmistice agreement, and this at a time when the arguments of the Fontainebleau Memorandum might have been used most effectively to overcome British obstruction.

Instead, Davis urged the French to compromise more. He proposed a ratio of 56 : 28, which was supported by Sumner. Loucheur would not go beyond 55 : 25, in spite of continued American pressure. ''I hope M. Loucheur will show the same spirit of conciliation'' as Sumner had shown, Davis declared; ''we have nothing further to propose.''[134] This was too much for Loucheur. ''Les Américains nous lâchent plutôt,'' he wrote in his diary, and to his fellow experts he declared: ''In my mind and in my soul, I cannot recommend what is not just. I made a great step forward; I regret that it has not been appreciated more, particularly by our American friends, and I regret to appear intransigent when I have gone beyond my instructions and beyond what I consider as strictly in conformity with justice.''[135]

The bargaining over figures sheds a certain amount of light on the relative severity of British, French and American reparation policy in 1919. But was all this a struggle over anything real? Perhaps all of these figures were so obviously impossible from a strictly economic point of view that this examination of the negotiations for a fixed sum is of very limited significance in itself, and that the real point to be made is that all the figures ''bandied about at the peace conference'' were so high as to be economically meaningless.[136]

What then do all these figures mean in real terms? The 120-milliard figure that the French and Americans were willing to accept in 1919 amounted to an annuity of about 6 milliard gold marks.[137] The figure was approximately the same for the main reparation plans for 1920 and 1921. The Boulogne Scheme of 1920 was worth about 100 milliard gold marks present value; the Paris Scheme of January 1921 and the Schedule of Payments of May 1921 were of the same order of magnitude.[138] It should be noted that it was never supposed that the full annuity would be paid at once, but would rather correspond to the reparation burden placed on the German economy after it had revived.

How then does the 6-milliard annuity figure compare to the national income figures for Germany in the late 1920s, after the German economy had recovered? Average GNP for Germany in the period 1925–1929 was 84 milliard gold marks.[139] The 6-milliard annuity was thus equivalent to about 7 percent of GNP.

Is an international transfer of this order of magnitude simply inconceivable? The experience of other countries with large unilateral transfers of wealth is relevant here. During World War I, for example, the American trade surplus expanded dramatically: a vast amount of real wealth was transferred across the Atlantic. After the United States came into the war, the trade deficits of the European Allies were financed largely by loans from the American government and money spent by the American army in Europe. In 1918 the government loans amounted to $4 billion, and direct military expenses came to $1 billion, or $5 billion in all. This compares with a figure of $76.4 billion for U.S. GNP for 1918.[140] Taken together these figures suggest that the unilateral transfer of wealth alone placed a burden on the American economy roughly equivalent to the burden the reparation annuity contemplated in 1919–1921 would have placed on Germany. It is also clear that the American economy in 1918 was bearing other exceptional burdens related to the war effort, and that even so its capacity for generating an economic surplus had hardly been exhausted.

There is, however, a problem with the American example. The merchandise export surplus in 1918 was only $3.3 billion, or 4 percent of GNP. The 1913 merchandise export surplus had been 2 percent of GNP. This hardly represents a vast shift of real resources. The relatively moderate trade figures are made consistent with the figures for capital movements only by the addition of an unusually large error factor. Perhaps the trade surplus was actually larger than the figures indicated, or perhaps the European Allies were somehow able to hoard their American loans for postwar purposes. But the discrepancy in figures deprives the American example of much of its force.[141]

The experience of the British economy before 1914 is perhaps of greater relevance. The net export of capital as a proportion of GNP varied tremendously in the course of the late nineteenth and early twentieth conturies. In the period 1900–1904, for example, the net British export of capital amounted to about 1.6 percent of GNP. For

1911–1913, the figure had risen to approximately 8.7 percent. The net shift was thus equivalent to 7 percent of GNP.[142] So without benefit of government intervention, the economy was able to effect a transfer of real wealth abroad roughly equivalent to what Germany was supposed to do under the reparation schemes contemplated in 1919–1921 without anyone worrying about or even being aware of any serious dislocation of international trade or finance.

It is necessary to be cautious here. None of this proves anything about what German capacity actually was or whether Germany could have paid reparation on the scale envisaged at the peace conference. The purpose of this discussion is simply to give a very rough idea of the meaning of the magnitudes involved and to disprove the idea that the figures of 1919 were "preposterous," "astronomical," obviously incapable of realization. It does not follow from this that the opposite idea that such reparations could unquestionably have been paid is true. The burden to be imposed on Germany was substantial, and a comparison with particular episodes in British or American experience in itself proves nothing about whether Germany could have paid since conditions were so different. The whole question of Germany's theoretical capacity to pay in fact is contingent on so many variables—demand schedules, quality of entrepreneurship, government policy and so on—many of which are measureable (if at all) only on the basis of somewhat arbitrary assumptions about behavior over time, that a rigorous and solid analysis might well be beyond the reach of economic science. An exact test of German capacity could only have been made by the Germans themselves: only if they had made a serious effort to pay reparation could the limits of their capacity really have been probed. But such an effort was not made—this point will be demonstrated in the chapters that follow—and as a result the political question of willingness to pay was much more important than the economic question of theoretical capacity. For this reason no attempt will be made to examine economic capacity in any detail—because of all the essentially unknowable variables involved, an attempt at precise analysis would in any case yield misleadingly exact conclusions. The struggle over reparation was political at its core; the political and not the economic side will therefore be the focus of the discussion here.

By the end of March, it had become clear that in all likelihood there would be no fixed sum in the treaty, not even a system of maximum and minimum figures. This was mainly due to inability to agree on figures. Instead a scheme had evolved for setting up a commission to add up the damages to be listed by category in the treaty, with power to decide how and when the bill would be paid. Variants of this plan had been suggested by French, American and British delegates. In its essentials, this was the scheme that was ultimately drafted into the treaty.

It was about this time, just after the hopes for a fixed sum had dimmed, that British representatives pressed strongly for the inclusion of a new category of damages: pensions and separation allowances. Sumner, on March 27, then the South African statesman Jan Smuts, on March 31, argued that these claims should be added to the bill. The French generally supported the British in this matter, but the Americans, for the most part, opposed the inclusion of pensions. Dulles argued that adding pensions to the bill would violate the prearmistice agreement—the same logic that ruled out war costs should also rule out pensions. But on April 1, Wilson turned this argument aside, exclaiming "Logic! Logic! I don't give a damn for logic. I am going to include pensions!"[143]

British insistence on the inclusion of pensions has always been somewhat embarrassing to those who believed that British ideas on reparation were relatively moderate, and that the lofty phrases of the Fontainebleau Memorandum were a true expression of British policy at the peace conference. Coming just a few days after the Fontainebleau Memorandum, and before any popular reaction could conceivably have forced Lloyd George to draw back from a moderate stance, the demand for pensions fundamentally contradicted the line of policy set out at Fontainebleau. For if an associate like the American government argued that the inclusion of pensions was a violation of the prearmistice agreement, the Germans would certainly feel that their inclusion in the reparation bill was unjust. Yet in spite of Lloyd George's principle that the Allies should avoid giving Germany the impression that she was being treated unfairly, the British delegation pressed forcefully for the inclusion of pensions.

It is widely claimed, however, that the demand for pensions was not in itself proof of the relative harshness of British reparation policy, for it was assumed that adding pensions would only affect the proportions in which German payments would be distributed, and would not affect the total amount that Germany would be asked to pay. Thus, in the mid-1930s, General Smuts declared that moderate delegates (presumably including himself) had supposed that Germany "would pay no more than a fixed amount"; including pensions, it was therefore supposed, would only affect apportionment.[144] Wilson's acceptance of pensions is defended in similar terms. "In conceding pensions," Davis declared in April 1919, "we did so on the theory that this would not increase materially the actual amount that Germany would have to pay, but would rather affect the method of distribution, because we regarded Germany's capacity as being agreed to as within the thirty-year limit."[145]

The evidence, however, does not support the contention that the British urged, and the Americans acquiesced in, the inclusion of pensions because of the apportionment consideration. Smuts's contention, in particular, is completely contradicted by a memorandum he wrote to Lloyd George on the indemnity question dated March 29, just two days before he wrote his memorandum on pensions. Smuts opposed a fixed sum and wanted all the damages included in the bill. "In the Peace Treaty," he wrote, "no amount should be specified, but the Germans should be responsible to make good all direct damage and loss inflicted on civilians, whatever that would amount to."[146] Nor does the evidence support Davis's contention that the Americans agreed to pensions because they believed doing so would only affect apportionment. In Dulles's memorandum of the meeting at which Wilson overruled his advisers and accepted pensions, there is no mention of the apportionment consideration. Maybe Wilson agreed to their inclusion simply because he felt Germany should, in justice, be obliged to reimburse the Allies for these costs. Perhaps he was simply caving in to a threat from Lloyd George to walk out of the conference if this demand were not met: on March 30, the British Prime Minister wrote Bonar Law that "Wilson does not like damage to combatants being included in the cost of reparation. I told him that unless this were included I might as well go home as I had no authority to sign unless this were admitted."[147]

Finally, a review of the negotiations that had already taken place on apportionment before the issue of pensions was raised completely discredits the idea that pensions were included for reasons of apportionment. On March 26, Sumner accepted 56:28, while Loucheur held out for 55:25: the British and French were not far apart. Is it seriously to be contended that the British pressed for the inclusion of a category of damage that would at the very least compromise the moral position of the Allies simply in order to gain a couple of extra percentage points? In fact, the British gained nothing from the inclusion of pensions. In December 1919, Great Britain and France agreed on a 55:25 ratio, the same proportion Loucheur had offered in March; this was reduced to 52:22 at the Spa Conference in mid-1920.

Why then did the British press for the inclusion of pensions? The evidence on this point does not permit a definitive answer. The chronology, however, suggests that pensions were included in order to provide a basis on which the apportionment of German payments which had nearly been accepted could be defended in the absence of a fixed sum—that is, in the system where Germany's debt would be determined by a list of damages: their inclusion came just after the abandonment of the fixed sum and the near-agreement on apportionment.

Davis, in arguing that pensions were included because it was supposed that this would only affect apportionment, claimed that the principle of limiting Germany's liability to her thirty-year capacity to pay had been accepted by the conference.[148] While there is no evidence that this principle had been accepted by the European Allies, the idea of letting Germany's thirty-year capacity to pay determine the bill had certainly been considered by the conference. In fact, for a long time there had been two competing bases of Germany's liability: her capacity and the list of damages.

In the end, it was felt that a choice had to be made, at least in the wording of the treaty, between the two notions. Originally it had been proposed that there be a provision requiring the enemy states "at whatever cost to themselves" to make reparation for damage done to the civilian population of the Allied states. The British and American delegates subsequently sought to substitute the phrase "to the extent of their utmost capacity."[149] Objecting to this change, the French took the question to the Council of Four on April 5. Lloyd George supported the French position that Germany would have to pay the entire debt no matter how long it took, although he felt the debt could be paid in thirty years. Finally both phrases were deleted, and it was Clemenceau who that day indicated the solution: Germany would be asked to make reparation for the enumerated damages. If, in the future, the Allies became convinced that this was more than Germany could pay, they could reduce the debt at that time.[150]

This is not to say that the notion of capacity to pay disappeared entirely from the treaty draft. Article 234 gave the Reparation Commission power, after considering periodically "the resources and capacity of Germany" to "extend the date and modify the form of payments," "but not to cancel any part except with the specific authority of the several Governments represented on the Commission." Article 18 of Annex II, furthermore, only recognized the right of the Allies to take measures against Germany in the event of *voluntary* default.

The idea of German capacity played such an important role in the whole reparation question that it merits close examination. The phrase "Germany's capacity to pay" is highly ambiguous, and the way it was interpreted tells a great deal about the way the whole reparation problem was approached in 1919. A study of this aspect of the question is therefore a useful way of ascertaining the intentions and concerns of the drafters of the treaty.

It is important to dwell on this aspect of the topic for another reason. Historians, adopting a particular approach to the question of "Germany's capacity to pay," have written as though it were an established fact of economics that large reparation payments were impossible. Events of the period are viewed in the light of Germany's perceived incapacity. The French have become figures of darkness; the attempt to extract reparation is generally condemned in unusually forceful language. The opponents of large reparations are treated with considerable sympathy, the heroes of the day. Their arguments are presented as indisputable, their beliefs declared vindicated by events.

The approach to the question of German capacity that dominates the historiography of reparation was also the approach that had the most prestige among the experts at the peace conference. It will be referred to here as the "transfer approach" because it stresses what was called the "transfer problem"—the problem, that is, of transferring goods and services across Germany's frontiers; or what amounts, broadly speaking, to the same thing, the problem of transferring the marks raised by the German government into the foreign currencies in which reparation had to be paid. The basic argument of the "transfer approach" was simple. What Germany could pay was essentially limited by what she could earn through foreign trade, for by and large in no other way could Germany obtain the foreign exchange with which to pay reparation. In other words, the measure of her capacity was the degree to which her exports exceeded her imports.

Thus stated, the argument appears irrefutable. It is nevertheless misleading, for the measure of what Germany *could* pay in any given year is not what her actual balance of trade *was,* but rather the most it *might* have been. For practical purposes, however, such a distinction appeared irrelevant. The existing balance of trade was accepted as a fact of life, determined autonomously, independent of such international financial movements as the payment of reparation. Only the vigor of a nation's commercial policy, the skill and drive of her exporters, and other factors of this sort, more psychological and political than economic in the strict sense, were seen as having a direct influence on the trade balance.

This kind of analysis led to pessimistic conclusions on the question of German capacity. From the point of view of the transfer approach, it did not matter how vigorous or productive the German economy might be; if, in a given year, German exports did not exceed imports, Germany could pay nothing in reparation through commercial channels that year. The existing trade situation was accepted as largely inevitable. Germany's capacity to make financial payments was for the most part seen as passive, a function of her actual commercial balance. Only to a small degree, and in a special sense, was it supposed that an effort to pay reparation could in itself influence the balance of trade: that through an aggressive commercial policy—harsh tariffs on imports, subsidies to exporters, careful organization for the "conquest" of foreign markets—Germany could act to create the necessary trade surplus.

At the peace conference, it was widely assumed that the Allies had no interest in inducing the German economy to develop along such predatory lines. A German trade surplus, it was felt, could only be created at the expense of Allied industry. The Allied export trade would suffer if Germany succeeded in capturing markets in third countries that the Allies coveted; national industry would be imperiled by a successful German "invasion" of home markets. If Germany cut her own imports, the Allies would lose yet another market.

The American delegation took the lead in arguing along these lines. Lamont, for example, wrote in late February that the German economy would have to remain on a "war basis" if it were to pay large reparations:

Germany must (as was the case during the war blockade) cut down all imports to the least figure commensurate with the amount of raw materials

which she actually requires from abroad, for the conduct of her domestic
and industrial life; and must turn herself into a nation of exporters, organized for the purpose of paying the reparation claims of the Associated Governments. . . .

The development by the enemy countries of such a policy as just described will inevitably mean the creation, especially in Germany, of an organization so highly developed and so skilled as calculated in the future to
have great influence for generations to come upon the markets of the world.
Therefore the question may well arise with the Associated Governments as
to whether, in the long run, grave economic disadvantages may not accrue
to the peoples of such Governments as a result of the methods which the
enemy countries must inevitably adopt in order to succeed (or even to stand
any chance of succeeding) in paying the figure of reparation set forth above
[120 milliard gold marks].

It must not be overlooked that such internal organization is based on a
minimum of consumption by the German population and that such reduced
consumption by 70,000,000 people may seriously affect the ability of the
Associated Governments to dispose of their surplus products.[151]

In mid-March the report of the Committee of Three, drafted by
Davis, emphasized the dangers to Britain and France of "closing
Germany as a market for their export products and making these
countries, together with other countries of the world, a dumping
ground for Germany's surplus products."[152] Since in 1913, the report argued, there was evidently "no unfilled demand for any further
products," Germany's ability to earn more through exporting more
without taking markets away from anyone else depended on how
much "the consumptive power of the world" could be increased.[153]
The committee estimated, without explaining its reasoning on this
point, that an indemnity of 40 to 80 milliard gold marks over a period
of twenty to thirty years was within reason. But as to the estimates of
"eminent bankers" (an obvious allusion to Cunliffe) that Germany
could annually pay 12 to 16 milliard gold marks, the three experts
could

. . . say only that we are satisfied that such a performance on the part of
Germany is utterly impossible, because in the first place she would never
agree to such an undertaking, and in the second place, even if she were able
to do so, which is improbable, it could only be done by absolutely destroying the trade of England and France and other countries of the world, and in
order to do so Germany would have to develop a state of efficiency such as
has never been known in the history of the world, and if she can do this,

there is nothing we can do which would prevent Germany from overrunning the world thereafter.[154]

President Wilson took up the argument in the Council of Four on March 26. "Germany," he said, "can only pay such huge sums by taking an even greater share of the world market than was the case before the war. Is that in our interest? Would it not be better to earn this money ourselves on these markets, instead of encouraging Germany to take them from us?"[155]

The French delegation was certainly alive to the supposed dangers of a swift revival of the German export trade and hoped to guard against it. Loucheur, as noted above, basically wanted raw materials from Germany. He was reluctant to allow German industry to participate in the work of reconstruction: "We had hoped to place our orders in France and with our allies."[156] Dulles reported that Loucheur told him that the treaty clauses (Annex IV) giving the Allies the option to call on Germany to supply reconstruction goods,

. . . were sought primarily for political effect. He stated that he was vigorously opposed to permitting Germany to supply the machinery and equipment to be reinstalled in the devastated regions. This, he said, would be to give Germany a stranglehold on the economic life of northern France, as, once German machinery was installed, all replacements and spare parts would have to be supplied by Germany, and orders for enlargements and new installations would similarly go to Germany."[157]

Dulles himself in January developed the arguments of the transfer approach with characteristic rigor. The Allies, he said, could seize many of Germany's liquid assets—gold, foreign securities, etc.—immediately. But the balance of the German debt should not be expressed solely in terms of dollars, but rather

. . . in terms of the commodities which we can advantageously receive from Germany, or the labor which she can render us. When desirable imports or services are thus estimated and balanced against imports into Germany which we will desire to make, or services which we will desire to render her, the difference will be the amount we should demand as deferred payment from Germany. Once this calculation is made, it should be expressly provided that indemnity shall be paid by commodities and labor in a specified form and no other; otherwise, we will again give Germany an ascendancy in our markets which, while it will permit of the ready payment of a large indemnity, will, when the indemnity has been paid, leave her a commanding position in the trade of the world at the expense of the merchants of the Allied countries.[158]

This was in fact the method preferred by Loucheur. To him, German capacity was to be determined by adding up the total value of all the "means of payment" specified by the Allies and imposed on Germany.[159] Under his guidance, the second subcommission of the CRD proceeded to estimate Germany's capacity. Would Germany not need to preserve her precious metals as "backing" for her currency?[160] Would taking too much coal not only paralyze segments of German industry, but also affect the ability of the British coal industry to continue selling large amounts of coal to the continent?[161] As for restitution by equivalent—the replacement, for example, of machinery taken by the Germans from factories in the occupied areas with machinery in use in German factories—Loucheur had serious reservations. This, he said, was continually being proposed by the German General Winterfeldt at Spa; the Germans wanted to establish this principle in order to "send us their junk" ("nous repasser leur camelote"). But handled intelligently and with restraint, restitution by equivalent was a real possibility.[162]

The use of German labor was another means of payment studied at the conference. Loucheur favored the use of such labor in reconstruction work, but Cunliffe pointed out some of the problems. "First of all," he said, "do France and Belgium really want to take in a great number of men who are, at the very least, undesirable, and who might even be spies? . . . I believe I know something of the psychology of our enemies, and I would not be astonished if they released their criminals from prison in order to send them."[163] The proposal to force Germany to supply labor was ultimately dropped, since it smacked too much of slavery.[164]

Another means of payment discussed at considerable length by the subcommission was the imposition of taxes on Germany. But this means of payment was essentially different from the others discussed. The paper marks raised by most forms of taxation were not an equivalent kind of real wealth, of direct utility to the Allies, but only represented possible real wealth, which, if the subcommission had been consistent in its method, should have been estimated independently. The subcommission ended up begging the question of taxation anyway. It was not the business of the Allies, Loucheur argued, to dictate how the enemy countries should tax themselves. This was best left for them to decide.[165] Consequently on March 24, the idea of specific taxes to be imposed on Germany was dropped by the subcommission; with this decision, the subcommission's study of the whole question of German capacity was in effect abandoned.

The general method of the subcommission, however, illustrates how an extreme form of the "transfer approach" led to pessimistic conclusions. In fact, as indicated above, Loucheur had used this method in the subcommission as a means of discrediting Cunliffe's baseless estimates, and of demonstrating the severe limitations on Germany's capacity.

The transfer approach, which at the peace conference was considered the sophisticated approach to the question of German capacity, tended more generally to discredit the idea of large reparations. From the belief that only vigorous commercial activity and an aggressive commercial policy could substantially influence the balance of trade, it followed that the obstacles to the creation of the German trade surplus necessary to pay large reparations were so great that it was unrealistic to expect that Germany could pay such enormous sums. Moreover, even if Germany could develop her export trade to the extent required to pay large reparations, such a development was not in the interest of the Allies: if Germany could pay, it was only at the expense of Allied industry itself.

Because of the importance of the transfer approach both at the peace conference and in historiography, it is necessary to examine this set of ideas at length in the light of economic theory. I hope to show that this approach to the question rests on fallacious reasoning, and derives historically from what even in the context of the economic theory of the time were misconceptions concerning the working of economic mechanisms. This must be demonstrated in order to clear the ground and provide a fresh perspective from which to view the history of reparation.

The first point is that the transfer approach is not the only way in which the question of capacity to pay can be analyzed. Capacity can also be defined, for example, as the maximum surplus of real wealth that the German economy is capable of generating. In its most extreme form, such an approach to the question of capacity assumes a willingness on the part of the German people both to consent to the greatest sacrifices in reducing consumption and to make a supreme effort to increase production. Perhaps such assumptions are unrealistic, since in fact the German people would refuse to make even the kind of sacrifices it made during the war in order to pay reparation. But the whole point of the notion of capacity is to abstract from the notion of will: it makes no sense to say that the Germans could not pay because they did not want to pay. In any event, such extreme assumptions are by no means necessary, and any set of conditions generates its own definition of "capacity to pay." One may assume, for example, that Germany has a right to a "reasonable" standard of living, and that a "reasonable" amount is needed for investment. The miximum surplus beyond this point that her economy is capable of generating, capitalized over a given number of years, would then define her "capacity to pay."[166]

Such an approach to the question was actually taken at the time by Wesley C. Mitchell, a prominent American statistician and economist, chief of the Price Section of the War Industries Board in 1918, and after the war a founder and first Director of Research of the National Bureau of Economic Research. In response to a request from Dulles, Mitchell wrote a memorandum describing how Germany's capacity to pay an indemnity could be estimated. Capacity was defined as the "excess of annual production of wealth over and above what is necessary to sustain" the population and industrial equipment, and was estimated by adding to the amount expended on the war in the last twelve months of fighting, the productive power of the demobilized soldiers and the advantage derived from the lifting of the blockade; but the figure had to be adjusted for the loss of territory, and allowance had to be made for the economic restoration of Germany and for a more adequate standard of living than that which prevailed in 1918.[167]

The French Inspecteur des Finances André Poisson analyzed the question of German capacity in similar fashion.[168] But analysis of this sort was rare at the peace conference, and such ideas had no discernable influence on the prevailing approach to the question of capacity. Did not the problems of transfer make this "economic surplus" kind of analysis plainly irrelevant?

The answer depended on the existence of a mechanism of transfer by means of which the domestic economic surplus could be turned over automatically, through ordinary commercial channels, to the creditor nations. The transfer approach recognized no such mechanism: the balance of trade was thought to be relatively autonomous—not determined by movements of capital and other financial transfers—and it was supposed that the *prior* creation of a trade surplus was a necessary condition for the payment of reparation.

But financial and real economic movements are clearly linked—a trade deficit is impossible if the means of financing it do not exist—and it is because of the linkage between the two that an automatic mechanism of payment does exist. Far from being dependent on the prior creation of a trade surplus, financial movements like the payment of reparation in themselves actually help shape the balance of trade, and in so doing tend automatically to effect the transfer of the real wealth they represent.

In the classical theory as it existed at the time—as for example in the writings of Taussig and Viner[169]—the mechanism of transfer was not complicated. Under the prevailing paper money regime, where currencies of debtor and creditor were not convertible into gold, the key feature of the mechanism was a freely moving exchange rate. The German government, continually purchasing foreign currency with paper marks raised through taxation or internal borrowing, depresses the exchange value of the mark below its "natural" level—the exchange rate, that is, that would exist in the absence of such financial pressures. Because of the discrepancy between internal and external values of the mark, German exporters are in a position to profit. They buy goods cheaply at the German domestic price and sell abroad at the world price. Because of the fall in the exchange rate, the foreign exchange raised in this way can be traded for a relatively large amount of German money, and exporters' profits tend to increase. Over the economy as a whole, the divergence between internal and external values of the marks thus creates a premium for export: lured by increased profits, capital and labor are attracted to the export trade. Goods traditionally sold abroad are now exported in greater quantity; other goods, which previously it had not been profitable to export, can now be sold because a profit can be made. In this way German exports expand; conversely imports contract. Foreign goods become relatively expensive, and demand for imports declines. Thus a trade surplus is created. Its size and the speed with which it is formed are largely dependent on the degree to which internal and external values of the mark diverge. Exactly the opposite process applies to the creation of the necessary trade deficit in the creditor countries.

Neither Taussig nor Viner claimed that the mechanism could handle a payment of any size. But it is important to note that the empirical work of Taussig and his students demonstrated that the mechanism was more efficient, and that the problems of transfer were more limited, than they had originally supposed. When Taussig looked at the statistical evidence, what surprised him was the ease and rapidity with which trade balances moved to conform with financial movements. The theoretical explanation for this came later, first with Ohlin's idea of shifts in "purchasing power," and then when the theory of international trade was developed to take account of the Keynesian theory of employment. The recognition of the role of "income effects" led economists to view the mechanism of transfer as even more effective, and the problems of transfer as more limited, than Taussig for example had supposed in 1920. But the transfer problem was never dismissed entirely, and it has always been clear that the greater the amount to be transferred, the more limited the efficiency of the system would be. In effect, there would be an increasingly large "secondary burden" on the debtors resulting from the presumed shift against them of the terms of trade.[170]

Even to the extent that real problems of transfer do exist, it is important to recognize that such problems are by no means insurmountable. To the extent that markets fail, the state can intervene and create channels for the direct transfer of real wealth; through a system of material incentives and disincentives the state can assist in the shaping of proper patterns of trade. Thus problems of transfer are essentially technical and not absolute; if the will exists, they can always be overcome.

Perhaps this is all beside the point. Perhaps the real problem was not Germany's capacity to pay, but the Allies' reluctance to take the goods. In a speech in 1921, Dulles stressed the distinction: it was not Germany's capacity to pay, which Dulles viewed as substantial, but rather the rest of the world's willingness to receive that was the limiting factor. For sound economic reasons, according to Dulles, the Allies were not inclined to accept a large influx of German goods and services. Why should German rather than Allied industry be allowed to satisfy Allied needs? The payment of reparation was not worth a depression: "The Allies during twenty months of practical experience [with reparation in kind] have come to a realization of the havoc which would be caused by receiving a great quantity of economic values direct from Germany."[171]

The idea that the transfer of real wealth hurt the nation that received it was nothing new. Dulles and the other "experts," especially in the American delegation, had often argued along these lines at the peace conference; the acceptance of this point of view had the effect of discrediting the idea of substantial reparations. Moreover, many historians have taken the validity of this line of reasoning for granted.[172] In fact, the assumption that only the most moderate ideas on reparation were consistent with sound economic theory, everything else being a delusion, is quite common in the historical literature. It is this assumption which, in large measure, accounts for the hostile tone in which reparation has, until fairly recently at any rate, been discussed.

Is it to be supposed that an influx of real wealth from abroad necessarily hurts a nation economically? From the standpoint of social economy, there is no reason why a nation should not actually find such a transfer advantageous; in principle, there is no reason why any resource at the disposal of an economy must be left unutilized. Classical economic theory assumed that under ideal conditions an economy absorbs all the resources at its disposal. In the real world such assumptions do not apply; nevertheless it remains clear that the market is a powerful instrument for the absorption of new resources. Just as over the great span of history the world economy has absorbed the vast increase in per capita production resulting from technological advance, the automatic working of the market mechanism—especially in an inflationary economy like that of France in the early 1920s—would tend to permit the reparation creditors to absorb an influx of manufactured goods from Germany without detriment to themselves.

The "experts" of 1919 generally ignored the market mechanism; to them, the economic system was rigid, not malleable. Davis, for example, spoke of a fixed "consumptive power of the world." Classical theory, however, recognized no limit on the world's capacity to consume—no limit, that is, other than the world's productive capacity. In other ways as well, the kind of analysis which appeared as sophisticated in 1919 cuts radically against the grain of traditional economic theory. It was not just that the analysis of the "experts" ignored the role played by the market mechanism in the settlement of international balances and the general allocation of resources; more than that, it was based on assumptions whose rejection lay at the heart of classical political economy. The payment of reparation meant the creation of German trade surpluses and of Allied trade deficits; it meant the loss of markets to German commerce and a German "invasion" of home markets. Such developments were universally condemned by the "experts" of 1919. But the classical economists from Adam Smith on passionately attacked the common assumption that such developments were detrimental to the national interest. An influx of real wealth from abroad—that is, an excess of imports over exports, or trade deficit—was in itself viewed as patently desirable (assuming, that is, that it would not have to be paid for later). The loose doctrine that had grown around the idea that nations should seek to create trade surpluses Smith called "mercantilism." By this he sought to imply that a policy of encouraging exports and restricting imports (of manufactured goods especially) was promoted in the interest of the merchant class at the expense of the true interest of the nation as a whole. Adam Smith, therefore, would not have been surprised to see the "experts" of 1919 arguing along the lines they did. They were businessmen, bankers and politicians—almost never academic economists—and it was natural for them to assume that for nations as for businesses, it was better to sell than to receive.

Even if the views of the "experts" were not based on a sound understanding of economic theory, it would be wrong to suppose that their fears were groundless. The process by which the creditor nation would adjust to an influx of German goods would perhaps be painful for certain elements in its economy. The extent of the discomfort, however, is difficult to determine, since it is hard to tell to what degree resources would be "pulled" into new fields (for example, reconstruction work) by the lure of high profits, and to what degree they would be "pushed" out of old ones by German competition. It is clear, however, that by means of tax credits and other forms of subsidy, the state would in theory be able to minimize these problems of economic transition. Moreover, to a country like France, with the cessation of the war and the termination of Allied economic support, there would be a great problem of transition in any case; a priori, it is impossible to say whether transition to a situation where Germany replaced the Allies as the source of a large and continuous influx of real wealth would be more difficult than to a situation marked by the absence of any foreign assistance.

There is a more basic reason why the fears of the experts should not be dismissed too quickly. Economic theory, with its assumption of perfect markets, is but an imperfect guide; in the real world, supply and demand do not automatically and swiftly move into balance. But even to the extent that such problems of adjustment existed, it does not follow that the creditors should have waived their right to reparation. Payments which were "unabsorbable" through normal commercial channels (in the sense that their absorption would create significant unemployment in the receiver nation), could have been used outside these regular channels: the German resources they represented could have been applied, for example, to the construction of public works, such as hydroelectric projects, that otherwise would not have been built. Similarly, if an influx of German imports created some unemployment of labor and capital in France, these domestic resources could also have been applied to projects that would otherwise have been left undone. Thus there is nothing intrinsically impossible or undesirable about the transfer of large payments: to the extent that the market mechanism is inadequate, the state can step in and take up the slack. The creation of such machinery for state action was, in fact, one of the more interesting directions in which French reparation policy evolved later on.

The way the economics of reparation was understood by the "experts" of 1919 cannot therefore be accepted as gospel. Historians must nevertheless recognize that these pessimistic ideas—that substantial reparation could not be paid, and that even if it could, the Allies would be hurt if they accepted payment—played an important role at the peace conference. To be sure, these views did not fully shape the reparation settlement, but this was not because they had been refuted, but rather because other factors—notably the political climate in Britain and to a lesser extent in France—also came into play. Still, the role this set of ideas played was nonetheless real. Seeing the problem in these terms, many of the experts were more concerned with creating the appearance of large reparations than with designing a workable system for engineering large payments. Hence the aura of unreality that enveloped the reparation clauses from the start: the hollowness of the reparation settlement derived from the anxiety of its architects concerning large transfer.

By the end of April, the reparation clauses had taken nearly final shape. A body called the Reparation Commission, representing the United States and the European Allies, was to be created; by May 1921, it was to set Germany's debt by adding up damages listed by category in the treaty. It would then decide how and when the debt would be paid, but the total period of payment to be prescribed was not to exceed thirty years. Another provision (Article 235 in the final treaty) would govern reparation in the period before May 1921: Germany would pay 20 milliard gold marks, but not all of this would go toward reparation. Occupation costs would come out of this sum, as would the cost of German supplies of food and raw material, to the extent such financing was approved by the Allied governments. Again, the Reparation Commission was to decide the time and manner for the payment of the 20 milliards. There were various provisions for reparation in kind, and in addition Germany was to issue 60 milliard gold marks worth of bonds at once, with more to follow when the Commission unanimously judged Germany capable of paying the coupon on these bonds. (Whatever part of the 20 milliard payment under Article 235 went toward reparation would liquidate an equivalent amount of the initial 60 milliard bond issue.)

The bonds were prescribed largely as a means of satisfying the French demand for at least a partial "mobilization" of the debt. The bonds could be sold mainly in America, raising the money the French needed immediately. In theory, the bonds did not cover the entire debt. But the status of the part of the debt not covered by bonds was unclear: was not the failure to issue bonds an admission that this part of the debt was beyond Germany's capacity to pay? In practice, bonds were often treated as the main channel of payment—aside, that is, from reparation in kind; such a practical limitation on Germany's real liability, under the cover of a large but perhaps purely nominal debt, fit in well with the fears and hopes of many of the experts. The reparation settlement would appear large to public opinion while the real arrangement would be modest: the creditors would only receive raw materials, and, through the sale of bonds, the American credits they really wanted—exactly the kind of solution French officials had sought since 1918. Thus the transfer problem could be completely evaded: ". . . it was assumed," Dulles wrote in 1938, that by means of the bonds "reparation could be permanently absorbed into an expanded world credit structure and there could be an indefinite postponement of the problem of actually transferring goods or services in payment of this portion of reparation."[173]

It is thus possible that under the cover of the formal terms of the treaty, the experts had laid the basis for a relatively moderate settlement. A definitive interpretation of the bond issue is, however, impossible to give; the treaty does not clearly define the role bonds were supposed to play. Perhaps such problems were deliberately put aside in 1919. Indeed there is much in the treaty that seems deliberately obscure—the vague language describing the powers of the Reparation Commission, for example, or the provisions of Article 248, which, taken literally, would oblige the German government to pay its treaty obligations in full before spending anything for any other purpose, even for ordinary administrative expenses, unless it had secured the permission of the Reparation Commission to act otherwise. It does not seem, however, that such provisions were meant to be taken literally, and the Allies were surprised when the German delegation took them at face value.

The point is that the peace treaty in itself did not rigidly determine the future course of relations between Germany and the Allies. Like all such documents, it was subject to interpretation. The Allies were free to decide how to execute it, and its drafters took care to avoid locking the Allies into one posture vis-à-vis Germany. The very looseness of the treaty, however, created serious problems. Because the Allies had not made up their minds about the kind of peace they wanted, the solutions contained in the treaty were more apparent than real. The reparation settlement finally drafted rested on contradictory assumptions—a circumstance which in itself tended to compromise its viability. Take the bond issue, for example, which in practice was one of the central features of the settlement. Bonds could be sold only if the German people at least semivoluntarily accepted the obligation to pay reparation; for if they repudiated the legitimacy of this obligation, what sensible investor would buy the bonds? But in spite of the critical importance in this regard of the German attitude, the Allies were relatively unconcerned with how Germany received the treaty as long as it was signed. There was little concern for German sensibilities, as the case of Article 231 shows, and little effort was made to negotiate the treaty with the Germans—an imposed peace was largely taken for granted. Thus a fundamental incongruity was contained in the reparation settlement: on the one hand, the treaty took German hostility for granted, while on the other hand, the system presupposed German good faith in carrying out the reparation provisions.

Beginning in March, the French made an effort to square the circle by holding out to the Germans the possibility of substantial revision to be worked out through direct negotiation; final agreement would be reached only after the treaty was signed. First through Professor Haguenin, the Berlin representative of the French Foreign Ministry, and then in May through René Massigli in Versailles, the French government made repeated overtures to the Germans along these lines.[174] Both Haguenin and Massigli indicated French willingness to talk about the peace settlement in general—even about the territorial clauses—but they stressed especially the French government's intention to discuss concessions on financial and economic questions, such as reparation, reconstruction and industral collaboration. Massigli, who did not hesitate to use the phrase "collaboration franco-allemand," pressed in these talks for "practical, verbal discussions" between experts, on the basis of German proposals; toward the end of May he even went so far as to suggest the lines along which such negotiations should proceed.[175]

It is clear from the substance and even more from the tone of these talks that what the French government had in mind went far beyond a mere business arrangement with Germany. It was in fact aiming at some kind of political arrangement, although it is unlikely that at this point it had a very clear idea of what the terms of this relationship might be.[176] Nevertheless, French willingness to contemplate such a prospect was very significant in itself, and has to be understood in the context of the Clemenceau government's disillusionment with its allies. For in these talks Massigli's remarks bristled with hostility toward the "Anglo-Saxon Powers." The impression in Germany that France was Germany's only real enemy, he said, was "entirely mistaken." Massigli instead stressed the common interest of the two countries in opposing "Anglo-Saxon" domination, declaring that "the deepening of the opposition" between France and Germany "would lead to the ruin of both countries, to the advantage of the Anglo-Saxon Powers." On reparation, Massigli admitted that

Germany's capacity to pay had been overestimated, but he felt that Germany and France could cooperate on reconstruction within the context of the Reparation Commission system.[177]

The problem of bringing about such a *rapprochement* was politically difficult, and both Haguenin and Massigli urged the Germans not to make matters worse by taking a defiant and intransigent position on the peace terms.[178] But the German leaders, with barely an exception, were not at first particularly interested in these French overtures or even in the idea of a policy of accommodation with France.[179] These French initiatives were suspect in German eyes. It was possible that France was deliberately raising false hopes just to get the Germans to sign the treaty as is. Or perhaps France was trying to divide Germany from America, the ex-enemy Power most likely to take up the German cause. The German Foreign Minister, Brockdorff-Rantzau, was so committed to this policy of aligning Germany with American policy—or at least with Wilson's policy as it was understood in Germany—that as a matter of principle he refused to engage in direct negotiations with any individual Allied power, and in particular, largely refrained from making the kind of concrete proposals that could test French sincerity.[180] One German diplomat even argued that Germany had no interest in encouraging French moderation, since France's excesses simply alienated her from her allies.[181] Rantzau himself ignored French pleas not to be overly concerned with the exact text of the treaty, and to work out arrangements which would in fact amount to a revision of the treaty after it was signed.

Instead the German Delegation, presented with the treaty in early May, raged in a stream of notes against the proposed settlement.[182] Thus the German Economic Commission, in a report sent to the Allies on May 13, declared that "those who will sign this Treaty will sign the death sentence of many millions of German men, women and children."[183]

The formal "Observations of the German Delegation on the Conditions of Peace" forwarded to the Allies on May 29 was another strident denunciation of the draft treaty. The reparation demands were a principal focus of German anger. In his covering letter, Rantzau declared that the treaty would condemn the German people to "perpetual slave labour."[184] The Reparation Commission would have

. . . dictatorial powers over the whole life of our people in economic and cultural matters. Its authority extends far beyond that which the Emperor, the German Federal Council, and the Reichstag combined ever possessed within the territory of the Empire. This Commission has unlimited control over the economic life of the State, of communities and of individuals. Furthermore, the entire educational and sanitary system depends on it. It can keep the whole German people in mental thralldom.''[185]

These themes were elaborated in the ''Observations'' themselves and in the ''Statement of the Financial Commission of the German Delegation'' that was delivered the same day.[186]

But at the same time, the Germans made certain attempts to see whether some sort of accommodation was at all within reach. Was it possible to save the coal-rich Saar territory—to be internationalized for a fifteen year period according to the treaty—by offering to cede to the French part ownership in the German coal mines? The idea had been suggested by Massigli; representatives of German heavy industry were willing to go along providing the principle of shared ownership could be extended to the iron ore fields of Lorraine. In a formal note on May 16, the German delegation made a proposal to share ownership of the German mines in exchange for being allowed to retain the Saar. But French policy had by now changed and this offer was turned down. Perhaps the problem was that this proposal was too public, and that for political reasons, secret negotiation after the treaty was signed was the only way to proceed. Certainly French interest in reaching a direct agreement with Germany on economic questions, and in particular coal and iron, did not end with the signing of the treaty; negotiations on these matters did take place in the latter half of 1919 and continued sporadically through 1920.[187]

On the larger question of reparation as well, the German delegation made certain efforts at this time to probe the chances for a settlement. In their ''Observations,'' the Germans offered to pay 20 milliard gold marks by 1926, and up to another 80 milliards after 1926. Toward the initial 20 milliard payment, however, were to be credited such things as the value of the armistice deliveries (including military material), state property in the ceded territories and their share of state debts, and of course deliveries in kind and other forms of direct reparation.[188] The total debt might not reach 100 milliard gold marks—it was to be restricted to reparation for ''damage caused by Germany to civilians in the occupied districts of France and Belgium,'' and such damage had to be ''determinate, material and immediate''—and in any case, there would be no interest charged on any part of this proposed reparation liability.[189] The real value of the proposed debt was much less than 100 milliards, perhaps as little as 30 or 40 milliards.[190] Precisely how much less it is impossible to say, since no precise schedule of payments was proposed. Annual payments were to be no higher than a percentage to be fixed of total German federal and state revenues; for the first ten years, Germany would not have to pay more than 1 milliard gold marks a year, and toward the end of this period a new ceiling would be set by mutual agreement.[191]

All this was subject to certain conditions. Germany demanded among other things the "restoration of its over-seas relations, and of its colonies overseas, of its commercial establishments, etc."[192] A proportionate part of the reparation liability, furthermore, was to be imputed to the new owners of ceded territories (thus because of the reannexation of Alsace-Lorraine, France would assume a certain share of the reparation liability.)[193] Within these limitations, the Germans made certain proposals designed to facilitate the payment of reparation. They suggested that a German commission face, as an equal, the Allied Reparation Commission, with points of interest to be settled by a "mixed Court of Arbitration under a neutral Chairman."[194] In this fashion, damages would be assessed, the annuity set, and the value of the payments in kind determined. The two commissions would jointly work out the procedure for economic cooperation, including plans for the use of German labor in the reconstruction of the devastated areas, and the participation of German firms in the restoration of French coal mines. Germany offered "to do all she can" to supply France with amounts of coal corresponding to the deficit resulting purely from the destruction of the mines; the large additional options to Belgium, France and Italy contained in Annex V were rejected as "physically impossible."[195]

The fundamental German contention was that peace had to be based on mutual trust—on a spirit of cooperation deriving from a peace of reconciliation based on principles of justice. The problem was that the Allies and the Germans did not have the same conception of "justice"; the German terms for reconciliation were unacceptable to the Allies, who viewed the war as a crime and whose sense of justice ruled out an easy, generous peace. The German attitude, moreover, was not likely to convince the Allies that they could work together with their former enemies in a spirit of mutual trust. Wistfully, President Wilson contrasted German resistance with Austrian acquiescence: "If the Germans had had the good sense to speak like the Austrians, the situation would be better. The Austrians said to us, 'We are in your hands; but we are not solely responsible.' "[196] If only the German people, he seemed to feel, had honestly taken the position, through their representatives, that they would do their best to fulfill the peace terms, they would then not find it impossible to do business with the Allies. So much depended on how the treaty was executed. If the Germans showed as much good faith as the Austrians, the Allies would reciprocate; but if they resisted, the development of a spirit of cooperation and mutual confidence would be impossible, and the poisons of the war would be perpetuated.

Wilson and his American colleagues felt that the German delegation had failed to understand how the peace settlement would operate in practice. It was true that in many areas the treaty granted wide powers of discretion to the Reparation Commission. The Germans had assumed that these powers would be used against them—that the Commission was essentially an "engine of oppression"—and in fact, the Commission could be used in such a way without leaving the legal framework of the treaty. But the Allies had no intention of acting in this way; the discretionary powers of the Commission rather served to introduce a measure of flexibility into the system that everyone assumed would be used in Germany's favor. The true intent of the Allies should be carefully explained to the Germans; this, Wilson hoped, would relieve their anxieties and induce them to take a more reasonable attitude.[197]

The American delegation therefore pressed for a declaration of intent, which was to be put in the form of a reply to the German "Observations." The French did not oppose this initiative and completely shared American views on the role and power of the Reparation Commission.[198] But to Clemenceau such questions were of secondary importance. The Allies had no intention of using the treaty to "crush" Germany, and there was no reason to avoid a formal and binding declaration of Allied intent. It was not Allied policy that threatened world peace. The real danger lay elsewhere. In Clemenceau's eyes, the ferocity of the German reaction to the peace terms served only to focus attention once again on the great, unresolved problem of the peace settlement, the problem of enforcement. To him, Germany's resistance to the reparation provisions symbolized her refusal to accept defeat and resign herself to a new status quo. The bitter German repudiation of the treaty terms confirmed him in his conviction that Germany had not changed and that ultimately sanctions would be essential: Germany, he predicted, "would sign the treaty with the intention of not executing it, she will raise difficulties on one point, then on another, and if we have no way of imposing our will, everything will slip away bit by bit."[199]

In contrast, Lloyd George was disturbed by the unsubmissive tone of the German reaction to the draft treaty. He feared that Germany would not sign. What would the Allies then do? Would it not be better to give some satisfaction to the German complaints? Under the cover of defiant language, the Germans had presented certain concrete counterproposals. These should be explored. Thus the German "Observations" occasioned an eleventh-hour attempt at treaty revision. With respect to two key issues—reparation and Upper Silesia—this effort at modification took the shape of a curious struggle between the British and the Americans; the French again proved to be surprisingly accommodating.

Many British leaders went much further than Lloyd George in proposing changes in the treaty. This greatly irritated the Prime Minister, and his reaction to his colleagues' suggestions indicates that he was still somewhat out of sympathy with the idea of "appeasing" Germany.[200] Nevertheless he allowed the critics to voice their misgivings in a series of meetings of the British Empire Delegation (BED) held between May 30 and June 1.

The reparation settlement was a principal focus of criticism, but even at this point the moderation of British reparation policy is open to question. When Smuts argued at the first meeting that the treaty should be exclusively based on the Fourteen Points, containing nothing that was not explicitly provided for in Wilson's program, the Labourite Barnes asked if the Allies were then wrong to include pensions, which he said were not contemplated at the time of the armistice. Lloyd George replied that "in his opinion, the Allies could have included much more, for example damages for loss of trade."[201] (Smuts himself later remarked that British taxpayers "were just as much entitled to compensation as a man whose house had been destroyed.")[202]

Lloyd George, moreover, remained adamant in his opposition to any scaling down of Germany's reparation obligation. In the BED on

June 1, he returned to the subject of reparation, which he called "the most baffling and perplexing of all." "He did not think the time had quite come for letting Germany off of anything," and discussed the provisions for allowing the Allies to reduce the debt should payment prove impossible. His remarks in this connection, however, were based "on the assumption that Germany could not pay, but he did not accept that assumption, when he found, as he did, most prominent business men engaged in foreign trade advising him that Germany could pay."[203]

He was still opposed to a fixed sum. Instead he proposed two plans. The first plan, which he preferred, was for the Germans to contract to come in and restore the devastated areas; other reparation obligations (such as pensions) could be readily estimated and a figure given. The second plan was to insist that the Germans sign the treaty as it was, but to invite at the same time an offer of a fixed sum within three months. If the figure then proposed was unsatisfactory, everything would revert to the system prescribed in the treaty. The other members of the delegation rallied to the support of these proposals.[204]

The next day in the Council of Four, Lloyd George declared that British public opinion wanted "peace before anything else and does not attach excessive importance to the conditions of the peace."[205] Worried lest Germany reject the draft treaty and plunge Europe back into war, the British delegation, he said, therefore insisted upon certain treaty modifications that might induce the Germans to sign. He disclaimed personal responsibility for the shift in British policy, which he portrayed as being forced upon him by his colleagues. The British Empire Delegation had met four times, he said, to consider the peace terms. Representing a broad range of British and Dominion opinion, those who took part in these discussions felt, he declared, that only if the treaty were altered in certain ways would a renewal of hostilities (including a reimposition of the wartime blockade) be justified in the event of a German refusal to sign. In particular, they felt that the reparation clauses had to be changed. It was the "indefinite and unlimited nature of the debt imposed on Germany" that he said was most severely criticized.[206] Later in the meeting, he outlined his two alternative reparation schemes.[207] Wilson and Clemenceau declared that they would like to consult their delegations before going into a detailed discussion of the British objections and proposals.

Some of the American and French leaders had learned through experience to distrust Lloyd George. In August 1918 House had written of "Lloyd George's inability to act in any but a thoroughly selfish way—a way, indeed, which approaches dishonesty"; two months later, he noted that Clemenceau "spoke in acrimonious terms of Lloyd George and of the English generally. He said they did not tell the truth."[208] And at the time of the Fontainebleau memorandum, House wrote that "Lloyd George is a mischief maker who changes his mind like a weathervane. He has no profound knowledge of any of the questions with which he is dealing."[209] This old distrust now welled up again.

Wilson was particularly bitter. As a man of principle, he resented arguments of pure expendiency; as a moralist, he rejected the argument that the treaty should be changed merely because it was harsh. According to Baruch, Wilson told Lloyd George on June 2 that "he was not willing to change anything in the Treaty simply because it was severe; that he wanted this to be a historic lesson, so that people might know that they could not do anything of the sort the Germans attempted without suffering the severest kind of punishment."[210]

The next day, the entire American delegation held an extraordinary meeting to discuss the situation created by the new British attitude.[211] As far as the British were concerned, Wilson said, reparation was the "biggest point." Now that the reparation question was being reopened, the American experts again urged the inclusion of a fixed sum "as high as we really could get Germany to agree to without having a bayonet at her throat."[212] Only in this way could reparation be integrated into the world credit system, and the means thereby provided for enabling Europe to return to work. A fixed sum was better than either of Lloyd George's proposals. A contract for restoration was impractical and economically unsound.[213] Lamont suggested that this was just a device for temporarily evading the problem. "With all respect to Mr. Lloyd George," he remarked, "he is simply trying to postpone the evil day, as far as public opinion is concerned."[214] Influenced by his experts, Wilson resolved to press again for a fixed sum.

To the Americans it seemed that the French were still willing to be conciliatory on this point. The American experts had met that morning with Tardieu, now Clemenceau's closest adviser on foreign policy, who had indicated that the French would consider a fixed sum.[215] Of course, Lamont noted, Loucheur had "more to say about that than Mr. Tardieu," but in the past Loucheur had been willing to come to terms with the Americans on this question: "If it had not been for the British 'Heavenly Twins' [Sumner and Cunliffe], we could have gotten together with Loucheur months ago."[216]

Thus the Americans blamed the British and not the French for the reparation clauses, and it is in this context that Wilson's famous (and generally misunderstood) outburst of disgust at the British must be seen:

THE PRESIDENT: Well, I don't want to seem to be unreasonable, but my feeling is this: that we ought not, with the object of getting it signed, make changes in the treaty, if we think that it embodies what we were contending for; that the time to consider all these questions was when we were writing the treaty, and it makes me a little tired for people to come and say now that they are afraid the Germans won't sign, and their fear is based upon things that they insisted upon at the time of the writing of the treaty; that makes me very sick.

And that is the thing that happened. These people that overrode our judgement and wrote things into the treaty that are now the stumbling blocks, are falling over themselves to remove these stumbling blocks. Now, if they ought not to have been there, I say, remove them, but I say do not remove them merely for the fact of having the treaty signed.

MR. WHITE: Do the French remind you of that?

THE PRESIDENT: Not so much as the British. Here is a British group made up of every kind of British opinion, from Winston Churchill to Fisher. From the unreasonable to the reasonable, all the way around, they are all unanimous, if you please, in their funk. Now that makes me very tired. They ought to have been rational to begin with and then they would not have needed to have funked at the end.[217]

As were his American colleagues, Loucheur was dissatisfied with the treaty. He told Baruch on May 20 that the reparation clauses were a "mistake, and that his acquiesence in them was due to the political conditions in France."[218] He suggested that Allied "business experts" meet with the Germans to "find out from them what they needed to give them some hope for the future." But, as Baruch noted the next day, Loucheur could make no headway with Clemenceau on this plan.[219]

Clemenceau did not, however, rigidly oppose treaty modification. He accepted Lloyd George's alternative reparation schemes, and even went further than the British toward meeting the American position on a fixed sum.[220] Minor changes in the border between Poland and Germany, he agreed, were possible.[221] On the questions of the Silesian plebiscite and German admission into the League, he took the same position as Wilson, at first opposing them but then finally accepting the plebiscite and holding out the possibility of League membership for Germany once her good faith in carrying out the treaty had been demonstrated.[222] There was but one point raised by the British on which his opposition was steadfast: the proposed dropping of the provisions for the fifteen-year occupation of the Rhineland. To Lloyd George's argument that an army of occupation would not be needed to defend France from a disarmed Germany, Clemenceau replied that this was not the point of the occupation: it was rather a way of forcing Germany to comply with the treaty, and in particular with the financial clauses.[223] His insistence on this principle, however, did not preclude a willingness to modify provisions of secondary importance. He was willing to limit the size of the occupation costs which Germany would have to pay, and to restrict the activities of the military authorities, even to promise that the occupation forces would be withdrawn faster than the schedule laid down in the treaty if Germany showed good faith.[224]

Thus French reparation policy even in June was characterized by a distinct willingness to compromise, but for political reasons the French position now hardened in one important respect. Like Lloyd George, Loucheur was reluctant at this point to actually put a fixed sum in the treaty.[225] What had been acceptable before the terms of the peace were made public was now inexpedient: the Allies could not openly appear to be giving in to German objections. It was therefore not the right time for formal agreement on a fixed sum. But Loucheur still favored eventual agreement on a figure, and the French accepted the British suggestion that Germany be invited swiftly to survey the devastation, make offers for direct reparation, and propose a figure for the balance of the debt.[226] With the groundwork thus laid, Loucheur went on to propose a specific figure and timetable for agreement. According to his plan of June 5, the reparation debt would eventually be set at 120 milliard gold marks, a sum also supported at the time by the American experts.[227] The Germans would apparently be asked to propose this by September. Then, with the "crisis of public opinion" behind him, Clemenceau, Loucheur implied, would allow "his people" to accept the arrangement in early autumn.[228] This projected policy was of course fully consistent with what Massigli and Haguenin had been telling the Germans.

The British government was never willing to go this far at the peace conference. Even those British moderates who privately discussed possible figures at this time were hardly willing to go much further. Bonar Law contemplated a figure on the order of 100 to 160 milliard gold marks, and Smuts suggested 100 milliards, adding, however, that this "was probably not enough."[229]

In the face of Anglo-French resistance, Wilson did not insist on the inclusion of a figure in the treaty.[230] Instead, Lloyd George's proposals, along with a clarification of the reparation provisions, were embodied in the Allied "Reply" of June 16 to the German "Observations." The terms of the treaty remained intact, but in issuing the statement of principle contained in the "Reply," the Allies formally committed themselves to a moderate interpretation of the reparation clauses, and insofar as the Germans could trust the Allies to keep their word, many of the criticisms leveled against the treaty were fully met. From the German point of view, this was almost as good as a formal modification of the treaty terms.

The Germans had protested that the Reparation Commission could dictate German legislation, determine the shape of the German budget, and demand the imposition of taxes in Germany. This the Allies denied. The treaty provided only that the Commission study these things in order to determine what Germany's capacity was, and to test whether Germany was making a real effort at compliance. The Germans themselves had accepted the treaty provision that taxation in Germany be at least as heavy as taxation in any Allied state; to test the application of this principle, the Commission had to study the German tax system. The Allied "Reply" explicitly noted that the Commission's power to modify payments would only be used to help Germany: there could be reductions in the annuity, never increases.

The German counterproposals were rejected. "A sum of 100,000,000,000 marks (gold) is indeed mentioned, and this is calculated to give the impression of an extensive offer, which upon examination it proves not to be."[231] Instead the Allies in their "Reply" declared their own willingness to consider more reasonable proposals, along the lines of the plans proposed by Lloyd George. Germany was invited to survey the devastation, and would have four months following the signing of the treaty to suggest ways of settling the Allied reparation claims, either by one lump sum, or category by category. In particular, Germany could offer to restore directly a given area or "certain classes of damages" in a specific region, or offer labor and materials for work not directly undertaken by the German government or by German firms. These offers could be made through a German commission—"no reason is perceived why such a commission could not work in harmony with the Reparation Commission."[232] There would be two months of negotiation following the receipt of the German proposals. To the extent that an accord would be reached, the corresponding treaty provisions would be superceded and Germany's liability made definite. In the areas of discord, the procedure that was outlined in the treaty would remain.

The Allies made two additional declarations. They announced that they were fully aware of Germany's need for food, raw material and shipping facilities and promised not to "withhold from Germany commercial facilities" necessary to the revival of the German economy—but this vague statement was so hedged by conditions that it in no way bound the Allies to pursue any kind of commercial policy.[233] A separate Allied declaration raised the prospect that the occupation armies would be withdrawn from Germany ahead of schedule if Germany would show good faith in the execution of the treaty and give "satisfactory guarantees to assure the fulfillment of her obligations." Moreover, as soon as Germany disarmed in accordance with the treaty, the costs of occupation for which she would be responsible could not annually exceed 240 million gold marks.[234]

Through these declarations and clarifications the Allies went as far as they could to meet the German complaints. Although there were certain concrete pledges, the Germans were being asked to trust the Allies and believe in the sincerity of their statements of principle, just as the German delegation had earlier pleaded for a peace settlement that presupposed German good faith. But mutual confidence did not exist at the time, and given the prevailing atmosphere of deep suspicion, an imposed settlement, upheld by coercion rather than by the desire to vindicate trust and to honor promises freely given, was probably inevitable.

Chapter Three

Indulgence

IN MID-1919 a deep and ill-defined sense of unease pervaded France. One inescapable fact dominated the French vision of international politics: forty million Frenchmen faced sixty million Germans, and the demographic gap was clearly widening. The disparity of population, taken together with Germany's unquestioned military genius and capacity for organization, meant that in the natural course of things Germany would overwhelm France—of the German will to domination most Frenchmen had little doubt.

The events of November 1918 had not modified this point of view. It was generally believed that defeat and revolution had not really transformed the German spirit. Clemenceau, in particular, felt that revolution had not broken the power of the old rulers of Germany. Her new Socialist leaders were "surrounded by the old bureaucratic personnel of the Empire, with Rantzau at its head,"[1] and the Social Democrats themselves he tended to distrust. During the war they had served the imperial government; only since defeat had some of their leaders come to take a moderate line. Even if these new sentiments were genuine, the authority of the new rulers of Germany had not been firmly established: the Social Democrats, he noted, had come to depend on the militarist party. In this unstable situation, there was no reason to suppose that democratic ideas and institutions would inevitably take root in Germany. It would therefore be foolish to base French policy on the supposition that Germany had radically changed her ways.[2]

Clemenceau believed that in the absence of restraint, Germany might well again threaten to dominate France. It followed that a set of constraints—the Versailles system—had to be interposed between France and the menace of a resurgent Germany. But by mid-1919, when the treaty came before the French parliament for ratification, there was already much doubt as to how solid a barrier the Versailles system was. The treaty, it was said, did not assure the security of France. To Clemenceau such attacks were ill-founded: it was an illusion to suppose in any case that peace could be automatic. A right-wing critic, Louis Marin, had complained that the treaty reduced France to a policy of vigilance. Clemenceau seized on this phrase and declared that yes, vigilance was necessary, and "the crisis which is open will last for I do not know how many years, I would almost say how many centuries." Difficulties were inevitable, and France must not delude herself: no treaty in itself could magically make her secure. It would take great and sustained effort to make the new system work. The treaty was but a "collection of possibilities" and could live only if an active national policy gave effect to these possibilities. But if the admitted defects of the treaty were too heavily stressed and the new system were discredited at its inception, the treaty would be "an instrument not of life but of death." In short, Clemenceau told the Chamber, the treaty "will be what you will make it."[3]

The problem, however, was not so simple, for France did not face Germany alone. As Clemenceau was keenly aware, the working of the treaty presupposed the effective continuation of the Allied coalition. He viewed Allied solidarity as the "motor" of the Versailles system.[4] In his mind, this was no defect, for it really could not have been otherwise. To Clemenceau, the Alliance was the only means to French security. Crushing Germany was out of the question—a powerful nation could not be destroyed, and ultimately France and Germany had to live together.[5] An effective Allied policy was therefore essential. But by late 1919 the fragility of the Alliance was evident. American ratification was seriously in doubt, and British loyalty to the Versailles system was already open to question: as Clemenceau noted, British suspicion of France was deep-seated.[6]

By early 1920, wide sections of both British and American opinion had turned against the peace treaty. In Britain, the shift was especially marked in Liberal and Labour circles. What had originally been the view of "advanced" elements (such as the Independent Labour Party) quickly gained wide currency, and by the end of the year, the treaty was routinely condemned even by the moderate left.[7] It was the frustration of the great hopes that the Wilsonian program had inspired in 1918 that, in America and Britain, lay at the root of disillusionment and hostility to the treaty. There had clearly been no peace of reconciliation—the Versailles system could only be maintained through force of arms. But real peace, a true reconciliation of peoples, could not be achieved in this way. The treaty, if it remained intact, would permanently poison international relations and destroy any hope of lasting peace. Therefore, the peace settlement had to be revised.

In the eyes of many, the treaty itself thus became the enemy, the root cause of all that was wrong in world affairs. Since France had become identified with the enforcement of the treaty, many critics turned against France, the one great obstacle to their hopes for a "Wilsonian" solution to the European crisis. Because the French were willing, it seemed, to use military force to preserve the treaty, France was condemned as "militarist" and "imperialist"—even President Wilson himself, in early March 1920, publicly condemned the "militarism" of the French.[8] If any proof were needed to support this judgment, recent events seemed to dissipate all doubt. For what, if not the vindictive policy of the French government, had been responsible for the frustration of Wilson's program at the peace conference? Everyone knew, moreover, that France had pressed for a Rhenish settlement in 1919 that conflicted with the principle of self-determination; it was assumed that the relatively harsh policy pursued in this area was characteristic of all aspects of French policy. This was after all a plausible assumption: French suffering had been so enormous and so direct that vengefulness seemed inevitable.

Thus the legend of a harsh France took hold. The assumption was that all aspects of French policy were part of a coherent whole, and that all aspects of policy were rooted essentially in one basic aim: the permanent destruction of German power. It was not that this point of view had no substance to it whatsoever; Clemenceau's Rhenish policy certainly provides evidence for an interpretation of this sort.

The problem was that it was simplistic, that it took no account of the change in motivation from issue to issue—that is, of what may be viewed as either the incoherence or the subtlety of French policy in 1919. For as we have seen, French reparation policy at the peace conference was too moderate to be construed as part of a well-integrated policy to ''crush'' Germany. Nor did this simplistic view take into account the fact that overall policy (to the extent that it existed) can change over time, and thus that the shift from Clemenceau to Millerand at the beginning of 1920 could make a difference.

But interpretations of this sort come into being not as the result of careful analysis, but because they have political functions. In this case, moreover, the simplistic interpretation of the peace conference was in large part perpetuated because those who were in a position to correct it came to have an interest in its maintenance. Tardieu, for example, whose articles in 1920 and book *La Paix* in 1921 provided the most important French firsthand account of the diplomacy of the peace conference, painted a picture of a tough Clemenceau government standing up to Anglo-American pressure for a moderate peace. In this way he sought to defend the treaty (and by extension himself) and to discredit the new Millerand government by contrasting its weakness with the firmness of the Clemenceau regime. Wilson and his followers, for their part, encouraged the idea that the peace conference was essentially a struggle between forces of darkness and forces of light, championed by the French and the Americans respectively: blackening the French was an essential element of the myth portraying the Wilsonians as goodness incarnate.[9] As for Lloyd George, he of course had an interest in forgetting the intransigence of British reparation policy at the peace conference once his government became converted to the view that a swift and moderate solution to the reparation question was vital.

The rise of revisionist sentiment in Great Britain suited Lloyd George's purposes. The stability of Europe was his aim: the important thing was to turn back the tide of revolution that menaced Europe from the east, to stabilize the existing sociopolitical order so that force would not be needed to uphold it. France was currently the strongest military power on the continent. But in the eyes of Lloyd George and his associates, France was too exhausted to be a real threat to the balance of power in Europe.[10] Ultimately Germany was far more dangerous, and the basic goal of British statecraft was to try

Keynes, the leading critic of the treaty, believed that he and Lloyd George shared essentially the same views, and differed only on how best to achieve the common aim: Keynes preferred a head-on confrontation of Truth and Falsehood, while Lloyd George, he believed, felt that a dishonest policy would be more expedient.[12]

These differences on tactics, however, obscured basic disagreement on the substance of policy. The revisionists were passionately concerned with the real problems of reparation; their critique was logically consistent, their proposals radical. Lloyd George, on the other hand, was inclined to treat international politics as a kind of game, the goal of which was to solve the problems that presented themselves while obtaining the maximum advantage for one's own side. To him difficulties were basically subjective in nature: the important thing was to bring France and Germany together, but the exact terms of agreement hardly mattered in themselves. His policy tended to be piecemeal and somewhat inconsistent. He believed, for example, that it would hurt the British economy to receive a large influx of German wealth, but unlike the revisionists, he refused to consider anything that approached a waiver of the British share—although such an action might have brought agreement on a fixed sum more within reach. Revisionists like Keynes ruled out from the outset the use of force. But Lloyd George never went so far; under certain conditions he was in fact willing to use coercion, albeit reluctantly.

These nuances meant little to Frenchmen in 1920. All they saw was that British opinion and British policy were quickly drifting away from the treaty. There was deep resentment, even in moderate, left-center French circles, at how swiftly France's erstwhile Allies had turned against her, and at how unfairly they now judged her actions. But more was at stake than hurt feelings. The new situation raised in acute form the basic problem implicit in the peace settlement: how could the Versailles system, which presupposed continued Allied unity, be made to work when that unity no longer existed? In 1920 and after, French statesmen feared that they were being presented with a fatal choice between the treaty and the Alliance. This was a choice no French statesman could lightly make, and much of French policy amounted to an attempt to evade it.

In this interplay of national policies the reparation question was central—the touchstone of international relations in the immediate postwar period. Reparation dominated Germany's relations with the West in the early 1920s, and the reparation policies of Britain and France were the clearest expressions of each nation's policy toward Germany at the time. It was in connection with reparation that the Versailles system received its most critical test, for on this issue Allied cooperation was most obviously essential, and Allied disunity most painfully evident.

In France, the essential problems were clear at the outset. The great criticism leveled against the reparation provisions of the peace treaty was not that they promised too little, but that they well might be empty promises. Critics inveighed most strongly against the absence of real guarantees of payment: without guarantees, and especially without an American guarantee of the reparation debt, it would be extremely difficult to convert Germany's reparation obligation into anything tangible for France.[13]

Socialists and moderates alike condemned the treaty for not including an inter-Allied or League of Nations guarantee. There was nothing new to their argument. French needs were immediate, while substantial German payments could only be made over a long period. Would the French people be obliged to advance the sums required for reconstruction pending eventual German payment? Would France, as a Socialist deputy put it, be required to be the "banker" of Germany? The alternative was the "mobilization" of the debt, the conversion of Germany's reparation obligation into bonds that would be sold mainly in America, thus raising the funds required immediately. But without Allied guarantees, the chances for a substantial mobilization would be slim.

Klotz and Loucheur, speaking for the government, sought to allay these criticisms by vaunting the advantages bestowed by the treaty. What huge sums would be forthcoming once the treaty took effect! Under the treaty, Klotz said, Germany would have to pay about 300 milliard gold marks, a figure endorsed by Loucheur.[14] But the submission of such a figure did not bear on the problem of guarantees; it did not answer the closely related question of what France would really get and when. To this question, Loucheur and Klotz gave no satisfactory answer. The presentation of enormous figures was rather a somewhat dishonest attempt to evade it altogether.

The question of gurarantees revived the old issue of Allied financial cooperation. It was not through any oversight or lack of interest that attempts to secure American financial cooperation had failed. It was due instead to the unrelenting opposition of the United States government to any scheme that looked to the American treasury for a solution to the financial problems of Europe. This was, however, something that the French government felt it could not publicly admit. Klotz alluded to his projects for Allied "cooperation"—his plan for a financial section of the League, his scheme for pooling war costs. Negotiations, he said, were continuing, and he insisted they might bear fruit.[15]

The government's declarations on the question of the fixed sum were equally deceptive. Loucheur and even Clemenceau himself declared that the French delegation at the peace conference had blocked the inclusion of a fixed sum. The figure that had been suggested at the conference, Clemenceau declared, "was completely ridiculous."[16] In fact, the French delegation had generally been willing to accept a fixed sum, and one far below the figure cited by Klotz and Loucheur during the ratification debate. The government again was deliberately deceiving the Chamber. No doubt this must be understood in terms of the impending electoral struggle: the Clemenceau government felt it had to appear as the defender of a "strong" line on reparation.

The effect of all this was to corroborate the view of many Englishmen and Americans that French reparation policy was harsh; and more important, these declarations allowed the French people to avoid the unpleasant task of coming to terms with the nation's real problems. In particular, in the absence of any recognition of the blunt American refusal to take on any part of the financial burden of Europe, the French people and their representatives in Parliament would not be able to consider policy in the cold light of a realistic analysis of the situation. It was so much more satisfying for people to call for "justice" in terms of an "equitable" redistribution of war costs or of forcing the aggressor to pay for his crimes, than to think coldly in terms of political expediency. In these circumstances, a clear and rational policy was difficult to frame or execute, for governments had to accommodate public sentiments by presenting their policies in a false light. Thus in 1920 the basic lines of French policy were somewhat obscured by the reiteration of the increasingly empty phrase "strict execution of the treaty." As a result, the French government was given no credit abroad for its moderate policy, and the disturbing charge that France was a militarist power quickly hardened into an article of faith.

It was apparent in late 1919 that the peace treaty would not be self-enforcing. The German government was obviously weak, and if left to itself would certainly not take the energetic measures necessary to comply with the treaty. To punish Germany only after she had defaulted would be futile. For force to be effective, it would have to be put behind an active policy, one which indicated to the Germans the precise actions that would meet their reparation obligation. In other words, channels of payment needed to be created. Such a policy would provide a test of German good faith: only after Germany had made the prescribed effort, which might be a fiscal effort, would the argument of incapacity due to insurmountable problems of transfer be an acceptable excuse for nonpayment. The question would thus be reduced from Germany's capacity to Germany's willingness to pay, the sole aspect of the problem in which force could be effective.

Only in the context of an active French policy could negotiations with Germany succeed. An underlying threat of an eventual use of force did not preclude businesslike negotiation. Indeed without it the German government would have no incentive to negotiate in good faith. The constant application of pressure, precisely channeled, would offer the greatest inducement to the Germans to cooperate in the solution of the reparation question, for only in this way might the pressure be removed.

Clearly, the exclusive reliance on a distant threat of inflicting a catastrophe on Germany, while leaving on her shoulders the burden of transfer, stood little chance of being productive. A passive policy, moreover, would mean that there would be strong pressure on France to be guided by British policy. Furthermore, the clear formulation and firm execution of a creative policy would be the only defense against the rising current of revisionism that was undermining the treaty. For from the beginning, recognition of the transfer problem and the associated idea of Germany's limited capacity to pay were used to discredit the idea of reparation.

In a polemic of genius, a brilliant blend of invective and seemingly unassailable economic argument, John Maynard Keynes gave classic expression to this point of view in *The Economic Conse-*

quences of the Peace, which appeared at the end of 1919. The central thesis of this book was simple. Germany could pay only by selling more than she bought, but there was no reason for thinking that such a huge trade surplus as was required could be created; and Keynes challenged those who thought Germany could pay a large annuity "to say *in what specific commodities* they intend this payment to be made, and *in what markets* the goods are to be sold. Until they proceed to some degree of detail, and are able to produce some tangible argument in favour of their conclusions, they do not deserve to be believed."[17] To replace the "impossible" provisions of the treaty, Keynes proposed a definite plan to restore the world economy. His plan contained a number of features favorable to France. Although reparation would be scaled down enormously—the payments would amount in terms of present value to less than 20 milliard gold marks—he would waive the British claim to reparation and wipe out all inter-Allied debts; and Europe as a whole would benefit from an international loan raised largely in America.

Keynes's book made a sensation. In France, there were constant references to it in Parliament and in the press throughout 1920.[18] *The Economic Consequences* became the Bible of the revisionists, Keynes their high priest.

In terms of historical significance, the tone of the book is at least as important as its substance. *The Economic Consequences* was hardly written from the viewpoint of a disinterested economist. Keynes's bias was evident: though he felt Germany had caused the war, he was inclined to be indulgent toward her; he had little sympathy for France.[19] Many who found Keynes's economic arguments irrefutable were led to accept his political judgments as though they followed with rigorous logic. In France, it was the unfair tone of the book that evoked hostility.[20] But to Keynes and his followers, this hostility seemed but further evidence of French unwillingness to listen to reason.

The attack on the reparation provisions of the treaty was the spearhead of a larger drive to demolish the Versailles system. Keynes's essential argument was that because of the transfer problem, Germany's reparation obligation exceeded her capacity to pay. The point was so effective, and so characteristic, that the very phrase "Germany's capacity to pay" became a shibboleth of revisionism.[21] This development reinforced those who were convinced by Keynes in their belief that it was absurd to expect Germany to pay more than her "capacity." Moreover, the idea that the transfer problem placed an absolute limit on Germany's ability to pay went unchallenged— even in France the validity of the transfer approach was generally admitted.[22] This was in large part because the economists, although they understood the weakness of Keynes's arguments, refrained from criticizing him for political reasons. Jacob Viner, who in the interwar period was one of the leading specialists in the theory of international trade, admitted as much in his 1947 review of Etienne Mantoux's attack on *The Economic Consequences of the Peace*:

> It is rather remarkable that so important a book should have had to wait for a quarter of a century before it was subjected to a full-scale, competent economic scrutiny from any quarter. As I recall it, economists at the time regarded its economics as undistinguished in general and technically defective at some crucial points, especially in its treatment of the alleged difficulties of "transfer" of reparations. But the political views which Keynes expounded with great force of exposition were those which Anglo-Saxon liberals of the 1920's, including the economists, shared almost to a man, and I suppose there then seemed little point in exposing technical flaws in an economic argument which had the virtue of leading to the desired political conclusions.[23]

An unchallenged belief, however, is the functional equivalent of a fact, and while difference of opinion is tolerable, a refusal to accept a fact arouses the deepest indignation. In this case, it excited suspicion as well. French reparation policy, so absurd if taken at face value, evidently had a deeper and more "rational" explanation. The French insisted on their demands in order to force a German default, and thus give themselves a pretext for dismembering Germany by force— or at the very least as a means of providing for French security by keeping Germany economically weak. Such were the only explanations of French policy that appeared to make any sense at all.[24]

Against the powerful tide of ideas that was discrediting the reparation settlement, and with it the whole treaty, an active French policy was the only possible defense. The creation of machinery for effecting the transfer of real wealth would have been the best way of refuting the idea that the difficulty of transfer was insurmountable. Reducing the problem in this manner to one of Germany's willingness to pay would have made it clear that it was a refusal to make the prescribed effort rather than an objectively defined incapacity to pay that the French objected to. This was the sole means, short of abandoning reparation as such, of allaying the growing suspicion of France.

In the latter half of 1919, even before the treaty legally took effect, the French government did pursue an active policy of direct negotiation with Germany. Although certain agreements were reached during this period, in the most important areas the negotiations failed. But this does not mean that a study of these talks is without interest. In fact, analysis reveals key features characteristic of both French and German reparation policy in the whole period down to 1923.

The negotiations on coal, iron and steel were particularly significant. Already during the peace conference Massigli had signaled the French government's willingness to reach an accommodation in this area, and on August 1 Loucheur proposed to the Germans the formation of a steel cartel, including France, Germany, Belgium and Luxemburg. He also suggested that industry conclude an agreement for the exchange of coal and iron ore.[25]

Loucheur was trying to deal with one of the most basic economic problems that plagued France during this period, the problem of coal. Even before the war, the French had to import over a third of their supply of coal—a net import of about 24 million tons out of a total consumption of about 65 million tons in 1913. If prewar levels of coal consumption were to be maintained, coal imports would have to be expanded to compensate for the loss of the mines destroyed by the Germans—at first by about 15 to 20 million tons annually, then diminishing as these mines were repaired. Furthermore, the reannexation of Alsace and Lorraine aggravated the problem—this added another 7 million tons to the annual deficit.[26]

During the war, the Comité des Forges, the main organization of steel manufacturers, had suggested the annexation of the Saar as a means of dealing with the problem. The idea of annexing the Saar —or at least of that portion of it that had been French during the period of the Revolution—had considerable appeal in high political circles in France. Regaining the "Alsace of 1790" was in fact a clear goal of two of the wartime governments, those of Briand and Clemenceau.[27] In January, at the very start of the conference, Clemenceau twice told Poincaré, then President of the Republic, that if France got ownership of the mines, the Saar itself need not be annexed—a 'small republic' would be an acceptable solution. He changed his mind in early February, according to the account in Poincaré's diary, but only because Lloyd George had urged him to annex the area. And in early April, just after the French had renounced direct annexation on March 29, Tardieu allegedly condemned as "folly" the inclusion of the territory in France.[28]

The acquisition of the Saar mines, however, would still not be enough to solve France's coal problem. The Saar coal surplus was 8 or 9 million tons a year, while the French deficit was 50 million tons. Nor was this the end of the problem. The French steel industry, which was greatly expanded by the reacquisition of Lorraine, needed metallurgical coke, but the coal in the Saar was not suitable for this purpose. The mines in the Ruhr basin, on the Right Bank of the Rhine, produced the right kind of coal, but the French government showed little interest in annexing this area, or even in acquiring title to its coal mines. Even the most ambitious French leaders, like the steel magnate Camille Cavallier and of course Marshal Foch, wanted the Rhine River to be the military frontier of France.[29] The Comité des Forges as a whole, it seems, was sympathetic to the idea of an annexation not just of the Saar but of the entire Left Bank.[30] As for the Right Bank, instead of annexation it asked that France receive title to at least some of the Ruhr mines. But it is a measure of the Comité's lack of influence with the government that this request appears never to have been taken seriously: Loucheur in particular strongly rejected the notion of acquiring mines without political control.[31]

Was it enough to force the Germans to supply the coal? Certainly the French were attracted to the idea of exploiting their military superiority to this end. Clauses providing for the delivery of coal as reparation were inserted in the peace treaty—France had the legal right to coerce Germany in this matter. But solutions resting on force rather than on consent and mutual interest are notoriously unstable. Even aside from the complications resulting from the inter-Allied nature of the enforcement mechanism, the French government preferred to spare itself the effort of continually threatening and perhaps actually employing military coercion as a way of solving economic problems. Besides, in the long run how permanent was French military superiority? Would it not be better to pursue a more moderate policy, and work out a permanent compromise arrangement with the Germans at a time when French military superiority and an ultimate threat of coercion could still condition the situation?

Moreover, even an adequate supply of coal would not completely end the problems of French heavy industry. With Lorraine again in France, French capacity to produce steel would expand enormously, once supplies of coke were secured. Yet where were the markets to absorb this output? The treaty contained provisions which sought to keep the German market open for five years, but again such legal rights, temporary in any case, were a fragile basis for the health of the metallurgical industry. An entente with the Germans was a more desirable solution.

Such a solution it seems was favored by an important part of French heavy industry. Representatives of Schneider-Creusot, one of France's biggest steel companies, participated in Loucheur's negotiations with the Germans in August, and in early 1920 steel industry representatives were willing to sidestep the treaty and buy coal directly in Germany. The French system for leveling out the price of coal derived from various sources ("péréquation") kept prices high; it would be cheaper to purchase coal directly in Germany. While this is not quite the same as saying that the big steel manufacturers wanted an entente with their German counterparts—and Jeanneney's recent study of de Wendel has demonstrated the great Lorraine industrialist's preference for a much tougher policy—still any move away from the treaty system implied negotiated arrangements with the Germans.[32] In any case, French industry wanted more than the mere right to buy coal in Germany—Robert Pinot of the Comité des Forges put forth a plan for a participation of French capital in the German mines, and in April 1920, according to the German ambassador in Paris, French "industrial circles sought an understanding with Germany in the near future"[33]

The French government, however, while sympathetic to the idea of industrial collaboration, felt that its favorable political position should condition the terms of agreement, and was reluctant to abandon its treaty rights. It believed, moreover, that it controlled an economic weapon capable of compelling the Germans to accept a suitable bargain on these matters: Germany, the French government believed, was dependent on French iron ore. French experts warned that this was not the case, that Swedish or Spanish or even Canadian ore could be substituted for the minette of Lorraine. Nevertheless, the

French government went ahead and cut off German supplies of minette when German industry proved unwilling to accept French terms. But, as was predicted, the minette was replaced by scrap metal and other sources of ore: the French, a German industrialist said in 1922, could "choke" on their minette.[34]

The failure of this attempt at coercion resulted from the fact that German heavy industry was in a much stronger position than its French counterpart—in particular, the Ruhr was simply much less dependent on minette than Lorraine was on Westphalian coke.[35] It was in fact this very inequality of strength that was the real justification for French policy: the idea was to capitalize on France's favorable political and legal position as a means of redressing this economic inequality.

Why was this policy unsuccessful, and why did matters develop to the point where the French took the extreme measure of stopping shipments of iron ore to Germany? It was not that political pressures in France forced Loucheur to abandon his policy of collaboration with Germany—he was in fact cheered in the Chamber when on September 11 he alluded to these talks and announced the French government's intention to be "broad-minded" in dealing with the question of heavy industry. Nor was it that the German government was blind to the opportunity being offered. The official German representatives in these talks appreciated Loucheur's businesslike approach and believed that Germany should reciprocate and pursue in good faith a policy of real economic cooperation with France. For this reason they urged that Germany offer to provide France with reparation coal right away—and in fact a protocol to this effect containing a schedule of coal deliveries varying in accordance with German production was signed on August 19.[36]

But it was one thing to sign such a document, and quite another to carry it out. The problem was that the representatives of German heavy industry, conscious of their own strength and of French economic weakness, showed little interest in Loucheur's overtures, or in their own government's attempts to maximize deliveries of coal to France. Government officials complained about the attitude of the Ruhr magnates. Schmitt, a Foreign Ministry official who had participated in the negotiations with Loucheur, noted in a long memorandum on October 28 that official relations with France "are right now thoroughly characterized by a tone of mutual understanding and a willingness to get along with each other,'' but then went on to criticize heavy industry for obstructing government policy:

The industry of the Rhineland and Westphalia during the war lost little of its sense of its own power. It is completely right in believing itself in the long run stronger than its French counterpart. It sees things, however, solely from the standpoint of comparative economic strength, and has no proper understanding of the general politico-economic difficulties of our situation. It still completely does not understand that for the very reason that France is industrially weaker in the long run, she would make a good partner.[37]

But the government was too weak, and industry too powerful, for the policy advocated by Schmitt and his colleagues to actually be implemented: the French attempt at collaboration was frustrated.

This affair set the pattern for Franco-German industrial relations down to mid-1922. Repeatedly the French made overtures which were rejected due essentially to the opposition of the Ruhr magnates.[38] Throughout this period there were those within the government and the administration who like Schmitt argued in favor of a more positive policy of cooperation with France. It was not that these people were resigned to the peace treaty. They were simply willing to accept the realities of the situation, in particular the ability of France to inflict a catastrophe on an intransigent Germany, and grasp the opportunity France was offering to work out some kind of accommodation. On the whole, this group was unable to determine policy. The autumn of 1919 was the high tide of their influence, but even then they proved largely powerless.

Schmitt and others complained that the big industrialists were oblivious to political concerns. But the attitude of the Ruhr magnates and their allies in the government in the whole period from the armistice down to the Ruhr occupation was political to the core. The industrialists and those officials who shared their views thought in terms of power—not the immediate, but the long-term distribution of power—and were willing to play for big stakes. Contemptuous of France, of French weakness and isolation, they felt that Germany in the long run could defy France with impunity. Germany could pay lip service to the treaty in public, but in fact should refuse to engage in a policy of cooperation with France. Thus Hugo Stinnes, the most prominent steel magnate in the period, in April 1920 opposed accepting any figure for reparation: the present situation was to Germany's advantage, he argued, since it meant that the continual depreciation of the franc would not be stopped.[39] And Carl von Schubert, a leading Foreign Ministry official (whose importance would be even greater under Stresemann in the late 1920s) opposed in January 1921 the relatively conciliatory policy temporarily being pursued by the German government. "I absolutely fail to see," he wrote, "any advantage for us in helping the French out of their present very precarious situation." If no acceptable sum was possible, it was better to let matters come to a head; Germany would ultimately overcome the difficulties that would ensue.[40]

The views of Stinnes and Schubert were somewhat extreme, but in attenuated form they seem to have been widely shared in influential German circles. Even the Socialist-dominated government of the peace conference period acted in many ways as though Germany were still a great power and had not lost the war.[41] Certainly the new republic was unwilling to play the role prescribed for it by liberals in the West and make a clean break with the imperial regime. On the war guilt question, for example, it refused to take an attitude of letting the cards fall where they may, and was more concerned with making a good case for Germany.[42] In addition, the old bureaucracy was carried over virtually intact and was allowed (together with prominent leaders of business and industry) to play a leading role in the formulation of policy, particularly on reparation.[43] But reliance on conservative elements is hardly a sufficient explanation for the kind of policy the new government pursued. In many respects, the new rulers of Germany and the old imperial bureaucrats who now served them saw eye to eye on matters of foreign policy.[44] The most curious example of the new leaders' attitude was their insistence that Germany not be held liable for damages to Allied merchant ships resulting from the submarine war. The prearmistice agreement had explicitly referred to "sea" damages, but this, a number of ministers argued, referred just to attacks from the sea on Belgium and northern France.[45] (An argument could be made because the reparation provisions of the pre-armistice agreement were presented as clarifications and not as modifications of the Fourteen Points, to avoid making it appear that Wilson's program was being altered.) Such a view simply ignored the strong feelings that the Americans had on the question: after all, they had come into the war over this issue in the first place. It also ignored the British interest in this category of damage—to rule it out would mean depriving Britain of any share in the indemnity. Such a policy might have made sense if the Germans intended to throw in their lot with the French, but it hardly corresponded tactically to a policy that rejected French overtures and looked instead to Wilson and Anglo-American capital for Germany's salvation.

Thus even in the immediate aftermath of Germany's defeat, the Socialist-dominated government was hardly willing to allow the fact of defeat to condition its foreign policy, and acted instead as though resistance and negotiation on basics was still possible. If this was the attitude of a government of this sort at this time, it is not surprising that later more conservative governments should have resisted the treaty and have dragged their feet on more positive efforts to work out mutually satisfactory arrangements with the French.

Late 1919 was the high point of German willingness to cooperate. Government efforts were frustrated in the key area of industrial collaboration by the opposition of big business, but in another area— that of the use of German labor in French reconstruction—it was a sudden change in French policy that prevented final agreement. An Allied body, the Committee for the Organization of the Reparation Commission (CORC), handled reparation during the period before the treaty took effect (and thus had no power to compel the Germans to do anything); it was the CORC that conducted the negotiations on the use of German labor. Loucheur, as president of the CORC, was the driving force behind these talks.[46] An agreement in this matter was clearly within reach when the French government unilaterally decided to suspend the negotiations. Why this abrupt change of policy?

André Tardieu, Minister for the Liberated Regions since November 6, 1919, had requested the prefects to advise him on the question of German labor: how many workers could be used in their departments, what kind of work was there for them to do, etc. He soon had the answers. "On the whole," he wrote Loucheur on November 27, "they do not show themselves to be extremely favorable to the use of this labor, most of them hesitating to put German workers in contact with the civilian population." The prefects' figures seemed to Tardieu "very feeble in view of the work to be done." He personally favored the use of German labor and wanted a contingent of 250,000 to 300,000 workers.[47] Loucheur noted laconically on the margin of Tardieu's letter on December 21: "Council of Ministers has decided to renounce provisionally the use of German labor because of political difficulties."

The phrase "political difficulties" is vague: just where did the opposition to the use of German labor come from? The inhabitants of northern France certainly disliked the presence of the Germans, but this problem had been taken into account early in the negotiations, and both sides had agreed that the German workers would be isolated from the indigenous population.[48] Loucheur later blamed French labor unions for sabotaging the introduction of a German work force. The unions took pains at that time to refute this charge of "xenophobia," but the attitude of labor was hardly clear-cut. Because of their internationalist ideology, but also because they did not believe themselves strong enough to dictate to the government, the leaders of the building trades union did not try to absolutely veto the use of German labor in reconstruction. But their attitude toward it was extremely cold. Chauvin, head of the French union, told his German counterpart Paeplow in Amsterdam on July 29 that his union could "guarantee nothing on this subject." A few days later, the French building trades union refused a government invitation to help deal with the question "as long as there were unemployed workers in France." The fact that the money used to pay these German workers would come from Germany, and would in no case be available to relieve French unemployment, was apparently not taken into account. Moreover, to the degree French unemployment was structural (and there were constant references to the "transportation crisis" at this time), the reconstruction work done by these Germans might actually relieve the problems of French labor; however, this possibility was never even considered by the French union. At the grass roots level, hostility was sharper still, as the discussions at the union's national congress in late November 1919 show. It is likely that this hostility had something to do with the government's decision to drop the negotiations with Germany.[49]

The decision left a bitter taste in Germany—the French, it seemed, were not willing to allow Germany to work off its debt—and the affair led to a certain turning away from the idea that direct participation in French reconstruction was the key to a solution of the reparation question. In the German union, this shift was particularly striking. In the year following the armistice, the leaders of the German building trades union were willing to recognize German responsibility for the war and thus accept a certain moral obligation for making reparation. Paeplow, in December 1918, even admitted the responsibility of the German people, saying it would "pay very dearly for its error."[50] But by January 1921 Paeplow noted the increasing reluctance of German workers to go to France for reconstruction work: "The workers' sense of a moral obligation to be helpful, both to the Reich and to their French brothers, in the reconstruction of the devastated areas, is fading away."[51] To be sure, an objective factor was also at work. The movement of resources, such as the transfer of German labor to France, is easiest to bring about in times of economic transition; the longer the delay, the more solid the economic situation becomes, and the harder it is to effect such a movement of resources. But the result was the same: as time passed, this mode of reparation became increasingly unlikely.

As far as French policy is concerned, the decision to drop the negotiations on German labor was a turning point. It was not that the French government changed its mind about the principle of cooperation with Germany. There were in fact negotiations taking place in Paris just before the Clemenceau government resigned in late January, and the Millerand ministry which took over made collaboration with Germany one of the key features of its reparation policy.[52] But French policy lost its vigor. The French government, except on the coal question, ceased to move forcefully to open particular channels of payment. French reparation policy would remain essentially passive until the end of 1920. This was in spite of the fact that the coming into force of the treaty in January created the legal basis for the exercise of pressure; the French government simply chose not to press Germany in this way. In large measure its reluctance to apply pressure was rooted in its moderate hopes, its desire to be "reasonable" and arrive at a "businesslike" solution through the mobilization of the debt. But this moderation, overshadowed by French demands for a Ruhr occupation to deal with the coal default, was never in fact recognized. Because French policy had not taken the initiative in reducing reparation to a question of Germany's willingness to pay, there was no way of demonstrating that French demands did not exceed Germany's capacity, and hostility to France continued unabated.

Alexandre Millerand formed his government in January 1920. It was Millerand who embodied the spirit of the *Bloc National,* which had triumphed in the legislative elections held two months earlier. The elections had been fought mainly on the issue of Bolshevism, and in principle the *Bloc National* was a grouping of all the "republican" parties—that is, excluding the Socialists and the monarchists. In reality, the parties of the right dominated the *Bloc,* and its victory marked a crushing defeat for the Radical party. The Radical group in the Chamber was reduced from 157 to 87 members. Right-wing representation, on the other hand, vastly increased in size. The Entente Républicaine Democratique, the main conservative group, jumped from 57 to 183 members—a potent force even in a Chamber of over 600 deputies. The elections had thus resulted in a pronounced shift to the right in the political composition of the Chamber.

The new prime minister, however, had no intention of pursuing a purely right-wing policy. Millerand took the ideal of republican union seriously: his policy would be a national policy, transcending faction. In line with this he chose the well-known Radical, Senator Steeg, as his Minister of the Interior. The choice of Steeg so distressed the conservatives that on a vote of confidence on this point, abstentions outnumbered votes for the government.[53] But having made this gesture, conservative groups soon reiterated their intention to back the new government.

On reparation as well, Millerand avoided taking the intransigent position espoused by certain sections of the right. The French government, he declared to the Chamber in late March, should not simply tell the Germans: "Here are my rights, here are your engagements; I ask you strictly to execute the treaty, I have nothing more to say to you." His policy was more reasonable. The government was willing to discuss with the Germans larger economic problems—he in fact welcomed "the idea of an economic collaboration" with Germany. But the German government had to show good faith in attempting to carry out the terms of the treaty; this, he said, was the basic condition of future relations with Germany.[54]

Millerand's chief advisers also held what, in 1920, were moderate views on reparation. The new Minister of Finance, banker Frédéric François-Marsal, favored the economic restoration of Germany, and wanted to set Germany's reparation debt at a fixed sum. A definite figure was necessary both for Germany to get the credit needed to rebuild her economy, and for France, through at least a partial mobilization of the German debt, to get the sums with which to finance her reconstruction effort.[55] To Marsal, the restoration of the machinery of international credit, for which a fixed sum he believed was essential, was the key to the economic revival of Europe. This was at the time the characteristic view of moderate Europeans and Americans; it was the central argument in all the principal expressions of liberal thought on the large economic problems that then faced Europe.[56] This was also the argument developed in May 1920 by Jacques Seydoux, the main Foreign Ministry official concerned with economic matters; Seydoux was to play a leading role in the elaboration of reparation policy for much of this period.[57]

The two main French reparation experts in the first half of 1920, Alexandre de Celier, director of the Mouvement Général des Fonds (and thus the highest permanent official in the Ministry of Finance), and the Inspector of Finance Joseph Avenol, also held quite moderate views. Celier in fact basically saw eye to eye with Keynes, with whom he had long been carrying on a very interesting correspondence. "On your basic ideas," he wrote Keynes in mid-1920, "you have known for a long time that agreement between us is not far from being complete. The settlement of the international debts left by the war, both the reparation debts and the inter-Allied loans, can only be conceived of on an extremely broad and liberal basis, and such a settlement is the only one which at the same time can be a realistic settlement."[58] Letters written in June and November 1919 in fact leave little doubt that Celier had long sympathized with Keynes's point of view.[59] As for Avenol, in 1919 he had endorsed the reparation plan Keynes had presented to the peace conference, a plan foreshadowing the scheme outlined in *The Economic Consequences of the Peace*.[60] In 1920 Avenol continued to take a moderate line on reparation. He wanted "to help Germany, to do business with her"—and his reason throws a good deal of light on the status of the Alliance in early March—"in order not to find ourselves dealing just with the English and the Americans."[61]

It is clear that disillusion with the Anglo-Saxons was one of the main things that had led the French government since the time of the peace conference to contemplate closer relations with Germany. The views of another important French official, Prof. Haguenin, are particularly significant in this context. Haguenin was the French government's first, though somewhat unofficial, representative in Germany after the war. With a wide range of contacts he was a key source of information on what was going on across the Rhine, and it seems that his views were taken quite seriously. Certainly he had the ear of Millerand and in early 1920 kept in close touch with him through his *chef de cabinet*, Albert Petit.

Haguenin had long been calling for an extremely active French policy in Germany. What he proposed in 1919 amounted in fact to the imposition of a French "tutelage" on Germany. Her sacrifices in the war and her continued vulnerability gave France the right, he argued, "to watch over, to dominate, to educate Germany."[62] In a February 1920 letter to Petit, Haguenin reiterated his argument. Germany had to be "led onto practical ground by the hope of collaboration. If not she will submit to the protection of England and immediately all the clauses of the treaty will slip away like sand through our fingers. I have been repeating it for a year: if Germany is not restored under our surveillance, by our efforts, for our advantage, she will be restored by others and against us." In other letters in March and April he made much the same argument.[63]

The views of people like Haguenin and Seydoux help shed some light on one of the more perplexing features of French policy toward Germany in 1920: the coexistence of harsh and moderate strains of policy. The eagerness to invade the Ruhr does not seem at first glance to fit in with the desire for economic collaboration and for a "businesslike" solution to the reparation question. Haguenin's desire for close relations with Germany did not prevent him from actively supporting Bavarian separatism (he was involved in talks with the reactionary Bavarian leader von Kahr, who was seeking French support for separatist or at least federalist policies). Similarly Seydoux was willing to talk with Germany, but this did not mean he was ruling out the eventual use of force; in fact in his view an element of constraint was essential.[64]

The kind of policy that Seydoux and Haguenin were pushing for is thus better characterized as "active" than as "moderate"; they were reacting against the passivity of French policy and in particular against French dependence on Britain. For all his moderate language, Seydoux especially was not willing to give up the treaty. This was not because he viewed it as sacrosanct. The treaty was for him rather a point of departure, something to be developed, and also both the symbol and the guarantee of France's position as a victor power. It was not something to be given up too quickly; the policy of "economic collaboration,'' whatever its long-term implications and possibilities, presupposed for the time being a large element of German good faith in carrying out the treaty.

It was toward an active policy of this sort that French policy as a whole evolved in 1920. However the situation that the French government had to deal with was difficult. By early 1920 it was already clear that Germany had no desire and little incentive to accept the Versailles system. There was no moral obligation to accept a settlement that had been imposed by brute force, a treaty that relegated Germany to a subordinate status for an indefinite period. The reparation terms were particularly odious. As even Anglo-Saxon opinion was coming to admit, the reparations obviously exceeded Germany's capacity to pay, and to make matters worse, they were based on the ''lie'' of Germany's war guilt. Reparation, moreover, was for technical reasons the most difficult part of the treaty to enforce, and the area where the Allies were most disunited. Germany, therefore, had an interest in focusing her resistance on the reparation clauses: if there was to be a struggle over the Versailles settlement, it made sense from the German standpoint that it should be fought in the area where the treaty was most vulnerable, and where Germany's advantages were relatively greatest. It was in this way that the reparation issue acquired its political significance, for what was a stake was not simply how much money would be paid. The real question—and this is what makes the analysis of the issue important—was whether the Versailles system as a whole would in essence remain intact, or if not, what kind of political system would replace it.

To French officials in 1920, German ''bad faith'' was most evident in the coal question.[65] The treaty gave France the right to receive 7 million tons of coal annually, plus up to 20 million tons a year in compensation for the mines destroyed by the German army in 1918. These shipments would diminish as the mines were restored. In addition, Belgium and Italy together were entitled to call for another 12.5 million tons in 1920. After ten years the options would lapse. The options specified in the treaty thus amounted to nearly 40 million tons a year, or 3.3 million tons a month. Deliveries on this scale were not, however, rigidly decreed by the treaty. Should the Reparation Commission judge that the ''full exercise'' of these options ''would interfere unduly with the industrial requirements of Germany,'' it was specifically authorized to set its own schedule of deliveries.[66] In

August 1919, the CORC had negotiated a protocol with the Germans governing coal deliveries that would temporarily supersede the terms of the treaty.[67] The deliveries called for under the protocol were substantially smaller than those provided for in the treaty: 1,660,000 tons a month, rising as Germany's output increased. But Germany did not carry out the provisions of the protocol. Loucheur bitterly complained at an Allied conference in December 1919 that the French were receiving less than one-third the coal they had been promised in the protocol and coal deliveries remained unsatisfactory through the first half of 1920.[68]

There are certain indications that the French were correct, and that the German government was not making a maximum effort to deliver reparation coal. In mid-June 1920, for example, when the Reparation Commission decided to decrease the German share of Upper Silesian coal, a meeting of high German officials was called to consider how Germany should react. Von Simson, the key Foreign Ministry official concerned with reparation, argued that if nothing were done, earlier German claims to the effect that a maximum effort was being made would be perceived as fraudulent. Therefore orders had been given to reduce coal deliveries to the Entente to make up for decreases in Silesian coal. He did not argue that it was economically or even socially or politically impossible to accept the reduction in Germany's coal supply. His views were supported by the coal commissioner, Stutz, and by state secretaries in the reconstruction and finance ministries. Chancellor Müller agreed to maintain the order reducing deliveries to the Entente. State Secretary Schroeder, of the Ministry of Finance, noted that because of the coal shortage Paris, as opposed to Berlin, was relatively dark after 10 P.M. He therefore recommended that light usage be curtailed, but only in cities where Allied commissions sat and especially in big hotels; the Chancellor also supported this suggestion. This was a small matter, of course, but again one which illustrates that the German government was more concerned with appearances than with making a real effort to do its utmost to comply with the treaty, for it now clearly avoided a cutback in unnecessary coal consumption in cities throughout Germany.[69]

The French, on the other hand, were by no means pursuing an intransigent policy in this whole matter. In spite of all the talk of "strict enforcement of the treaty," never in 1920 did the French government demand that the Germans deliver all the coal provided for in the treaty. Instead, the generous principle of equal satisfaction of coal needs was implicitly accepted by the Reparation Commission in February 1920 as a basis for deliveries.[70] The problem was that the rate at which German needs were being met was substantially higher than the corresponding French rate.[71]

In mid-February Millerand brought up the question of Germany's coal default at an Allied conference in London. He argued that the default was due not to inability to deliver the coal—Germany disposed of substantially more coal per capita than France. In the face of this egregious violation of the treaty, he proposed that the Allies occupy the Ruhr Basin "with a view to forcing Germany to carry out her undertakings, which at the present time she was deliberately avoiding."[72]

From the peace conference down to the London Conference of May 1921 and beyond, the idea of occupying the Ruhr appeared to the French government as the one truly effective measure it could take to overcome German resistance.[73] Not only were the great German coal deposits in the Ruhr, but this area was the industrial heart of Germany: occupation would enable the Allies to cripple Germany economically if she refused to accept their terms. Moreover, the Ruhr was the power base of the "Pan-German" industrialists, who in French eyes were the real force behind German resistance.[74] Finally, the Ruhr was within easy striking distance of the French army on the Rhine.

It was British policy, however, to support the "moderate constitutional government" in Germany. An occupation of the Ruhr would stir up the country, and make the position of the government difficult, perhaps untenable. So Lloyd George, who definitely did not want to see the present regime collapse and be replaced by a Communist or militarist government, therefore opposed the French demand for action on the coal default, insisting successfully that the matter be referred to the Reparation Commission for further study.[75] This, it should be noted, was a change from his attitude in December 1918, when he strongly suggested to Foch the occupation of the "coal basin of Westphalia" as a guarantee for the payment of the indemnity.[76]

The French increasingly resented British policy, for it seemed to them that the British were more sympathetic to Germany than to France. The British were blocking action designed to secure German coal for France, yet at the same time were pursuing what seemed an exceptionally selfish policy with regard to the sale of their own coal abroad. Within Britain, the sale of coal was still controlled by the government, which saw to it that British industry had first claim on the output of the British mines, and that it received it at artificially low prices, lower than those that would be set in a free market. That part of Britain's coal output not earmarked for domestic consumption could be sold abroad at prices set by supply and demand. The export price rose rapidly; because supply was restricted by government controls, the British export price appeared to the French artificially high.

French opinion was convinced, as Lord Derby, the British Ambassador to France at the time, put it, that Great Britain was "reaping undue advantage and gathering extortionate profits from the supply of British coal to France." Derby urged a more generous coal policy, and even Lloyd George wondered whether something more could be done for France. But the Board of Trade refused to make any concession, and the cabinet approved the Board's policy on May 6, 1920.[77]

British coal policy was taken in France as proof that Great Britain cared little for French needs, and by February 1920, for this and other reasons, there was an upswell of hostility toward Britain in France. This sense of bitterness was born of disillusion: the great hopes of the war years that real Allied solidarity would persist in time of peace had clearly been misplaced. The Alliance, it seemed, was little more than essentially temporary diplomatic alignment, a chance product of momentarily overlapping interests.

French opinion was concerned above all by the rising current of revisionist sentiment in Britain, which seemed responsible for the rapid shift of government policy away from the treaty; the ease with which French "imperialism" and "militarism" were condemned was particularly disturbing. The right in France reacted with anger and despair to the shift of British opinion and policy.[78] Even the most moderate French circles, those in which, for example, Keynes's ideas had been sympathetically received, were disturbed by the swift turning of British opinion against France.[79] It was in this context that a series of events took place, the resolution of which was to profoundly color Anglo-French relations for the rest of the period.

On the night of March 12 right-wing elements headed by a minor official named Kapp carried out a *coup d'état* in Berlin. By March 17 the Kapp Putsch had collapsed, but not before touching off a left-wing uprising in the Ruhr. The constitutional Bauer government renewed a request made earlier on behalf of the Kapp regime for permission to send troops in to suppress the uprising. (The Ruhr area was in the "neutral zone" on the right bank of the Rhine, in principle forbidden to German troops by the peace treaty, yet not under Allied occupation either.)[80]

The French government had opposed this request when made on behalf of the Kapp regime, and continued to oppose it when it was renewed by the Bauer government. Instead Millerand and Marshal Foch proposed that the Allies send troops into the Ruhr to "restore order" themselves.[81] But the disorder was essentially a pretext: for a month Millerand had been seeking to occupy the Ruhr in order to get the coal that France needed, and these events now seemed like the perfect occasion for pressing his case.[82] The other Allies refused to support this action; the British government strongly felt that the Bauer government should be allowed to crush this "Soviet revolt" itself.[83] In the face of this resistance, the French government gave up its plan for "using the disturbances in the Ruhr valley as an excuse for sending in Allied troops," as Derby put it in a letter to the Foreign Secretary, Lord Curzon.[84] On March 20 Millerand told Derby that German troops could enter the Ruhr if Allied troops were allowed simultaneously to occupy new areas of Germany until German troops left the Ruhr.[85]

Lloyd George rejected this new French proposal as pointless and dangerous, and in an Allied conference on March 22 again argued that the German government be allowed to suppress the "communist" insurrection itself. The Allied negotiations were deadlocked, but the German government, anxious to take action, approached the French to negotiate directly. The German representative in Paris proposed that German troops be allowed into the Ruhr on condition that if they were not out within two or three weeks, then the French could occupy Frankfurt and Darmstadt until they were withdrawn. On the evening of the 29th a high Foreign Ministry official (Paléologue) agreed to these terms, but on March 31 Millerand changed his mind and unconditionally rejected the German request to send in troops.[86]

The British were furious that the French had negotiated independently with the Germans, instead of acting in accord with the Allies.[87] At the same time, however, the Foreign Office decided, on the basis of reports from its agent in the Rhineland, that the situation in the Ruhr was not in fact serious enough to warrant the despatch of

German troops. Curzon therefore notified Derby that the British government was "quite prepared for the moment not to press for authority to be given to the German Government to despatch their troops into the neutral zone."[88] The German government remained anxious to act, and informed the Allies on April 3 that it would send in troops without prior Allied consent.[89] Allied diplomats in Berlin warned German officials against such action.[90] In fact, the military operation had already begun; and German troops had penetrated the Ruhr on April 2.[91]

At the beginning of April, when the British were angry about private French negotiations with Germany, Millerand had repeatedly promised that France would not act alone.[92] He now tried to consult with Britain on what "immediate sanction" to take. The British sought to argue him out of taking immediate action, but to no avail. The Allies had been defied, and the French government could not allow Germany to act in this manner with impunity.[93] On the night of April 5 French troops occupied Frankfurt and four other German towns without incident.

The British government exploded with anger, directed exclusively against France. On April 8 the cabinet met to discuss the question. "This is a very serious departure by the French Government from united action," Lloyd George declared. "We may," he added, "be landed one day in war with Germany through French action. Or we may have to repudiate our allies. They have sent black troops to Frankfort. If the Germans sent niggers from German Africa to Newcastle? Frankfort is a proud city!" "Like Manchester," Austen Chamberlain interjected. "Yes, or Birmingham," Lloyd George continued. "People here would say we can only die once, we won't stand this insult. I am sure there will be street fighting and bombardment in Frankfort. In a couple of years the Germans will have fed themselves up with sausages and be as virile as ever and they will recall their having fought for five years against superior forces and held their own. The French will go on and on like this and the Germans will become more and more formidable." This kind of thing, he believed, would lead ultimately to war. "The French," he said, "think they can whistle for us and call us up if war breaks out." It had to be made clear to them that if they took isolated action, "they must do it on their own responsibility." Again he focused his outrage on the use of African troops: "There are ugly tales going round of the behaviour of the black troops towards German women. We must make it clear that we won't spill British blood to defend that sort of thing. We must do it dramatically or it will make no impression on the French."[94]

The cabinet decided to withdraw the British representative on the Conference of Ambassadors as a signal to the French that if they acted alone, they could not count on eventual British support—that isolated action, in other words, was inconsistent with the maintenance of the Alliance. A stiff note was despatched to the French government condemning their action, and announcing the withdrawal of Derby from the Ambassadors' Conference.[95] Curzon wrote Derby that he "personally" felt that the French government should apologize for their behavior—in private, of course.[96] The French prime minister did in fact come as close as he could to admitting that he had been wrong, for on April 11 he formally promised that henceforth on questions related to the treaty, the French government "had no intention of acting save in accordance with its Allies."[97] Soon afterward, when the insurrection was crushed and German troops were withdrawn from the Ruhr, the French army evacuated Frankfurt and the other four towns it had occupied.

Throughout the affair French policy had been confused, equivocal and at times deceptive. On the two basic questions Millerand had wavered: Was the entry of German troops into the Ruhr negotiable or absolutely unacceptable? Would France ever act alone, or would she act only in conjunction with her allies? On April 1 Lord Derby wrote that Millerand "impressed on me time after time that he had no intention, and never had had any intention, of acting except in thorough accord with the Allies."[98] When the French did act alone, the British felt justified in their view that Millerand "was not candid"— especially as the French ambassador in London had been deliberately kept "almost completely in the dark by M. Millerand" as to what French policy was.[99]

If French policy had wavered both in appearance and in substance, this was largely because Millerand felt himself called upon to make an impossible choice between the Alliance and the treaty. That this was on his mind at the time is clear: in a March 20 meeting of the Conference of Ambassadors, he excitedly accused the British of having decided "to take no account of the violations proved and not in any case to take measures to cause the Treaty to be respected."[100]

The French had finally given in to the British, but this did little to remove the impression that France was incurably militaristic. Instead the whole affair served to confirm it. Moreover, Lloyd George became convinced of the basic unsteadiness of the French government—a firm guiding hand, directly applied by the British, was necessary to correct this unfortunate tendency. Negotiation through intermediaries had proved unsatisfactory. Now Lloyd George would insist that the Allies resolve their differences in conferences of heads of government; his earlier willingness to allow the Reparation Commission wide latitude now disappeared.

The heads of the principal Allied governments met in San Remo in late April. The hope was that in the face-to-face meetings at this conference a common Allied policy on questions related to the execution of the treaty could be worked out; the unity of the Alliance, so recently imperiled, would thereby be reaffirmed. Reparation was one of the key issues discussed, and at the conference Lloyd George and Millerand reached agreement on the basic lines along which Allied policy would proceed toward a solution of this question.

The French government two months earlier had set out a reparation policy that on essential points was in complete accord with British ideas. At the London Conference in February the French Finance Minister François-Marsal had welcomed the idea of German economic revival. He agreed with the British that the restoration of the normal mechanism of international credit was essential, and that to secure it Germany's reparation liability had to be set at a definite figure.[101] This view was then embodied in the Economic Memorandum adopted by the Supreme Council on March 8. The memorandum twice called for a fixed sum, and to this end declared that the four-month deadline on German proposals set in June 1919 "should be extended."[102]

Millerand on March 26 therefore wrote Raymond Poincaré, former President of the Republic and now the French delegate on (and president of) the Reparation Commission, requesting him, in accordance with the decision of the Supreme Council, to support the formal extension of the four-month limit on German proposals. Poincaré resisted this suggestion. "I am first of all," he wrote Millerand on April 3, "forced to make, as far as I am concerned, the most formal reservations on the 'decision' taken at London."[103]

The question had been discussed by Millerand, Marsal and Poincaré on April 2, as the Ruhr crisis was reaching a climax. Marsal still favored a fixed sum, providing it would lead to a mobilization of the debt. But Poincaré, as a matter of principle, was opposed to the sacrifice of treaty rights that a fixed sum would entail. For the moment, Poincaré's views prevailed.[104] But the reason for this given in the minutes of the meeting reveals a striking lack of French self-assurance: the proposal for an extension of the time limit for German offers was rejected because "we would expose ourselves in fact to seeing the debt put at an extremely low figure by the Germans and above all to seeing this figure accepted at once by the Reparation Commission"[105]—an odd point since unanimity was essential on this issue, and a French veto could legally block any reduced figure.[106]

It was Lloyd George's idea at San Remo that a more active Allied policy was vital. Matters related to the execution of the treaty, he said, "could not be allowed to drift."[107] The German government was weak, and had "to be pulled together" by Allied pressure.[108] But he vetoed Millerand's suggestion of an immediate occupation of the Ruhr; instead, he would press the German government on questions related to the execution of the treaty in face-to-face talks: "The best plan would be to have a straight talk with them and find out what could be done."[109]

This Millerand accepted subject to two conditions. The Allies would have to agree in advance on "the precise character of the demand that they would make and insist on" and on "what they would do if the German Government did not execute their promises within the prescribed limits of time."[110] Lloyd George at once accepted these terms. He even proposed that the military be asked to suggest various measures of coercion for the consideration of the Supreme Council.[111] All this, however, should not be taken at face value. It was evidently Lloyd George's plan to bring the French to accept his policy one step at a time. His tactic was simple: at each stage, he would minimize the divergence between his ideas and those of the French. Faced with the choice between endangering Allied unity and making relatively small compromises, the French would move to accept his position. Then a subtle change would occur. British policy would become just a bit more conciliatory toward Germany, pulling Millerand yet further into the paths of moderation. In this process the minor Allies played a definite role. The Belgian government, anxious above all to preserve the Anglo-French entente, was always ready to propose compromises to bridge ever-recurring Anglo-French differences. The Italian Prime Minister Nitti, who at the time strongly sympathized with Germany, also played "a very useful role," according to Lloyd George, placing Great Britain "in the position of being a moderator between two extreme views represented by the Italians, on the one hand, and the French on the other."[112]

Lloyd George thus accepted Millerand's conditions, happy to have attached the French government (however tenuously) to his policy of direct negotiation with Germany. He soon receded from his promise to agree on measures of coercion ahead of time.[113] In spite of the importance of this point Millerand did not really press it, and all that remained at the end of the conference was a vague threat in the Allied declaration to Germany to occupy more German territory, if that were necessary to ensure the execution of the treaty.[114]

Lloyd George began at once to reshape the French idea of precise Allied demands for the correction of treaty violations. What emerged under his guidance, but with the full acquiescence of Millerand, was a plan that in all but name amounted to a revision of the treaty. In theory, the Allies began to formulate a reparation plan that would serve as a standard by which to judge the acceptability of German propositions for the execution of the reparation provisions. In practice, however, what now took shape was a plan that could serve as a basis for negotiation with Germany on a solution to the reparation question.

During the San Remo conference, Lloyd George, in contrast to Nitti, took what appeared as a strong line on reparation—on this question "he meant to be quite unyielding."[115] Millerand, as usual, insisted on the full execution of the treaty. Lloyd George fully agreed: "He was entirely opposed to any disucssion about the revision of the treaty."[116] What he proposed was nothing more than the application of the treaty—or at least of the protocol that had been attached to the treaty at the last moment embodying the modifications that he had demanded.[117] In that document the Germans had been invited to propose a fixed sum, and it was the setting of a global figure that Lloyd George now pressed for. This, he insisted, was the key to the problem. Without a fixed sum Germany could get no credit and could therefore pay nothing.[118]

Millerand was reluctant at first to accept this idea. Inviting Germany to make such an offer, he pointed out, would be viewed in France as willingness to see Germany's liability reduced, since any figure proposed would clearly be less than what the Reparation Commission would set by adding up damages. Light-heartedly, Lloyd George replied that Millerand's reluctance "was, in itself, a departure from the treaty" because he was in effect repudiating the invitation extended at the end of the peace conference for the German government to propose a figure. Millerand for his part declared that he would "accept any arrangement" consistent with the treaty.[119]

He did in fact soon accept the principle of a fixed sum.[120] Indeed, he took the initiative in proposing further negotiations among the Allies. He himself proposed that, as an alternative to merely setting a figure for a capital sum, the idea of a scheme of annuities varying in accordance with changing economic conditions in Germany be considered.[121] Lloyd George liked this idea, and the two prime ministers referred the whole question for further discussion to the experts—Avenol, who had originally proposed the sliding annuity plan, and the British and Belgian delegates on the Reparation Commission, Bradbury and Theunis.[122]

The matter was not delegated to the Reparation Commission itself for negotiation with Germany. Millerand then opposed the very idea of such negotiations. The Allies, he told Lloyd George, should simply fix a figure among themselves, and "then send for the Germans and reply 'Yes' or 'No' to the German offer, according to whether it was equal to, or below the figure fixed by the experts."[123] Lloyd George did not at this time argue with Millerand on this point, but simply passed to another subject.

The bypassing of the Reparation Commission is understandable enough at this time. Both Millerand and Lloyd George felt that Allied reparation policy had to be under the direct control of the governments. Although this need not in principle have been an obstacle to acting through the Commission—each government could simply have instructed its delegate to act according to its wishes—at the time this was difficult. Poincaré was sure to resist the policy of having the Reparation Commission set a figure, and Millerand did not at the moment wish to oppose him head on. For his part, Lloyd George, trusting in his great powers of persuasion, felt only "summit" negotiations could achieve speedy results.

Yet if the aim was to solve the reparation problem, the decision to bypass the Commission had certain disadvantages. A body composed of specialists negotiating on a daily basis with their German counterparts was better able to pursue an effective policy. Negotiating out of the limelight, there was no need to posture, nor to reach hasty solutions. The prestige inherent in the word "expert" would in itself win support for any arrangement reached at these relatively low-level negotiations. Furthermore, acting through the Commission was the sole means of putting legal pressure on Germany, in the absence of which the German government had no incentive to bargain in good faith and every incentive to temporize. Yet the Allied governments in 1920 made little effort to apply this pressure through the exercise of the principal rights prescribed in the treaty, something which could be done only through the Reparation Commission.

Article 235 was the main provision in the treaty governing reparation in the period before the definitive schedule of payments would be handed to the Germans (in May 1921 at the latest). It provided that "Germany shall pay in such installments and in such manner (whether in gold, commodities, ships, securities or otherwise) as the Reparation Commission may fix, during 1919, 1920 and the first four months of 1921, the equivalent of 20,000,000,000 gold marks." In other words, the Reparation Commission had the right to set a schedule of payments, giving the date for each installment and the form each payment would take. Such a schedule would put pressure on the German government to make a real effort and negotiate in good faith with the Commission on the practical machinery of payment. Without a schedule, the Allies would have no legal right until May 1921 to force compliance with the reparation clauses as a whole; it was only with respect to those areas such as coal where a precise obligation already existed, that a default could be declared and coercion legally applied. Nevertheless no Article 235 schedule was ever prescribed, and in spite of Millerand's calls for the "strict execution of the treaty," the French government in 1920 never insisted on the elaboration of such a schedule.[124]

The second part of the article provided that out of the 20 milliard sum would be financed such supplies of food and raw material as the Allied governments judged "to be essential to enable Germany to meet her obligations for reparation." This implied that the Germans would submit for Allied (and this came to mean Reparation Commission) approval schedules of supplies deemed essential. It was in fact at first assumed that such schedules would be submitted. But none ever were. Germany nevertheless received credit after the fact for her purchases of food and raw material. Again, the French never proposed in 1920 that the provision for prior approval be invoked, nor did they make any effort to block a liberal interpretation of this provision when accounts under this article were being drawn up—hardly the attitude of a power eager to "enslave" Germany, or of one bent on a narrow interpretation of the treaty in order to force a German default as an excuse for crushing her.[125]

Furthermore, the Reparation Commission made no real attempt to invoke Article 248 which provided, subject to exceptions granted by the Commission, that reparation and other costs arising from the treaty were "a first charge upon all assets and revenues of the German Empire." This article supplied the legal basis for an active policy of pressing the German government, inclined to view reparation as a "last charge" on its revenues, to make the necessary fiscal effort. Again, the Reparation Commission, including the French delegate, tended to take an indulgent attitude and avoided too literal an interpretation of the treaty.[126]

The Millerand government's failure to press for the execution of these key treaty provisions is in itself proof of the moderation, or at least the passivity, of its reparation policy. But a moderate policy is not necessarily an intelligent policy, and the effectiveness of French policy was compromised by the confusion of the ideas on which it was based. There was no precise conception of the role that force would play. French leaders spoke, for example, of the occupation of the Ruhr not so much as a "sanction" (which would imply that its function was to oblige the Germans into making a clear effort to pay), but as a "guarantee," as though the occupation would itself bring in huge sums. In this light, it was easy for Lloyd George to discredit the idea of seizing the Ruhr: the costs of occupation would outstrip the sums this operation would raise.[127]

For much of 1920, there was no recognition of a related consideration, the importance of reducing the question to one of Germany's willingness to make a prescribed effort. This was the only defense against the argument, raised for example by Nitti at San Remo, that French demands exceeded Germany's capacity to pay.[128] By not limiting his demands explicitly to what lay within Germany's capacity, Millerand left France open to the charge that she was asking Germany to do the impossible. Yet so great was the importance of the phrase "strict execution of the treaty," and so enormous was the horror felt in France at the phrase "Germany's capacity to pay" which had become a kind of by-word of revisionism, that Millerand dared not frankly admit the principle which most nearly corresponded to the substance of his policy.

With this gap between words and practice, and with no clear conception of how to proceed, Millerand was unable to take a firm stand and was thus open to British manipulation. But Lloyd George's policy was equally ill-conceived. He subordinated everything to arriving at a fixed sum. Without real Allied pressure, however, it soon became clear that Germany never would offer a figure approaching what the Allies would find acceptable.[129] Lloyd George, however, was extremely reluctant to use military coercion to obtain Germany's consent. Even putting aside the legal difficulties—since Article 235 was not being applied, there was no default and hence no legal basis for the application of force—there was the more fundamental problem that imposing a figure on Germany would be tantamount to a second Treaty of Versailles. The obligations arising from another dictated settlement would not be viewed by Germany as morally binding. The problem of default would persist, and the problem of mobilization would be unresolved, for no one would buy the bonds of a debtor bent on evading payment.

It was this that made the reparation question so difficult. A freely negotiated agreement was impossible, while an imposed settlement was relatively worthless. Was there any way out of this dilemma? If a solution were at all within reach, it could be achieved not through threats and coercion, but only through continual pressure on Germany to gear her economy to produce the maximum surplus for reparation—the kind of pressure best applied through a vigorous Reparation Commission. Germany would be allowed to escape from this pressure only through agreement on a fixed sum; with this incentive, a semivoluntary acceptance of a reasonable, definite reparation liability might be extracted. But Lloyd George, like Millerand, made no effort to apply pressure in this way. He instead counted on pressing the Germans in face-to-face meetings with their leaders. Thus at San Remo, the Germans had been invited to meet with the Allies to discuss the application of the treaty; it was eventually decided that this conference would take place in Spa. But even such an exceptionally forceful personality as Lloyd George proved unable to push the Germans far enough at these meetings, and his whole strategy for reaching for agreement on a figure turned out to be largely an exercise in futility.

Two weeks after the San Remo Conference adjourned, Millerand and Lloyd George, accompanied by their Ministers of Finance and various experts, met again at Hythe. Marsal had set out the French line in a long letter to Millerand a few days earlier. A fixed sum was acceptable, Marsal wrote, but only under certain conditions: "Before listening to appeals addressed to our good will with respect to an immediate determination of Germany's obligations, we want to receive definite assurances as to what we will obtain. Before examining whether or not it is possible to set the debt right now, we want to obtain guarantees that our share will be paid in its entirety, as well as the guarantee that we will be able to capitalize it and convert it into cash. Finally, at a time when we are being asked to make an effort of moderation, we must not be the only ones to consent to sacrifices; we must find, in the very arrangements that we are now being invited to discuss, ways of making the financial burden we will have to bear more equitable."[130] Marsal left little doubt as to the three major concessions he felt the Allies should make. He wanted the French to be given a kind of priority, even if this meant a revision of the percentages previously accepted; he wanted Allied assistance in the mobilization of the debt, and called for measures that would relieve France of her war debt to Great Britain and the United States.[131]

When the Hythe Conference opened on May 15, Millerand at once stated the French point of view. In spite of political difficulties, he was willing to agree with the Allies on a fixed sum. But, he said, "I cannot do so unless, in exchange for a hope (though it be in part illusory), I am given a reality, even mediocre, but concrete."[132] Millerand thus revealed his true feelings about the treaty: French rights under it were largely empty, and could only be made real through a policy of completing and developing the treaty in cooperation with the Allies.

In this and subsequent meetings Millerand and Marsal pressed the British for the concessions outlined in Marsal's letter of May 13. Millerand hoped in this way to extract something real from the treaty.

But Allied concessions were also needed for political reasons. The government, Marsal stressed, had "to be able to present the Chamber with certain advantages as compensation" for giving up the right to have the Germans pay for all the damages in accordance with the treaty.[133]

The French demand for concessions was largely frustrated. Lloyd George, stressing the intangibility of agreements already made, firmly resisted proposals for priority that would reduce the British share of German payments. Why, he argued, should Britain have to pay France a price for acting intelligently? The proposal for a fixed sum was not being made "for the sake of Germany. Any suggestions we made were solely with the object of getting the money. The Allies were dealing with a bankrupt estate. . . . If one creditor among several proposed a method of obtaining some part of the debt, he ought not to be asked to make a concession to the other creditors."[134]

Millerand at first reacted strongly to this rigid British veto. He declared that if the French proposals were unacceptable, a return to the treaty (i.e., letting the Reparation Commission set the debt through totaling up damages) was the only alternative, and he threatened to break off negotiations for an Allied agreement on a fixed sum.[135] But Lloyd George did not despair of reaching some arrangement with the French. What they really wanted, he said,—and this corresponded to Marsal's second point—"was to get an immediate use of what came from Gremany for the purpose of reconstruction."[136] He proposed a scheme for the mobilization of the French share of the debt. For five years Great Britain would refrain from directly or indirectly mobilizing her share, thereby increasing the chances for a successful French mobilization. This suggestion struck Millerand and Marsal as "a very inferior collaboration to what they thought indispensable."[137] The next morning Millerand proposed as an alternative a plan to associate the other Allies, and perhaps also some neutrals, with France and Germany in the issue of the loan, the proceeds of which would go in part to Germany and in part to France. The French share would in effect represent a partial mobilization of the reparation debt.

The language of the French proposal was vague—it did not, for example, call explicitly for a British guarantee of part of the loan— but the principle was sufficient to rouse Lloyd George's hostility: "This proposal seemed to be going back on the arrangements already reached, and to constitute an endeavour to set up an arrangement of quite a different character."[138] He was willing to allow the experts to examine the general question of the mobilization of the debt; but when the question was next discussed by Millerand and Lloyd George on June 20, it became clear that the British would go no further toward meeting French views on this point than they already had.[139]

In the third area in which the French pressed for concessions—the linking of the war debt question with reparation—the British were inclined to be more liberal and accepted the principle of a "parallel liquidation" of both kinds of debt.[140] But here it was American and not British resistance that proved the stumbling block. In the informal meetings of experts that followed the first Hythe Conference, and again at the second Hythe Conference on June 20, the British indicated their desire to deal generously with the French debt. In an experts' conference British officials led the French to believe that they would be asked to repay only the capital of the debt: interest would be forgiven. This, a French report noted, "would cut in half the annuities to be paid by France."[141] At the second Hythe Conference, Lloyd George gave the assurance "that France need not be anxious about our insistence on our full rights when she had difficulties over her devastated regions."[142]

Lloyd George wanted, however, to avoid a formal agreement regulating the debt issue with France. The reason he gave was that this might prejudice the general cancellation of inter-Allied indebtedness favored by the British government.[143] It is quite possible that he also hoped to retain British loan rights as a means of maintaining pressure on France. In May 1920 two leading cabinet ministers, Winston Churchill and Austen Chamberlain, stressed that the debts could be used in this way.[144] Even the Americans tried to use the debt issue "as a weapon to compel what they considered proper conditions as regards the German indemnity," although the concessions they were willing to make in exchange for Allied moderation on reparation were absurdly small.[145] Lloyd George himself was of course not above considerations of this sort.

The British thus held back from the formal remission of the French debt—favored, incidentally, by the Treasury, the Foreign Secretary and the British Ambassador in Paris.[146] Although the

French did win British acceptance of the principle of "parallel liquidation," the meaning of this concession was vague. For the British insisted that the French debt to America must not be given any preferential treatment: the debt to Britain had to be settled on as favorable a basis as the debt to America.[147] And the Americans, when approached on the subject, were as rigid as ever.[148]

So the French had really won very little from the British at Hythe.[149] Millerand nevertheless continued at the conference to work toward a fixed sum. For reasons that remain obscure, he dropped the Avenol plan for sliding annuities that he had presented at San Remo.[150] He instead somewhat ambiguously proposed a fixed sum "that cannot be less than 120 milliard gold marks."[151] This figure had seemed quite moderate in 1919, but to Lloyd George it now seemed too high, and he attempted to bargain Millerand down.[152] In the absence of an agreement, however, the whole question was referred to the experts.[153]

Unlike Clemenceau, Millerand did little to conceal the thrust of his reparation policy from the French people. At San Remo, Hythe, and after, the press carried reasonably accurate accounts of the reparation negotiations. In particular, Millerand's proposal for a "minimum fixed sum" of 120 milliard gold marks was widely publicized—and if the word "minimum" had been added to confuse people, few were really taken in.[154]

Millerand's opponents were quick to react. Even before resigning from the Reparation Commission, Poincaré began to attack the policy of the fixed sum in biweekly articles in *Le Matin* and the *Revue des Deux Mondes*.[155] Tardieu, the other arch-opponent of Millerand's reparation policy, hit hard against the movement toward a fixed sum in an important series of articles in *L'Illustration*. The new government, he argued, was abandoning French treaty rights without getting anything in exchange.[156] It was not the fault of the treaty if French hopes were being frustrated; rather, Millerand was to be blamed for not knowing how to execute the treaty, and for his inability to stand up to the British. Tardieu liked to contrast Millerand's weakness with Clemenceau's strength: at the peace conference, France's allies had made similar proposals for a fixed sum, but the French delegation had successfully turned back these attempts. Now, although the Allies were honor-bound to respect the treaty they had signed, the Millerand government was abandoning without any real compensation the rights that had been defended so tenaciously by the Clemenceau government.[157]

Tardieu's purpose in these articles was transparently political. If Millerand did not know how to enforce the treaty, Tardieu himself did. The conclusion was evident: In this hour of crisis, France should return Tardieu and his friends to power. There was a strong element of dishonesty in the *clemenciste* polemic against Millerand. It was dishonest to contend, as Tardieu often did, that the French delegation had consistently opposed a fixed sum, when in fact it had accepted the principle of a fixed sum, only to see it blocked by the British.[158] It was a distortion to imply, as Tardieu did, that Millerand bore responsibility for the failure of American financial cooperation, when it was abundantly clear to all who would look that the rigid attitude of the Wilson administration and the United States Congress was responsible for the frustration of plans for American financial involvement.[159] It was certainly disingenuous for Tardieu and Loucheur, who in 1920 participated in this polemic, to attack Millerand in the Chamber on the 120 milliard figure, when it was precisely this figure that they both had been willing to accept at the peace conference.[160]

The polemic in any case was not successful in its immediate aim. Millerand was eager to defend his policy on precisely the grounds staked out by Tardieu. The discussion in the Chamber in late May quickly took the form of a debate over the merits of the treaty. It was impossible, Millerand argued, simply to rely on "texts heavier in promises than in realities."[161] A more active policy was essential if France was to get anything real, and France could pursue a positive policy only in cooperation with the Allies. This was the regime set up by the treaty; France had but one vote on the Reparation Commission and simply could not make demands in isolation.

The right wing shared Millerand's view that the treaty was to blame, and it was in large part for this reason that rightist deputies and the conservative press now supported Millerand's reparation policy. The idea of the fixed sum was accepted grudgingly, but accepted nevertheless—a distasteful but unavoidable consequence of Clemenceau's failure at the peace conference. Indeed Millerand's policy was supported at this point by a wide spectrum of bourgeois opinion. *Le Matin, Le Petit Parisien, Le Journal du Peuple, Le Gaulois,* even *L'Action Française*—all supported the government on the question of the fixed sum.[162] In Parliament, Millerand half-denied his commitment to the 120 milliard figure, but it is clear from the debate that few were taken in by his equivocation. By an enormous majority of 501 to 63, with only 32 abstentions, the Chamber voted at the end of May to support the government.[163]

Practically all the opposition came from the Socialists. Vincent Auriol, explaining the Socialist attitude, insisted that the 120 milliard figure was insufficient.[164] A fixed sum was acceptable only if completed by Allied "guarantees of financial solidarity."[165] In addition, the Socialists demanded priority for France. Auriol condemned at one point the "double error committed by the French negotiators" at the peace conference—having failed to insist on priority, and "having renounced inter-Allied solidarity."[166] Loucheur challenged the word "renounced," but Auriol defended it. In this he was supported by Briand, who declared that Allied solidarity "should have been imposed, since promises had been made" (he was referring to the Paris Economic Conference of 1916!)[167] The Socialists felt such conditions could still be imposed, and their proposed *order du jour* indicated they would accept a fixed sum only if it were supplemented by the kind of inter-Allied arrangements that Auriol had indicated.[168]

After the Hythe Conference negotiations with the British moved swiftly. By the time Millerand again met Lloyd George on June 20, the experts—Celier, Avenol, Blackett, Bradbury and Theunis—had prepared what with certain minor modifications came to be known as the "Boulogne scheme"—although the conference at Boulogne in late June was but one of several conferences at which the plan was discussed. The French did not insist on the 120 milliard figure; indeed by mid-June Millerand had indicated to the British that he "was convinced that the 120 miliards of francs [sic] previously proposed was not reasonably to be expected."[169]

The Boulogne scheme instead called for a series of annuities, rising from 3 milliard gold marks in 1921–1922 to 6 milliards in 1926–1927, and finally to 7 milliards in 1930–1931.[170] The annuities were to remain at this level until the reparations ended in 1963. There was, however, an element of flexibility in this system: the Reparation Commission could postpone the payment of part of the annuity after 1926, but in no case would the annuity in any year drop below 3 milliard gold marks. Germany was given a certain incentive for swift payment: sums paid by May 1922 would liquidate annuities discounted at 8 per cent. Thus a loan that raised 65 milliard gold marks ($16,250,000,000) would completely liquidate the German reparation debt; the swift payment to France of less than 35 milliards (less than $9,000,000,000—even in those days no "fantastic" figure) would totally wipe out her claim on Germany.

For purposes of comparison with other reparation plans, it is necessary to compute the "present value" or value in capital of the Boulogne scheme. But this cannot of course be given in any absolute sense. Like any set of annuities, the present value of this scheme can only be calculated with reference to a particular rate of interest. At 5 percent the Boulogne annuities would have a present value of almost exactly 100 milliard gold marks; at 8 percent they would be equivalent to a capital sum of 65 milliard gold marks; at 0 per cent—assuming, that is, no interest at all—the figure would be 269 milliards. There is nothing sacred about any particular interest rate; the important thing is to be consistent in using the same rate of interest when comparing figures corresponding to different plans—a simple enough precaution, but one neglected by historians from time to time, with curious results.[171] Here the 5 percent interest rate will be the basis for the computation of the present value of reparation plans. This was taken as standard at the time, and was inscribed in the treaty itself.

The Boulogne scheme thus amounted to a fixed sum of 100 milliard gold marks. On June 23 the semiofficial paper Le Matin announced this figure in a headline. But there was more to the plan than just a schedule of annuities. Germany would continue to pay occupation costs as a first charge.[172] Moreover, Germany was to try to float loans in order to make the "anticipatory payments" outlined above; she could keep up to a fifth of the proceeds of these loans for her own needs. The loans, and more generally the reparation debt, were to be guaranteed by certain German revenues and assets, notably the customs.

Millerand did not intend to insist on the Boulogne scheme as an absolute minimum. He agreed with Lloyd George that should the German offer prove totally inadequate, this plan was a "good starting-point" for negotiation, and admitted that a further reduction of the debt was possible.[173]

In view of the widespread belief in the intransigence of French reparation policy in 1920, it is instructive to examine the Boulogne agreement more closely. It is clear that the French government was willing to accept an immediate payment of 35 milliard gold marks as completely liquidating its share of reparation. From the French point of view, a swift and total mobilization of the French share was in fact the ideal solution: it was better to take the 35 milliards at once than to wait for the annuities, even though the latter amounted in terms of present value to a higher sum. Moreover, Millerand recognized that the Boulogne scheme might be reduced further, in the course of negotiation with the Germans. Therefore what France would have gotten under the most favorable conditions from the Boulogne scheme was hardly more than what she would have gotten from the plan proposed by Keynes—less in fact when the questions of the inter-Allied debt and the British share are taken into account. Keynes would have waived the British claim to reparation, which at Boulogne remained intact; under his scheme, therefore, it was more likely that the French share would have been paid in its entirety, because the total German debt would have been substantially smaller. Keynes furthermore would have canceled inter-Allied indebtedness, which at Boulogne also remained intact. The French debt to Britain and America amounted to 25 to 28 milliard gold marks (the estimates differ); under the assumption that the German debt, as set at Boulogne, were paid in full, the Allied debt would also have had to be paid in full. This was evidently what the principle of "parallel liquidation" implied. Thus under ideal circumstances France would net only 7 to 10 milliard gold marks from the settlement of international accounts. She would dispose of a further large sum of 28 to 31 milliards at a time when it was most needed, although this would eventually have to be paid back in full. Under the opposite assumption, ruling out a swift and substantial mobilization, the French share would be 52 milliards, meaning that over a forty-two-year period France would net sums (after the payment of the Allied debt) amounting to a present value of 24 to 27 milliards. Thus, under the Boulogne agreement, France would end up with between 7 and 27 milliard gold marks, the exact amount depending mainly on the speed and size of mobilization; and while a rapid mobilization of the entire debt was out of the question, French officials did not rule out a swift mobilization of a substantial portion of their share of the debt. Whatever the figure, Millerand was willing to reduce it still further in negotiation with the Germans.

Even the maximum figure of 27 milliards was by no means unreasonable. This was about what France would obtain from the plan Keynes advocated in *The Economic Consequences of the Peace*. It follows that to the extent that a willingness to conform to Keynes's proposals is an acceptable measure of moderation, the French were paradoxically more "moderate" than the British and the Americans; indeed the French were somewhat justified in feeling that Anglo-Saxon moderation in 1920 consisted of a willingness to make concessions essentially at the expense of France.

Lloyd George was not much concerned with figures as such. To him, the important thing was to bring France and Germany together on a fixed sum. It hardly mattered what it was, so long as France and Germany accepted it. Increasingly autocratic, it was his will alone that determined British policy on this question.[174] British Treasury officials might argue whether Germany could pay the Boulogne annuities—Basil Blackett, for example, the most important permanent official concerned with these matters, thought that she could—but Lloyd George was not interested.[175] A fixed sum was what was needed, and France and Germany had to be half-coaxed, half-coerced into agreement. With the French attitude he was now generally satisfied; the problem was to get Germany to bargain realistically. The German government, however, was not disposed to suggest a figure.[176] Lloyd George therefore proposed to frighten the Germans into taking the right position on reparation. He agreed with Millerand that Britain should appear to take the initiative in pressing for German compliance with the disarmament clauses. "This," he argued, "would help to create the necessary atmosphere at Spa. He [Lloyd George] was seriously perturbed at the possibility that Germany might think that the Allies were divided. It was very important to create the necessary atmosphere of alarm on the part of Germany, in order to induce her to put forward reasonable proposals in regard to reparation, and not such proposals as would not even form a basis of negotiation."[177]

The Conference of Spa, which convened on July 5, climaxed this phase of the diplomatic maneuvering over reparation. Owing to the German elections, the conference had been much postponed since San Remo. The elections had, however, considerably altered the composition of the Reichstag, and had resulted in the formation of a new government in which the Socialists did not participate. The new

Fehrenbach government, in fact, had only been in power for about a week when it met with the Allies at Spa. As the new German Foreign Minister, Dr. Simons, admitted, his delegation had come to Spa unprepared, without a definite plan on disarmament and without concrete proposals on reparation.[178]

Lloyd George was disappointed that on disarmament, instead of getting down to business and offering specific proposals, the Germans only offered "vague promises, nebulous assurances and appeals."[179] If this was their attitude on disarmament, where the Allies were most united, it was obvious that on the more tangled issue of reparation Germany would propose nothing of real substance. By July 7 Lloyd George and Millerand both doubted that a solution to the reparation question could be reached at Spa. They readily agreed that after hearing out the Germans, the Allies should have the Reparation Commission, joined by a minister or ambassador from each government, negotiate with German experts on the basis of the Boulogne accord.[180] It was Millerand who took the initiative in proposing these relatively low-level discussions. But at the same time he urged that the Allies should develop a plan for military coercion should the Germans prove uncooperative on the whole range of questions associated with the execution of the treaty.[181]

The German attitude appeared to justify Allied fears that Germany would hold back from specific proposals on reparation. Dr. Simons admitted as much on July 10. So far, he told the conference, the German reparation proposals existed "only in skeleton form" but he promised a "detailed scheme" would be submitted within the next two days.[182] By July 12 the German delegation did in fact send three notes to the Allies outlining its ideas on reparation, but these proposals hardly amounted to a "detailed scheme."[183] In the first note, the German delegation described a plan for a financial settlement, without, however, mentioning any figures (other than to register the claim that the 20 milliards called for in Article 235 had already been paid). The financial scheme resembled in structure both the Avenol plan discussed at San Remo and the American plan at the peace conference for a system of minimum and maximum annuities to be operated by the Reparation Commission. The German note spoke of a fixed minimum indemnity, a fixed maximum, and an index to make the actual payment each year depend on improvements in the "economic and financial situation of Germany." Everything would be on the basis of Germany's thirty-year capacity to pay. The second note proposed a system for the reconstruction of the devastated areas. It called for a "vast international enterprise" in which businesses from all nations would participate, but it gave no indication of how such a scheme would be financed. Finally, the German government proposed an arrangement for payment in kind. German industry would be organized so as to produce the required goods; the receiver nations would also be organized to accept and distribute these goods.

Why were these proposals not more precise? It was not that the German government had given no thought to the question. The Müller government had been reluctant to propose a fixed sum: Müller had preferred to allow experts to come up with a figure in confidential discussions.[184] The big industrialists were strongly opposed to a definite offer: Wiedfeldt (from Krupp) thought Germany was virtually incapable of paying anything, while Stinnes, on tactical grounds, felt a definite settlement was not in Germany's interest.[185] The more moderate Carl Bergmann, head of the Kriegslastenkommission (KLK), the body set up to deal with the Reparation Commission in Paris, also opposed a concrete offer at this time: there was no point in making proposals that the Allies would reject out of hand. Furthermore, Germany's ability to secure credit, he believed, had nothing to do with agreement on a fixed sum for reparation.[186]

Bergmann, after a conversation with the British and Belgian representatives on the Reparation Commission, changed his mind and supported a proposal of the banker Melchior: Germany should offer a minimum annuity of one milliard gold marks, and should suggest some scheme for increasing the annuity as Germany's situation improved.[187] The Allies—at least the British and the Belgians—would not view such an offer with contempt. The new Fehrenbach government now rallied to this proposal, but under the proviso, Foreign Minister Simons stressed, that Upper Silesia remain German and that no additional sums would be paid for occupation costs.[188] But at the Spa conference, Simons changed his mind and decided not to propose any figures at all, because, he said, "public opinion in France and England was still not sufficiently prepared for modest figures of this sort." Consequently, the German delegation had only proposed their "sketchy" reconstruction scheme.[189]

Even Lloyd George, after reading these documents, lost hope that an agreement on figures could be reached. But at least, he felt, the Allied experts might try to get the Germans to define their proposals more precisely.[190] Millerand still felt that the matter was best left to the experts to examine; however there were so many questions raised by the German proposals that he felt the experts could not come to any meaningful conclusion in the next few days.[191] When the experts were through, the conference could reconvene, he suggested, "to found conclusions upon their work."[192]

But Lloyd George persisted in his view and got his way. The "experts"—the Reparation Commission delegates, the British and French ambassadors to Germany and one minister each from Britain, France and Belgium—met the next morning with members of the German delegation. The Germans refused to suggest any figures; the meeting, however, did clarify certain technical aspects of the German proposals.[193]

By this time, the coal question had completely overshadowed the larger problem of reparation. The German government refused to make any offer on the size of the annuity until the coal question was cleared up.[194] When final agreement on that was painfully worked out, everyone was too exhausted to tackle the more difficult general problem of reparation. It was therefore decided to refer the question back to the "special commission"; in two or three weeks there would be another conference in Geneva to "exchange views and explore the whole question." The delegates at Geneva would "then report again to the Spa Conference."[195]

The Geneva Conference never took place, and it was not until December that the experts really got down to business. To understand why the Millerand government shifted course, it is necessary to turn to the issue that dominated the Spa Conference: coal. In 1920 the French need for coal was more pressing than their need for reparation in general. Hence in this area their policy was more active than on larger financial questions; in particular Millerand's eagerness to apply coercion focused on the coal default. Yet even on this point French policy was still somewhat ambivalent: figures for the amount of coal to be delivered were not extreme and were open to negotiation not just with Britain but with Germany as well. The important thing was to enforce whatever delivery plan was ultimately established.

On the question of coal, moreover, the French government felt it had a particularly strong case. Up to this point the Allies, acting through the Reparation Commission, had not fully invoked the coal options specified in the treaty. Instead a protocol had been negotiated with the Germans in August 1919 establishing a schedule of coal deliveries much less rigorous than that provided in the treaty. Actual deliveries, however, fell far short of the figures indicated in the protocol, and beginning in December 1919 the French government pressed for action. These demands were successfully resisted by Lloyd George. But by mid-1920, in spite of a further alleviation of Allied demands on April 29, the coal default had become more glaring. The rate at which French needs were being satisfied was substantially less than the corresponding German rate.[196] Moreover, as German output had increased, deliveries of reparation coal had fallen off. On June 30 the Reparation Commission therefore notified the Allied governments of Germany's default.[197]

This notification, Millerand told Lloyd George on July 2, was intended "to be the preliminary to a claim for a better delivery of coal."[198] The French government wanted to institute a tight control over the distribution of German coal, but Lloyd George believed this would be too drastic. Instead the Allies agreed on a compromise plan for a somewhat looser system of controls.[199]

Millerand met with Stinnes on July 4 to press him directly on the coal question. At the very least, Germany should deliver enough coal to replace the output of the destroyed mines. This, Stinnes said, was an impossible demand. If France insisted, he told Millerand, the result would be war: "A people driven to despair will and must attempt to free itself from the impossible conditions which have been forced upon it."[200]

The Spa Conference itself formally took up the question of coal on July 9. Bergmann made certain excuses. Millerand refuted some of these arguments and passed to the attack. Germany was still better supplied with coal than France. To prove the point, he compared corresponding rates of satisfaction: "The figure for France at the present time was 59 per cent., and in Germany 79 per cent."[201] This situation could no longer be tolerated. Millerand presented the Germans with the Allied plan to control the distribution of German coal upon which he and Lloyd George had earlier agreed.

The German delegates replied the next morning. Dr. Simons and the representative of the miners, Herr Hüe, were relatively moderate in their comments. But the mighty industrialist Hugo Stinnes—"a most sinister figure with a black beard and hideous sensual face''—delivered an insulting, highly emotional speech for which Simons and Chancellor Fehrenbach soon apologized.[202] Lloyd George was indignant; he felt that ''for the first time he had met a real Hun.''[203] Nevertheless, he urged that instead of breaking off talks, the German and Allied experts be allowed to discuss figures and come up with a plan. Millerand readily accepted this proposal, and in his remarks to the conference that afternoon, he informed the German delegation that the Allies agreed to refer the whole question to the experts.[204]

Millerand in fact preferred to avoid a completely imposed solution. He was in complete agreement with Lloyd George ''that it would be better to have the German Government's consent to the 2 million tons than to impose a claim for 2,400,000.'' (This latter figure represented the demand of the Reparation Commission.) Although Millerand felt that the figures regarding coal output, on which the Commission demand had been based, ''had never been challenged,'' he would nevertheless make the sacrifice of accepting the lower figure if he won in return for German cooperation in the delivery of the coal.[205]

When told of this proposal on July 12, the Germans argued that satisfaction of Allied coal demands depended on increasing coal production; to increase output, the miners had to be better fed. Lloyd George and Millerand accepted this point of view and hoped to find in it the basis for an agreement on coal deliveries.[206]

The outlook for a settlement, however, remained bleak, since the coal figures proposed by the Germans fell far short of what the Allies felt they could consider.[207] Millerand and Lloyd George both blamed Stinnes for the impasse.[208] It was because of his power and intransigence that, in Millerand's words, ''the policy of moderation and co-operation towards Germany'' that the Allies ''had shown themselves ready to adopt'' was being frustrated: the Allies ''had held out their hand, but it had not been grasped.''[209]

The negotiations seemed about to collapse, and the Allied leaders asked Marshal Foch to recommend measures of coercion on July 14.[210] Foch wanted to control the Ruhr from the outside by regulating its food supply. Lloyd George ''could not help feeling that the Allies had now reached a stage when it was necessary to decide between abandoning the Treaty of Versailles, or taking steps to enforce it." He had "very reluctantly" concluded that an occupation of the Ruhr was the only "method available for enforcing the treaty."[211]

Lloyd George thereupon proposed the following plan. The Allies would set "the most moderate contribution" of German coal they were demanding in accordance with the treaty. Then they would occupy the Ruhr and "say that no coal was to leave it for Germany until that minimum had been supplied. Then the Allies would be in a position to let the Germans come to them and ask that coal might be released. They would reply: 'Yes, on certain conditions.' "[212] But Lloyd George would support this policy only if the French first agreed to seven conditions. His key demand was that, contrary to the terms of the treaty, Germany be credited on reparation account for the coal at the "world" price. This, of course, meant the British export price. The principal effect of this would be to increase the British share of the cash payments that Germany would eventually pay, since a high valuation on reparation coal would account for a large portion of the 52 percent of the German annuity that was assigned to France, thereby decreasing the proportion of cash to which France would be entitled.[213] Millerand at first resisted this condition, although he agreed to all the others. But Lloyd George was persistent. To evaluate the coal as the treaty prescribed, he claimed, would bring France a profit of £2 a ton. "Speaking for the British Government, he said that it was impossible to contemplate the shooting of German miners so as to secure such a profit for the French Government or anyone else; and if the matter was based on a profit to France he must wash his hands of the whole affair." The discussion became heated, and Lloyd George said that the French were taking the position of Shylock—a remark that struck his close associate Sir Maurice Hankey as "brutal and rude."[214]

Lloyd George, meanwhile, in a secret meeting with Dr. Simons, had urged him to offer 2 million tons a month. He suggested that this offer be made contingent on the supply of credits for food for the miners, and proposed specifically that the "difference between the internal German price for coal and the export price" be used for this purpose. Later that evening, Lloyd George discussed with Millerand a number of questions that Dr. Simons had just sent him, suggesting precisely the kind of solution that Lloyd George had just secretly outlined to Simons; the next morning, the German delegation submitted a definite proposal along these lines.[215]

The French were by no means hostile to the idea of supplying food to the miners. Jacques Seydoux, the principal Foreign Ministry official concerned with reparation, wrote Millerand on July 8 that "French authorities have been long seeking a way of furnishing foodstuffs to the working population of the Ruhr"; negotiations with Stinnes linking food deliveries to increased coal shipments had in fact been taking place.[216] It was on the basis of this general idea that an accord was finally worked out, and an occupation of the Ruhr averted. For the next six months Germany would provide two million tons of coal a month, and would get credit for it on reparation account at the treaty rate (i.e., at the internal German price). In addition, she would get a cash premium of 5 gold marks a ton, supposedly in return for the right of the Allies to specify the qualities of coal they were to receive. Finally, the Allies would lend Germany an amount equal to the difference between the price they were "paying" (the internal German price plus the 5 gold mark premium) and the world export price. These advances, to be repaid at the end of the six-month period, were to enjoy an absolute priority over all other German debts to the Allies. The advances were to be furnished in accordance with the proportions determined by the definitive arrangement, also adopted at Spa, for the distribution of German reparation payments: Britain, for example, entitled to receive 22 percent of the reparations, would furnish 22/92nds of the advances, even though she received no reparation coal at all.[217] The five gold marks premiums, however, were to be paid in accordance with how much coal each nation received. Britain, therefore, would pay nothing in this way. Finally, it was understood that both the premiums and the advances were to be used to finance food supplies for the miners, although in the written agreement with Germany this provision was only mentioned with regard to the premiums.[218]

In his desire to preserve the Alliance and avoid the use of force, Millerand had made substantial concessions. On coal, as on the general reparation question, Millerand had given in a great deal. After months of default, France would get substantially less coal than the Reparation Commission had considered equitable on the basis of comparative rates of satisfaction. Moreover, the French government had actually agreed to pay for this coal, partly in the form of cash premiums and partly in the form of advances that, until they were repaid, would place an additional burden on the already hard-pressed French treasury.

The Spa accord was thus greeted in France with dismay. Millerand's whole reparation policy was once again attacked by Poincaré, Tardieu and Loucheur. But the Chamber, persuaded that there had been no real alternative, continued to support the government. The Alliance had to be preserved. This was a point that even Millerand's opponents conceded. To attack his government, therefore, they had to contend that resistance to British demands would not have broken the Alliance—an argument that simply did not convince the majority of the Chamber.

Millerand admitted that the coal agreement was disappointing, and the majority of the Chamber, in approving Millerand's policy on July 20 and in voting credits for the Spa advances ten days later, seems to have shared this point of view.[219] The right-wing ideologue Maurice Barrès was one of the very few deputies to approve wholeheartedly: providing the miners with food was a way of cultivating ties between France and the Rhenish workers.[220] The Socialists as usual voted against Millerand, still insisting that the only acceptable solution was one based on an Allied guarantee of the debt.[221] All the bourgeois parties overwhelmingly supported the government although the greatest support proportionately came from the right.[222] It was with a heavy heart, however, that the Spa accord was accepted by the representatives of the *Bloc National*. Its adherents were repelled by the chain of concessions that France had been called upon to make; these bitter feelings for the moment prevented Millerand from carrying through his reparation policy.[223] Spa, it was felt, must be the last concession; France must not go to Geneva to make yet another sacrifice on reparation. For the moment this view prevailed: the Geneva Conference was never to take place.

At Spa Millerand had clearly pursued a relatively conciliatory policy, and it was this that ultimately made the coal agreement possible. Was the larger international situation a determining factor in the outcome of the Spa conference? Poland was at the time fighting for its life against Russia (in a war that Poland to be sure had originally provoked): did the fear of a Soviet victory lead the Allies, and the French in particular, to be more conciliatory toward Germany than they would otherwise have been? The surprising thing here is how little impact the Polish crisis had on developments in the area of reparation and on relations between Germany and the West more generally. There was no sharp departure in French policy at Spa that needs to be explained by reference to an exogenous factor: all along the French government had taken more or less the same line on these matters. Similarly, as far as Lloyd George is concerned, there is no need to refer to the Polish crisis to explain his eagerness for an accord with Germany: other more permanent factors adequately explain why he pressed so vigorously for an agreement that would avert an occupation of the Ruhr. For the Allies the fact that the Spa conference was held at all at this time indicates that they were relatively unconcerned with the impact of the Polish affair on the negotiations with Germany. If they were worried, they could easily have pointed to the newness of the German government as an excuse for postponing the conference until matters in the east cleared up. Moreover, at Spa the Allies had in the final analysis been willing to coerce Germany on coal and even on disarmament: Allied insistence on these particular demands at a time when Bolshevik armies were sweeping toward Germany's borders is in itself a striking illustration of the disjunction between policy on the Polish war and policy on Germany.

Although French policy on Poland was not at this time directly linked to French reparation policy (something which in itself is symptomatic of a certain lack of realism in French policy generally), French behavior in the Polish affair exhibits characteristics and had certain effects which did bear on developments in the area of reparation. First, Millerand's passivity on Poland illustrates the general weakness of France: at Spa, even Lloyd George was willing to do more for the Poles than Millerand and Foch, who in no event were willing to send any French troops to prevent a Polish collapse.[224] And yet in this case a complete Soviet victory would have had the most far-reaching effect on the whole European political situation: in particular, the presence of Communist troops on Germany's border would have obviously doomed the disarmament provisions of Versailles and led to the military resurgence of Germany. On the other hand the coming into being of a common Russo-German border would have had definite advantages from the point of view of the West: both Russia and Germany, afraid of each other, would have had a great interest in staying on good terms with Britain and France.

Yet there was apparently no attempt to weigh these factors and think through the effect of a collapse of Poland; French policy in the whole affair smacks of improvisation.

The French government's unwillingness to send troops to prevent Poland's destruction did not prevent it from resenting what it viewed as British willingness to sacrifice Polish independence in negotiations with Russia. In a somewhat related move, the French government in August accorded de facto recognition to the dying White Russian government of General Wrangel in the Crimea. All this led to a fresh deterioration of Anglo-French relations.[225] But conflict with Britain gave the French government a double incentive to improve its relations with Germany. Germany was a possible counterweight to Britain: cultivating Germany would reduce France's dependence on her Ally. At the same time, a more moderate policy on German questions would remove the chief obstacle to good Anglo-French relations and thus strengthen the Entente. So in spite of the reaction to Spa at home the French government had good reasons in the fall of 1920 to strive for at least a partial resolution of the reparation problem. These general considerations, taken together with a certain evolution of thinking on reparation problems in the French government, led at the end of 1920 to a dramatic and vigorous effort to reach a solution: the Seydoux Plan.

The Seydoux Plan
Chapter Four

ALTHOUGH AFTER Spa Millerand could no longer rapidly proceed toward a fixed sum, this did not mean that French reparation policy was paralyzed. In fact, for the first time since the treaty had taken effect, French policy came alive. For there was more to the reparation problem than just the question of the figure at which Germany's liability would be set. Equally important was the problem of the mechanism of transfer: the question of how much Germany could pay could be answered only once it was understood in what manner reparation would be effected. It was in this area that the French now pushed ahead. The three vague notes the German delegates had submitted at Spa were in a sense a point of departure, since their very inadequacy convinced French officials that they could no longer expect acceptable German proposals, but must themselves seize the initiative in pressing for a solution.

The German notes, and German opinion in general, stressed the importance of direct reparation: reparation in kind and German participation in French reconstruction. While its financial situation was such that the German government could not hope to pay reparation on the scale demanded by the Allies, the German people were willing to work and turn over the product of their labor in satisfaction of Allied demands—such was the line generally taken by the German press at the time.[1]

The middle-ranking French officials who had been most directly involved with reparation in kind had a somewhat different perspective on German willingness to pay in this manner. At Spa they were asked to examine the German notes, and on July 12 reported that nothing new was being offered. The German plan for reparation in kind was not even as advanced as the arrangements already agreed upon in conversations between Reparation Commission and Kriegslastenkommission experts in Paris.[2] The problem, as they saw it, was that Germany was showing no eagerness to pay reparation in kind. This applied particularly to the options for reconstruction material under Annex IV of the treaty. Instead of simply invoking these treaty rights, the French government had preferred to negotiate. Beginning in April, lists were submitted to the Germans, who were invited to make offers as to which of the enumerated goods they could deliver, when, and at what "price" (that is, how much reparation credit they would get for these deliveries). The Germans held off from replying as long as they could; their offers, when they finally came, struck the French experts as absurdly inadequate, while the "prices" proposed were "3 or 4 times as high as world prices."[3] Thus by mid-1920 it seemed to even the most moderate French experts that largely because of German obstruction, the treaty provisions for direct reparation were unable to work; in particular, as a leading French official later wrote, Annex IV was rapidly becoming a "dead letter."[4]

The French experts were convinced that the procedure under Annex IV was too slow and too bureaucratic to be effective. The proof was that an organ of the French government, the Comptoir Central D'Achats, acting on behalf of the *sinistrés,*[5] actually bought reconstruction goods directly from German firms for cash: "Thus as a consequence of the practical impossibility of executing the provisions of the treaty, we have come to buy in Germany outside of reparation and we will end up destroying the whole Annex IV regime."[6]

This analysis of what was wrong with the treaty system shaped proposals for a new mechanism of payment which might serve as a basis for a solution to the whole reparation problem. The key conclusion drawn by the French experts at Spa from their critique of the Annex IV regime was that it was essential to "de-bureaucratize" the procedure for the payment of reparation in kind. In several memoranda written at the time, these experts outlined an ingenious plan for putting the payment of such reparation on a commercial basis. The

German government would pay paper marks into a special account. The French could draw upon this account to pay German firms for reconstruction goods. The German government, upon proof that an order had been placed, would replenish the account with an equivalent sum of paper marks, so that a revolving fund of set size would be automatically available. The Comptoir Central d'Achats and corresponding organs in Germany would continue to function, forming the basic channel through which orders would be placed, but the French could deal directly with individual German firms if they preferred.

The advantages of this flexible scheme for a revolving fund were immediately evident. If the plan took effect, reparation would be put on a business basis; the possibility of bureaucratic delay and obstruction would be minimized. Material interest would replace the threat of coercion as the guarantee for satisfactory delivery.[7] Questions of price would be settled automatically. Indeed, it was assumed that in practice the *sinistrés* would often deal directly with German firms, and the sole function of the Comptoir in that case would be to oversee the machinery of payment.

There was, the French experts stressed, yet another advantage to the procedure. German businessmen, benefiting directly from reparation orders, would use their enormous influence to get the German government to expand the revolving fund.[8] As the hostility of German industry was, in French eyes, one of the principal factors obstructing a reasonable solution of the whole reparation question, the winning over of this powerful segment of German society through a commercialization of direct reparation would speed a satisfactory resolution of the entire problem.

The experts' proposals were well received in higher official circles. The Ministry of Finance had long favored the importation of German goods and in particular the payment of reparation in kind as a means of relieving pressure on the franc. Celier, for example, argued in a note to Clemenceau in late October 1919 that because of the difficulty of obtaining American credit on reasonable terms, France should import even finished goods "from those countries where we dispose of the means of payment, and in particular, from Germany and Austria."[9] To restrict French purchasing to Allied and neutral countries, he wrote a month later, would mean that Frenchmen would be forced to pay unnecessarily high prices. He proposed instead that it be French policy to buy wherever goods were least expensive—a point of view wholeheartedly endorsed by Sergent, the Under-Secretary of State in the Ministry of Finance.[10]

By July 1920 the importance of direct reparation from Germany had sharply increased in the eyes of French leaders. The reason was that at Spa it was finally recognized that the preferred way of getting reparation, by means of a mobilization of the debt in America, simply would not work. Agreement on a fixed sum, the first condition for mobilization, was evidently not possible. The only alternative, therefore, was to extract wealth directly from Germany.

Clearly the new plan for reparation in kind would benefit the French treasury: to the extent that the *sinistrés* received direct satisfaction from Germany under the proposed system, their claims on the treasury would be reduced. French leaders, however, did not judge the new proposals purely in terms of narrow financial considerations. They saw in the proposed scheme an opportunity for putting relations between France and Germany on a new footing—a chance to lay the foundation for a lasting and mutually beneficial collaboration of French and German industry.

In 1920 Millerand often expressed his hope for "economic collaboration" with Germany, providing always that Germany made an honest effort to comply with the treaty. In line with this policy he had chosen Charles Laurent as the new ambassador to Germany: "In choosing M. Charles Laurent for this difficult post in Berlin, I have sought to throw into relief the character of the policy that we intend to follow with regard to Germany. It is above all an economic policy. I am certain that the surest way of re-establishing between the two countries a peace worthy of the name is by working to join together their material interests."[11]

This was in fact how Laurent's nomination was generally interpreted in France. Laurent had had a long and distinguished career in the highest strata of the administration and of private industry and finance. In 1920 he was among other things the head of the Union des Industries Métallurgiques et Minières de France. Alphonse Merrheim, secretary of the Fédération des Métaux, and thus Laurent's counterpart in the trade union movement, applauded the nomination. In an article entitled "The Defeat of Political Nationalism. The Revenge of Economic Necessities," which appeared in the important syndicalist organ *L'Information ouvrière et sociale,* Merrheim wrote that Laurent's nomination meant that the French government had chosen the path of economic collaboration with Germany, a choice of which he approved.[12] The nomination was interpreted in the same sense by the extreme right. Léon Daudet, the voice of Action Française in Parliament, attacked it for this very reason. Laurent was not—and here Daudet used the English expression—the "right man in the right place." He symbolized an economic policy, but what was needed was a policy of military coercion: "It is more important than ever to bridle Germany; and there is only one way to do that, namely by bridling her economic development with the aid of a military policy."[13]

But this was an extremist view. The government, on the contrary, hoped that some kind of reconciliation was possible. Of course, the idea of "economic collaboration" was vague. To Millerand, it seems, a policy of collaboration meant a policy which took as axiomatic the view that the Allies and the world in general had a real stake in the economic revival of Germany; it meant in essence a policy that aimed at the creation of a community of material interest between France and Germany. In this context it would be the goal of French reparation policy to draw the two economies together. Millerand in fact had long been trying to reach some kind of economic accommodation with Germany, particularly on metallurgical questions. But the negotiations that did take place in the Spring of 1920 were largely unsuccessful: German heavy industry had refused to take part in these talks.[14] The outcome of the Spa conference confirmed Millerand in his conviction that "the literal execution of the Treaty is a chimera," and that an accommodation with Germany was the best solution.[15] It is therefore clear that the new plan for reparation in kind was well within the orbit of Millerand's ideas.[16]

Secretly, and through unofficial intermediaries, the French signaled their willingness to work out an arrangement acceptable to both sides. On August 26 an unidentified "personality of French nationality, of whose reliability there is no question," approached a private German citizen with an extraordinary message. The German, after having him put it down on paper, at once forwarded it to Dr. Simons in Berlin. The Frenchman wrote that Marsal

. . . was desposed to *talk* unofficially with the German government about the application of the financial clauses of the Treaty of Versailles.

It would not be a question of revision in the strict sense of the clauses in question, but of a "modus vivendi" to be sought in common, in such manner as to facilitate the execution of what is executable, while putting aside what would appear as incapable of realization. The French government would abandon a part of its treaty rights, if in exchange for this very great concession the German government decides to give it satisfaction on other points. In brief, the treaty of Versailles appearing to many sensible people in France as "not being able to stand on its own two feet," at least from a financial point of view, it would be desirable to go over it chapter by chapter in private conversations between representatives of the two governments, and in a spirit of mutual confidence. This would be but a first step toward a more far-reaching economic entente, which the French government has in mind, and which is in the interest of the two countries.

The mysterious Frenchman was certain that these were the real views of the French government. Marsal's *chef de cabinet* had twice confirmed to him that these were the intentions of the Minister of Finance, and that Millerand himself also approved. Laurent, the *chef de cabinet* had noted, had received the necessary instructions: "Should a qualified member of the German government approach him, he will find the ground prepared and favorable. But the initiative not being able to come from the French government, it had been judged expedient" to get in contact with the Germans in this more discreet way.[17]

In fact, when Simons approached Laurent in early September to propose such conversations, Millerand quickly consented.[18] Simons's views in these talks could only have encouraged French officials to develop their policy along the lines proposed by the reparation experts at Spa. The German foreign minister, Laurent reported on October 1, was concerned with getting some cash in return for deliveries in kind, a wish that fit in well with the French hope for basing reparation on interest rather than on force. Moreover, when Laurent pointed out that Germany's economic problems at the moment derived not from a lack of coal, but rather from insufficient demand, Simons readily agreed. Factories needed orders, but German commercial policy—a rather rigid and confusing system of controls on foreign trade—had tended, Laurent said, to exclude foreign buyers from the German market. "The minister declared that I was right," Laurent noted, "and blamed Socialist influences for this ruinous error."[19]

By October 4 Laurent had received fresh instructions from Georges Leygues, who had just succeeded Millerand as Premier and Minister of Foreign Affairs. (Millerand himself had become President of the Republic, a post he had agreed to assume only after political leaders had assured him that he would be no mere figurehead. He intended to play an active role, particularly in foreign policy. Leygues, his hand-picked successor, retained his cabinet and was generally taken to be a pliant tool through whom Millerand would continue to govern.) Leygues readily accepted the idea of giving the Germans a certain material interest in paying: "We understand . . . the necessity of giving incentives to German manufacturers—a premium over and above the 'reparation' price paid them by the German government, but the sums going to this premium must remain under French control."[20] Following Simons's earlier remarks to Laurent, Leygues pointed out how accepting manufactured goods in partial satisfaction of Germany's reparation debt favored the interests of German industry. Reparation demand would create work in Germany, factories would get the orders they needed. "It is thus in the interest of the German government," Leygues wrote, "to expand as much as possible this category of reparation."[21]

Meanwhile the British were pressing for a resumption of the procedure agreed upon at Spa. Lloyd George was furious that the French government was backing out of its commitment to continue negotiations on a fixed sum.[22] It was essential, he thought, that the Geneva conference take place as planned; a coalition of Great Britain, Belguim and Italy would oblige France to give way and accept a figure.[23] Beginning in late August, he set about building such a coalition.

At the same time, the British government stepped up its pressure on France. The French had proposed abandoning the Geneva conference and letting the Reparation Commission in Paris study whatever proposals Germany had to make.[24] As Millerand privately admitted, this change was due to the hostile attitude of public opinion.[25] To "save the face of the French Government," Curzon suggested "a preliminary meeting between the Germans and the Reparation Commission"; but the Geneva conference had to follow swiftly. Lest this "concession" be misinterpreted in France, Curzon was quick to follow it up with a threat: if the French, he wrote Derby, stubbornly ignored the wishes of the British government in this matter, "we shall be obliged seriously to consider withdrawing from co-operation with them on the reparation question."[26]

Curzon's remark indicates how much Anglo-French relations had deteriorated since Spa. There were other indications as well: the hostile and bitter tone of Lloyd George's allusions to France at this time; the increasing level of anti-British sentiment in what Lloyd George called "the wind and rabid French press"; the excited reaction in France to the unilateral renunciation by Britain of the right to seize private German property in the United Kingdom in the event of a voluntary reparation default—a reaction far out of proportion to the importance of this episode.[27]

As relations were bad, even agreement on procedure was difficult. Through September and October and half of November, these negotiations dragged on. For most of this time, the French sought to defend the prerogatives of the Reparation Commission; they insisted in October that the experts who, prior to the Geneva conference, would examine the German proposals must be members of this body.[28] The British government, which at first had offered to accept only a perfunctory examination by the Commission, finally moved in late October and early November toward accepting the French point of view—possibly because reports from the British delegate on the Commission and talks with the Belgian Prime Minister had convinced Lloyd George that the commissioners could be counted on to take a moderate line.[29]

But just after the British had agreed to the idea of appointing the Commission delegates as the experts charged with discussing the question with the Germans, the French government changed its mind and decided that the governments should be free to choose whomever they wanted as their representatives. The British now readily agreed, and the whole procedure was sanctified by an exchange of notes on November 11 and 12; the experts' conference, it was further decided, would take place in Brussels.[30]

Why the sudden shift in the French position? It seems that the Leygues government had come to the conclusion at this time that if it asserted itself, the Brussels Conference could be really productive; the French leaders, that is, hoped to seize this opportunity to put their new policy on reparation into effect. On October 21 Laurent told Simons that the French government wanted to replace the bilateral talks in Berlin with a "more open meeting of technicians in Brussels." He thought, however, that he should continue in Berlin "to prepare an economic *rapprochement* between the two countries," and told a receptive Simons that he intended to go on discussing these questions with representatives of German industry.[31] Since the

French government hoped to get down to business at Brussels, it insisted that it not be bound to select Dubois, its delegate on the Reparation Commission, as its representative. Quite possibly, Leygues and Millerand had instead already decided to appoint the official who in late 1920 had become perhaps the principal architect of French reparation policy, Jacques Seydoux.

Seydoux, a high-ranking official in the Foreign Ministry, had become the champion of the new policy. The victim of a painful disease that had confined him to a wheelchair, Seydoux had nevertheless risen high at the Quai d'Orsay. His own struggle seems to have shaped a firm belief in the power of the will to overcome seemingly insurmountable obstacles, a belief that his clear and well-disciplined mind now applied to the reparation question.[32] On reparation, his views had long been relatively moderate. A German diplomat in June characterized him as a "convinced advocate of a policy of economic understanding with Germany."[33] He certainly was capable of talking in "reasonable" tones. In April, for example, he told an American diplomat that because France and Germany "had to live in the same house," he was "doing all in his power to bring about better commercial and economic relations." The trouble was that Germany was unwilling to make a corresponding effort—"the Germans should show 'Entgegenkommen' (he used the German word) which so far, they had not done." Nevertheless, he declared, he was working with Millerand's full support to bring about "cooperation in reconstruction work."[34]

But Seydoux did not identify moderation with passivity. In fact he urged that France pursue a vigorous policy and force a solution, preferably through accommodation with Germany, but through coercion if necessary. An active policy was necessary, but so far the Reparation Commission had failed to pursue such a policy. "The Reparation Commission," he wrote in May, "at the very beginning should have set up a Financial Commission in Berlin, taking in hand the control of all the resources of Germany, immediately imposing on that country a budget a share of which should have been assigned to reparation. . . . As long as the Allies limit themselves to waiting for the benevolent execution of the peace treaty from Germany, they will get nothing: the treaty is capable of execution, but it is necessary to put it into effect and no measure seems to have been taken to this end, especially by the Reparation Commission." In other words, he called—explicitly in another document written a few weeks later—for Article 248 to be taken seriously and enforced by the Reparation Commission, but it seems he was skeptical about whether a vigorous policy of that sort could be practiced with the existing machinery: "There is no chance of putting the peace treaty into effect if the present system is continued: it is too heavy, too slow, it is inoperative. Germany does not pay because no one forces her to, and no one seems to have the means of forcing her."[35] It followed from this that a simplified, less bureaucratic system for reparation in kind along the lines suggested by the experts was highly desirable.[36]

It is clear that in the last analysis Seydoux was willing to coerce Germany, and he felt that instead of compromising on coal at Spa, France should have imposed its will on Germany through an occupation of the Ruhr.[37] Of course, the larger question of reparation had not been touched at the conference, and in this regard after Spa Seydoux was more convinced than ever that events could no longer be allowed to drift. Little could be expected from Germany—or from England for that matter. It was therefore vital that France pursue an active policy and seize the initiative in pressing for a resolution of the reparation question.

His views at this point come out very clearly in a letter he wrote to Millerand's secretary at the end of October. "If we want to arrive at a friendly understanding with Germany acceptable to the Allies," he argued, France would have to accept some manufactured goods from Germany, and could not limit reparation in kind to raw material, as the Minister of Finance had proposed. To regulate trade with Germany so that the adverse impact of an influx of German products would be minimized and French industry compensated for any possible loss of trade by a share of the German market, it was desirable that French and German industry reach a series of direct understandings. This plan was "the only reasonable one, if we want to arrive not at a new *bouleversement* of the world but at the reestablishment of peace and at real economic collaboration with Germany." But such a solution might be beyond the reach of France, and therefore a policy of outright coercion might be ultimately necessary:

Of course there remains the possibility of our taking possession of the Ruhr basin: the violent solution, which would settle everything and render us master of Germany, independent of England, and make us into an industrial power of the first order. I know that in France a good number of people consider this the necessary solution. But it carries such risks, as much from the external side as the internal, that I believe it indispensable to first exhaust all formulas of conciliation and understanding that we can accept.[38]

Seydoux insisted that an active policy was necessary because the German government was too weak to make any real effort of its own to comply with the treaty. He was not alone in this belief, which was widely shared in French official circles.[39] Nor was this view limited to the French. At the beginning of October, Herr Urbig, a German banker and the second member in the German delegation at the Brussels Financial Conference then in session, approached a French diplomat and declared that Germany needed "the domination of a strong government and of a vigorous administration." The present regime was too weak; therefore, Urbig said, it was up to France "to impose on Germany the firm direction she needs." "He more or less called for our intervention in the internal affairs of Germany," the French diplomat noted; "I did not follow him onto this dangerous terrain."[40]

Seydoux, however, agreed up to a point. Reflecting on Urbig's remarks, he wrote in mid-November: "The German government is too weak to make German industry and finance accept anything but a simple tenacious resistance. It is up to us to substitute our will for its will, keeping our demands within the bounds of possibility." Since the Germans had essentially negative ideas and the British could be trusted to act selfishly, the French, he felt, had to take the initiative in pressing for a creative solution to the reparation problem: "It is up to France, principal, and as one can now say, sole interested party, to have a practical, executable plan and to impose it first on her allies and then on Germany."[41]

In another letter written at about the same time, Seydoux revealed his feelings on the larger questions of foreign policy. France could lead Europe, he thought, but only if she succeeded first in dispelling a certain mistrust of her, "which derives from the mistrust that she herself feels toward others." This French attitude resulted from a lack of self-assurance. The French did not feel themselves to have won the war; they did not have the confidence of a victorious nation. "It seems in fact that we are lacking in confidence and boldness," he wrote; "these alone will give us in Europe a large and balanced conception of things and will enable us to exercise the ascendancy that the peoples of Europe are ready to accept as in the great centuries of our history."[42]

Seydoux's analysis is important because his views sum up the spirit of the dominant strain in French policy at the end of 1920; it also throws some light on the future evolution of French reparation doctrine down to 1923. For people like Seydoux and Millerand, "moderates" in the context of 1920, were to take a more extreme position than even Poincaré by the end of 1922. Yet there was no break in their thinking. They knew Germany could pay and tried to create channels to facilitate payment and work out what seemed to them unquestionably fair arrangements; the failure of these efforts was to give them by the end of 1922 a very clear sense of Germany's bad faith and thus the strong conviction that coercion and a real test of will with Germany were unavoidable. Their willingness to resort to coercion was linked to their awareness of the precise uses to which it could be put: the same economic arrangements which they had sought unsuccessfully to create through mutual agreement could be imposed through force.

Even in 1920 Seydoux realized that the use of force could not be excluded a priori, and his aim was to put France's superior power behind an active policy designed to bring about a real and not just a theoretical solution to the reparation conflict. But what kind of solution did he, and the French government in general, have in mind? Was it just a matter of helping Germany accept French political and perhaps even economic superiority? Or was the policy of "economic collaboration" associated with the eventual dismantling of the Versailles system and the substitution of a more equal system of relations between the two powers? The issue is important because it raises the question of whether there was a "lost opportunity" here—that is, whether a real Franco-German reconciliation was possible, and thus whether events could have taken a fundamentally different course after World War I. The question of the implications of the policy of economic collaboration cannot, however, be answered categorically. But certain claims can be tested and tentative conclusions reached.

Consider first the notion that the French government was reaching for economic superiority over Germany. An argument of this sort, limited, however, to 1919, has in fact been made by Jacques

Bariéty.[43] Bariéty looked at the text of the treaty and saw that those parts of it bearing on economic and especially metallurgical questions added up to a system: all of Lorraine was returned to France, and German steel mills there were turned over to new French owners; the way was opened for the Saar and Luxemburg to be integrated into the French economic system; Germany was to supply French industry with coal and markets, at least in the first few years. That the reannexation of Lorraine and the provisions inserted in the treaty to assure its prosperity would shift the balance of industrial power is obvious. But Bariéty goes beyond this simple point to argue that it was the French government's ambition to replace Germany as Europe's leading steel producer. He claims that in demanding large amounts of coal for France, the French government aimed at forcing a cutback in German steel output during the first critical years when the structure of the industry was being reestablished. It was the government acting on its own, Bariéty argues, that elaborated this "projet sidérurgique." The French steel industry took a much less ambitious line and sought to avoid a conflict with its German counterparts.

Insofar as this argument goes beyond the obvious, how well established is it? Bariéty presents no evidence of an aggressive economic policy from internal French documents; the treaty itself is his fundamental source. The coal demands can be explained sufficiently by France's own needs. The moderate policy on coal pursued by Loucheur—that is, by the principal maker of French economic policy throughout 1919—in August of that year shows that the coal figures embodied in the treaty were *maxima*. The overtures to the Germans through Haguenin and Massigli at the peace conference signaled a much more conciliatory attitude than one would deduce from a mere reading of the treaty, and the German officials who negotiated with Loucheur in the latter half of the year were convinced of his moderation and his willingness to arrive at an acceptable settlement. It is important to bear in mind that it was still too early to impute French moderation at this point to British restraint; the British representative clearly played little role in restraining or otherwise guiding Loucheur in these talks. In general, the coal figures the French demanded even into 1920 when the treaty formally took effect were not too much greater than what France would have been allotted by the principle of equal rates of satisfaction of coal needs (on the basis of 1913 consumption of areas within the borders of 1920): this points less to an aggressive economic policy than to a conservative, relatively conciliatory one. Finally the notion that French industry was more moderate than the government is definitely mistaken. The demands of the Comité des Forges were more extreme than those of the government: the steelmakers wanted France to be given ownership of at least some of the Ruhr mines, and if the government were serious about a "projet sidérurgique" it would probably have supported proposals of this sort designed to thwart German resistance. That these demands were ignored points again to the government's preference for negotiated arrangements with Germany on metallurgical questions, and thus to relatively moderate aims in this area.[44]

If the idea of an aggressive French economic policy can therefore be excluded—and even Bariéty does not apply it to the period after 1919—there remains the possibility that while accepting a kind of economic equality (equal assess to raw materials and especially coal, French and German industry operating at the same level, and so on) the French might have insisted in exchange that the Germans accept a permanent position of political inferiority. The economic clauses might be substantially revised, but the treaty system would be preserved intact in the crucial political sphere. But again the evidence for such an interpretation is not compelling. The Germans of course were never offered a deal of this sort, and French officials apparently never analyzed the situation along these lines even in internal memoranda. Moreover, it was evident that economic and political questions were objectively and fundamentally linked, and that a real economic entente could not last unless it were followed eventually by some form of political reconciliation. The logic was so clear and the minimum demands of the Germans in the political area so evident that it is very unlikely that French policy makers were unaware of them. That the overtures to Germany were linked to deteriorating relations with Britain is also clear, not just from the chronology, but also from some of Seydoux's (and others') remarks; the fact that the policy took shape in this particular political context implies strongly that the initiatives were designed not just to solve a technical problem, but rather had a larger political purpose: namely, to create the possibility of a Franco-German political alignment, which would obviously have been impossible if the French were to insist that Germany accept a subordinate political status for an indefinite period.

Furthermore, the documents give the distinct impression that in fluential circles in France were from the outset skeptical about the stability of the Versailles system. Clemenceau himself was very much aware of the centrifugal forces within the Alliance, and in his view without the Alliance the treaty could not work. In 1920 the Versailles system lost the effective support of both the United States, and, as it was becoming increasingly evident, Great Britain as well; the conviction that existing arrangements could not last then grew much stronger. France was too weak to enforce the treaty by herself, and if it were not enforced it would collapse. The disarmament provisions, ultimately the crucial constraint on German power and thus the heart of the Versailles system, were perhaps the main focus of long-term anxiety. French official circles as a whole doubted whether these provisions could be permanently enforced: the French were significantly more skeptical in this regard than were their British counterparts.[45] The sources, moreover, convey a sense of the thinness of French military superiority, and thus of the tenuousness of the Versailles arrangements. According to a November 1922 report submitted to the Conseil Supérieur de la Défense Nationale, the highest military policy-making body in the country, after only six months of rearmament Germany's military strength would equal that of France, and from then on the margin of German superiority would widen rapidly.[46] As for reparation, the documents already cited indicate clearly enough the French government's lack of confidence in the treaty system and its desire to replace it with more workable arrangements. Millerand himself declared toward the end of 1920 that "the literal execution of the treaty is an illusion."[47] This implies, however, only that the French government was willing to consider changes in the Versailles system; it does not say anything about the particular nature of the changes contemplated.

Finally, there is the evidence of the German sources. If the French had hoped to get the Germans to accept an inferior political status in exchange for economic concessions, one would expect the Germans to have sensed it and to have resisted the French overtures on these grounds. But this was not the case. The German foreign minister and his closest associates, it will be shown, like the German negotiators a year earlier, took the French proposals very seriously and did not want to reject the "outstretched hand"; given the whole tenor of German policy in this period, this reaction would have been very unlikely if they had viewed the French suggestions as just a device to facilitate the execution of the Treaty of Versailles. One of these German officials (von Buttlar) even argued that a political compromise would follow the economic entente. Finally it was not as though those elements within Germany that effectively obstructed a really positive response to these French overtures—most notably the Ruhr magnates—did so with the argument that the proposed terms were not fair, or that Germany was being asked to accept French political domination and that this was impossible. One is struck instead by the violent tone of their argument: they wanted to push the French against the wall. One industrialist's remark in 1922, "Let them choke on their minette," is in fact characteristic of the Ruhr magnates' attitude from late 1919 on.[48]

There is one final matter that should be considered. If the Versailles system was seen as unstable, then this was a problem that in theory had more than one solution. An eventual rapprochement with Germany was not the only one. From the outset another strain in French policy existed: to a certain extent the French government tried not so much to impose as to facilitate a weakening of German unity; at times—for a brief moment in 1920 and much more seriously beginning in August 1923—this turned into a desire to bring about the "disaggregation" of the German Reich. This policy focused on the Rhineland, but it is important to see French Rhenish policy as part of a wider policy of weakening Germany by encouraging federalist, autonomist and (it was hoped) eventually perhaps even separatist forces. French policy in Bavaria is very significant in this connection.[49]

Does the existence of this side of French policy in itself disprove the idea that the French were willing to contemplate a kind of *rapprochement* with Germany? The issue is not clear-cut. On the whole France pursued a long-term policy in the Rhineland. The basic aim was to win over the Rhinelanders in spirit rather than to impose new political structures through force. Clemenceau in particular was hostile to military personalities like General Mangin who spoiled things by siding too openly with separatist elements like Dorten—essentially fringe groups in the Rhineland. His successors basically shared this attitude. The proof is that they kept in office Paul Tirard, French High Commissioner in the Rhineland, and the personality in the government most closely associated with an active Rhenish policy; but at the same time the government in Paris remained cool to Tirard's more vigorous proposals. One has the impression that through the middle of 1922 this strain of French policy, while continuing to exist, was more or less put on the back burners; its merging with reparation policy in late 1922 will be analyzed in some detail later.

Did this aspect of French policy fundamentally contradict the more moderate side symbolized by the phrase "economic collaboration"? The degree of contradiction is not as great as one might expect. Since the aim of the French authorities was to win the sympathy of the Rhinelanders, the occupation regime was deliberately mild; for many strong advocates of a Rhenish policy, the Rhineland ideally was not so much a barrier as a bridge linking Germany with France. Proponents of an active Rhenish policy did not necessarily see a moderate stand on reparation as conflicting with their goals; it was not as though they automatically wanted a rupture with Germany over reparation to provide an excuse for applying measures to cut the Rhineland off from the rest of Germany. Maurice Barrès's strong support of the Spa agreement on coal is very significant in this connection.

In spite of all this, it would be foolish to contend that there was no real choice here. But to the extent a contradiction existed, reparation and the policy of "economic collaboration," for the period down to January 1923 at least, took priority over Rhenish policy; when Rhenish questions became really important in late 1922 it was as an outgrowth of the evolution of reparation doctrine, and not because the structure of power or even the fundamental concerns within the French government had changed—Seydoux was always more important than Tirard. So the conclusion comes down to this: French officials believed that the existing system was unstable, but they had by no means resolved to replace it with a policy that called for a violent disruption of German unity.

What then does the whole analysis amount to? It is first of all unlikely that the policy of economic collaboration was not supposed to have any basic political consequences—that the French government calculated that through concessions in the economic sphere Germany could be reconciled to an inferior political status. But if it was understood in some vague way that an economic *rapprochement* was in the long run intimately linked to a radical change in political relations between the two countries, it does not follow from this that French officials had a definite idea of exactly what concessions would be made to Germany, how rapidly the Versailles system would be transformed, and what kind of system it would be replaced with. It is clear in fact that the French government was reluctant to abandon the Versailles guarantees before Germany had proved herself—but by this was meant probably a lot less than acceptance of the full political order of 1919. What the French probably wanted was for Germany to integrate herself into a stable European system, to abandon hope of turning the clock back to 1913 and accept instead what both sides could view as "fair" arrangements. This was all very vague, and it is unclear whether the essential differences between the two countries were mild enough to have permitted a solution of this sort. In any case it was probably considered premature to work out ultimate goals or strategy before the Germans responded positively, and because their response was not positive the whole question was put off. But French caution, and the French inclination to play it by ear, do not contradict the idea that there was a good chance that the French initiatives in late 1920 provided a real opportunity for putting European politics on a fundamentally different footing.

What then exactly happened at the end of the year? To understand the affair, it is necessary to turn to the more mundane features of Seydoux's analysis and examine in greater detail the development of French policy. In Seydoux's mind, reparation was basically a problem of German willingness to pay—of the willingness, that is, of the German people, and especially of the German industrial magnates, to make the necessary effort.[50] French officials in general did not feel that their demands exceeded Germany's capacity. For capacity was an economic concept, a function of the maximum surplus of real wealth that Germany could produce. It was widely recognized, in fact, that in spite of the appalling state of public finance, economic life in Germany had revived vigorously—aided often by the very subsidies responsible for the budgetary deficit.[51] The financial and political difficulties of the German government had no bearing on the economic question of capacity. For in theory there is always a way for governments to tap economic surpluses—a priori the purely technical problems of tax collection can always be solved. Budgets, in a sense, are always balanced: the printing of paper money is, as a British official put it at the time, "only an unscientific method of taxation."[52] Since it was being done unscientifically, there was no reason why it could not be done more intelligently—no reason, that is, except the unwillingness of influential elements within Germany to bear the bur-

den. Thus the German financial crisis was seen as proof of the unwillingness of important elements in Germany to make a real effort to
pay reparation, an impression tied to the strong suspicion that the
Germans were deliberately letting their financial situation deteriorate
in the hope of thereby evading Allied reparation demands.[53]

Broadly speaking, Germany's capacity was thus seen as a function of the strength of the German economy; the financial problem
was viewed mainly as a measure of German willingess to pay. There
was also, of course, the transfer problem, the problem of getting the
surplus wealth created by the German economy across national frontiers. A solution to this problem depended not just on Germany's
willingness to pay but also on the Allies' willingness to receive. And
it was precisely in this area, the ultimate obstacle according to
Keynes, that the French government now pressed most vigorously for
a solution. For the French admitted, as far as they were concerned,
that reparation would in the first few years be limited to deliveries in
kind; to govern this form of payment, the French government elaborated a scheme based on the plan for a revolving fund suggested by
the experts at Spa.

Seydoux endorsed the new scheme when it was first proposed
and played a leading role in its development.[54] In early August he
urged the Germans to enter into direct negotiation on reconstruction,
saying that the reconstruction plan Germany had presented at Spa was
too bureaucratic and "over-organized"; this of course already suggested the more simple, commercial scheme he hoped to bring into
being.[55] It was he who presented the new ideas to the Germans at
Brussels, and the proposed arrangement came to be called the "Seydoux Plan." The basic idea was to place paper marks at the disposal
of the reparation creditors, who would in turn use this money to buy
directly what they wanted in Germany. The plan would have a double
effect. On the one hand, it would solve the transfer problem by placing the burden of transfer on the Allies. On the other hand, it would
reduce reparation to a problem of internal finance, since the German
government would have to raise the necessary fund of paper marks.
Consequently the Keynesian myth of German incapacity due to insurmountable problems of transfer would be broken, and reparation
would at last be reduced to a question of Germany's willingness to
tax itself sufficiently.

The basic lines of the Seydoux Plan seem to have been first

openly discussed in the third part of Etienne Weill-Raynal's article, "The Reparation of War Damages and World Peace," which appeared in the October 7 issue of *L'Information ouvriere et sociale.*[56] But it was not until December 12 that the new thrust of French policy was revealed to a large public in *L'Europe nouvelle,* an organ with which Seydoux had close ties. The anonymous article entitled "How to Make Germany Pay" evidently reflected the official point of view, for it outlined in broad terms the plan the French delegation was about to present at Brussels. According to this article, the "essential problem" was *how* Germany could pay. Reparation in kind was the answer, but it had to be organized along commercial lines; a variant of the revolving fund idea was outlined. The author noted in the usual fashion that such a system meant "the organization of Franco-German economic collaboration"; this implied among other things that France would supply German industry with, for example, "iron ore and colonial products," so as to encourage the economic revival of Germany. The advantages of an active, realistic policy were pointed out: in particular, such a policy would help dispel foreign suspicion of French intentions, and thereby increase the willingness of Allied governments to act together with France in the event of a voluntary German default.[57]

L'Europe nouvelle itself enthusiastically welcomed the new plan. In an editorial the prominent journalist Philippe Millet regretted the passivity, the "negative look," of French policy since the armistice. This was at the root of Allied and German distrust of France. But at last here was a bold plan, the product of "creative imagination," that would restore confidence in France and pave the way toward a realistic solution of the reparation problem.[58] Millet was not alone in his enthusiasm for the new active policy that France, it soon became clear, was to pursue at Brussels. Using the same reasoning, another leading journalist, Pertinax (André Geraud) eagerly endorsed the new plan in *L'Echo de Paris* on December 12; *Le Gaulois* followed suit the next day.

Even the arch-proponents of a "strong" line on reparation, Tardieu and Poincaré, after some initial hesitation, finally came out in favor of the new scheme.[59] Pierre Cheysson, the second French delegate at the Brussels Conference, in fact assured Bergmann on December 16 that Tardieu, Loucheur and Poincaré and his circle "have now wheeled around and come to the conviction that economic collaboration with Germany is necessary,'' and Mayer, the German ambassador in Paris, the same day reported that Poincaré had approached him at dinner and spoken reasonably about reparation.[60] Poincaré and Leygues had long been political friends, and it was perhaps this fact that had led to a certain softening of Poincaré's general attitude. In any event he continued to take a moderate line through the whole period of the Brussels Conference: when Cheysson met with him on January 8, he declared his ''readiness to tell Germany that he would examine with 'benevolence' her capacity of payment in order to set the sums that the Allies would ask for,'' and even approved the plan for a provisional five-year settlement which had just been proposed as a basis for Germany's actual payments.[61]

When the Brussels Conference convened on December 15, France ironically was the only Allied power that did not include a member of the Reparation Commission in its delegation. Instead the French government was represented by Seydoux and Cheysson. The two delegates were instructed to avoid the question of a fixed sum; indeed, according to their instructions, the experts at Brussels were to avoid arriving at any final decisions at all. Consequently, the instructions indicated, there was no need to reach any definitive agreement at Brussels, neither with the Germans nor among the Allied delegates. Rather, the Conference was to ''examine'' various aspects of the reparation question, notably the question of deliveries in kind. The first Boulogne annuities could be paid in kind; 2 milliard gold marks worth of raw material could be delivered, and this could be supplemented by another milliard gold marks worth of reconstruction goods, finished products and labor. To finance this latter category of deliveries in kind, the instructions of course suggested the plan for a revolving fund of paper marks, reiterating the standard arguments for ''economic collaboration with Germany.''[62]

This document did, however, contain some new ideas. In exchange for providing a market for German industry by means of this plan, the import of French goods into Germany should be favored. Negotiations based on this principle, it was hoped, would ''lead to the working out of a commercial accord between the two countries.'' Moreover, the plan for a fund of paper marks as outlined in the instructions was more flexible than the original scheme the French experts had suggested at Spa. The earlier plan was limited to reconstruction goods; now the paper marks might be used for a wide range of purposes, notably for hiring German labor and for investing in Germany businesses. To advocates of economic collaboration, the idea of a "participation" in German industry through the ownership of stock in German enterprises was particularly attractive: in this manner the French would have a stake in, and profit from, industrial revival in Germany. Such an arrangement would pave the way for direct cooperation between large French and German firms—a situation the French government, as well as a certain segment of German opinion, evidently viewed as desirable.[63]

The plan as it now stood was more flexible than the original version in a second respect. Before, purchases were to be financed entirely from the fund of paper marks. Now, in accordance with the idea of giving the Germans a certain interest in cooperating with the system, orders would be financed mostly in marks, but partly also in francs provided by the French purchasers—a device somewhat similar to the 5-gold mark premium on coal deliveries. The same principle applied to the proposed arrangements for the use of German labor, and for the transfer of stock in German firms: payment in both cases would be made partly in francs supplied by the French government or French business interests.[64]

The ideas developed in this document were clearly rooted in the notion that it was vital to give Germany a certain incentive for paying: the provisions relating to partial payment in cash and the extension of reparation in kind to German manufactured goods derived from this assumption. The need to compensate French industry for this influx of German goods led to the hope that an expansion of commerce would be guaranteed and regulated through direct agreements between corresponding branches of French and German industry. Nowhere was this more important than in the area of heavy industry, which for this reason became a central element in the Brussels negotiations. In September, for example, François-Marsal, the French Minister of Finance, had stressed the importance of assuring through agreement with Germany a market for the minette of Lorraine, which, he said, could be easily replaced by Swedish and Spanish ore: ". . . our biggest heavy industrialists have not concealed from me their anxiety on this subject."[65] Of course—and this was certainly understood by the Germans—the problem went beyond that, since French industry also needed to find a market for semiproducts like pig iron.[66] It was in all probability for this reason that Seydoux wanted to extend the negotiations beyond the question of raw materials and reach an agreement that would settle a much wider range of industrial problems.

Although Seydoux and Cheysson were not permitted to reach any definite agreements at Brussels, it is clear that they hoped to arrive at preliminary arrangements with their German counterparts on the key question of the machinery of reparation. They avoided any talk of figures; instead they sought to work out a mutually satisfactory set of principles on which a series of industrial ententes and an eventual settlement of the reparation question might be based. Was there any chance for such a preliminary agreement? Seydoux, at least, was convinced that there was. On December 16 he urged Carl Bergmann, now head of the German delegation at Brussels and in French eyes one of the most reasonable German officials involved in reparation, to seize this opportunity to work out an amicable settlement of the reparation problem. Bergmann's reply was encouraging, and his views on reparation in kind, Seydoux stressed, were very close to those of the French government: in a conversation with Cheysson, and again in his speech to the conference the next morning, Bergmann specifically suggested the creation of mark credits to be used to finance French purchases in Germany.[67]

Seydoux was delighted with Bergmann's general attitude: "The impression produced by M. Bergmann's speech has been very favorable: he has approached the questions very frankly and in a spirit permitting us to find a practical solution." It was true that Bergmann had discussed a number of problems connected with the payment of reparation—the costs of the armies of occupation, the fate of Upper Silesia, German property abroad, commercial reciprocity, and the German merchant marine. But Seydoux did not feel that Bergmann had brought up these issues in order to obstruct agreement. Rather, these were problems that did in fact bear on reparation, and which might legitimately be examined at the conference.[68] By December 20, however, Seydoux was disappointed with Bergmann, who was now seeking "to evade our suggestions." Although the German attitude improved the next day, Seydoux and the other delegates concluded that it was best to adjourn the conference for a while, so that the German delegates might discuss the French proposals with their government.[69]

Was there a real change in German policy due to the fact that the

British had in the interim outbid the French in moderation?[70] Certainly the British and Belgian delegates had suggested reduced figures to Bergmann, but this is no adequate explanation of any change in German policy. The Germans at this point were not interested in figures, and in any case, there was hardly anything new about British moderation in these matters. Perhaps there was no substantive shift at all. Maybe Germany had all along been merely playing for time, feigning for tactical reasons an interest in Seydoux's ideas while in reality intending to avoid any positive commitment on this matter.[71] Again, although the evidence is somewhat ambiguous, this does not seem to have been the case. Both Bergmann and Simons, as their correspondence with each other shows, really wanted an effective agreement with France on reparation in kind. On December 17, Bergmann wrote from Brussels that he had no doubt

. . . that an important shift in the French position has actually taken place, and it would be a serious mistake through a purely negative policy to nip in the bud all hope for an early understanding. We cannot discuss the size of our payments right now; cash payments must for the time being be refused. What then remains but a practical settlement for reparation in kind, especially the deliveries to France? If the French will be content if we basically meet their desires for a settlement of the Annex IV deliveries, and if this leads to a further improvement in the French attitude, then we should not reject the outstretched hand.[72]

In his reply the next day, Simons agreed that the scheme for a fund of paper marks was a good basis for a practical solution of the question. But, he stressed, his political difficulties were such that great caution was necessary: "For the time being, we have not only the Reconstruction Ministry, but also the Länder, especially Prussia and Bavaria, against us." It was this situation, rather than any bad faith, that was responsible for the German government's concern to keep the pace of negotiation slow.[73]

For months the German Reconstruction Ministry had been leading the opposition to the idea of facilitating payment in kind before agreement on an acceptable fixed sum had been reached—the efforts Germany made in such a case would be useless, since they would do nothing to liberate her from any real debt. If her liability was set at a tolerable figure, it would be in Germany's greatest interest to pay in kind instead of cash, and in that case the system for reparation deliveries should be "as clear and as simple as possible"; but in the absence of such a figure, the "cumbersone, bureaucratic organization" was preferable.[74]

The Economics Ministry took the opposite line, and argued for a demonstration of good faith in this matter. It advocated a simplified system of direct, commercial contacts between the *sinistrés* and German suppliers, which, it said, should be put into effect even if no final agreement on a fixed sum were reached. But if the first annual payments could be set, Germany could pay a considerable amount in this way—nearly 2 milliard gold marks the second year, and that figure did not even include standardized commodities like coal and dyes which would be covered in separate agreements, and which up to then had accounted for the bulk of Germany's reparation payments.[75]

The matter was fought out in the interministerial committee set up after Spa to work out the German proposals for the Geneva Conference. Von Simson, the important Foreign Ministry official who chaired the committee, argued that an agreement with the entente was necessary: if no accord were reached, the Entente could in any case force Germany to make large payments; he believed that an economic *Diktat* had to be avoided.[76] The Finance Ministry, the Reichsbank, and the Prussian Ministry of Commerce, on the other hand, supported the hard-line Reconstruction Ministry.[77] The majority on September 28 recommended in favor of the Economics Ministry plan, provided an agreement on annuities was first reached. Nevertheless the Reconstruction Ministry continued to object to the scheme: it was now argued that the execution of the plan would result in a dishonorable competition for French orders, and that the French might use the scheme for their own political ends, particularly in the Rhineland.[78]

This internal conflict prevented the direct negotiation with the French from getting off the ground in the fall, and as the instructions to the Brussels delegation show, the cabinet in 1920 was never able to fully resolve the question. The instructions ignored the problem of what was acceptable for reparation in kind in the absence of a fixed sum, and, as the defensive tone of his letter to Simons shows, Bergmann realized he was going beyond his authority in reacting so positively to Seydoux's ideas.[79]

Because of the narrowness of their political base, Simons and Bergmann realized that they could not go very fast, and were therefore pleased when the conference adjourned on December 22. It was supposed to reconvene in Brussels on January 10. In the meantime, the informal discussions with the Germans were to continue on the same basis, and Seydoux and Cheysson succeeded in getting adopted what was in effect "a very precise program of the work to be undertaken." Among other things, this program, as developed in a related note by Seydoux, sketched out an arrangement for the payment of reparation in kind along the lines favored by the French government. The system of a revolving fund of paper marks was to be extended to *non-sinistrés,* but in this case a large part of the purchase price—30 to 50 percent—would be paid in the national currency of the purchaser. To facilitate this system, trade barriers would be reduced on goods transferred in this way: each creditor would negotiate with Germany a reduction of tariffs imposed on such imports, as well as a corresponding reduction of German export duties. Finally, in line with a proposal made by the German delegation, a given percentage of the cash proceeds from the export of certain important German commodities (such as coal and potash), would go into the reparation account. This, Seydoux noted, would not only raise desirable foreign exchange, but also had "the advantage of increasing the annuity in proportion to the economic development of Germany."[80]

The adoption of this program was significant, for, as a French official noted a few days later, it marked Allied acceptance of the French reparation plan.[81] To French officials, it seemed that the British had long been suspicious of the idea of reparation in kind, and had blocked French attempts to apply the provisions of the treaty relating to this form of payment.[82] Now the British attitude had changed, and this might be of decisive importance. British acceptance of the French plan meant that a workable arrangement on reparation was at last within reach, for with the Allies acting together the Germans could surely be brought to accept a plan that in principle at least accorded so well with their own ideas.

Thus Lord D'Abernon, ambassador to Germany and principal British delegate, raised no objection when, after private discussions with the German delegates, Seydoux on January 7 formally handed Bergmann a relatively detailed version of the plan for reparation in kind—essentially the scheme outlined by Seydoux in his note of December 20 described above, but modified to take account of certain German observations.[83] The British delegates implicitly endorsed the French plan by putting their signatures on the January 18 report of the Brussels Conference, a document in which the revolving fund scheme was described in detail.[84]

The progress of negotiations on the plan for a fund of paper marks naturally drew attention to the problems of German finance. Clearly the German government would have to raise the fund of marks itself; yet how could this be done when its budget was already so strikingly out of balance? Thus at Brussels the problems of German state finance came to be viewed as central. Obviously, it was not the transfer problem that set the most stringent limitations on German capacity to pay, as Keynes had supposed—an assumption that lay at the heart of his attack on the treaty. The transfer problem had been solved by the French proposals. Rather, it was the German budgetary deficit that was the real obstacle to the payment of substantial reparation.

The Allies had presented the German government with a lengthy questionnaire probing the intricacies of German finance.[85] On the basis of the German replies, and following discussion with the German experts, a report on German public finance was drafted and adopted by the conference.[86] The report stressed the willingness of the Allies to cooperate in the restoration of German finance. From a perceptive analysis of the German budget, the conclusion was drawn that budgetary equilibrium was within reach and could be reestablished in the near future, if only the German government exerted itself sufficiently. The Allies would not compromise such an effort, the report implied; the French in particular showed themselves willing to work out a businesslike arrangement governing the size of the reparation payments that Germany would make in the near future.[87]

These apparently technical matters—arrangements for reparation in kind and the intricacies of the German budget—did not much interest Lord D'Abernon. In the discussion of these questions he played a relatively minor role—thus the report on the German budget was not written by D'Abernon, as originally planned, but by the French expert Cheysson.[88] D'Abernon had already made up his mind on the larger questions of reparation, and he seemed rather bored by problems of detail. A close associate put his views this way:

As you know, Lord D'Abernon's view, which is borne out by the plain facts of the case, is that Germany is practically bankrupt, and that any idea of getting, for the present, large payments over and above what she is already doing, is fantastic; but he considers that this fact cannot be brought suddenly and brutally to the knowledge of the public in Allied countries, and therefore something must be done meanwhile to make it appear that Germany is, in fact, giving values to the Allies, so as to enable the Allied Governments—and especially the French Government—gradually to accustom the public to the idea that our original claims are impossible of realization. In short, he thinks that the best policy is, as it were, to drag the matter out, using the press judiciously, to bring home to the public what Germany is doing, and how unlikely it is that she can do much more, so that when the time comes when it can be more definitely ascertained what we hope to extract after conditions in Germany shall have become more stabilized, there will not be the intense disappointment which would be aroused if the true facts of the case were published now.[89]

Although D'Abernon personally wanted to avoid a swift final agreement on a fixed sum, he nevertheless pressed hard at Brussels for a figure. One must therefore presume that Lloyd George had instructed him to proceed in this manner.[90] D'Abernon at once enlisted the cooperation of the Belgian government, whose views on reparation, he noted, "appear to coincide very closely with our own."[91] During the first week of the conference, he and the Belgian delegate Delacroix in secret repeatedly urged Bergmann to offer a definite figure. They said that 85 milliard gold marks was a good starting point for negotiation. Bergmann successfully evaded these overtures.[92]

At the end of the month, D'Abernon met Millerand, who informed him that the French government was "quite open to a speedy arrangement on sensible lines." "If you propose something practical," Millerand declared, "you will find us ready to agree." D'Abernon then brought up the idea of the Boulogne terms, but reduced by "10 percent or 20 percent or more." (The 85 milliard figure was Boulogne minus 15 percent.) "Without assenting to this," D'Abernon noted, "the President appeared to be not surprised and did not in any way protest," and in general, he wrote Curzon, Millerand's whole attitude "was distinctly friendly to reasonable compromise."[93]

Seydoux had known about D'Abernon's attempts to reach agreement on a fixed sum since December 29; it was in fact Delacroix who had told him. At that time he had expressed his displeasure that the British delegate had seen fit to proceed in that fashion: it was simply not the business of the Brussels Conference to deal with matters of that sort. When on January 7, at a meeting with Delacroix, D'Abernon and the second British delegate Bradbury, he found out about the 85 milliard proposal, he declared that the French government would never go along with any such scheme.[94]

Seydoux, like Bergmann, tenaciously resisted the pressure for a fixed sum. As he pointed out, both he and Bergmann had often recognized that for political reasons agreement on a figure was at present impossible: "if the Boulogne figure, for example, were now accepted, the governments presenting this figure, both at Berlin and at Paris, would immediately fall."[95] What was needed, Seydoux stressed, were practical results, direct and visible German cooperation in the French reconstruction effort. Once this was under way, the French attitude toward Germany would soften, and agreement on a fixed sum would be possible.[96]

D'Abernon remarked that it was essential that Germany know how much she would have to pay each year in the near future in order to prepare her budgets; Bradbury thereupon suggested a provisional settlement. Germany would pay 3 milliard gold marks a year for five years, and the final debt would be set in the meantime. Under the proviso that Germany's final liability would still be set as swiftly as possible, Seydoux accepted this suggestion, and it was agreed that Bergmann would be informed of the new proposal later that day.[97]

When Seydoux met Bergmann later that day, he argued forcefully for a provisional settlement. An arrangement of this sort was needed, he argued, to govern the situation until American intervention could effect a final settlement: "If America does not intervene, the finances of Europe cannot be rehabilitated.[98] This was in fact exactly the argument Simons had used in instructing Bergmann on January 1 to oppose the British attempt to arrive at a fixed sum: "The wagon under Lord D'Abernon's whip is moving too fast and is going down the wrong road. I think we should try to put off a final understanding on the size and nature of our payments until the United States of America is in a position to intervene in the negotiations." England, he said, now wanted a quick solution, because it hoped to "feather its nest" before America came in.[99]

In this letter, Simons again stressed his interest in working out practical arrangements for reparation in kind: reparation orders would create business at a time when it was sorely needed, and payment in kind instead of cash would significantly relieve the burden on Germany's foreign exchange. But he was worried that the German industrialists might sabotage his policy: "We have to reckon, however, with the most boundless distrust and a kind of obstructionism on the part of our industry, and must be extremely cautious with promises." This document clearly shows that Simons wanted a substantive agreement, and was not just pursuing negotiations for tactical reasons; it was this hope, in fact, that led him to insist on a slow pace. It also demonstrates that in spite of Simons's own close ties with organized business, he was by no means their tool, but viewed the industrialists as opponents of his policy.

The position of the Ruhr magnates was strong because of the key role that accords on metallurgical questions played in the proposed system. Simons and a number of other high German officials went to Essen on January 8 to meet with the leading industrialists and win their cooperation. The Reichsverband der deutschen Industrie, he said, had promised to take part in the negotiations if no figures were to be involved. This condition had now been met. Germany could drag its feet in the negotiations on annuities, he implied, but "the question of reparation in kind cannot be handled in a dilatory fashion." The representatives of the Economics Ministry (Hirsch, von le Suire, von Buttlar) went further and stressed that concrete results in this area could not be avoided. Von Buttlar insisted on the political implications of a real agreement: "The French in their proposals are evidently striving for an interlocking of German and French industry, out of which a political compromise between the two countries will later arise."

The industrialists accepted the idea of direct industry-to-industry talks. They hoped, however, to avoid too close a connection with the government-level negotiations in Brussels, in order to allow Germany's economic superiority free play in shaping the most favorable terms of agreement. The industrialist Klöckner, supported by Wiedfeldt (Krupp) and Hasslacher (Rheinische Stahlwerke), urged that the industrial talks be moved away from Brussels to Aachen or Cologne: a physical separation would be a good way of making sure that political and economic questions would remain largely isolated from each other. The tone of their remarks, moreover, indicates that the steel magnates did not want to give up much in these negotiations. Klöckner wanted to keep French products, except some minette ore and possibly pig iron, out of Germany, and Stinnes was all in favor of exploiting the weak points in the French position: "The French remain under the burden of a swollen iron industry that lacks adequate markets. We have the greatest interest in allowing this incongruous situation to fully work itself out, and thereby gain time.''[100]

In promising to avoid any commitment on figures, Simons could not have been totally sincere: for an agreement to have a practical effect, it was obviously necessary to specify quantities and include precise figures. Probably he had made this promise to avoid a break with the industrialists; the evident logic of the situation, which they themselves would come to see as they were increasingly coopted into the negotiation process, would bring about their acquiescence in figures for the annuity, or at least for the yearly amount to be paid in kind, when the time was ripe.

At the same time as Simons was meeting with the industrialists, the French were starting to press for results on all fronts. Laurent, supported by Lord Kilmarnock, the British chargé in Berlin, urged Simons to accept the proposed arrangements for a provisional settlement "in principle"; the actual figures could be discussed in Paris.[101] In the area of industrial ententes, the French also moved ahead. A commission of the biggest names in French heavy industry was formed to carry on negotiations for the formation of industrial ententes with Germany, and French representatives in Berlin were urged to facilitate these efforts. Seydoux wrote Haguenin, also on January 8, that Bergmann simply did not have the stature to impose the French plan on Germany, but there were other "Germans intelligent enough to know what I want." Haguenin was just about the only one who knew these men: could he help pave the way for contacts with the group of French industrialists?[102]

With the French and even the British breathing down his neck, Simons again met with the representatives of the Ruhr in Berlin on January 14. He and Bergmann now expressed—"feigned" is probably a better word—hostility toward the five-year plan, but argued that for this reason, it was essential to make real progress on "Seydoux's other ideas": the plan for reparation in kind and the proposal for industrial ententes. Stinnes for his part urged that, on the question of the provisional settlement, the German government should avoid an outright rejection of the plan, but should instead adopt dilatory tactics: "It must come down to this: above all, in the next few years we pay nothing. A settlement of our liabilities should be put off as much as possible, because the development of political and economic relations in the world is moving in a favorable direction for us.'' The consequences of such inaction would not be serious: he did not believe that a new Diktat would be handed down by the Allies on May 1, by which time, according to the treaty, Germany's total debt was to be set. Like Simons and Bergmann, Stinnes still accepted the idea of direct contacts with French industry; he cautioned only that these negotiations should be conducted in such a way that "we do not run the risk of losing England and America as financiers and as markets.''

Then Klöckner spoke, taking exactly the opposite line: "It is not in the interest of our industry to begin negotiations soon.'' If the excess output of the French steel industry were absorbed by the German market, a third of Germany's blast furnaces would have to be shut down. If industry were not rushed or subjected to any political pressure, a favorable agreement with France was possible: by "favorable,'' he meant an arrangement where German industry would control France's exports of steel and iron. But right now these questions were so interlocked with the general political situation that such results were unlikely. Stinnes now changed his mind and along with several other industry representatives supported Klöckner's new point of view.[103]

Thus the industrialists had suddenly changed their tune, and this shift in position had apparently nothing to do with any change in government policy—Simons at this point had done nothing to indicate that he was giving in to the Allies on the question of figures. It was only the next day, January 15, that Laurent virtually forced him to accept a provisional settlement. In their meeting the French Ambassador emphasized the importance at this time of a demonstration of German good faith: "Here is a unique occasion which, in the interest of both countries, but especially in Germany's interest, must not be allowed to slip away.''[104]

Simons, however, attempted to bargain. In abandoning her right under the treaty to learn the extent of her liability, Germany, he argued, was making a great sacrifice. In exchange Simons asked for Allied concessions, relating notably to Upper Silesia, the fate of which was soon to be determined by a plebiscite. Laurent refused to be drawn into this kind of discussion. Would the German government, he asked, really prefer the strict execution of the treaty? Simons quickly retreated and accepted the "Seydoux proposals'' for a provisional settlement and on reparation in kind as a basis for discussion. According to Laurent, the only important condition raised by Simons was that the exact figures were subject to negotiation. The demand for related concessions, on Upper Silesia and so on, was apparently dropped.[105] The German account of the interview, however, indicates that not only did Simons continue to insist on all the preconditions set out by the German delegates at Brussels, but also that Laurent had specifically proposed that Germany could make these reservations.[106]

Perhaps Laurent and Simons had misunderstood each other. In any event, the misunderstanding, if that is what it was, persisted as negotiations resumed in Paris. Having won an acceptance "in principle" of his reparation proposals, Seydoux proved quite reasonable on figures. Two milliard gold marks a year, he conceded, was acceptable for the first two years, rising to 3 milliards beginning in the third year in accordance with an index of prosperity to be established.[107] Bergmann "personally" felt that this was acceptable; both D'Abernon and Seydoux were therefore convinced that agreement was within reach—something hardly possible if they had been aware of German obstinacy on conditions relating to Silesia and so on, for it was clear that the Allies could not surrender on many of these points.[108] Furthermore, as late as January 23, Laurent was convinced of the good faith of the German government in pursuing the negotiations. His despatches up to that point carried no information that would correct the impression conveyed by his earlier account of Simons's views that the question of "preconditions" had been dropped.[109]

Seydoux at this time also continued to push ahead, and pressed for "immediate talks with Wiedfeldt and Vögler in Paris."[110] Simons wired Wiedfeldt on January 24 to see if he could go: apparently Simons had not taken Klöckner's declarations at the January 14 meeting as the industrialists' final word.[111] But Wiedfeldt and Stinnes, who was also invited, now refused to go, and in spite of a new request from Simons the steel industry again in late February refused to enter into talks with its French counterpart.[112]

The uncooperative attitude of heavy industry was not Simons's only problem. He also had to face stiff opposition from within the government itself. Presumably the Reconstruction Ministry and its allies continued to view plans for facilitating the payment of reparation without sympathy, and Simons was also opposed by a leading official in his own ministry, Carl von Schubert. Schubert rejected the idea of a provisional settlement: putting off a final settlement to a time when the general economic situation improved would result in a higher final figure. Moreover, Schubert argued, Germany would have no interest in putting her finances in order until a definitive settlement was reached: a vigorous fiscal effort, solving her financial problem, would only increase her final reparation burden. A swift settlement was vital. But if the Allies would not agree to a low enough figure, then Germany should allow the crisis to come to a head—unlike Stinnes he had no illusions that Germany could get away with a purely negative policy. The great difficulties this would involve, he believed, could ultimately be overcome.[113]

Probably Simons felt obliged to accommodate hard-liners of this sort. This would explain the position he took in his interview with Laurent on January 15 and the ''semiofficial'' German note released to the press on January 26: this document insisted that figures for the annuities not be discussed, and demanded counterconcessions on the points raised earlier at Brussels (Silesia, German property abroad, etc.).[114] But this did not necessarily mean the end of the new reparation policy pursued at Brussels. Gestures like the release of this note were designed above all for internal consumption, and did not lock German policy into an intransigent course. The refusal of the Ruhr magnates to cooperate was another matter, but while this ruled out the idea of an industrial entente, other features of the French program could still be put into effect. Setting up a revolving fund of paper marks to finance reparation in kind and the purchase of shares in German industry might in itself lead eventually to the kind of Franco-German industrial relations that the great industrialists had for the moment vetoed. The French for their part had come to expect German obstruction as a matter of course, and had long felt it could be overcome if the Allies persisted in forcefully pressing for a realistic solution to the problem.

But before the depth of German obstinacy could really be probed, the Brussels program was killed by the Allied leaders themselves. For at yet another Allied conference, this one held in Paris at the end of January 1921, Lloyd George demanded action which, he supposed, would lead to a final solution of the problem. A fixed sum was vital, he contended; and when Briand, the new French prime minister, argued in favor of the provisional settlement worked out by the Brussels experts, Lloyd George harshly rejected this alternative. "Briand is rather like Asquith," he remarked a few days later. He was "lethargic and wanted to postpone disagreeable duties. I had to force him to face realities."[115] Thus, in spite of both the British government's acceptance in mid-November of a rather deliberate procedure for the settlement of the reparation question, and of its recent support in Berlin and Paris of the five-year plan, Lloyd George now insisted that the French at once present proposals for a definite settlement of Germany's liability. Lloyd George was not reminded of these earlier commitments, and Briand gave in without much of a struggle. Once the French proposals were made, it was only a question of time before a plan was worked out. The Paris "agreement" provided for annuities composed of fixed and variable parts—the latter would be equal to 12 percent of the value of Germany's exports. In terms of present value, it amounted to slightly more than the Boulogne scheme; the prescribed initial annuities were also slightly larger than the corresponding annuities of the earlier plan.[116]

The Allies, however, could not simply set the German debt at the level prescribed by the Paris agreement. Under the treaty the Reparation Commission was to fix Germany's debt by totaling up damages, and no alternative procedure could legally be adopted without Germany's consent. It was clear at the time, however, that the Paris agreement was something more than a mere proposal that Germany was free to reject. On January 29, the Paris Conference decided upon a number of sanctions, including a further occupation of German territory, that would be applied in the event that Germany did not accept the Allies' terms regarding both disarmament and reparation. News of these sanctions was leaked to the press in early February, and the *Times* went so far as to treat German assent as a mere formality.[117] Lloyd George, in his Birmingham speech of February 5, was more scrupulous: Dr. Simons had the right to prefer the "full bill," although such a preference was absurd. The German government could also present alternative plans, providing they represented "a *bona fide* effort to liquidate" the reparation debt. But at the same time he warned Germany that if her alternative proposals were "a mere attempt to evade payment, we cannot put up with that."[118]

When it learned of the Paris "decisions," the German press exploded in anger.[119] The Allies, it seemed, were still attempting to impose a settlement regarded by the great mass of German opinion as absurd and impossible. Relations between Germany and the Allies rapidly deteriorated; in this poisoned atmosphere the resumption of "businesslike" negotiations was impossible. In early February Simons, Laurent and D'Abernon grasped at straws. Perhaps all was not lost, perhaps the Seydoux proposals and the Paris "agreement" could somehow be reconciled. "Would it not be possible to salvage at least something from the Seydoux project?" Simons wondered. There was no "absolute incompatibility," Laurent replied.[120] After all, as D'Abernon pointed out to Simons, the first annuities prescribed by the Paris agreement were not much higher than those endorsed by the Brussels experts.[121]

These hopes were all in vain. The atmosphere of impending confrontation created by the Paris Conference was obviously incompatible with the businesslike spirit that had prevailed at Brussels; the demise of this spirit meant that, for the time being, there was no longer any possibility of working out realistic arrangements based on at least semivoluntary German cooperation.

For this fateful turn of events Seydoux bitterly, but with evident justification, blamed the British government. England, he wrote at the end of March, had jealously blocked reparation plans that would have led to Franco-German industrial collaboration. The British feared that if French and German industry joined forces in this way, they would rule the European market, and to them this was intolerable. On the other hand, Great Britain was also "afraid lest France, weary of not being paid, apply increasingly violent measures of coercion which would end up by putting Germany at her mercy, from an economic point of view." Thus, he concluded, England had "an interest in the maintenance of a situation which she has prolonged for a year, which retards the payment of reparation and leaves us, vis-à-vis Germany, in a state of semi-hostility, preventing any direct entente between the two countries, but excluding any violent action on our part."[122]

To Seydoux the British cared only for their own immediate interests, and he was right in thinking that the British government showed little concern for the interests of France. Preoccupied with national and imperial problems, Lloyd George and his associates found the idea of withdrawal from European affairs increasingly attractive. Hankey, for example, was pleased that Lloyd George, in an important Cabinet discussion of general policy on December 31, 1920, had come out in favor of a policy of "aloofness" from Europe—"a selfish policy, perhaps," Hankey noted, "but the cheapest and best for our own people."[123]

Real withdrawal from European affairs was impossible. Lloyd George pressed therefore for the next best thing, a quick solution to outstanding problems. Such a policy was hardly malicious, as Seydoux, assuming a rational explanation for what appeared to him as otherwise unintelligible, was inclined to suppose; but there is scarcely any doubt that as a direct result of British policy, the best chance for eventual settlement along lines acceptable to both France and Germany had been allowed to slip irretrievably away.

Impatience

IN EARLY 1921 Lloyd George was more convinced than ever that a quick solution to the reparation problem was vital. By "solution," however, he meant little more than agreement on how much should be paid. He was willing to pay heavily for Germany's acceptance of a figure, but there was a limit below which he would not go. If Germany's proposals were unacceptable, he would coerce her into agreeing to the payment plan set by the Allies.

He believed the reparation scheme "proposed" at the Paris Conference of January 1921 to be within reason—he said so at the time both in public and in private [1]—and in early 1921 British representatives pressed the German government to propose a settlement of that order of magnitude. But the German proposals, when they were made at the London Conference in March, struck both British and French statesmen as absurdly inadequate. To punish the Germans for their "bad faith," sanctions were imposed. Finally, in May 1921, a rather moderate schedule of payments was dictated to the German government. Threatened with an occupation of the Ruhr should they prove recalcitrant, the Germans "accepted" it a few days later. Thus Lloyd George had achieved his goal: the reparation problem had been "solved."

Lloyd George's anxious grasping for a figure must be understood in the context of economic conditions in Britain at the time. A severe depression had struck the country in the latter half of 1920; it was widely believed that unsettled financial and economic conditions in continental Europe were responsible. For this Allied and especially French reparation demands were blamed. Reparation, it was supposed, had prevented a return to normal conditions of trade; it was reparation, therefore, that was the root cause of Britain's economic difficulties.[2]

The argument, however, was weak. It cannot be assumed a priori that foreign conditions were directly responsible for the depression of 1920–1921. The general economic situation in Europe, and especially in Germany, was improving at the time, and the statistics seemed to show in fact that a decline in foreign demand had not touched off the depression. As the *Economist* noted on October 16, 1920, the September export figures were actually higher than those for August, in spite of the decline of trade within Britain. It was not until January 1921 that the *Economist* "at last" saw some reflection of the trade depression in the export figures.[3]

From a more theoretical point of view it is clear that a rupture of international trade need not reduce aggregate demand: foreign demand lost in this way may by largely offset by the gain in demand resulting from the "eviction" of foreign commerce from the domestic market. A country, however, may well suffer from the dislocation that a shift in demand resulting from a sharp reduction in international trade would in any case cause. The extent of such dislocation is primarily a function of the importance of international trade in the economy.

The problems generated in the foreign sector are thus essentially problems of conversion—that is, of reallocation of resources in response to changing patterns of demand. The usual market mechanisms facilitate adjustment to the new situation resulting from the loss of foreign markets—a process which might be easier in the commodity markets than in the investment market, but which nevertheless over the economy as a whole tends automatically to fit national patterns of output and consumption into the new conditions of international trade. Partial withdrawal from the world economy of course limits the international division of labor and thus generally tends to reduce a nation's real wealth, but labor and capital at home might be used just as fully as before. The ease of conversion depends to a large extent on the adequacy of demand, and this in turn is largely a function of the government's fiscal and monetary policies: inflationary policies ease the process of resource reallocation, deflationary policies have the opposite effect.

The problems deriving from the situation in Europe were not the only problems of conversion that the British economy would face after the armistice. The fundamental changes in the economy which had taken place during the war—in the allocation of resources and in the distribution of wealth, in Britain and on the continent—would in any event have prevented a smooth return to the trading patterns of 1914. The British economy would have to adjust to these changes no matter how vigorously the continent revived. In view of these changes, it is by no means certain that a return to the prewar system of international commerce—assuming that foreign conditions were such that that were possible—would have been any less difficult than conversion to a more closed economy in which foreign trade played a significantly smaller role than it did before the war.

Thus the easy assumption of the day that conditions on the continent of Europe were the root cause of Britain's economic difficulties ignored the complexity of the problem—the possibility that other factors, like the changes wrought by the war, or the fiscal and monetary policies of the government, might have had a significant and perhaps dominant bearing on Britain's situation. Great Britain might have had severe problems even if Europe had revived more swiftly, even if there had been no reparations. But nostalgia for the pre-1914 world and the belief in the "solidarity" of the international economy were such that it was easy to blame Britain's problems on the plight of Europe and the contraction of the continental market.

From the government's point of view, it was convenient to blame the foreign situation for Britain's troubles—certainly more convenient than accepting responsibility for the failure of Great Britain to make full use of her resources. Yet it is clear, and was clear at the time, that the depression was intimately related to the government's own financial policies.

As a consequence of the inflationary methods universally used to finance the war, prices in 1919 and early 1920 were much higher than they had been in 1913; it was widely assumed that prices must be made to fall back to their prewar levels. Only in this way, it was supposed, could the "soundness" of the currency, and thus the health of the economy, be assured. In 1920, a policy of deflation was the official policy of the British Treasury.[4] British officials had few illusions as to the effect of such a policy on trade. As the highest permanent official in the Treasury, Basil Blackett, noted in July, "the policy of gradual deflation involves long months during which commerce and industry is a prey to despondency."[5] For in a period of falling prices, profits contract, since costs of production are high in comparison with the final price obtained. This generates an attitude of pessimism among businessmen, inclining them to restrict output.

Treasury officials and bankers were aware that a deflationary policy hurts the economy. Nevertheless, they tended on the whole to view it as an "heroic" policy. The nation, to be sure, would endure a period of economic stagnation, but would emerge from it with a strong currency—the sure foundation for an era of prosperity, the real guarantee of genuinely healthy economy.[6]

There seems little doubt that the policy of deflation, which was pursued in America as well as in Britain, was closely related to the severe depression that struck in mid-1920.[7] But reparation, and not deflation, was made the principal scapegoat for Britain's economic problems, and in the latter half of 1920, hostility toward reparation deepened. In another, more indirect way, deteriorating economic conditions had the effect of further discrediting the claim to reparation. Increased unemployment and trade stagnation generated pressure for protection from foreign competition. The clamor for protection was directed above all against Germany, whose "collapsed exchange," it was said, gave her industries an unfair advantage over their British competitors.[8] But reparation could be paid only by means of a net influx of German goods into Britain (or its equivalent, if channels of payment ran through third countries); it followed from this that the payment of reparation was not in the interest of the British economy. But while the Lloyd George government shared the concern of businessmen and hoped to protect British industry from German competition, it did not consider abandoning the British claim to reparation. Sir Robert Horne, president of the Board of Trade, put the matter bluntly in a February 1921 speech in Sheffield: "Germany had to meet her reparations to the Allies, but we should not permit her to make those reparations in goods."[9]

By early 1921 the government seemed to have adopted a policy aimed at protecting against imports from Germany; it was inconsistent, and therefore absurd, to demand at the same time large reparations from Germany. What was doubly absurd was that Lloyd George tried to use reparation itself to provide this protection against German competition. In the Paris agreement, the scheme for a variable annuity had called for an additional payment, over and above the specified base figures, equal to 12 percent of Germany's exports. The French wavered on the interpretation of this provision, but the British government clearly understood it as calling for the imposition of a 12 percent tax on German exports.[10] The Paris scheme was not accepted, but Lloyd George persisted, and as a result of his efforts, one of the sanctions adopted at the London Conference in March was the imposition of a tax on imports from Germany. To give effect to this measure, Parliament enacted the Reparation Recovery Act, which aimed at collecting reparation by having British purchasers of German goods pay up to half of the purchase price into the reparation account.[11]

Lloyd George found the idea of taxing German exports particularly attractive because it seemed to solve so many problems at a stroke. The tax would raise money for reparation, and do so in a way that solved the "transfer problem," while at the same time providing a measure of protection for British industry.[12] Not everyone shared his commitment to this device. To many well-informed people, the imposition of a tax on German exports as a means for the payment of reparation appeared as an attempt to square the circle. Payment depended on the expansion of the German export trade, while the kind of tax Lloyd George wanted to apply would tend to restrict the development of Germany's foreign commerce. The measure was therefore widely opposed even within Lloyd George's own government, and Loucheur laughed when he first heard about it.[13] And although neither the Reparation Recovery Act nor the "collapsed exchanges" provisions of the Safeguarding of Industries Act passed later in the year were ever fully put into effect,[14] the protectionist orientation of British policy served further to discredit reparation: it was absurd to demand that Germany pay and at the same time seek to deprive her of the only means of earning the money with which to make payment.

This further discrediting of reparation was somewhat unjust to the French, for in fairness, it was Lloyd George's policy and not reparation as such that should have been discredited; the logical conclusion to be drawn from the argument that an influx of German goods hurt the British economy was that the British share to reparation should be waived. The French at Brussels had demonstrated their willingness to take the goods. But in January 1921 prejudice against reparation was so strong that the evidence was neglected. Indeed, in spite of the importance of the transfer problem, the direct bearing of the work of the Brussels Conference on this problem was ignored, and the idea that nonpayment was due to incapacity resulting from insurmountable problems of transfer rather than to an unwillingness to make real sacrifices continued to be accepted as an article of faith.

It was evident at the time that Lloyd George bore primary responsibility for the Paris accord, and thus for the failure of the Brussels arrangements. But the new French government had offered him little resistance. Why this was so remains somewhat baffling. The change of government is in itself an inadequate explanation. The fall of the Leygues cabinet was not due to parliamentary opposition to its relatively moderate reparation policy: of the 116 deputies (all non-Socialist) who voted in favor of Leygues at this time, 36 percent had either voted against the government or abstained on at least one of the three earlier votes (May 28, July 20 and July 30) testing Millerand's reparation policy. The corresponding figure for the non-Socialist deputies in the Chamber as a whole is 37 percent; one would expect a much greater discrepancy if reparation were the decisive issue. Both Poincaré and Tardieu, moreover, were inclined to be indulgent toward Leygues, and Tardieu was in the small minority that supported him on the fatal vote of nonconfidence. After all, Tardieu wrote, Leygues had not voted for the Spa advances, and "his personal feelings are not in doubt."[15] The discontinuity normally associated with a change in government is no adequate explanation either, for Millerand, as President, and important permanent officials like Seydoux, provided a certain continuity. Loucheur, again in 1921 a leading maker of French reparation policy, certainly was not opposed in principle to a moderate settlement based on a kind of Franco-German "economic collaboration."

Was it perhaps the hostility of influential French industrialists toward reparation in kind that accounts for the slight enthusiasm of the Briand government for the Seydoux arrangements? For the same reason that businessmen clamor for tariff protection, it may be assumed that the business community on balance would exert pressure to curtail reparation in kind.[16] But as the vicissitudes of tariff legislation show, there is no a priori way of knowing how effective this set of pressures is. Certainly there is no one-to-one correspondence between the interest at stake and the pressure exerted; countervailing factors—an ideological commitment to free trade, for example—limit the free play of interest-group pressure with varying degrees of success. In this case, it does not seem that industry was very concerned with the impact of the Seydoux plan: the *Journée Industrielle,* which reflected the concerns of the business class, was not much interested in the Seydoux scheme. This proposal certainly generated nothing to compare with the storm of opposition aroused later in 1921 by the Wiesbaden accords on reparation in kind, as even the most cursory comparison of the *Journée Industrielle* for the two periods demonstrates.

This difference is partly to be explained by the great care Seydoux took to frame his proposals in a way that would neutralize the opposition of business. It was part of his plan to compensate French producers for any loss of trade at home by winning for them increased access to the German market. Moreover, businessmen were to be coopted into the negotiation process itself—a group of industrialists had been set up in early January to carry on, in conjunction with the government, discussions with the Germans on metallurgical questions. Finally, for psychological reasons, the commercial scheme for a fund of paper marks was bound to arouse less hostility than the more bureaucratic system the Wiesbaden accords proposed to set up. In Seydoux's plan, German reparation goods would actually be bought for money which the *sinistrés* were free to spend on corresponding French products if they so wished; in the Wiesbaden scheme it would be impossible for French businessmen to compete with a flood of "free" German goods coming in through bureaucratic channels.

Seydoux's skill in neutralizing potential opposition was important, but there is a deeper reason for the government's relative freedom to shape reparation policy. The nature of the French political culture was such that both government and business on the whole shared a common conception of the role of business in making foreign policy: this was to be the government's sphere, and providing it did not overstep the bounds and interfere too directly with the material interests of business, it was free to do as it saw fit in this area. This certainly was not the case in Germany, where the views of industry carried great and at times irresistible weight even on the broadest questions of foreign policy, and where businessmen, especially since the revolution, played a direct role in making policy on questions like reparation.[17]

It thus seems clear that the opposition of business was not responsible for the demise of the Seydoux Plan. How then is French policy at the Paris Conference to be explained? Another possible explanation is that the Briand government simply was not aware of what was at stake in January 1921. This is not particularly compelling but it seems to be the best interpretation available.

It was in fact easy to ignore what was at stake at the Paris Conference, since Lloyd George's demand for a figure did not clearly contradict the line of policy which had culminated in the Seydoux proposals.[18] For French policy operated on two levels. There was on the one hand the question of the figure at which the reparation debt would be set, and on the other hand, the question of the actual payments Germany would make. The two questions were considered distinct, although ultimately, it was assumed, the total debt would be formally reduced to the level that corresponded to actual payments. In this context, French officials felt that it was important to set the formal debt at a level not much higher than the final figure representing Germany's real payments.[19] Therefore, these officials argued, the French evaluations of damage should be on the low side; German objections would thereby be minimized, and French public opinion would not be outraged when the figure set by adding up damages was reduced to the final figure.[20]

The Boulogne Scheme apparently represented the final settlement at which French policy aimed; the level of payment prescribed by the Boulogne accord also corresponded to the actual payments the French were prepared to receive via the Seydoux Plan, at least in the first years. Seydoux himself called for a formal figure to be set by totaling up damages by May 1. He felt that the French evaluations of damage should be on the modest side. He specifically suggested a figure of 76 milliard gold marks as the French claim: 52 milliards— the French share of the Boulogne figure—plus 24 milliards, corresponding to the war debt. Eventually, the Reparation Commission's figure would be reduced to the Boulogne level; but in exchange for this concession, the inter-Allied debt would be forgiven—or at the very least, France would be granted very liberal terms for repayment.

All this, however, did not supersede the plan for the five annuities, which was to govern actual payment: the shaping of the formal German liability was distinct in Seydoux's mind from negotiations on real deliveries.[21]

The new government fundamentally shared this point of view. As the notes of a high-level meeting of January 23, 1921—that is, just before the Paris Conference—make clear, Millerand, Briand and their associates made the same distinction between the theoretical German debt and actual German payments. Millerand in particular felt that the procedure for setting the formal liability, as laid down in Article 233 of the treaty, was "indispensable." The figures for damages, he said, should be set on a completely "solid, moderate" basis; whenever there was a question where the Reparation Commission had to exercise discretion, Millerand declared that it should decide in favor of "the most reasonable and the most moderate hypothesis."[22] Briand agreed, pointing out "the danger of presenting an exorbitant figure, one impossible to realize; the sum total of our damages must be near the figure at which the German debt will be set. We will be inevitably led to make sacrifices, for which compensation must be offered us by our allies." But nobody seemed to feel that the setting of a fixed sum by May 1 had any bearing on the Seydoux arrangements, nor even on the plan for a provisional settlement.[23]

It is clear from the discussion at this meeting that the new Minister of Finance, Senator Paul Doumer, was totally isolated in the government. He wanted a large debt figure of 212 milliard gold marks; Briand and Millerand pointed out that the British would not go along. Millerand alluded to the "very great impatience" of the British for a fixed sum, and while he felt that because of the state of French public opinion, it was best not to determine the debt right away, he also said that if Lloyd George insisted, the French would have to give way. Briand agreed: to both men, the preservation of the entente was the most important consideration.[24]

Thus the French government was disposed, even before the Conference convened, to fall in with Lloyd George's second attempt to reach a fixed sum. Because of its own two-level conception of policy, it was not aware that new action to secure a figure would result in the collapse of the line of policy pursued at Brussels. Nor did the frustration of the hopes aroused by the Seydoux Plan in December make much of an impact on French public opinion: these hopes just faded away. In Great Britain, the significance of the Seydoux arrangements had never really been recognized, and their passing hardly created a ripple.

The Paris agreement itself was received with satisfaction in France. The Chamber supported Briand just as it had approved Millerand's reparation policy after Spa. The vote itself was similar—363 to 114, with 102 abstentions—and opposition was distributed across the political spectrum in much the same way. The debate was basically a replay of the reparation debates of 1920: Tardieu attacking the government for not applying the treaty, the government replying that the treaty itself was to blame and that the alliance had to be preserved.

At Paris, the Allies had been unable to actually set Germany's reparation liability. German assent was necessary. To this end, another conference was scheduled, this time in London, to reach final agreement on a figure. In spite of British efforts, there were no preliminary conversations among experts. It was therefore at the full conference on March 1 that the German counterproposals were first outlined. To the argument that the economic revival of Germany placed her in a position to pay substantial reparation, Dr. Simons countered with a curious metaphor: "A decaying fruit tree was able to produce fruit in large quantities just before it died," and although German industry was at present very productive, "in point of fact it was about to collapse in ruinous fashion." The financial problem was the key difficulty, and upon a restoration of German finances depended the economic future of the country.[25] In effect, Simons was making excuses in advance for the patently inadequate proposals he was about to present.

Simons had been warned that the German proposals "must not leave the framework of the Paris decisions," and those proposals purported to take the Paris arrangement as a point of departure.[26] The fixed annuities of the Paris plan, discounted at 8 percent, amounted to a figure of 50 milliard gold marks; subtracting the 20 milliards alleged to have already been paid, 30 milliards were left. Up to 8 milliards of this would be paid by means of a loan Germany would raise in the near future; the rest would bear interest at 5 percent, and would be retired by payments which at first would be only 1 milliard gold marks a year. The 12 percent export levy would not be imposed, since the underlying idea of allowing the Allies to participate in German economic revival had already "been taken into full account." The whole plan was subject to Germany's retention of Upper Silesia, and to the restoration of a regime of commercial equality and freedom.[27]

The plan, with its juggling of figures and interest rates, struck the Allies as completely unacceptable.[28] Without even waiting to hear the German proposals in detail, Lloyd George, as President of the Conference, rejected them out of hand.[29] The Allies had to take some action in the face of these German proposals; on this point Lloyd George and Briand were agreed. The problem was that, owing to the nonapplication of Article 235, there had as yet been no default on reparation account. Was it proper to use Germany's violations of other parts of the treaty as a pretext for punishing her for her defiant attitude? Lloyd George at first had his doubts, but eventually came to the conclusion that the war criminal question provided an adequate legal basis for Allied action.[30] He agreed with the other Allied delegates that the hostile spirit of German policy provided the real justification for sanctions.

What measures then could be taken? At the Paris Conference the Allies had agreed on a set of sanctions to be applied in such a case. The two most important ones were an extension of the occupation and the application of "customs or other measures in the occupied Rhenish territory."[31] Lloyd George now said these measures "could be discussed," but he was opposed to an extension of the military occupation and he did not like the proposal for a customs line along the Rhine.[32] He pressed instead for the imposition of an enormous duty on German goods imported into the Allied countries. 50 percent of the value of German imports would be paid to the Allied treasuries. If the German industrialists did not accept these terms, they would be faced with "the loss of 70 to 80 percent. of the markets of the world." They would then urge "their Government to carry out the Paris resolutions. They would say that this new measure was 'worse than Paris.' "[33]

Briand, however, insisted on a modest extension of the occupation—just a small-scale occupation of certain key towns in the Westphalian industrial district: "A few battalions sent to Mannheim would bring Herr Stinnes quickly to his senses." Duisburg, "the tap for the outflow of the coal areas," would also be occupied; once it was "in the hands of the Allies the activities of Hugo Stinnes and other captains of industry could thereby be regulated; and as a result those great financial experts would very quickly discover all sorts of means to get rid of the control."[34] Whether this had any concrete meaning is unclear. When Lloyd George objected that the French apparently wanted to extend the occupation in order to exploit the occupied area economically, and that the "British Government viewed with the utmost fear anything that looked like the effective occupation of a part of German territory," Briand did not even try to argue the point and sought to reassure Lloyd George instead.[35] The next day the idea of occupying Mannheim was dropped; it was proposed instead to send troops to Duisburg, Ruhrort, and Dusseldorf in order to control most of the coal coming out of the Ruhr. But it was unclear what function this control was to have and it was not evident how it would be exercised.[36] It seems in fact that the new occupation was to be basically a gesture—Briand certainly insisted that the political situation within France made some military sanction essential.[37]

The other French proposal was for the seizure of the customs in the occupied areas and for a customs line between occupied and unoccupied Germany. Briand at first called for a "custom and fiscal organisation" which aimed at the exploitation of the Left Bank.[38] What this involved is also somewhat unclear—according to Chamberlain the French plan called for "the economic and financial administration by the Allies of the occupied territories"—but Briand apparently did not object when the scheme was quickly pared down to the customs line proposal.[39]

Lloyd George was hostile to both of Briand's proposals, and in private sharply condemned the French preference for military over economic measures: "The French can never make up their mind whether they want payment or whether they want the enjoyment of trampling on Germany, occupying the Ruhr, or taking some other military action. It is quite clear they cannot have both, and they have to make up their minds which they desire. As far as we are concerned, we are strongly against any military adventure. I prefer economic pressure to military."[40] Nevertheless he agreed to threaten Germany with all three sanctions, the two proposed by France and his idea of a big tax on imports from Germany.[41]

On March 3 the British Prime Minister delivered a speech to the conference rejecting the German proposals and warning that if the Germans did not come up with a satisfactory plan in four days, these sanctions would be imposed.[42] The Germans soon proposed to go back to the plan for a provisional settlement; this now appeared as the sole avenue of escape, and Lloyd George, who had sabotaged the plan a month earlier, now endorsed it.[43] But it was too late: the entire atmosphere had changed since Brussels. Simons had decided in early February that the time had come to "raise the question of revision in all its clarity," and in a February 16 speech at Karlsruhe, he specifically repudiated German responsibility for the war.[44] The Germans, it was clear, simply did not accept the Treaty of Versailles as binding.[45] They would perhaps pay for five years, Briand thought, but it was now evident that they hoped that when this period was up, they could not be forced to pay any more.[46] In any case, the German proposal was hardly acceptable as it stood: most of the money was to come from a loan Germany would try to raise abroad, and any payment was subject to the usual reserves, notably the retention of Upper Silesia.[47] Thus the attempt to fall back on a provisional settlement failed. The other schemes Lloyd George came up with were unable to serve as a satisfactory basis for negotiation. The conference failed to reach any solution and the sanctions outlined by Lloyd George were, to one degree or another, eventually put into effect.[48]

Hostility toward Germany had long been building up in official circles in France. There were many signs that the Germans refused to accept the peace treaty in good faith, that they were playing for time and were doing all they could to escape their obligations.[49] The French government felt it had made a great effort to pursue a reasonable policy, but that Germany had not reciprocated. The German government had dragged its feet at Brussels, and at London had made proposals which even the British felt to be ridiculous. Actual payments appeared ludicrously inadequate: of the 20 milliards called for under Article 235, Germany had only "paid" about 8, approximately half of which was the credit granted for her purchases of food and raw material. The balance credited to Germany was not large enough to cover various charges having priority over reparation: occupation costs, expenses of Allied control commissions, and repayment of the Spa advances. For France in particular, the payment received from Germany by May 1, 1921, amounted to 1,585,000,000 gold marks, virtually all of which was in the form of armistice deliveries (especially rolling stock), coal, paper marks for the armies of occupation, and the Saar coal mines. But occupation and commission costs and sums needed to liquidate the Spa advances amounted to 1,517,000,000 gold marks, so that France netted almost nothing on reparation account.[50]

For all these reasons, patience had worn thin by the spring of 1921. Reluctantly, French leaders came to the conclusion that force was the only answer now that conciliation had so clearly failed, and by April 1921 official opinion had turned bitterly against Germany. The tone of Laurent's despatches, for example, became increasingly hostile toward Germany at this time.[51] Seydoux's attitude hardened dramatically, and he now advocated the occupation of the Ruhr.[52] Millerand himself was no longer in a mood for further concession.[53] As for Briand, he wrote on April 7 that the Reparation Commission would officially declare Germany in default in May; at that point the Allies would act to "triumph over the increasing bad faith of Germany and to impose upon her the payment of the reparations through appropriate, effective measures."[54] At the same time, the French government was developing a plan for the occupation of the Ruhr and the extraction of wealth from Germany by means of the imposition of a tax on the Ruhr coal.[55]

The feeling that the time for action had at last come was fully shared by parliamentary and press opinion. In a series of tough pronouncements, the government gave vent to the widespread mood of anger, frustration and impatience. Briand, in a famous phrase, declared that "a firm hand would fall on her collar" should Germany continue to evade her obligations.[56] Germany could pay, but refused to; on May 1, after her default had been registered, her creditors, he declared, had the right under common law to use coercion against her.[57] To give force to these threats, the government dramatically increased the size of the army.[58]

At about this time, Simons moved to head off an occupation of the Ruhr. In an interview with *Le Matin* he indicated that Germany would make further proposals.[59] But French officials were wary. Laurent reported on April 11 that D'Abernon was still hoping to reach some arrangement with Germany: the Paris figure could be accepted in principle and the question could then be referred to the experts for further discussion. The British ambassador was "visibly disturbed" by the prospect of sanctions, and internal difficulties—a reference to the British coal strike—obliged his government, he said, to pursue a policy of conciliation. Laurent replied that further discussions were possible, but only if the Germans "made precise engagements guaranteeing the Allies against the usual dilatory maneuvers."[60] Briand shared Laurent's views on this point, and urged him to warn D'Abernon against pursuing a "policy of weakness" toward Germany. The French government had gone "to the extreme limit of the spirit of conciliation. This had only resulted in reinforcing the German decision to shirk her obligations." British domestic problems had nothing to do with the question of whether force should be applied: only if France had asked Britain to deploy a sizable military force against Germany "could British internal difficulties be invoked: in fact the French government is only asking for the moral support of the English government." Reparation was of "vital importance" for France; it was necessary, he concluded, to break out of the cycle of "talks, experts' meetings and endless discussions, and arrive at real immediate payments, in cash and in kind, imposed if need be by force, since all attempts at conciliation have failed."[61] But this did not mean that he would turn a deaf ear to any proposals that Germany would make; he only insisted that the German plan be precise and concrete.[62]

The German proposals were presented not to the Allies directly, but rather to the American government. On April 20, the Germans offered to accept American arbitration: they would accept as binding any figure designated by the President of the United States.[63] Charles Evans Hughes, Secretary of State in the new Harding government, immediately rejected this proposal, but he did offer to act as intermediary between Germany and the Allies and even agreed to participate in any reparation negotiations that took place.[64] On April 24, the Germans presented a reparation plan to the American government, on the basis of which negotiations might proceed. It called for a liability of 50 milliard gold marks present value, which would be paid in annuities totaling as much as 200 milliards.[65] This was more than Germany had ever offered. But it does not seem that the plan was seriously put forward as a basis for eventual settlement.[66] The whole plan was subject to the usual conditions, including one which apparently referred to the retention of all of Upper Silesia in Germany. The French government was certainly in no mood to negotiate on the basis of these vague proposals at this late date. Laurent's view was typical—the German plan was "hastily drawn up, full of ambiguities deliberately inserted to deceive sometimes German and sometimes

Allied opinion, if not both at the same time. It stands out very clearly as a dilatory maneuver on the part of the government of the Reich.''[67]

The German proposals did not in the least shake the conviction of the French government that the time for action had come. A plan for the occupation of the Ruhr and the concurrent imposition of taxes and various economic controls on Germany had been developed, but Briand had no intention of acting alone.[68] He asked to meet Lloyd George in order to discuss joint action in view of the impending default.[69] The meeting took place at Hythe on April 23 and April 24. Briand presented the French plan for the occupation of the Ruhr.[70] There would be a tight control of industry and heavy taxation of the output of the mines and factories in the Ruhr basin. Germany would then have the incentive to negotiate in good faith. When acceptable proposals were made, the military occupation would end; but a paper promise to pay was not good enough in itself. Real guarantees were essential, and the military "guarantee" (i.e., the Ruhr occupation), would have to replaced by economic and financial guarantees. In this connection, the French plan called for the permanent imposition of a 40 gold mark per ton duty on coal: "This is not exactly a tax on coal, but it is intended to compel Germany to pay according as a source of riches is created, of which she will be deprived if she does not acquit herself of her undertakings.''[71] This would raise 3 to 4 milliard gold marks a year, but this money would be in the form of paper marks. Therefore, this was complemented by an arrangement for a "Control Office for Foreign Securities." All the foreign exchange earned by German exporters would be paid into this office, part of which would be used to finance imports, also to be controlled by the office. The control would be effected by means of a system of licenses, and imports would be so restricted as to create a surplus of foreign exchange which could be applied to reparation. For the system to work, exporters had to be reimbursed in paper marks for the foreign exchange they turned over. A certain proportion of this would be raised through the sale of foreign currency to licensed importers. The rest, presumably,—the plan is particularly vague on this point—would be the fund of paper marks created through the coal tax. Indeed it seems that the plan for control of foreign trade was primarily a device for transferring sums raised through the coal tax into foreign currencies.[72]

The British government had expected the French to demand this kind of action, but was divided as to how to react. Churchill strongly opposed the very idea of a Ruhr occupation.[73] But Lloyd George, worried that a flat refusal to take further measures in the face of German default might drive France to Poincaré and a policy of independent action, felt that Britain should go along with the idea of a Ruhr occupation under certain conditions: the Allied demands could not exceed the Paris scheme, the French would have to agree to accept reparation in kind, and military action must not be used to dismember Germany.[74] The prime minister's point of view prevailed, and was embodied in a counterproject presented to Briand at Hythe.[75]

The conditions relating to the dismemberment of Germany and to reparation in kind clearly reflected continuing British distrust of French intentions. Indeed British policy as a whole reflected this mistrust. Whereas Briand wished to go into the Ruhr and then wait for the Germans to make proposals, Lloyd George believed that the Allies should make their precise demands clear in advance: the Germans should know exactly what terms they would have to accept to secure the withdrawal of Allied troops. "There must be no blank cheque to the French," he said.[76] It followed that before the Allies went in, they should present Germany with an ultimatum demanding acceptance of these terms. Only if the ultimatum were rejected would the occupation take place.

What Lloyd George was really counting on was that the threat of a Ruhr occupation would induce Germany to accept the Allied terms. In this way he hoped to avoid an actual occupation. His intentions on this point were quite clear. The prospect of a Ruhr occupation, he told Briand at Hythe, "was like a threat to kill; by such a menace a man might be induced to do many things; for instance to hand over all his money, or give you his boots; but it was no good killing him, for his carcase was useless."[77]

Briand was not convinced, and the matter was still unresolved when a formal Allied conference opened in London on April 30. But the gap between British and French ideas was not as great as it seemed, and Briand only weakly resisted British pressure for an ultimatum. He suggested only that it was pointless: the bill fixed by the Reparation Commission—132 milliard gold marks—was greater than the debt provided for in the Paris agreement. "How could it be thought," Briand asked, "that Germany would accept the greater when she had refused the less?"[78]

This was not the kind of criticism that went to the heart of the issue. Briand, for example, did not remind Lloyd George of his earlier remarks concerning the relative worthlessness of an imposed settlement—the limited value of "another Versailles Treaty"[79]—and he did not put up much of a fight before agreeing to Lloyd George's proposal for an ultimatum. The reason seems to be that Briand had no real desire to go into the Ruhr. He certainly had no yearning for an occupation for its own sake. The French, he said, "only desired to occupy the Ruhr in order to make the Germans capitulate. If they succeeded in obtaining the guarantees, without occupying the Ruhr, so much the better."[80]

Again on the question of figures the Briand government demonstrated a striking willingness to compromise. The French delegates quickly agreed to a plan calling for an annuity of 2 milliard gold marks plus 26 percent of the value of German exports—an arrangement based on an earlier British plan. At first, it was proposed to offer this plan to the Germans as an alternative to a tougher schedule of payments to be established by the Reparation Commission in accordance with the treaty. The plan would thus be a final attempt to settle the reparation question through "agreement" with the Germans.[81] But then it was decided that it would be more expedient to have the Reparation Commission formally adopt the Allied plan as the schedule of payments called for in the treaty.[82] After some resistance, the Commission did just that, and after an ultimatum a new German government accepted the Schedule of Payments on May 11.

The debt, as set by the Schedule of Payments, was certainly a good deal less than the 132 milliard figure it purportedly amounted to. At Lloyd George's insistence, even the pretense of a formal debt bearing interest at 5 percent was dropped. Interest would only accrue on that portion of the debt corresponding to the annuity level in a given year.[83] The system was worked by means of a variable bond issue. There would be 50 milliard gold marks worth of bonds—the "A" and "B" bonds—bearing interest at 5 percent, plus 1 percent for amortization. This would amount to an annuity of 3 milliard gold marks. As the annuity set by the export index exceeded this level, further bonds—called "C" bonds—would be issued. The service of the additional bonds would correspond exactly to the increase in the annuity. No matter how long it took for these bonds to be issued, their nominal value at time of issue would be deducted from the total remaining debt, until bonds to a nominal value of 132 milliard gold marks—the original 50 plus a further 82 milliard gold marks worth— had been issued.[84] Once these bonds were paid, the entire debt would be canceled. There would be no interest, in other words, on the uncovered portion of the debt, and the present value of Germany's liability would therefore be considerably less than the 132 milliard figure. Exactly how much less it is impossible to say, but even under the most optimistic assumptions, the Schedule of Payments did not amount to more than a capital sum of 108 milliard gold marks.[85]

It was for this reason that D'Abernon wrote in his diary that the Schedule of Payments was "a document of moderation and wisdom," and Lloyd George, in urging acceptance of the scheme, declared to the German ambassador Sthamer on May 5 that the terms of the Schedule "were, in fact, the best terms that had been proposed yet to Germany."[86] The point was not missed in France. The economist Charles Rist called the Schedule a "solution which, seen up close, does not differ by much from that which Mr. Keynes had proposed," and Poincaré noted that the liability set by the Schedule was much less than the 132 milliard figure promulgated by the Reparation Commission.[87] Yet once again, by a large majority, the Chamber endorsed the government's reparation policy.

A New Beginning?

Chapter Six

FOLLOWING THE London Ultimatum, the German Fehrenbach Ministry fell and was replaced by a new cabinet under Joseph Wirth, a member of the Center Party who had served as Fehrenbach's Minister of Finance. The old cabinet did not resign in protest against the Schedule of Payments. Simons in particular felt that the ultimatum should have been accepted, largely in order to increase Germany's chances of retaining Upper Silesia. The problem was that the political parties, and especially the moderate right-wing Volkspartei, had lost confidence in the government even before the ultimatum had been handed down.[1]

The coming to power of the Wirth cabinet marked no basic change in German reparation policy. Wirth and Walther Rathenau, his principal collaborator on reparation policy, urged more forcefully than their predecessors the need to conform to the treaty as a way of demonstrating its impossibility and the subsequent need for revision. Germany would comply with the treaty up to the limit of her capacity—but this principle was so vague and so flexible that it had been the constant basis of German reparation policy from June 1919 on.[2]

A promise to pay to the limit of Germany's capacity did not amount to very much. The notion of "capacity" was elastic: noneconomic factors such as domestic political opposition were often taken as limiting "capacity." Thus when Germany's leaders spoke of her "incapacity," even among themselves, this should not be taken as proof that they actually believed substantial reparation payments were economically impossible. The distinction between a declaration of incapacity and an outright refusal to pay, moreover, is not clear-cut: indeed, an avowal of inability is the conventionally polite way of turning down a request. Thus even in these internal discussions, it was psychologically preferable to talk of Germany's incapacity instead of her unwillingness to pay, especially since using the idiom of incapacity would help reconcile real policy with public pronouncements and thus tend to undercut, even in the minds of the policy makers themselves, any possible charge of dishonesty.

In dealing with the Allies, given Germany's weak position in May 1921, the more moderate idiom of incapacity was obviously preferable for tactical purposes, and Rathenau stressed this consideration in his very revealing remarks to the cabinet in March 1922. At this point, the Wirth government proposed for the first time to reject outright certain Reparation Commission demands and Rathenau used the occasion to review the policy the Wirth government had pursued since it had come to power. At the outset, when England had been ready to approve an occupation of the Ruhr, a policy of "fulfillment," he said, had been a necessity. It had kept the French out of the Ruhr and had preserved the unity of the Reich. A certain danger of French intervention still existed, but the general situation was more favorable to Germany now than before. A firmer and more direct policy was therefore possible. Between the government and its right-wing critics, the difference had been essentially tactical in nature. Rathenau stressed that there had never been any question of pursuing an "Erfüllungspolitik sans phrase"—"a policy of fulfillment pure and simple." From the beginning, he said, it had been realized that the policy of fulfillment had its limits which one day would have to be revealed. The problem was that "a purely positive policy of fulfillment could not lead to a modification" of the treaty. The parties of the right were correct when they made this point, but they could not be publicly contradicted lest Germany's enemies be provided with any ammunition against her. He stressed that the policy of fulfillment was "no end in itself"; the problem of the government was to see how far it could go without unduly provoking the Allies—to see "how far the ice is capable of bearing the load."[3]

During 1921 the Wirth government, for essentially tactical reasons, had, in fact, refrained from stressing Germany's incapacity and spoke instead in softer tones. One of the government's chief concerns was to avoid antagonizing the West at a time when the fate of Upper Silesia was hanging in the balance. In a more direct way as well the Wirth government tried to use its reparation policy as a means of retaining Upper Silesia. Wirth publicly warned in July that an "unjust" (i.e., unfavorable) decision on Silesia would bring an end to Germany's will to execute the treaty, and Rathenau tried unsuccessfully to link the two questions in his talks with Loucheur at Wiesbaden in June.[4]

Following the October League of Nations decision on the partition of Upper Silesia, German reparation policy did harden, but even before that point the Wirth government had not made a maximum effort to comply with the treaty. For Germany to make a serious and continuing attempt to execute the Schedule of Payments, it would be necessary to find the internal resources to cover those payments. To resort to the printing press would simply accelerate the rise in prices and the parallel fall in the value of the mark on the foreign exchanges, and lead inevitably to a German plea to be at least temporarily relieved of the burden of her reparation liabilities. Immediately after the acceptance of the ultimatum, the German Economics Ministry, which felt that the balancing of the budget was essential as an end in itself, pressed for the adoption of a scheme that would provide the resources to cover the payments. This plan, inspired by certain socialist ideas for a "seizure of real values," met with strong opposition even within the government. Both Rathenau and leading officials in the Ministry of Finance were opposed, and Wirth himself stressed the political difficulties of getting the plan enacted into law.[5]

The key question, however, was not whether this particular scheme should be accepted, but rather whether Germany should make a real effort one way or another to balance her budget. Julius Hirsch, the state secretary in the Economics Ministry, insisted that this was the central consideration: did the government have the political courage to force a resolution of the budgetary problem?[6] But those who rejected the Economics Ministry plan proposed no alternative scheme to cover the deficit. The government as a whole did press for increased taxes, but its fiscal program was not nearly enough to solve the budgetary problem. It nevertheless met with great opposition from the Reichstag, and it was not until January 1922 that a "taxation compromise" was adopted.[7]

After making all allowances for the government's political difficulties, it remains clear that Wirth had not gone all-out to cut expenditures and increase taxation. A vigorous policy of that sort might have stabilized the mark and put reparation payments on a firm basis, but a sound system for the execution of the treaty was not what Wirth and Rathenau desired.

The inevitable crisis was not long in coming. On May 31, 1921, Germany handed over the equivalent of a milliard gold marks in cash. This was to be "the only significant cash payment made by Germany" in this period.[8] The next cash payments were due in January and February 1922. By November 1921 it was clear to the German government that these two payments could be met only if it could borrow what was needed. But negotiations first with private German industry, whose large foreign holdings the government had been unable to tap through legislation, and then with the London banks, both failed. This, together with the dramatic and continuing collapse of the mark, led the Wirth government on British advice to request relief from the Reparation Commission. Could the January and February 1922 payments, it enquired on December 14, be postponed?[9]

The first request for a partial moratorium was a predictable consequence of German monetary and fiscal policy, and yet Briand had done little to direct French efforts toward a resolution of the problem of the mark. Instead, the French government concentrated its attention on another area, and pressed for an ambitious system for the organization of reparation in kind. Whether it was Rathenau who approached Loucheur or vice versa is unclear—the documents contradict each other on this point—but what is certain is that when the two men met at Wiesbaden in June, Loucheur took the initiative in setting out a detailed plan for deliveries in kind. Negotiations were continued in Paris, and by the end of August Loucheur and Rathenau had initialed a convention outlining the new system; a final and more complete accord was signed at Wiesbaden on October 7.[10]

The basic idea of the scheme was to set up a bureaucratic organization to manage the delivery of vast quantities of reconstruction material. Orders would be centralized on the French side by a technically private body grouping the *sinistrés;* this organization would then place the orders with a central German body, also technically private, which would distribute them to German industry. Prices would be set by direct agreement between the two bodies, or, if that were impossible, through arbitration. In the period up to May 1926, total payments in kind—that is, reconstruction material delivered through this system and other goods like coal whose delivery was governed by Annexes III, V and VI of the Treaty—could amount to 7 milliard gold marks. (Loucheur had originally wanted a 10 milliard figure for reconstruction goods alone.)[11]

The main problem here was that the value of such payments in kind would exceed the French share of the annuity. Unless something were done, France would have no right to any part of Germany's cash payment, which would go completely to the other creditors. To get around this difficulty, the Wiesbaden system provided a limit to the amount of reparation credit Germany could get in any year for all her payments in kind: no matter how much was delivered, the French reparation account would not be debited more than a milliard gold marks, and in no case would Germany get reparation credit for more than 45 percent of the value of reconstruction goods delivered through the Wiesbaden system. The balance would bear simple interest and would be repaid out of the French share of the reparation annuities over a ten-year period beginning in 1926.

A system of this sort was astonishingly favorable to France. For that very reason, it would have been surprising if it had ever taken effect without France having to pay some additional price both to Germany and to the other reparation creditors, who would obviously be penalized by what was in effect a disguised priority in favor of France. The British immediately objected to the scheme: they were not dissuaded by the French argument that only "private" bodies were involved, and therefore no one could legitimately oppose a "private" German loan to France.[12] Evidently, Loucheur had hoped at first to ignore British objections and put the plan into operation even without British assent, but when the Germans insisted on bringing the matter before the Reparation Commission for its approval, he changed his mind and accepted this procedure which in effect gave Britain a veto.[13] But the British insisted that before discussions for a revision of the Wiesbaden arrangements could even begin, the French government would have to ratify a convention for the apportionment of the first milliard paid by Germany.[14] On August 13 the French Minister of Finance, Doumer, in what was unquestionably a blunder, had signed this convention *ad referendum* (i.e., contingent on government approval). But because it contained provisions which would have prevented France from getting any share of the cash payment, the French government had refused to ratify it. It was not until March 1922 that these inter-Allied complications were finally resolved.[15]

Did the Germans also expect to be paid a price for their willingness to see the Wiesbaden accords actually put into effect? In so far as they were serious about their Wiesbaden promises—and Rathenau's relative indifference to the problems of financing these enormous deliveries at a time when budgetary problems were already unusually critical does suggest that his willingness to sign texts was not entirely serious—their aim was to relax the tension and pave the way for a "reasonable" settlement of the whole reparation question through a demonstration of good faith.[16] A direct exploitation of the Wiesbaden policy for other political ends was ruled out by Rathenau and Wirth; the relation of Wiesbaden to political questions like Upper Silesia was apparently to be more subtle. Instead of making the execution of the Wiesbaden agreement formally dependent, for example, on Germany's retention of all of Upper Silesia, Rathenau hinted at the desirability of French moderation on the latter question. When the decision on Silesia turned out to be unfavorable, German reparation policy hardened, and despite French pressure in 1922 the Wiesbaden agreement was never actually put into effect. Unless one assumes a surprising degree of discontinuity in the Wirth government's policy, it seems fair to suppose that a certain linkage between the Wiesbaden policy and larger political questions had existed all along.[17]

French policy is also somewhat unclear: given the absence of documentation, Briand's motivation at this point is largely a matter for conjecture. What were the implications of the Wiesbaden accords from the French point of view? It is unlikely that Briand pursued this policy as a means of preparing the way for a political entente with Germany: France did not take a pro-German line in the Upper Silesian affair, which next to reparation was then the most important political issue between France and Germany. French officials generally felt, moreover, that their willingness to facilitate German payment and provide orders to German industry was compensation enough for the great concessions Germany was making: there was no recognition of any need to pay an additional political price.[18] Nor is it probable that Briand's prime concern in pursuing the Wiesbaden accords was to improve relations with Britain: it was obvious that the accords would adversely affect British interests if they were ever put into effect.

Nevertheless, in a more indirect and less ambitious fashion, Briand's diplomacy was rooted in a desire for a relaxation of tensions with Germany and an improvement of relations with Britain. Tangible results, in the form of reparations in kind, would tend to lessen political pressure for extreme measures such as the occupation of the Ruhr: a direct confrontation with Germany, with Britain morally in the enemy's camp, was something that Briand sought above all to avoid. And indeed in late 1921 Briand turned more and more openly toward a policy of conciliation, praising Wirth and stressing France's moderation and the need to preserve her alliances.[19] His parliamentary majorities became increasingly centered on the moderate left. Much of the *Bloc National* majority was becoming alienated from the government—all the more so as it became clear that Briand's policy had failed in its objectives. As the hostile treatment of France at the Washington Conference on naval disarmament in late 1921 demonstrated, French moderation had not been appreciated by America or Britain. It was evident, for example from a speech that Curzon gave at the end of November, that relations between France and Britain were continuing to deteriorate. As far as Germany was concerned, the request for a moratorium showed that moderation had not worked: without outside pressure it seemed that Germany would never put her house in order and make a serious effort to pay.[20]

Briand was also increasingly isolated within his own government: the most important figures concerned with reparation—Loucheur, Seydoux, Millerand—were moving in exactly the opposite direction toward a more forceful policy. Even before the final Wiesbaden accord was signed, Loucheur and Seydoux vigorously condemned the prospect of a German default—a "faillite frauduleuse" they called it. A claim of bankruptcy would be fraudulent, they believed, not because the collapse of the mark had been deliberately engineered by the German officials. Rather, weak governments had passively drifted into those loose fiscal and foreign-exchange practices that were responsible for the decline of the mark—inefficient tax collection and lax control of capital exports, large subsidies, swollen bureaucracy and reliance on the printing press as a means of covering the deficit. Only after the fact had German leaders come to see the foreign-policy benefits of a collapse in foreign exchange. Seydoux stressed the responsibility of the "party of the big industrialists," who profited from the decline of the mark and were able to sabotage efforts to bring it under control: "as long as this situation lasts it is useless to hope to obtain from the German government a clear policy of paying the reparations."[21]

If this was the case, what then could France do about it? The answer was, in a word, "control." France should insist on a program of outside supervision, including controls over the German budget, on German foreign trade, and especially on the "scandalous" export of German capital—the "flight from the mark"—which was playing such an important role in the collapse of the mark. There was no question, of course, of outright intervention in the administration of Germany: the French word "contrôle" is somewhat looser than its English counterpart, connoting something closer to a right of observation than authority to give orders. But the institution of control meant the exercise of continuous, firm pressure on Germany to put her finances in order and save the mark.[22]

There is little doubt from a technical economic point of view that the French analysis was essentially correct. The creation of new money to meet budgetary deficits was the root cause of the German inflation. To be sure, this view was contested in public, at least by the Germans: it was not the increased supply of money but the trade deficit that supposedly was ultimately responsible for the decline of the mark.[23]

There is no need to resort to a study of trade statistics—of dubious validity in any case—to refute this thesis.[24] A trade deficit need have no effect on the exchange rate if the means exist to finance it; it is the overall balance of payments and not just the balance of trade which is the operative force in determining the exchange rate. But at any given point, actual payments are necessarily in balance (assuming, of course, that everything that amounts to a "payment" is taken into account). Any "deficit" has to be covered in some way, if only by the willingness of the rest of the world to increase its reserves of the debtor nation's currency or to postpone the time of payment—either eventuality is the equivalent of an outright loan.[25] Thus the actual balance of payments is zero—measurable credits equal measurable debits—for the same reason that more generally when markets clear supply and demand are equal. Thus no *actual* balance of payments deficit can explain the collapse of the mark because in the broadest sense no such "deficit" can even exist.

The *tendency,* however, for payments to exceed receipts was the immediate cause for the decline of the mark: if this were not the case, the mark would not have fallen. The real question here is the degree to which the potential payments deficit was an autonomous cause independent of fiscal policy and of changes in the supply of money. The answer is that it was only partly autonomous. For example, the decisions of investors and speculators to export capital were not entirely a function of monetary and fiscal policy, although the overall behavior of the authorities clearly had a significant bearing on the "flight from the mark." But equally obviously, there are limits to how far such "autonomous" factors can in themselves depress the exchange rate. A vigorous policy of monetary and fiscal restraint is certainly able to hold down internal prices. Generally speaking, to the degree that "autonomous" factors depress the exchange rate and create a gap between the internal and external value of a currency, countervailing forces are released which tend in the usual fashion to equalize prices and profits between foreign and domestic trade, thereby reducing the gap—the greater the divergence, the more powerful these forces are.[26]

Moreover, even to the degree that "autonomous" factors played a role in determining the exchange rate, the problem of the mark was not beyond the reach of government policy. The problems deriving from the export of capital, in particular, could be checked through the institution of tight controls over international investment and trade. Such controls are common in wartime, and a very complete system of licensing and border inspection to regulate trade and suppress the export of capital can easily be imagined.[27]

There was nothing impossible, therefore, about a stabilization of the mark from a purely technical economic point of view. The real question was its political and social feasibility. A deflationary policy is painful: high taxes, reduced services and large-scale unemployment are rarely popular. But could the evil day be put off forever? If the accelerating inflation was not to continue indefinitely—and few thought it could—was it not better to proceed to a stabilization of the mark at once? To wait for a complete collapse might be more painful in the long run.

Suppose, however, that a certain rate of inflation is desirable for social reasons. How does this affect the reparation problem? The greater the budgetary deficit deemed acceptable, the easier it is to finance reparation payments: resources devoted to reparation will maintain aggregate demand as well as any other sort of expenditure. If a level of inflation corresponds, moreover, to deliberate government policy, its existence is not a legitimate excuse for the non-payment of reparation. One cannot have it both ways, condemning reparation for being an element in the inflation while insisting that the inflation is necessary for social reasons.

Just as the stabilization of the mark was always theoretically possible, the imposition of a solution from the outside through the establishment of Allied financial control was conceivable from a purely technical economic point of view. Moreover, many in France believed that the Allies had the right to impose controls precisely because Germany was using the collapse of the mark as a way of evading her reparation obligations: such an excuse would have been valid only if these financial difficulties had been unavoidable. Again, the real problem was political: a control would be effective only if an intimidated Germany cooperated at least passively with it. But the general political situation seemed to be drifting in Germany's favor. Britain, America and Russia were increasingly sympathetic to Germany; France was weak and isolated. If this situation resulted in German obstruction, the control would fail no matter what texts were signed.

The question of control was to be at the very core of the politics of reparation for much of the period down to the beginning of 1923. Given the logic of the situation, the issue of control should have been even more important than it in fact was. It is clear that other aspects of the problem—a system for reparation in kind, the establishment of ''guarantees''—were subordinate to a resolution of the problem of the mark. What good was it to press for agreements like the Wiesbaden accord if the German government was unable to finance vast deliveries in kind on account of the budgetary crisis? What good was it to take over particular revenues for reparation while the inflation continued unchecked? If a ''guarantee'' raised paper marks, these sums could not be transferred to any significant degree lest the Allies be blamed for accelerating the collapse of the mark. If on the other hand, as in the case of the customs receipts and the export levy, foreign currency were raised, Germany would be deprived of resources which otherwise would have helped, in effect, to support the mark. In either case, the reparations would be blamed for the problems in the foreign exchange market. Moreover, depriving the German government of any of its revenues would in itself directly aggravate the budgetary problem. At best, the idea of "guarantees" was a partial solution, permitting the extraction of only bits and pieces of German wealth. A solution of the budgetary problem was necessary if the economic surplus that Germany as a whole was capable of producing was to be transferred through established government channels. Since there was no question of the creditors going in and directly exploiting the entire German economy themselves, a solution to the problem of the mark was essential. Given the inability or the unwillingness of the German government to solve it itself, the establishment of some degree of foreign control was the key to a resolution of the whole problem.

The logic of the problem was clear enough for the question of control to have been important in late 1921 and throughout 1922, but there were limits to how fully it was grasped. French efforts in this matter did not adequately correspond to its intrinsic importance: instead of concentrating their attention on implementing control, French officials allowed themselves to be distracted by other concerns, and repeatedly opportunities in this area were allowed to slip. After a while, because no effective control had been established, the idea itself came to seem increasingly chimerical; by July 1922 it had nearly fallen by the wayside. The idea of a direct seizure of guarantees became correspondingly more attractive. In this way, the failure to institute a system of control had a direct bearing on the decision to go into the Ruhr in January 1923.

But in late 1921 hopes were still high, and both Loucheur and Seydoux strongly urged that the French government elaborate a precise program of controls. Millerand, who in May had been irritated that Briand had abandoned plans for an occupation of the Ruhr, agreed with their analysis and urged that the Reparation Commission be allowed to go to Berlin only if a "complete program" had been put together.[28] Seydoux stressed the importance of France's taking the initiative; otherwise France would either have to defer to English wishes on the subject or see an Anglo-German bloc take shape: "It is the entire policy of France in Europe which is currently at stake."[29]

But what if the British resisted the policy of control? If the past was any guide, it was likely that the British government would oppose France on this matter. The idea of foreign control of German revenues and expenses had been in the air for some time—such a system was suggested by the example of the foreign debt commissions imposed on weak countries like Turkey and Egypt before the war.[30] But British opinion had rejected the "Ottomanization" of Germany—it was inconceivable to treat a nation like Germany in that way. Even provisions for "guarantees" (that is, for particular revenues, like the customs duties, specifically assigned to the payment of reparation), which implied the institution of certain controls to detect cheating, were resisted by British officials.[31] The argument was that such controls were not authorized by the treaty, but the real concern was not juridical: the British government was anxious as a matter of principle to avoid measures which might "infringe on German sovereignty."[32] It was for this reason that those provisions of the treaty which could be used to justify the institution of controls, Article 248 especially, had remained a deal letter.

The British attitude was particularly clear at the London Conference of late April and early May 1921. In return for agreeing not to go into the Ruhr, the French had apparently won British approval for a system of guarantees and controls: Article 7 of the Schedule of Payments provided for a subcommission of the Reparation Commission, the "Committee of Guarantees," to be set up to oversee these arrangements.[33]

Seydoux, who had called in mid-April for the imposition of budgetary controls on Germany, was pleased with the new scheme: he believed the "guarantees" would cover the whole debt, and Article 248 of the peace treaty would at last be taken seriously.[34] On both points he was to be disillusioned. There was nothing in fact in the text of the Schedule of Payments that required the guarantees to cover the whole debt, and the reference to Article 248—a simple provision charging the Committee of Guarantees with its enforcement—had not been taken seriously even by the French delegation at the London Conference.[35]

From the legal point of view, the Committee of Guarantees had no greater power in this regard than the Reparation Commission itself, since it was decided to present the Schedule of Payments as an application of, and not as a departure from, the treaty. Moreover, a clause was inserted providing that the Committee was not "authorized to interfere in German administration"—a similar clause in the Allied "Reply" to the German "Observations" in June 1919 had been to a large degree responsible for Article 248 remaining a dead letter.[36] In any event, the main problem was not legal and cannot be deduced from a textual analysis of the Schedule of Payments. The most limited "right of observation" could be used, if so desired, as a basis for the exertion of strong pressure: legally innocuous "remarks" or "suggestions" would have tremendous impact if it was evident that such views would, if ignored, lead to a declaration of voluntary default and thereby to an occupation of the Ruhr; on the other hand, the broadest grant of formal authority would lead to utterly ineffectual policy if the will to exercise it was absent. It was all a question of the spirit in which the new provisions were executed. In this respect the Schedule of Payments and the setting up of the Committee of Guarantees marked no change whatsoever. The committee concerned itself almost exclusively with the establishment of machinery for the control of export statistics and especially of the specific guarantees mentioned in the Schedule (the proceeds of which were not nearly enough to cover the annuity); on the more important question of the German budget, in spite of its obvious bearing on the whole reparation question, the pressure the committee was willing to exert was very mild indeed.[37] Even the French member of this body disliked the idea of suggesting the particular measures the German government might take to straighten out its finances: to complain about the inadequacy of German efforts was legitimate, but to go beyond that and say what should be done would be to take on a responsibility that more properly should remain with the German government.[38]

It was the failure of the Committee of Guarantees, already apparent to Seydoux in June,[39] that underlay efforts in late 1921 for the institution of a serious control of German state finance. Loucheur, who had publicly advocated such a policy on the eve of his coming to power in January 1921, was willing now even to break with the British over this matter. If they refused to go along, he said, "this would not be a sufficient reason for us to give in." Hopefully, this could be avoided, and he advocated a propaganda effort to win over British opinion: "The real source of the difficulty is the absolute lack of understanding of the situation on the part of most of those who speak of this question." But if these efforts proved futile, it would be necessary "to study a program of isolated action."[40]

Loucheur was bitter about the hostile British reaction to the Wiesbaden accords, and this perhaps explains why he was willing to go so far.[41] Seydoux had no love for the British either—their reaction to Wiesbaden confirmed his own hostile interpretation of their policy as designed as much to block Franco-German *rapprochement* as to prevent an outright confrontation—but he was still reluctant to contemplate a break over reparation.[42] He felt that some kind of compromise was essential, and proposed on December 5 that in exchange for French willingness to scale down the Schedule of Payments, the British should cancel the inter-Allied debt and agree to measures of control. A permanent control, he wrote on December 17, was necessary in any case to "replace military measures that we can no longer take"; in return for a French renunciation of force, the British would guarantee France military aid in the event of aggression.[43]

In December 1921 the immediate problem was how to deal with Germany's request for a partial moratorium. The British government sympathized with this request and indeed wanted to go further and give Germany "a considerable breathing space—say two years without payment other than deliveries in kind."[44] It hoped at first to circumvent any possible French obstruction by imposing a moratorium through a majority vote of the Reparation Commission; a Treasury official named Fass was sent to Brussels and Rome to organize what amounted to an anti-French coalition.[45] In addition, Bradbury threatened that Britain would withdraw from the Reparation Commission if she did not get her way.[46] The Fass mission was an utter failure. The Belgians were extremely hostile, and the Italians tried to sell their support at too high a price. The British were thus obliged to deal with France directly. On December 5, just after Fass's report from Brussels was received, Loucheur was invited to cross the Channel for a "preliminary personal and informal discussion."[47]

Why was the British government so eager for a moratorium? It was not that it disputed the French analysis of the German inflation. British officials generally, with the important exception of Lloyd George himself, agreed that the budgetary deficit was the root cause of the inflation, and that the German government was to blame for not doing enough about it. Proud of their own vigorous fiscal effort, they had little sympathy for the German argument that nothing more could be done. British representatives on the Reparation Commission and the Committee of Guarantees held Germany responsible for the problem. Bradbury in particular argued, in a letter to the Chancellor of the Exchequer in early November, that the moratorium should be used to oblige Germany to make a real effort: the moratorium could be suspended if it were found that Germany was not making adequate progress toward a stabilization of the mark.[48] Lord D'Abernon similarly argued over and over that the budgetary deficit, and not reparation, was responsible for the collapse of the mark, and that the Reparation Commission was "fully entitled to demand from the German Government pledges of serious financial reform as a return for the requisite alteration in the schedule of payments."[49] The Treasury as a whole had long seen things in the same light, and at the end of November and in early December Sir Robert Horne, the Chancellor of the Exchequer, proposed making the partial moratorium contingent on Germany's pursuing a deflationary policy.[50]

Neither Horne nor Bradbury realized how close their ideas were to the views of the French government. Their efforts were inspired by the mistaken belief that France really wanted to go into the Ruhr. It was for this reason that Horne tried to organize a coalition with Belgium and Italy so that a moratorium could be established by a majority vote, in spite of French opposition.[51] It was for similar reasons that Bradbury had gotten the Reparation Commission to press the German government to enter into negotiations for a loan. "The fact that the Commission has given the credits question so much attention makes it very difficult for us to say later, if the credits prove impossible to obtain, that it is possible for Germany to pay without them. If, on the other hand, the credits prove, owing to the position taken up by possible lenders, to be possible only upon a promise of a moratorium, the commission will, if it refuses to entertain the suggestion of a moratorium, find it difficult to report Germany for voluntary default." A moratorium was essential because a finding of voluntary default would "make drastic action by France almost inevitable," and although the threat of a Ruhr occupation was the "only pressure we can exact on the industrials," an actual occupation was of course to be avoided.[52]

Although British and French officials analyzed the problem of the mark in much the same way, there were important differences between the two governments on the question of actual policy. What could the Allies do to force Germany to mend her ways, and how tight a control should be imposed? The French were always willing to go much further than the British in this area. In the French view, mere warnings were futile: Germany had been warned repeatedly by the Reparation Commission and the Committee of Guarantees—the Reparation Commission, for example, had declared formally on December 2, 1921, that a default would have "serious consequences"—but when the moment of truth came, the British objected even to a finding of voluntary default. The imposition of new sanctions was completely out of the question. What incentive did the Germans have to respond to Reparation Commission pressure when experience had repeatedly demonstrated that threats and warnings had ultimately proven emply?[53]

The British objection to a finding of voluntary default was rooted in the belief that such action would inevitably lead to a "disaster of a most appalling character, the consequences of which no man can estimate."[54] Of course, there had been declarations of voluntary default before which had had little effect on the situation. But now it seemed that the Briand government had locked itself into a rigid position of using force in the event of default: in such a case, Briand had publicly asserted in May, sanctions would be applied automatically, if necessary by France alone.[55] It was hardly likely that these declarations had been meant seriously, nor does it seem probable that after all their experience with Briand in the first part of 1921 that the British government took them at face value. Perhaps the British were worried that after a finding of default the political pressure to invade the Ruhr would be irresistible in France.

In any case, the British attitude effectively ruled out a finding of default, and the result of this was to weaken the Allies' hand in exerting pressure on Germany. For suppose there had been a declaration of voluntary default (and according to the British analysis the default had been a result of German policy and therefore voluntary). The Allies could then have said that they were legally entitled to impose territorial sanctions, but if Germany agreed, they would be willing as a concession to settle for a system of control instead. If, however, there were no voluntary default, but only a moratorium conditioned on Germany's making an "adequate" effort in the budgetary area, the exercise of pressure would be much more difficult. How could the moratorium be revoked and Germany be required to make an enormous immediate payment, the Germans would certainly argue, when the Reparation Commission had only granted the moratorium in the first place because it recognized Germany's incapacity to pay? Without a formal finding that Germany had defaulted voluntarily and thus had violated the treaty, what legal right would the Allies have to go beyond the treaty and encroach on German financial sovereignty?

In holding back from the kind of policy that could have laid the basis for an effective control of German finances, the British government of course had more in mind than the effect on France of a finding of voluntary default. Whatever the French reaction, the British were reluctant to impose a tight control on Germany, and it is important to realize that political and not economic considerations dictated British policy in this area. The economic analysis suggested that outside control was the only answer; but the British attitude was, as one Foreign Office official put it (with regard to a particularly severe and detailed condemnation of German financial policy issued by the Committee of Guarantees in late October) that broader political considerations should take priority over "the somewhat technical arguments of the financial experts."[56] Because its policy had all along been concerned, in the words of another British official, with avoiding "any appearance of intervention in German domestic affairs," the British government was always inclined to give Germany another chance to work out its problems itself. Default was an argument not for increased pressure, but for a "breathing space" and for cutting down Germany's obligations to a "reasonable" level so that Germany would finally have an incentive to put her finances in order and pay off her debt.[57]

The obvious criticism here was that such a policy, which in effect rewarded noncompliance in the past, would give Germany an incentive for continuing to evade her treaty obligations. But those who advocated a policy of trust believed that apart from all considerations of foreign policy, Germany had an overwhelming interest in the resolution of her financial problems. If the reparation figures were sufficiently scaled down, the German government, encouraged now that a solution was within grasp, would proceed at once to voluntarily put her finances in order. It was scarcely conceivable that the German government could deliberately allow the mark to collapse; given the utter imporance of stabilization to Germany itself, it would not take all that much to turn the situation around.

French views were more pessimistic. Loucheur, who came over to London twice in December, the second time with Briand, on each occasion brought up the question of control.[58] Lloyd George and his principal collaborators agreed that Germany had to put her affairs in order, yet they did everything they could at these meetings in London and at the formal Allied conference held in Cannes the following month to water down the French proposals. Lloyd George admitted that legally France was entitled to go further and occupy the Ruhr. But if France did this, or even only insisted on Loucheur's more moderate proposals for control, "France must go alone on the way which she had chosen for herself." If, on the other hand, Anglo-French cooperation was to be maintained, there could be no "fresh ultimatum," no "violent pressure on Germany" which "would simply result in hurling that country into bankruptcy" with "incalculable" effects "throughout the world." In no case could an Allied commission be granted "the kind of powers which it would be necessary to give to a financial body entrusted with the control of finances in countries like Turkey and China." Loucheur tried to evade the problem: the French, he said, did not propose "to 'Turkify' Germany. The only question was how to secure effective control." The experts should be able to work out a suitable formula.[59]

Two days later the experts Blackett and Tannery had been able to reach agreement on a draft of the terms for the moratorium. Their report called for a vigorous German policy to balance the budget and "stop abuses in the matter of export of capital." As far as control was concerned, this document provided for only one thing, the appointment of a "technical advisor" mutually acceptable to the Reichsbank and the Reparation Commission with power to veto the creation of new money.[60] Although this represented a considerable reduction from the original French program, this provision was potentially of overwhelming importance: the limitation of the money supply was the key to the stabilization of the mark.

Lloyd George did not like this provision. It "seemed to him to amount to internal interference in Germany." Nevertheless, although nothing was actually signed so as to avoid antagonizing Belgium and Italy, it is clear that the entire document was accepted as binding by Britain and France.[61]

However, when the Allies met in Cannes in January 1922 to agree formally on the terms of the moratorium, British delegates began to express second thoughts about the control provision contained in the London Memorandum, as the experts' report was called. On January 6, Bradbury opposed the plan for a "technical adviser" with real power, and in general he felt that the Reparation Commission's responsibility for, and therefore authority over, Germany's finances should be minimized. The next day Horne took a similar line: he was "opposed to stringent control." Loucheur replied that "it was necessary to have the courage to assume one's responsibilities. . . . To confine oneself to giving advice to Germany was no solution of the problem. Within a year the same situation would arise. The French delegation could not then agree to the grant of facilities for payment in the year 1922 unless at the same time new guarantees were exacted. It could not be forgotten that the present German government was too weak itself to take measures which were imperative unless they were dictated to it by the Allies."[62] But two days later, on January 9, when Horne openly opposed the idea of a "technical adviser"—"he wanted as little control and as much goodwill as possible"—Loucheur gave in. He agreed that the alternative of making the Reichsbank autonomous (i.e., free of direct government control), should be explored first in talks with the Germans.[63]

Thus France, in deference to Britain, had given in again. The cycle which had culminated in the Schedule of Payments had just been repeated. Before a default was formally registered, the French were told they had no legal right to force Germany to make a real effort to pay; after payment ceased, they were told nothing could be done about the past and that Germany should be given another chance. Control, the British argued, could do no good; direct coercion was out of the question; if France did not comply with British wishes in these matters the Alliance would come to an end. It was a measure of France's weakness that she had deferred to Britain for so long. A stronger nation would not have hesitated to break out of the cycle.

To be sure, it was not that Briand had gotten nothing in return for his concessions. The British were now willing to accept a modified version of the Wiesbaden agreement, and, more important, to sign a formal treaty of guarantee with France.[64] The French, who had brought up the question of a treaty in early December and were very eager for such a pact, wanted, in Briand's words, "a very broad Alliance in which the two Powers would guarantee each other's interests in all parts of the world, act closely together in all things and go to each other's assistance whenever these things were threatened."[65] The French aim was to extend the alliance to the case of "indirect aggression"—that is, to assure British assistance in the event Germany moved east against Poland or Czechoslovakia. But Lloyd George consistently refused to undertake any commitment for the defense of the "unstable and excitable" nations of eastern Europe. As a way out of the impasse, Briand on December 21 suggested the idea of a consultative agreement. Such a pact, he said, might even include Germany.[66]

Meanwhile Lloyd George had been trying to win French support for a new proposal of his for international cooperation on reconstruction. Governments for too long, he believed, had been preoccupied with relatively narrow questions such as reparation. The really important problem of the economic reconstruction of Europe had been neglected. The time had come to organize a frontal attack on that problem. It was essential to open up the markets of eastern Europe, and of Russia in particular, to foreign trade. He proposed a scheme for an international corporation to finance and carry out the work of reconstruction. Germany would participate, with part of her profits from the work in Russia going to pay her reparation debt. For Germany to pay in general she would need to secure markets for her exports, and thus in the long run the sole answer to the reparation problem was "to open up Eastern and Central Europe to German trade." Only by going beyond the immediate problem of a provisional arrangement with Germany could the problem of reparation, and indeed the whole European economic problem, be solved.[67]

Lloyd George's basic idea was that the way to solve problems was to link them up with each other. Unemployment in Britain, reparation, and the economic difficulties of eastern Europe were mutually interdependent and had to be dealt with in a single, all-encompassing negotiation process. For a time he felt he could bring in the question of the inter-Allied debt as well. It was likely, he told Loucheur in early December, that America would cooperate on these larger economic matters. If she did, Britain would cancel France's debt to her and waive most of her share of the reparations. Indeed, American participation was "an absolutely essential condition" for the success of his scheme—a view he later abandoned when the United States refused to take part.[68]

He continued after the turn of the year to pursue his basic tactic of solving problems by connecting them together. Now a broad array of the most important political questions was brought into the picutre. Economic assistance to Russia was a way of facilitating her drift back to capitalism (Lloyd George was deeply impressed by the implications of Lenin's New Economic Policy) and encouraging her reintegration into the European political order.[69] Diplomatic recognition, and eventual Russian participation in the European security system, were tied to provisions for reconstruction assistance and the protection of foreign capital.

The original British scheme in fact went further and insisted in more general terms that "the rights of private ownership in real and personal property and private enterprise must be recognized"; at Cannes, Russian participation in the plan was made conditional on Soviet acceptance of the property rights of foreign investors.[70] The reconstruction syndicates would have extensive powers of control over Russian railways. In return, the Soviet regime would be officially recognized—providing it accepted the conditions the Allied Powers laid down.[71] There was no point, Lloyd George thought, in being too categorical about this; it was unwise to insist that the Soviets accept the conditions before they were allowed to attend the international conference to be held in Genoa that was to work out the plan. But the Soviet representatives would have to accept the Allies' terms in the end: the economic situation in Russia was so desperate, he told the Czech statesman Beneš in February, that "if Lenin came back from Genoa with nothing in his hands, he would be overthrown."[72]

Another condition, brought up for the first time in Cannes in January, was of an intensely political nature: "All countries should join in an undertaking to refrain from aggression against their neighbors."[73] This proposal, which was to be binding on everybody, was apparently a response to Briand's earlier idea of a broad consultative agreement, the heart of which would be a renewed entente between Britain and France.[74] This did not mean, however, that a general nonaggression pact was conceived as an alternative to a more binding commitment—that Lloyd George, in other words, was willing to go only this far and no further. When Briand at Cannes proposed that the nonaggression agreement could be expanded into a general European consultative pact, Lloyd George agreed, insisting only that "the dangerous powers like Russia, Germany, Poland and Hungary" be parties to the accord. Such a system, Briand said, would "be a powerful system to stop war." Both Briand and Lloyd George agreed that this system would be "more practical than the League of Nations."[75]

A renewed Anglo-French entente, Briand said, would be the keystone of the new system. "A solid and serious agreement of long duration", he said, was essential, and Lloyd George agreed that a bargain on a grand scale, on the lines of the famous 1904 agreement, was what was needed. Britain would guarantee French security and give France certain advantages in the apportionment of reparation (mainly by approving the Wiesbaden agreement); in return France would have to limit submarine construction, and cooperate with Britain on the question of Greece and Turkey, on Tangier, and on European reconstruction. In particular, France would have to agree "to the summoning of a European economic conference" at which the Soviet regime would be represented.[76]

Lloyd George spoke of the 1904 agreement, and it is true that the new bargain he proposed was similar in scope to the original entente. But the spirit of give-and-take epitomized by the 1904 agreement no longer characterized British policy. Britain was not willing to concede very much in 1922: her position was so strong that she felt she did not have to. In the event of a German thrust to the west, Britain in her own interest would have come to the assistance of France even without a treaty.[77] In the more likely event that Germany used force to change the status quo in the east, Britain still would not be committed to pursue any particular policy. The concession on reparation meant little: both Germany's willingness and ability to put the Wiesbaden arrangements into effect had been dubious since late 1921.

On the other hand, the advantages to Britain would be enormous. French policy in the Near East, long a great irritant to the British, would now be brought into line.[78] At least since late 1920, the French had been trying to use the Eastern Question as a lever for obtaining British support in their dealings with Germany. This attempt would now be frustrated.[79] The Treaty of Guarantee would in fact be a powerful means of influencing French policy in every area. Lloyd George had already warned the French in December that independent action toward Germany could break the entente; in March he frankly told the cabinet that "he hoped to use the Anglo-French Pact to make the French behave decently toward the Germans on the question of Reparations."[80]

Thus at the beginning of 1922 Lloyd George was pursuing an extremely ambitious and wide-ranging policy. Within Britain his political position had been deteriorating since the armistice, and he scarcely concealed the fact that the success of at least a large part of his program was of great domestic importance to him.[81]

In France, on the other hand, the drift of events had generated increasing concern. France, it seemed, was in danger of becoming a British satellite. The growing opposition to Briand now came to a head. While his prime minister was at Cannes, Millerand led what amounted to a revolt in Briand's own cabinet. The President of the Republic, who had long been unhappy with Briand's policy, now objected strongly to two features of the agreement setting out the conditions for an international economic conference. He complained that Soviet representatives would not have to accept the Cannes conditions in order to take part in the conference, and he was worried that a general nonaggression pact would deprive France of the right of taking military sanctions against Germany. A sharp exchange of telegrams followed. The two men also disagreed on the moratorium question. Briand wired Millerand on January 9 that the cabinet should have the final word in this matter. He did not want to take responsibility for a rupture with Britain which a refusal of the moratorium would entail. The next day Millerand convened the cabinet. It supported the President on all points; in particular, the moratorium conditions were inadequate. (Loucheur had given in to Horne on the question of guarantees the previous day.) This decision, Millerand wired Briand, would create problems, especially with the negotiations for a guarantee pact. But Millerand no longer had much faith in the British, and in his eyes the guarantee pact was of limited value anyway.[82]

Briand immediately replied that his question had not been answered: should he break with Britain over reparation or not? The following morning the cabinet met this point head on. It accepted the principle of a moratorium. But in exchange, Millerand wrote Briand, it insisted on something more solid than just a new "piece of paper" guaranteed only by the "word of Germany." It still believed that guarantees were essential. If the negotiations were to fail as a result of this attitude, the cabinet would accept full responsibility.[83]

Briand returned to Paris on January 12. The views of Millerand and the anti-Briand group of ministers apparently reflected the feelings of the Parliament as a whole, and Briand saw at once that the situation was hopeless. His departure from office was dramatic. With great skill he defended his policy to the Chamber, but suddenly, to everyone's surprise, he declared: "Others will do better." He immediately left the hall; there was no vote. On that very evening, January 12, the newspapers announced the resignation of Briand's seventh ministry.[84]

Poincaré
Chapter Seven
in Power

AFTER BRIAND'S resignation, Millerand asked Poincaré to form a new government. He was the obvious choice. The tough line that Poincaré symbolized conformed to strong sentiment, particularly in Parliament, for a more forceful policy on reparation. In the past, it was felt, France had given in repeatedly. But these concessions had only served to weaken France's general position, and had not even prevented the continual deterioration of relations with Britain. Now at last something would be done to turn the situation around. In Britain, however, the prospect of a hardening of French policy generated a certain anxiety; and in Germany, the press reaction to Poincaré's coming to power was so violent that Laurent was instructed to intercede with the German government.[1]

These expectations—hopes in the one case and fears in the other—were to prove exaggerated. In his first months in office, Poincaré showed no inclination to break with the British, and even continued to negotiate for an Anglo-French alliance.[2] Like his predecessors, he hoped to solve the reparation problem by means of a vast credit operation: reparation bonds would be sold to foreign investors. This was in fact to be a constant and central aspect of his policy from the very beginning right down to the eve of the Ruhr occupation in January 1923.[3] Linked to this was his insistence on the establishment of a control of Germany's finances. Loans could be floated only if it was clear that Germany was not heading toward bankruptcy, and since Germany had been unwilling to solve her budgetary problem herself, Allied intervention in this area was essential. Some infringement on Germany's fiscal autonomy was, in his view, the price she would have to pay for even a partial moratorium, and in the first half of 1922 Poincaré concentrated his attention on the question of control.[4]

This emphasis on financial control and on the "mobilization" of the debt through a large-scale credit operation marked no new departure in French thinking on reparation. Clemenceau in 1919, Millerand in 1920, and Briand in 1921 had all found the idea of a "mobilization" attractive. The idea of an Allied financial control had of course been developed within the Briand government by Loucheur and Seydoux. In other areas as well, the continuity of reparation doctrine from 1921 to 1922 is striking. On reparation in kind (to Poincaré a "secondary but important" means of payment),[5] the new government for the most part continued the policy of its predecessor. The new Minister of the Liberated Regions, Charles Reibel, endorsed Loucheur's general policy and declared in the Chamber that the Wiesbaden accords "must be upheld."[6]

The Wiesbaden system, however, was to be altered somewhat. Reibel, like Seydoux, wanted a less bureaucratic and more commercial regime.[7] The accords on reparation in kind were modified accordingly through new agreements with the Germans on March 15 and June 6–9, 1922.[8] And, in another area as well, doctrine on reparation in kind underwent a certain development. In the middle of the year Yves Le Trocquer, the longtime Minister of Public Works, proposed a scheme of large-scale public works projects for Germany to carry out as a way of paying reparation.[9] This scheme was endorsed by Poincaré himself.[10]

But the new plans for payment in kind were not put into effect. This was not due to any lack of interest on Poincaré's part. Beginning July 12, he repeatedly pressed for the application of the agreements on reparation in kind and for negotiations on the Le Trocquer plan: repeatedly, the German government, on one pretext or another, evaded these requests. It was not until December 22 that the French ambassador in Berlin wired Poincaré that in the view of the German government the modified Wiesbaden accords had finally taken effect. Negotiations on the Le Trocquer plan had still not even begun.[11]

In the past, reparation in kind had been linked to the idea of industrial collaboration, and the Poincaré government, like its predecessor, was apparently interested in this question as well. In the spring of 1922, the French steel industry twice made overtures to its German counterpart. It is unlikely that it was acting entirely on its own initiative. In dealing with Germany, French industry could redress its economic inferiority only by exploiting France's politically advantageous position: French industry—timid in any case, as the Upper Silesian affair had shown[12]—was structurally dependent on government support. Moreover, the Comité des Forges leadership had close personal ties with Millerand, Laurent and Seydoux. It is therefore hard to believe that the Poincaré government was not in some way involved with these overtures. The reaction of the Ruhr magnates was just as intransigent as it had been when earlier French governments had been in power: there would be no negotiation as long as the occupation lasted.[13]

By the late summer French officials had apparently ruled out the idea of a friendly agreement with German industry. A more forceful policy was needed to lay the groundwork for an eventual industrial entente. Le Trocquer wrote in July that France should take control of the Ruhr mines: this would have "a happy influence on projects for a Franco-German economic rapprochement, the importance of which is not in question."[14] And Seydoux in August argued that "after having demonstrated our willingness to use force if necessary, we will be able to use the method of 'energetic collaboration.' "[15] When at the end of the year, with the prospect of a Ruhr occupation in sight, Stinnes finally proposed to come to Paris, Poincaré refused to receive him.[16] It was too late: the test of strength had to precede an industrial understanding.

Thus in all the main areas, French reparation doctrine was not fundamentally changed by Poincaré's coming to power, and the view that Poincaré sought from the beginning to break with Britain and Germany is clearly untenable. There was no headlong rush toward an occupation of the Ruhr: in Poincaré's view, such a move would not be lucrative[17] and was to be used only as a last resort. Similarly, the Poincaré government hoped at first to pursue a common policy with

Britain. Discord was due to misunderstanding. Once the British saw what the new ministry really wanted, Allied cooperation would once again be possible. Seydoux, for example, argued on February 2 "that if we present to our Allies a practical, constructive and possible plan for the payment of reparation, they will be the first to support us, and we will then be able to get the Germans to accept it voluntarily.[18]

In the area of reparation doctrine, therefore, the replacement of Briand by Poincaré had little effect. What set Poincaré apart from his predecessors was the increased vigor he demonstrated in trying to apply his policy. At the beginning of 1922 control was the central issue. Lasteyrie, the new Minister of Finance, as a deputy in December 1921 had called for a tough program of controls; Poincaré said he had been brought into the government in order to put this program into effect.[19]

For legal reasons, however, this was difficult. Following Briand's resignation, the Reparation Commission, acting on its own authority, had granted a partial moratorium for the January and February 1922 payments. No concessions regarding control were exacted; all the German government had to do was submit within fifteen days "a scheme of budget and currency reform, with appropriate guarantees, as well as a complete programme of cash payments and deliveries in kind for the year 1922." The period of partial moratorium would end when the Commission took a decision on this program.[20]

The Commission felt it had no choice but to act in this way. A default had to be prevented, and because of the political crisis in France, there was not enough time for the governments to act and lay down the conditions for the year-long moratorium. The Commission felt that it lacked sufficient authority to decide such a crucial matter itself. In theory, only a short period of time would be lost: the terms would be laid down when the Reparation Commission took its decision on the German program. A threat to revoke the moratorium and oblige Germany to pay her entire back debt under the Schedule of Payments would force the Germans to accept these terms. But in practice the Allied position had been weakened. Once granted, the moratorium proved difficult to revoke: by granting it had the Allies not admitted Germany's incapacity to pay? It was easier for the Germans to reject Allied conditions after the moratorium had been accorded than it would have been if the original granting of the moratorium had been made contingent on acceptance of the Allies' terms.

In spite of these difficulties, Poincaré began to press in February for a more forceful policy of control. The German program of reform, submitted on January 28, was viewed as patently inadequate, particularly on the question of control.[21] On February 2, Poincaré ordered Dubois, the French delegate on the Reparation Commission, to press for the establishment of a system of budgetary, monetary and foreign exchange controls; if the necessary reforms were not effective by a certain date (e.g., June 1), sanctions would immediately enter into play. The legal basis for this was the Reparation Commission's letter of December 2, 1921, which had warned of "serious consequences" in the event of nonpayment: "The Commission certainly understood by that that if it granted a delay, it would in exchange impose conditions on the Reich which, at least to a certain degree, would infringe on the fiscal autonomy of Germany. I can even affirm *confidentially* that this was at the time the opinion of your British colleague Sir John Bradbury, who wrote to me in this sense."[22]

Dubois, convinced that the British would obstruct any attempt to institute controls, did little to comply with Poincaré's wishes.[23] On February 25, he told a meeting of high French officials that the French Delegation did not even have a program of controls: "If it is demonstrated that Germany can pay, he will request purely and simply the application of the Schedule of Payments. Beyond that he cannot at present affirm anything."[24]

This point of view ignored the whole evolution of official thinking on the way of dealing with Germany's default, and Poincaré began to handle Dubois roughly. At a meeting on March 4, Poincaré, focusing on the question of control, declared that "we are at a most critical turning point. If the Reparation Commission does not succeed in establishing a control, it will be broken by the French Government itself. He will go before the Chambers. This is said in a definitive manner, and he will not accept any more discussion on this point."[25]

In letters of March 7 and March 17, Poincaré continued to hammer away at Dubois. He was upset at the constant loss of time: Dubois knew the importance the government attached to the swift organization of a system of controls.[26] By the time he received this second letter, Dubois had given in to the pressure. On March 17, his program for controls was ready.[27] This scheme provided for a relatively tight set of controls, particularly over the money supply. The proposed budgetary controls were somewhat looser: the Reparation Commission would not be able to veto German expenditures.

The actual scheme adopted by the Reparation Commission on March 21 was watered down further. Although the Commission ordered a vast increase in German taxation, the provisions for control did not go beyond the establishment of an Allied right of observation. The Reichsbank was merely to be made autonomous; no foreign authority would be able to veto an expansion of the money supply. Germany was to try to reduce expenditures, and was asked to submit a plan to regulate the export of capital. Under these conditions, a partial moratorium for 1922 would be temporarily granted. On May 31, the Commission would decide how well these conditions had been met, and whether the moratorium should be maintained or revoked—a revocation would virtually force a default.[28]

The procedure instituted by the March 21 decision conformed above all to the wishes of the British. Bradbury was especially pleased with these "quite moderate proposals not extending beyond the right of examination, criticism and censure." "The French," he said, had "fought obstinately for incorporating a lot of fantastic machinery which would probably have come near to bringing German foreign trade to a standstill without effecting their purpose," and he was glad that their attempt to control the export of capital had been defeated.[29] For the moment, the Allies had again chosen to trust the German government to make the necessary financial effort. If it failed to do so this time, Bradbury wrote, Germany would be exposed to Allied coercive measures, "which, however disastrous in their results they may be to all parties concerned, are the only ultimate sanction for intractibility." If "reasonably satisfactory results are not immediately forthcoming," the Allied governments would be obliged in particular to take action that "cannot leave intact the fiscal autonomy of the German people."[30]

Although to Bradbury the March 21 decision was a moderate document, its publication set off a tremendous protest in Germany. The very notion of "control" was enough to excite nationalist fury, even though in practice no authority was to be surrendered. Wirth and Rathenau felt the time had come to oppose the Allies openly. A violent Allied reaction would compromise the Genoa Conference. Lloyd George would therefore not permit it. On April 7, the German government formally rejected the Reparation Commission's terms.[31]

Now a real crisis was brewing. May 31 was the new *date fatidique*. If the Reparation Commission decided to force a default, France would act. Plans for the occupation of the Ruhr were elaborated in detail.[32] If Britain resisted, and the Reparation Commission declared a voluntary default only by a majority vote, France would act even in defiance of Britain: this was the message Poincaré proclaimed in a much-quoted speech at Bar-le-Duc on April 24.[33]

The tension had been greatly increased by the dramatic signing of the Treaty of Rapallo on April 16. The French right reacted violently to this "act of provocation." The two enemies of France, it seemed, had now joined hands; their ultimate aim was to destroy the Europe of Versailles.[34]

The Rapallo treaty, moreover, had apparently wrecked the Genoa Conference—although it is dubious whether much could have come out of the conference in any case. American non-participation meant that nothing could be done on the war debt question. Reparation had been ruled out even before Briand's fall, and Poincaré rigidly blocked attempts to bring it in formally; private talks on the subject at Genoa between Bergmann and Seydoux, fruitless in any case, did not bear on the key question of control.[35] As for the basic idea of an international syndicate for the reconstruction of Russia, this was fiercely opposed by the Soviet leadership itself: their fundamental aim of dividing the capitalist world was not exactly consistent with attempts to bring the capitalist powers together in a consortium for Russian reconstruction.[36] Nevertheless, in Britain, France was blamed for the collapse of the Genoa talks.[37] If only France had been more conciliatory toward Germany and Russia, those two powers would not have resorted to their defiant gesture. The French were bitter that Britain had reacted in this way. German and Russian responsibility was so obvious, that pinning the blame on France revealed Britain's complete absence of sympathy for the French point of view. There was not much hope that the British attitude would change—if Rapallo could not convince the British that France had been right about Germany, nothing would. Poincaré began to abandon his earlier illusions about the possibility of British cooperation.[38] His sensational speech at Bar-le-Duc was a clear indication of the evolution of his attitude toward France's chief ally.

The British point of view at this time, however, was by no means clear-cut. Germany, in fact, was blamed for the reparation crisis. "The root of the trouble," Bradbury declared at a cabinet meeting on May 23, "was the gross mismanagement of Germany's public finances." D'Abernon agreed: "The management of German finances was extraordinarily bad." Churchill, earlier the most pronounced Germanophile in the government, had now reversed his position: "The tale of German woes left him cold, and he wondered how far it might be Germany's policy deliberately to deprive us of what she could and ought to pay." But what should be done? Continued indulgence hardly seemed the proper policy, but coercive measures might do more harm than good. "It was difficult to take a definite line," Austen Chamberlain said, "in view of the fact that the reason why Germany cannot pay is Germany's own wasteful handling of her resources." Lloyd George, however, was afraid that forcing a deflationary policy on Germany would result in a "terrific collapse," and possibly in revolution—the efficient Germans would "run their revolution in ways which would be much more attractive to our people" than the Bolsheviks had.[39]

Thus on balance the British government still inclined to the side of moderation, and its representative on the Reparation Commission took the lead in working out arrangements to resolve the crisis. A solution was possible because the German attitude had softened. The more moderate Germans had seen all along that the March 21 terms "upon closer inspection proved to be more or less empty phrases and no really effective control of revenue and expenditure was demanded."[40] Negotiations on the basis of the Reparation Commission note were not inconsistent with German honor; if coercive measures could thereby be averted, such negotiations were utterly desirable.

It was Andreas Hermes, the German Minister of Finance, who now championed this relatively moderate point of view. Wirth and Rathenau still wanted to take a more defiant line. The split in the cabinet was unusually sharp, heightened by a fierce conflict over the Rapallo treaty. Nevertheless Hermes was allowed to go to Paris to see what could be done. He was able to work out an agreement with the Reparation Commission providing for a mild control of German finance, really nothing more than a right to observe and make comments. Various loose promises were made with an eye to limiting the expansion of the money supply; the demand for an immediate vast increase in taxation was dropped. All of this was contingent on Germany's getting a foriegn loan: if no loan came through, a new arrangement would be necessary.[41]

These arrangements were obviously favorable to Germany. Wirth and Rathenau, though angry that Hermes had made policy without consulting them, were finally willing to accept the scheme. Wirth felt the government had no choice: if the plan were rejected, foreigners would say that Germany was not doing its utmost. Rathenau was more sympathetic. The prospect of a foreign loan was attractive, and it now seemed that contrary to what an important British official (Blackett) had told him, the French might actually be ready to march.[42]

In Britain these new proposals were viewed as very generous to Germany. Bradbury's one "misgiving was that his proposals erred on the side of kindness."[43] He set out his reasoning in a letter to the Treasury written a couple of months later. He felt strongly "that effective guarantees must be obtained for the stoppage of further inflation." But he remained "completely skeptical as to the usefulness of endeavours either to dictate the details of German fiscal legislation, to exercise a veto over public expenditure or actively to interfere in administration. Control on such lines would, if it were made really complete, involve the government of Germany by the Allies as a conquered country: if incomplete it would be ineffective." The best policy, therefore, would be "to set Germany a task which is capable of accomplishment and to leave her responsible for the precise methods by which it is to be accomplished, but to take drastic action if she fails to carry it out."[44]

Bradbury was, it seems, willing to force Allied acceptance of his proposals through a threat of resignation.[45] And it seems clear that in general the British still felt strong enough to impose their views on France. Curzon, for example, noted in a May 22 memorandum that the British position was "not without advantage." If the French, even with Belgian support, acted without Britain, "the onus and the odium of breaking the *Entente* would then devolve publically upon them. They will not do it. For Poincaré would at once fall."[46]

It is impossible to tell whether Curzon was right. The Belgians supported the arrangements worked out with Hermes. There was thus no possibility of a majority Reparation Commission decision to declare a voluntary default. (If Belgium had sided with France against Britain supported by Italy, the tie vote would have been broken by the vote of the French chairman.) Poincaré was still unwilling to act outside the legal framework established by the Treaty of Versailles: without a formal declaration of voluntary default, France would not go into the Ruhr.

Moreover, Poincaré's own policy at this point is somewhat unclear. He certainly was not happy with the course and outcome of the negotiations with Germany. On May 26 he wrote Dubois that the arrangement was inadequate; the control of German finances had to be "completely precise and rigorous." Procedures for the exercise of control needed to be specified in such detail "that no misunderstanding can later arise on this subject." On May 28 he wrote that "it would be useless to reach agreement with the German government on how to apply laws authorizing the squandering of the Reich's resources." Finally, on May 31, he objected to the provision making the restoration of budgetary equilibrium depend on Germany's first getting a foreign loan. This was putting the cart before the horse. First Germany should balance her budget; only then could she conceivably get a loan to stabilize the mark. He condemned the "loopholes" ("*échappatoires*") in the draft agreement—the usual phrases regarding German sovereignty and noninterference in German administration. It was true that in the past the British interpretation of such provisions had prevented any serious control from being implemented. The establishment of control was now so important that this could not be allowed to happen again in the future; "the most minute precautions on this subject are necessary, for there is no doubt that only measures of control will allow us to prevent the government of the Reich from finding new ways of getting around the rules which we impose on it and the payment plans which we have prepared."[47]

To Poincaré, extreme caution in drafting the provisions relating to control was necessary because Germany could not be trusted. Bradbury of course tended to agree, and for that reason had made the ultimate resort to coercion an essential part of his approach to the question. But by this time French leaders had come to believe that when the moment came British leaders would always draw back; to acquiesce in their policy would simply encourage Germany in her defiance. Lloyd George and his associates, Poincaré was coming to believe, simply could not be trusted. His anxiety for precision at this time was rooted as much in distrust of the British as in his belief in Germany's bad faith: "I insist once again that the conditions in which the Committee of Guarantees will exercise its control be perfectly precise and unambiguous: without that, the Germans and our Allies themselves will be able to use textual interpretations to reduce to nothing the guarantees supposedly granted us."[48]

In spite of Poincaré's misgivings, the Commission adopted the proposed scheme without change through an exchange of notes with Germany on May 28 and May 31.[49] The partial moratorium was confirmed for the rest of the year. Is it to be inferred from all this that the arrangements were adopted by a majority of the Commission, contrary to the express wishes of the French delegate? The Commission's vote was unanimous. It is possible that this was for show and that the real vote had come before, in unofficial talks. But there is no reference to even the *propsect* of France's being outvoted in the relevant documents at the Quai d'Orsay or in the archives of the French delegation to the Reparation Commission.[50] There was no outburst of anger at this time over any Belgian "desertion"; sharp complaints about the behavior of the Belgian delegate were only made a few weeks later, when he sided against France in another matter.[51]

Was the compliant behavior of France in the Reparation Commission then due to the fact that Dubois was pursuing his own policy independent of the government? Although Dubois personally felt more positive about the new arrangements than did Poincaré (as their correspondence at this time demonstrates),[52] this explanation is hardly tenable. The delegate on the Reparation Commission was essentially a tool of the government, bound by official instructions. There is no evidence that Dubois actually defied the government—no reprimand, for example, for voting to adopt the new arrangements.

The best explanation for French policy seems to be that Poincaré's attitude was not quite as clearly defined as his correspondence with Dubois might indicate. He does not appear to have fought very hard for the point of view expressed in his letters. It seems in fact that the solution reached at the end of May, while distasteful and inadequate, was by no means intolerable to him. Perhaps he felt that the loose system of controls called for had to be set up first before a tighter system could be instituted, if only to convince the British that stronger measures were ultimately necessary; in spite of everything, some remnant of trust in Britain's good faith may have still remained. The agreement worked out with Hermes was more acceptable, at least for the time being, than the only real alternative available to him—that of immediate rupture with Britain.

Poincaré and his government, moreover, still believed that a large-scale credit operation—mostly for the "mobilization" of the reparation debt but also partly for the stabilization of the mark—was the only way out of the problem. The new arrangements were predicated on Germany's getting a loan. While Poincaré might have felt this was a tactical mistake, still there was at the time a certain chance that a loan might be granted even prior to the restoration of Germany's finances.

A committee headed by Delacroix, the Belgian delegate to the Reparation Commission, and including a number of prominent bankers, had been appointed by the Reparation Commission in April to study the whole question of a loan. The committee began its deliberations on May 24. It was only after the May 31 deadline that it became evident that the work of this committee would not bear fruit. The bankers, with the exception of the French representative, clearly felt that a loan was possible only if the reparation debt were scaled down, and this Poincaré refused to accept.[53]

Delacroix had sided with the majority, leaving his French colleague isolated in opposition to the Committee's point of view. The result was a sharp application of pressure to bring Belgium back into line. The day after the committee handed down its report, Poincaré told his ambassador in Brussels to protest Delacroix's attitude and threaten economic reprisals; these instructions were carried out the next day.[54] On June 23, Seydoux met Delacroix personally. The real cause of the problem, Seydoux said, was "Germany's ineradicable bad faith." If the Anglo-American bankers sided with Germany, that was because they had no interest in reparation; "we therefore have every kind of reason to distrust their game and their arguments."[55]

Confidence in Britain's good faith had worn thin by June, but enough remained to prevent a real rupture. When Poincaré met with British leaders in London on June 19, he took a very moderate and reasonable line on reparation; clearly, he still hoped to work out a solution in cooperation with Britain. Control, he said, was "the most important and the most urgent question." It had been a mistake to convoke the bankers before a real control had become effective. Perhaps a loan would be possible later, after the control had borne its fruit. Right now, control was limited to a right of observation; the Committee of Guarantees had no real authority over Germany. This form of control, he said, was perhaps a "necessary first step." Maybe a tighter control would be needed in the future.

Lloyd George agreed that "some measure of control" was in order, but stressed that Germany's difficulties might be beyond the control of her government. German capacity, he said, "would not improve until the world situation improved." Let the Reparation Commission make a report. If it were found that Germany "deliberately and fraudulently" was avoiding payment, then Britain would support "all reasonable measures necessary for the result desired." But for now coercion had to be ruled out.

With this Poincaré agreed: "for the moment it was necessary to be patient." He did not object to Lloyd George's suggestion that the Reparation Commission be asked to make yet another report on the ground, for example, that enough material was already known, and that similar reports issued in the past had led to no action. Nor did he try to pin down Lloyd George on what action would be taken in the event the Reparation Commission blamed Germany for the problem. He merely agreed that they should meet again after the Commission issued its report.[56]

Perhaps Lloyd George, pleased that Poincaré was now taking such a reasonable attitude, and convinced that this demonstrated just how dependent France was on British support, felt strong enough to push for a basic change in the arrangements covering reparation. At the June 19 meeting, Horne had already hinted at the need for a more radical moratorium than the one currently in effect: he warned about the danger of killing the goose who laid the golden eggs and called for "latitude" on the question of Germany's payments.[57]

The British Treasury had in fact long favored giving Germany "a considerable breathing space—say two years at least without payment other than deliveries in kind."[58] Now Blackett, in "semiofficial" meetings with von Simson in London on June 30 and July 1, encouraged Germany to apply for just such a moratorium. Von Simson had suggested that Germany not have to pay any cash in 1923 and 1924; reparation in kind would total 1,750,000,000 gold marks annually. Blackett's "purely personal opinion" was "that the British Government would be sympathetic to any plan which offered a real prospect of stabilizing the mark." If a moratorium such as von Simson had outlined was necessary to prevent a collapse of the mark, then the question should be "raised at once rather than after the crisis had developed." To avoid a wide extension of the existing control the German moratorium request "should be accompanied by some definite undertakings" on fiscal and monetary questions. "In view of these interviews," von Simson "was disposed to recommend to his government to make an application for an extended moratorium without delay." He was inclined not to sound out the other Allied Governments in advance, but rather "to launch the application without further parley."[59] The request for such a moratorium was in fact made on July 12.[60]

It is hard to believe that Lloyd George did not have a hand in this. The matter was too important, and Blackett too low in the hierarchy, for that official to have been acting entirely on his own. Von Simson had obviously understood Blackett to be speaking for his government. The pretense of "purely personal opinion" is often used in diplomacy when governments want to evade responsibility for their actions. In this case, the British government probably wanted to forestall the charge that it had acted without consulting its Allies: it could be said that Blackett had acted independently and if necessary the document could be produced to prove it.

If Lloyd George had taken this initiative out of the belief that Poincaré's conciliatory attitude at their June 19 meeting had demonstrated continued French dependence on Britain, events were to show that he had seriously miscalculated. In June Poincaré had suppressed his own strong feelings, clinging to the hope that Allied cooperation was the best way to resolve the problem. But by late July, after this hope had been worn down still further, he was willing to give freer vent to his feelings.

French policy at this time changed dramatically. The shift was most striking in two areas: an increased willingness to accept a break with the Allies, and the emergence of the idea of *"gages"* ("pledges," "guarantees," or "collateral"—no English word is really adequate). There was nothing new, of course, to the idea of independent action, if by this is meant a willingness to occupy the Ruhr in spite of British opposition, but following a majority decision of the

Reparation Commission declaring a voluntary default. Now, however, the prospect was that Belgium would be on the other side and
vote to extend the moratorium. If that was the case, as the semiofficial *Le Temps* wrote on July 18, then the Reparation Commission
would itself be guilty of violating the treaty, since its powers in this
regard were not completely arbitrary; France would then be entitled
to act independently, even without Reparation Commission sanction.
Lasteyrie, one of the more moderate figures in high policy-making
circles, had made a similar point on July 15. An attempt should be
made, he said, to reach a compromise agreement with the Allies. But
if this effort was unsuccessful, "it would be better to withdraw from
the Reparation Commission and reclaim our freedom of action rather
than accept a two-year moratorium which would signify the end of
reparation, and cause such difficulties that the recovery of the country
and the future of the regime would risk being compromised."[61]

By the end of the month, Poincaré was willing to brandish this
threat to act independently should the majority on the Commission
grant a new moratorium unacceptable to France. He instructed his
ambassador in London on July 28 to warn the British government that
France "would re-assume complete freedom of action" in such a
case.[62]

Poincaré's main intention at this point seems to have been to put
pressure on the Allies, and in particular on Belgium, not to vote a
moratorium opposed by France. He does not seem to have actually
wanted to act independently. At an Allied conference on the question
held in London in early August, he began by talking tough: "I have
not come here to bargain, but to state the French point of view after
long reflection and under imperious necessity."[63] But in fact he was
willing to bargain; the terms he was finally willing to accept were
much milder than the ones he had originally called for.[64] He never
actually attempted to force a finding of voluntary default by a threat
of independent action. Indeed, as will be shown, the whole French
strategy at the August conference was rooted in the assumption that
the Allies could not be pressed to declare a voluntary default, even by
a majority vote.

In August, Poincaré was reluctant to actually abandon the legal
framework the Treaty of Versailles had set up. He wanted to prevent
a new moratorium so that he would not be forced to decide on such a
step. But as he repeatedly threatened to act alone this consideration

probably diminished in importance. The August conference was to collapse; a week later, Poincaré gave another speech at Bar-le-Duc, this time openly warning that France would act alone if French views on the moratorium question were ignored.[65] In September, the French chargé in Brussels warned the Belgian Foreign Minister that France would move independently, if necessary, whatever the Reparation Commission decided.[66] And at the end of November, Poincaré personally warned the Belgian leaders that he would occupy the Ruhr by himself if the Allies did not cooperate.[67]

The combined weight of these assertions was in fact changing the direction of French policy. The French government was becoming increasingly resigned to taking action even without Reparation Commission sanction. Thus, even in internal discussions Poincaré came to indicate his willingness to act alone if necessary.[68] And Seydoux, his chief advisor on reparation,[69] now finally embraced independence from Britain as the way out of what he had long seen as the root of the problem: Britain had prolonged the crisis by both vetoing coercion and sabotaging attempts at Franco-German economic cooperation. Now France, free to resort to force, would also be better able "to use the method of 'energetic collaboration.' "[70]

The issue on which French leaders were prepared to break with Britain was a peculiar one. It was over the French demand for *gages* that the August conference broke up. The idea of assigning particular revenues to reparation went all the way back to the peace conference. In the past, it had always been a matter of secondary importance. Now, however, it had suddenly become the key French demand. In the context of the moratorium, *Le Temps* first mentioned this idea on July 20. Lasteyrie's memorandum of July 15, suggesting French policy on the moratorium question, had made no mention of *gages;* he proposed, as a compromise with the Allies, accepting a short six-week to two-month moratorium accompanied by a tightening of control.[71] These suggestions were accepted by Poincaré and embodied in formal instructions to Dubois on July 19.[72] There was still no mention of *gages* in that document.

But at the end of the month, the cabinet adopted a policy that insisted on obtaining *gages* as a counterpart to any new moratorium. This decision of July 27 was confirmed on August 3, and on that day Poincaré gave instructions to Dubois in this sense.[73] When Poincaré went to London a few days later, the call for *gages* was his principal demand.

The issue of a moratorium on further cash payment in 1922 was the immediate concern of the conference. The other Allies evidently wanted to grant Germany this relief. But Poincaré insisted that no matter how short the moratorium was, *gages* had to be created.[74] What were the *gages* and what role were they supposed to play? The occupation and exploitation of the Ruhr, Poincaré said at London, was the measure France preferred. As a compromise, however, he proposed some alternative steps which might be taken: the reestablishment of the customs line east of the occupied Rhineland possibly extended to include the Ruhr, the handing over of state mines and forests, the transfer of a majority of the shares of chemical and dye companies on the left bank of the Rhine, the direct collection of taxes in the occupied areas, the continued control of Rhenish imports and exports, and the actual collection of German customs and a percentage of German exports.[75]

It was not that these measures would be applied only in the event Germany violated the terms of the new moratorium. At least at first, Poincaré's views on this question were quite clear. The measures adopted were to be *gages productifs,* raising money during the period of the moratorium. The debate at the beginning of the conference in fact turned on the question of how effective these measures would be in raising money. It was indicative of the confusion surrounding the whole question at this point that a proposal setting out the conditions under which Germany would be allowed to pay nothing in cash was being debated on the issue of how much cash those conditions would raise. Only Schanzer, the Italian Foreign Minister, noted that "these two policies seemed to him not quite consistent."[76]

Later in the conference, French views on the functioning of the *gages* appeared to change somewhat. Lasteyrie, long dubious about the money-raising possibilities of such measures, preferred to conceive of them as instruments of coercion.[77] In the committee of experts appointed to examine Poincaré's proposals, he argued that the handing over of the mines "would constitute an asset which would be at the disposal of the Allies in case of default by Germany in the fulfillment of her obligations."[78] Poincaré himself moved toward such an interpretation. At first, he had suggested vaguely that the Allies either just run or actually take title to the mines and forests;[79] later he asked only for "some control in the widest sense of the word so as not to be confronted with something null and void," and said these properties would be put up for sale only in the event of a default.[80] Eventually he was willing to admit that title could be transferred only if Germany defaulted on coal or timber. The Belgians accepted this proposal. If the British had accepted it, agreement would have been within reach. Poincaré had dropped most of the other French proposals.[81]

Lloyd George at this time was not in a particularly pro-German mood. In a meeting of the Cabinet Finance Committee on July 31, he bristled at suggestions that he was Germany's advocate. "He had no wish whatever," he said, "to let Germany off. There was a real danger in Germany's being relieved of her liabilities. She was responsible for the present state of financial and economic chaos, and there was no reason whatever why Germany should be treated in a different manner to that which innocent creditors would treat a wilful and dangerous debtor."[82]

These sentiments, however, did not make him pro-French. The atmosphere of the London Conference was unusually strained. With the prospect of a break with France in sight, the cabinet met on August 10 to consider British policy. Curzon worried about the repercussions of a breach, particularly in the Near East; "If there was a rupture, Great Britain would have to face a France bitterly and openly hostile in every part of the world." But Lloyd George "did not wholly share" Curzon's views "respecting the impotence of Great Britain vis-à-vis an enraged Poincaré." He was clearly willing to contemplate a rupture: "Any policy involving the handing over of Europe to the tender mercies of M. Poincaré and the French militarists would be distinctly contrary to the traditional interests of Great Britain and would be fatal to the reconstruction of Europe and highly dangerous to the British Empire. In his view, there was evidence to indicate that France was endeavouring to re-establish that supremacy in Europe which she had exercised from time to time in her history." To give in to a French ultimatum would mean that Britain "had yielded up the control of Europe not to France, but to M. Poincaré and his chauvinistic friends. He was absolutely against any such policy, which, he was convinced, would not be tolerated by the industrial population of Great Britain or by the representatives of finance and industry in this country.''[83]

He therefore refused to accept Poincaré's much-reduced proposals on the eventual transfer of German state property. The most he would accept was a ''supervision'' of the mines and forests in the event Germany defaulted on deliveries of coal or timber.[84]

Thus no agreement was reached at London, and it seems that the unclear nature of Poincaré's policy was largely responsible for this. It was reasonable to conceive of the *gages* as sanctions, to be applied in the event that Germany failed to conform to the dictates of the Allied bodies charged with overseeing the restoration of German finance. But other theories of the role of the *gages* were in no sense compelling. Did it make sense to try to raise money as a condition of a moratorium, or to insist vaguely that something be done for psychological purposes?[85] Poincaré's somewhat confusing position on this point thus tended to discredit his views and increase French isolation.

A policy, on the other hand, which viewed the *gages* as sanctions would have been a logical development of prior French policy, which had stressed the importance of control. Now the idea of control was somewhat eclipsed; the notion of *gages* had taken on a life of its own. For Poincaré, even at the end of the conference, never fully accepted the idea that the *gages* were fundamentally sanctions. The establishment of *gages,* in his view, was an application of Article 248, which held that reparation was a first charge on German resources, and not of paragraph 18 of Annex II, which provided for sanctions.[86] This theory was of dubious legality, since a first charge was not the same as a mortgage.[87] The proper legal procedure in the event Germany failed to comply with Article 248 was to declare a voluntary default and apply coercion.

If Poincaré failed to take this path, it was in large part because he felt he had to bow to the refusal of the other powers on the Reparation Commission to declare a voluntary default. Convinced that even the Belgians were anxious to avoid this step, he felt he could not ask for measures which were possible only after a finding of default. Hence his somewhat labored attempt to find alternative ways of ''getting something''—exactly what did not seem to matter much.

But this is not an adequate explanation for the shift in French policy that had taken place. Things had moved off the track. Control was no longer the primary issue. If it had been, Poincaré would have been concerned with measures to tighten the control and render it effective by linking it to measures of coercion which would be applied if Germany evaded compliance. But this was not the case. The British at the conference actually acceded to French wishes on the question of monetary control, an important shift in policy on their part. The power of the Committee of Guarantees to limit the floating debt was to be greatly expanded. But this now did not seem very important to Poincaré. Measures of control, he said, were nothing new. Even the control of the Reichsbank "had been agreed to before. It was only now proposed to apply the agreement. Public opinion would say that up to now the Allies had been asleep and that they ought to have done it months ago." Even without a moratorium, the control would have to be tightened; if a moratorium were granted, the Allies should demand something new in exchange and that was why he insisted on obtaining *gages.*[88]

How is this shift in French policy to be explained? Why had French leaders lost faith in control? Part of the answer, as Poincaré had indicated, was that constant delay in putting effective measures of control into effect had discredited this solution. In London in May 1921 and at Cannes in January 1922, the French government had given in on the question; even in May 1922 only a mild form of control was accepted in principle, and it was not until the end of July that the Committee of Guarantees reached agreement with the German government on the procedure for the exercise of its right of observation.[89] As Lasteyrie wrote on July 15, "so far the control has just been pure façade."[90]

A strategy of pressing for a gradually tightening control might have worked if it had been applied earlier, but by August too much time had elapsed. German inertia and British obstruction had sabotaged French attempts to institute an effective control in the past. Would things be different in the future? It was true that the British in August had appeared to change their policy and were willing to give the Committee of Guarantees a veto power over German monetary policy. But were they to be trusted to carry out this promise? They had made a similar promise in December 1921, only to go back on it at Cannes the next month. Even if they had kept their word this time, would an overindulgent British representative on the Committee of Guarantees not be able to sabotage it in practice? By August French leaders no longer believed in the good faith of the Lloyd George government. After all, the British on the whole did not dispute that Germany was responsible for her financial problems, and still they refused to even declare a voluntary default.[91] How then was trust in Britain possible?

Moreover the British government had just made two moves which had particularly alienated the French. The day after the Germans had requested a moratorium, Lloyd George publicly endorsed the idea, without even consulting the Allies.[92] And on August 1, the British had issued the Balfour Note, raising the question of the French war debt to Britain. The United States was insisting on the repayment of the money she had lent Britain; Britain now stated her intention to collect as much from her debtors, including Germany, as she had to pay to America.

This move was directed mainly against the United States. If the American government could be shown the repercussions on Europe of insisting on repayment, maybe they would ease their demands on Britain. The idea, Churchill said, was to force the Americans "to search their consciences." Sir A. Geddes, the Ambassador to the United States, opposed being "unduly lenient" with America: "He thought it necessary to hit back and hit hard at once." Lloyd George shared this point of view. Not much would be gained by "cringing." The best thing was to pin responsibility on America for the consequences of her action, even if this meant aggravating the situation of the continent; it was clear that one result of this new British policy would be to force France to be tough on Germany.[93]

Although the primary purpose of the Balfour Note was to influence America, the new policy on the French debt was not pure bluff. "With regard to France," Lloyd George said, "she was one of the richest countries in Europe, and he was not sure that we should not obtain something from France."[94]

Lloyd George had known that France would be angry at the Balfour Note.[95] No one likes to be asked to pay debts, and major capitalist countries do not like to have to repudiate them either. But Poincaré's hostile reaction went beyond normal considerations of that sort. The timing of the Balfour Note, he said, was "at the very least regrettable."[96] At the same time that the British were pressing for a moratorium for Germany, France was being asked to pay.

The timing of the Balfour Note was in fact inept in another way as well. According to the note, Britain would only demand from her debtors—principally France and Germany—what she needed to pay America. This meant that the less Germany paid, the more France would have to. It hardly made sense to give France an additional reason to oppose the moratorium on the eve of negotiations on the subject. But Lloyd George was not basing his policy on calculations of that sort. Increasingly, he was pursuing a more emotional policy. The documents of this period record sharp outbursts of anger at France, America and even Germany—a clear indication that Lloyd George was losing his grip on events.

As for Poincaré, he had another reason for resenting the Balfour Note. The French had a plan for a parallel reduction in the German and the inter-Allied debt. But this could no longer be presented after Britain had laid down her policy.[97] Not that there was much chance of the French proposal being accepted in any case: as it was put to the British cabinet on August 14, probably by Lloyd George, "the plan in question was a ridiculous and insulting one, and it was clear that M. Poincaré, after reading the Balfour Note, realised that it was useless to produce it."[98] The Balfour Note, moreover, impeded attempts to work out an agreement at the London Conference on the basis of the concessions on inter-Allied debts. Balfour himself noted on August 12 that "he was not convinced that an offer of abatement of debt could be made at the present moment which would not weaken the position the cabinet had taken *vis-à-vis* America; nor, on the other hand, could an offer be made of an amount sufficiently substantial to evoke the gratitude of the Allies."[99] There was an additional political consideration which tended to rule out compromise in this matter. As Horne put it on August 10, "it was important to avoid giving the impression that M. Poincaré had achieved great success from his London visit."[100]

Despite British reluctance to enter into serious negotiations on the subject prior to a softening of the American attitude, Poincaré still hoped that a solution of this sort would be possible. At the end of the conference he cabled Millerand that due to the failure of the Allies to reach agreement, a moratorium would result in a definite break. "We will be abandoned by everyone, including the Belgians, in an isolated action, and the 'gages' which we will take will not yield much. In these conditions, it seemed to us that the best solution would be to refuse a moratorium now and have a meeting in the near future to consider as a whole the problem of loans and inter-Allied debts.''[101] This in fact was to be a central goal of French policy for the rest of the year.

But for the time being, it is important to note how France had been alienated by British policy, particularly by policy on the debt question. Disillusionment with Britain had been an important cause of the turning away from control. The political situation in France, as Poincaré himself had indicated, was a related factor. There had been too much hesitation in the past. Now the Parliament in particular was in the mood for some solid results. Serious opposition to Poincaré from the right had recently arisen. He had taken a particularly moderate line in a Senate speech on June 29, stressing that sanctions would not bring in much money and endorsing the idea of an international loan as a way out of the problem. This "evolution" of his thinking was now held against him by a significant portion of the *Bloc National.*[102] On July 23, *Le Temps* actually defended Poincaré by putting him between two extremes.

The clemenciste group, small in numbers but very energetic, was the cutting edge of this right-wing opposition. Tardieu was the leading figure here. Undoubtedly his opposition was partly personal, a carryover from the very strong animosity that Poincaré and Clemenceau had felt for each other during the war and in 1919.[103] But personal and political factors were so tightly intertwined that they are impossible to separate. In May 1920 Poincaré had made an attempt to join forces with Tardieu. At that time they had both strongly opposed Millerand on the question of a fixed sum. Tardieu rejected these advances. Poincaré's criticism of the treaty, he wrote, had fed defeatism in France: "You support the treaty, but without believing in it. . . . You occupy the trench while proclaiming that it is bad and virtually indefensible.''[104] (In fact, as chairman of the Reparation Commission Poincaré had done nothing to establish machinery for the payment of reparation—he had done nothing to enforce Article 235.) When he came to power in 1922, Poincaré made new overtures. Again Tardieu turned him down.[105] But his opposition to Poincaré's reparation policy only became strong during the second half of the year as Poincaré's fortunes correspondingly declined.[106]

If these factors explain Poincaré's desire to shift course and produce something new and dramatic, they are nevertheless not enough to account for the particular program he adopted. Was French Rhineland policy the missing factor? It was of course obvious that most of the *gages* he requested at London had to do with the Ruhr or the Rhineland. The British government certainly suspected that these demands had to do with Poincaré's Rhenish ambitions: the Rhineland, according to a Foreign Office memorandum of August 10, was "the objective of French expansionist policy."[107] Publicists in Britain and elsewhere had long claimed that the real goal of French reparation policy was to gain a foothold in the Rhineland; French officials and newspapers were continually objecting to this "calumny."

The actual link between the Rhenish and reparation questions is complex.[108] There is no doubt, first of all, that the French government had ambitions in the Rhineland. But its aims were not well-defined. The structure of the problem did not force a definition of policy. Instead of a black or white choice, there was in theory a continuum of alternative solutions: a unitary state, various "federal" solutions, autonomy of one degree or another, outright separation, varying degrees of integration into France. During the war, no firm Rhenish policy was adopted, and after the armistice the government still preferred to put off a decision. Clemenceau wrote Lloyd George on November 15, 1918, that German questions should wait until "things settled down a bit."[109] A Foreign Ministry document of November 26, which called for both the "dissociation" of the German states from the Reich and for a "federalist" solution, indicates the confusion of French policy at this point.[110] At the peace conference the French government pressed for the political separation of the Left Bank of the Rhine from Germany. This demand was of course frustrated by Anglo-American opposition.

Judging from documents which have recently come to light, a more basic aim of French Rhenish policy at this time was somewhat more subtle: whatever political status was assigned to the Left Bank the French government hoped to cultivate the friendship and sympathy of the Rhenish population. The Rhinelanders were not quite German; the Left Bank itself was therefore to be treated differently from the rest of Germany, so as to create a buffer zone not so much in law as in spirit. The population in the occupied areas might not be won over through propaganda and gestures of friendship alone. Objective forces would therefore be brought into play: economic bonds between the Left Bank and the rest of Germany would be loosened, and commercial ties with France and the West correspondingly tightened.[111]

The Rhenish provisions of the Treaty of Versailles and the Rhineland "Arrangement" adopted at the conference by no means signified the end of this policy. An Inter-Allied Rhineland Commission with limited powers was set up, but the largely French administrative apparatus which had been created during the armistice period remained intact. Paul Tirard, who had been chosen by Foch to head that bureaucracy, had argued most forcefully in early 1919 for an active policy of encouraging the "autonomy" of the Left Bank; Tirard remained in the Rhineland as French High Commissioner.[112]

As Jacques Bariéty remarks, Tirard pursued a long-term policy.[113] He intended to "favor, without interference in the internal politics of the country, the efforts of the Rhenish population to free themselves from Prussian tutelage." This policy was approved by the government in late 1919.[114] If it were not for the nefarious influence of "Pan-German propaganda" spread by the nationalist press, and the hostile, obstructive tactics of the Prussian bureaucrats who governed the country, the Rhinelanders, Tirard believed, would have responded positively to French policy. He stressed the importance, therefore, of counterpropaganda, "intellectual action," and hoped through subsidies to encourage closer cultural relations. Economic action would be even more effective: "The Rhenish problem is above all a problem of an economic nature" and only special economic relations with France could allow the Rhinelanders "to free themselves even partially from the German grip." Therefore, he wrote in his report for 1920, "in conformity with the program I have submitted to the government and which has received its approval, I have pursued the methodical development of intellectual and economic action, designed to strengthen the peaceful *rapprochement* between the French and Rhenish populations." But German bureaucrats had obstructed these efforts. He therefore wanted to be able to "evict" them, and replace them with Rhenish officials. He also pressed for a strengthening of the Allied High Commission. Did the Allies want to reduce the size of the occupation force? This was acceptable, he wrote, providing the Rhineland Commission was given greater power. A military presence could to a certain degree be replaced by stronger administrative control.[115]

The Rhenish question did not present French leaders with a black or white choice between immediate independence or continued acceptance of a unitary state. Autonomy could be developed by degree; a gradual policy which aimed at separation in the distant future was thus possible. Radical, violent measures, and open support for separatists like Dorten, were foreign to the spirit of Tirard's policy, which aimed at making the situation evolve organically in a favorable direction. The Clemenceau government as a whole seems to have shared this point of view: General Mangin, who had encouraged Dorten, was sharply rebuked by Clemenceau's deputy Jeanneney on May 24, 1919.[116]

Clemenceau's own attitude comes out with sufficient clarity in his July 1919 testimony before the Chamber's Commission on the peace treaties:

As for the inhabitants of the Left Bank of the Rhine—I am not telling anyone anything new—they are Celts, more or less Germanified; they suffer a lot from being ruled brutally by Prussia, but it is not less true that an infiltration of blood has taken place, and that they are Germans. You have heard it said that scissions might take place, they have even begun to take place already. It is an operation that for my part I would like to facilitate but with the discretion needed to avoid useless observations.

And again he returned to the theme:

I said that the inhabitants of the Left Bank of the Rhine are Celts, that without being French, without being Gauls, they are not Germans. . . . We must not intervene in these questions. If our hand is suspected, the Allies' mistrust will be aroused. Already imprudent acts have been committed—not by me—and they have cost us an international commission for the occupation of the Rhine, which, without them, we would not have had. They are keeping an eye on us because they believe we want to annex the Left Bank of the Rhine.

So we have a policy on this Left Bank. But it is a policy of good relations and straightforwardness; I do not dare pronounce the word "friendship," but I would even say that it is a policy of benevolence toward these people who are responsive to the expression of good feelings, more than Prussia naturally and her annexes. We must have a policy of helping these people—this must not be put in the newspapers!—to free themselves from Prussia. . . .

We have a policy: to serve France in occupied Germany, to serve her with discretion, but with a great continuity of effort, of benevolence toward these people.[117]

Although somewhat contradictory, these remarks speak for themselves and need little commentary. Suffice it to say that if someone as down to earth, as hostile to abstract notions, as Clemenceau accepted the idea that the Rhinelanders were not quite German, then this notion must have been very widespread indeed. It was on this assumption that the rest of French Rhenish policy was built: the mild occupation regime, the belief that it would be counterproductive to push things and that it would be better to allow the Rhinelanders themselves to take the lead, and so on.

It is in this context that one can also see the degree to which Mangin was an isolated figure—isolated not because the government had abandoned all hope of a Rhenish policy, but rather because the government's policy and Mangin's worked at cross purposes. The army as a whole, it seems, was more in sympathy with Tirard's policy, at least after the Treaty was signed. General Degoutte, the commander of French armies on the Rhine, the most important military figure in these matters, was opposed to German unity.[118] But to detach the Rhineland from Prussia, he advocated in February 1921 the same kind of economic and administrative measures that Tirard was continually calling for.[119] Similarly he thought an aggressive propaganda campaign could be effective. German periodicals were hard-pressed financially, he wrote in May 1922, and it would not be difficult to purchase influence.[120] And in 1922 he explicitly ruled out violent means of changing the internal political structure of the Reich. The occupation of the Ruhr, he wrote on June 1, was to be "a simple seizure of a 'gage' "; "*for the moment* no political consequences [were] to be drawn from it." Three years after the treaty, "any attempt to proceed to an immediate political separation of the Rhineland from the Reich . . . seems doomed to failure. The consequences could be irremediable." An indirect policy would be more effective. "The mere fact of showing our force, and the long-term occupation of the Rhenish territories, will be much more effective in reorganizing Germany on the basis of federalism or separatism than premature attempts at political upheaval. . . . Let us complete this occupation with a series of administrative, financial and economic measures. In particular, let us develop to the greatest possible extent economic links and trade between the Rhineland and France. And we will not fail to attain our goal; the Rhineland will separate from Prussia, perhaps from the Reich, as a ripe fruit falls from a tree.''[121]

The government in 1920 and 1921 gave only lukewarm support to an active Rhenish policy. In the spring of 1920, the Millerand government briefly contemplated a scheme designed to break up the Reich.[122] But French officials had misperceived the real aims of those Germans they were in contact with; when these aims became clear, the French government abandoned the scheme. Aside from that, the most Millerand did was to support Tirard's idea of a ''political and economic *rapprochement*'' with the Rhinelanders. A mild Rhenish policy was in 1920 subordinate to, but not inconsistent with, Millerand's hope for economic collaboration with Germany.[123]

Was Briand's Rhenish policy any different? One of the sanctions imposed in March 1921 had to do with the establishment of a customs line between the occupied territories and the rest of Germany; did this mean Briand had opted for a more vigorous Rhenish policy? If so, the establishment of a tariff barrier on the Rhine would have to be complemented by a lowering of duties between the Left Bank and France. This had been Tirard's goal all along, and a note of his dated February 10, 1921, framed in conjunction with Seydoux and a representative of the Ministry of Finance, had in fact called for such action on the part of France.[124] The government, as a whole, he later wrote, had consented to this policy.[125] But, as Tirard later complained bitterly, the French government moved in exactly the opposite direction: ''At the same time as the Allies set up a customs barrier at the Rhine, France tripled her protective customs duties.''[126] As a result, only nominal duties were exacted between the Left Bank and the rest of Germany: if Rhenish industry was being shut out of France, it could not very well be shut out of Germany as well.[127]

Tirard, with Foch's support, again pressed in April 1921 for new measures relating to the Rhineland. With a German default on reparation about to be declared, the Allies would be entitled to impose these measures as sanctions. The Rhineland Commission should control the collection of taxes and state enterprises on the Left Bank; the occupied territories should have their own budget; most important of all, the Commission should be able to ''evict'' Prussian bureaucrats.[128] The first and last of these measures were in fact included in the official project for the Ruhr occupation of April 22, 1921.[129] But they did not form an integral part of the French plan. At this stage, control of the coal resources of the Ruhr was seen as overwhelmingly important; nothing else really mattered much.[130] These plans were of course not put into effect, because Germany accepted the Schedule of Payments. But it is clear that the Briand government did not incline to the sort of active Rhenish policy that Tirard stood for.

Under Poincaré things were to change dramatically. Poincaré himself in 1919 had opposed Clemenceau on the question of the Rhineland. He wanted the occupation to last as long as the reparations were in effect, and even tried to keep the door open to eventual annexation to France.[131] Lasteyrie, in his important report to the Chamber of December 10, 1921, in spite of the treaty stated that France should stay on the Left Bank until the entire reparation debt had been paid off.[132] Nevertheless the shift in Rhenish policy does not seem to have been instigated directly by Poincaré or his Minister of Finance. It had its own internal logic and evolved at a lower level of the government.

It was not until the middle of 1922 that the shift in doctrine had taken place. A new default might be declared on May 31, and the French army might be called upon to occupy the Ruhr. The act of occupation was of secondary importance; the real question was what the French would do when they got there. The shift in Rhenish policy was rooted in the analysis of this problem.

General Degoutte was not happy with the plans for a Ruhr occupation that had been elaborated under Loucheur's guidance the previous year. The plans of April 1921, he later wrote, had called for ''an extremely detailed control, carried out . . . by a whole body of engineers, officers and secondary agents, spread out in the mining districts, and even inside the big industrial establishments.''[133] At the beginning of May 1922, and again in early June, he set out in detail his ideas on the projected occupation. A Ruhr operation, he said, would have been relatively easy in 1920 or 1921. Now after Rapallo the Germans, encouraged by the increased isolation of France, were defiant. Action now was more difficult, but it was the last chance to save the fruits of victory. He proposed a wide range of covert measures designed to buy off the leadership of various factions and facilitate the success of the operation: ''Experience shows that in no other country can one so easily obtain assistance in every camp, providing

that one is willing to pay for it.'' In the Ruhr especially, the workers
"blindly'' followed their union leaders. The Socialist unions could be
approached through their French counterparts, the Christian unions
through Rome. Influence over the press should also be purchased.
Massive contact between French troops and the workers should be
avoided; the encirclement of the Ruhr was a better strategy. The
French authorities should aim to maximize production. This would
rule out a direct exploitation of the Ruhr mines and factories. It
would be "idèal'' to leave industry to its present operators.

But what would the French authorities actually do once their
troops had moved into the area? Degoutte urged that the industrialists, "the true masters of the Reich,'' then be convened in Dusseldorf, together with government and labor representatives. The
French would present a moderate reparation plan; negotiation was
possible within limits. These talks would probably succeed, since the
French demands were reasonable. But it was necessary to make a
show of force in advance—the Ruhr industrialists would negotiate
seriously knowing that "we hold their fate in our hands''—and it
would be necessary to remain in the area even if the talks succeeded.
Only an "effective occupation,'' which he preferred to carry out
without Britain, would allow the French to "keep up the pressure''
and "move from promises to results.'' Events had shown Germany's
signature to be worthless, but this time Germany's submission would
be "real and lasting.'' "Germany,'' he said, "only respects force.
She will agree to an honest collaboration with us only when she
senses our strength. Any entente not preceded by a clear affirmation
of our strength in my opinion would just be a delusion.'' But suppose
the talks did not succeed. If the Germans refused to give in, Degoutte
argued, a customs line should be drawn around the whole of the occupied territories including the Ruhr. "This measure,'' he wrote,
"allows us to starve Germany economically by depriving her of the
manufactured goods and the raw material of the Ruhr, and in particular of coal, which we can prevent from leaving; thus the industrial
life of the entire Reich will grind to a halt.'' The Germans might take
countermeasures and import foreign coal. But even if they did, "we
will undoubtedly be able to respond by orienting the occupied areas
toward France, Belgium and the neutral countries.'' The Rhineland
would be able to hold out longer than the rest of Germany. Economic
and financial measures in the Rhineland would be complemented by

the usual administrative measures Tirard had long been calling for. The Rhineland would eventually separate from the Reich "as a ripe fruit falls from a tree."[134]

Degoutte's ideas are important because they were the point of departure for the elaboration of Ruhr doctrine in 1922. These documents mark the transition from the Ruhr policy laid out under Loucheur in 1921 to the plans which were to guide the actual occupation in 1923. Degoutte still stressed coal, but he also emphasized the importance of exploiting the Ruhr economically, of "sharing the profits" earned by industry in the occupied areas. It was this latter idea that was to be developed in the last half of 1922. In that year, coal was no longer in such short supply; the control of coal was therefore no longer such a powerful instrument of coercion.

Degoutte's suggestions also marked the beginning of a real merger of Rhenish policy with policy on reparation. In 1921, the measures proposed for the Ruhr were not organically linked with those for the Rhineland. Now there were the first indications that the Ruhr and the Rhineland together were coming to be conceived of as an economic bloc, to be exploited directly by France, oriented to the West commercially, and eventually separating from Germany politically.

This was a departure as much from earlier Rhineland policy as from existing reparation policy. In December 1918, when Lloyd George had suggested that the Ruhr be occupied until the reparations were paid off, Foch had objected that this was beyond his competence: from a strictly military point of view, it was preferable that the Rhine river itself be the frontier. All he wanted was the Left Bank; even in internal French documents he made no claim whatsoever to the Westphalian coal-mining area.[135] Nor did Tirard in 1920 or 1921 call for anything more than a more active Rhenish policy in the presently occupied areas.

Degoutte's proposals, however, marked just a first step in this evolution of policy. In his eagerness to cut through to a solution, he had overlooked a number of problems. Would France be able to assure adequate markets for the industry of the Ruhr and the Rhineland in the event that the German market was closed off? how would the goods—especially foodstuffs—currently imported from the rest of Germany be replaced in the event of a rupture? How could a stable system for the economic exploitation of the area be established if the unstable German mark continued to serve as currency there? In fact at this point he rejected the idea of a new Rhenish mark as too political.[136]

The next step was taken by Seydoux's friend Emile Coste, an Inspecteur Général des Mines in the Ministry of Public Works. Coste had been in charge of the Allied commission set up after Spa to supervise the distribution of German coal; when the Ruhr occupation was undertaken, he was made the head of the Allied mission in charge of the economic exploitation of the area, the "MICUM."

Coste's superior, Minister of Public Works Yves Le Trocquer, was particularly interested in the Ruhr mines. On July 26, 1922, he urged that France use the reparation default to demand title to enough of the mines to satisfy the French need for coke: "An intense economic struggle is certainly going to begin on the world iron market. In this struggle, France has but one advantage, her iron ore—a limited advantage at that; Germany possesses the coke, which is everything. Freed [after the lapse of the coal options contained in the treaty] from all obligations to supply coal after ten years, Germany will have no concern but to kill our metallurgical industry, by refusing to sell us coke, or by selling it to us only at a prohibitive price."[137] Le Trocquer's arguments were an important element in shaping Poincaré's demands at the London Conference of August 1922 and they were to have their effect in shaping Ruhr policy at the end of the year.

But Coste's point of view was rather different from that of his chief. After hearing the views of some of the highest French officials—Foch, Tirard, Weygand, Lasteyrie, Le Trocquer—he set out his ideas in a very important memorandum of June 15. He approved the notion of a cession of the state-owned mines, but such a transfer he felt would have only a very slight effect on the reparation problem. The main thrust of his plan lay in a different direction. The idea that a cutoff of Ruhr coal would bring Germany to her knees, he argued, was an illusion. Germany could buy coal elsewhere, and France would be unable to use or market the available coal. (She was "already incapable," he noted in August, "of absorbing the present output of the Saar basin.") What if Germany, furthermore, retaliated by cutting off her own supplies to the Ruhr? Radical measures simply would not work. "The only measures that one can adopt," he concluded, "are measures of a fiscal nature." A military occupation in itself would not be enough to force the Germans to give in; as France had learned in 1871, it was necessary for the occupation authorities to "weigh rather heavily on the occupied country in order to lead it gradually to give in." He insisted that these measures be applied not just in the Ruhr, but throughout occupied Germany. Measures limited to the Ruhr alone would not yield adequate results.

Coste was well aware that the policy of heavily taxing the entire occupied area—Rhineland plus Ruhr—would amount to a break with existing Rhenish policy:

There is, moreover, no reason at all to continue to allow the Rhineland to benefit from the favorable regime which has been accorded it for nearly four years. The Rhinelanders continue to remain—and no one can reproach them for this—loyal subjects of the Reich, but it is necessary that they bear the consequences of their loyalty to their country and that they be the first to participate in its liberation. Until now they have only seen the advantages of a foreign occupation; let them now see its disadvantages. Their situation will then perhaps lead their brothers from eastern and southern Germany to fulfill the engagements they accepted in signing the Treaty of Versailles.

Is it possible to go back on what has been done for four years in the Rhineland? It is not up to me to say. But what I can affirm is that we will get nothing from the Ruhr if the regime of the Ruhr is not at the same time applied to all the occupied territories.[138]

This document thus marked an important development of French doctrine. The Rhineland and the Ruhr were to be treated as a bloc; the aim was to exploit them economically through fiscal measures. This strategy was set out most clearly by Coste during the occupation itself: "we seek . . . neither coal, nor the labor of the miners, nor the capital of the employers, but the whole of these elements, the complete economic apparatus with all its mechanisms and its full yield."[139]

But problems remained. Were the measures to be taken to be permanent or temporary? A sense of permanence might be essential for the operation to succeed: the Rhinelanders would be more disposed to cooperate or at least acquiesce in the new status quo if it were clear that officials of the central German government would not soon be back in control, able to take reprisals. As Degoutte had argued, permanent measures were necessary because Germany's word could not be trusted. On the other hand—and this was Coste's argument—ultimate withdrawal was a necessary part of a larger settlement, based on a "mobilization" of the reparation debt. To Coste, the occupation was a provisional measure: the aim was to raise as much as possible pending a larger settlement.[140] To Degoutte, the direct exploitation of the occupied areas in the event of German resistance was more an alternative to the collection of reparations from Germany as a whole; the more serious this policy was, the more permanent these measures would have to be, and the chances for an effective agreement with the Reich as a whole would diminish correspondingly.

In opting for such a policy, Degoutte was willing to settle for less money from Germany. The compensation would be political, in the form of a separate Rhenish entity now including important territory on the right bank. This was the real issue that separated Degoutte from Coste. A separatist policy was linked to the idea of a permanent occupation; but Coste, who respected German unity, preferred essentially temporary measures.

Was the course of policy then determined by a struggle between these two tendencies, between a "political" approach that sought to create a Rhenish entity, and an "economic" approach that aimed at maximizing reparation receipts?[141] The important thing to note about the discussions of the question in the second half of 1922 was that the two points of view tended to converge. For technical reasons, people like Seydoux and the Ministry of Finance expert Jean Tannery were led, albeit reluctantly, to embrace a Rhenish solution; by the end of the year, their position was in fact considerably more extreme than that of Poincaré.

The key issue here was the question of the Rhenish mark. Could the occupied areas—the Left Bank plus the Ruhr—be exploited effectively if the inflation were allowed to continue unchecked? Monetary control was an essential element of economic control; monetary stabilization was necessary if the sums raised in the occupied areas were to be transferred. The logical conclusion was that a stable currency— the French franc, or to avoid overtones of annexation, a new Rhenish mark—should be introduced into the area. French leaders were extremely reluctant to take this step, but the logic of the situation was too strong. By the end of December, the Rhenish mark, with all it connoted about the permanence of the occupation and the limitations on German sovereignty in the occupied areas, was apparently accepted by the moderate, economically oriented group headed by Seydoux.

On July 12, the same day the Germans submitted their request for a moratorium, Poincaré asked that an interministerial committee be set up to examine the whole question of the Ruhr occupation.[142] The Ruhr committee, headed by Seydoux, met for the first time on August 9. The Coste memorandum was taken as a basis of discussion. The monetary question came up, but because of the "delicate problems" involved was left unresolved at this meeting.[143]

Lasteyrie was the chief opponent of the idea of replacing the mark. Shortly before taking office, he had argued that unless the franc were introduced the Rhenish *gage* would not be profitable. But, he added, "this is a serious undertaking which can only be attempted if our presence on the Rhine is of long duration." The occupation of the Ruhr might work as a military sanction, but, he said, from an economic point of view, it was an entirely different matter.[144] When the question came up again in mid-1922, his position was even clearer. The Ruhr occupation was a means of coercion. It could not raise money. Figures which purported to prove that such an occupation could be profitable were "purely imaginary." The fiscal measures proposed would only raise paper marks: "what will we do with these mountains of paper?" A new stable Rhenish currency would solve the problem, but Lasteyrie was firmly opposed to such a course. Any such currency he said would be "counterfeit."[145]

The argument about the profitability of the proposed fiscal measures was thus ultimately more political than technical. The measures would work if there were currency reform. The legalistic reason Lasteyrie gave for opposing the issue of a Rhenish mark reflected a belief that a radical policy of that sort would be politically dangerous. A Rhenish solution presupposed a virtually permanent occupation; a vast credit operation, to Lasteyrie the sole solution of the reparation problem and thus also of France's own financial problems, was possible, as Coste himself had argued, only in the event of eventual withdrawal from the Ruhr. Lasteyrie remained true to this position. In December he was still arguing along these lines.[146]

But by then Seydoux's attitude had evolved significantly. On November 21 he set out his ideas in a long memorandum. He still preferred to solve the reparation question with Germany as a whole, but it is clear that he had lost all confidence in the good faith of the German government. France, he argued, should not "accept any plan for the stabilization of the mark and for foreign assistance to Germany, of whatever variety, if this plan is not linked to a reparation system, and above all to a completely strict and clear-cut program of financial and administrative reform in Germany, linked to a very precise system of control." Unless Germany paid, France would have no interest in German economic revival. In fact, freed of her reparation obligations, a revived Germany would be a threat to France. He then drew an astonishing conclusion: "If therefore all guarantees in this area are not given us, we must, to the contrary, disinterest ourselves in Germany's fate." He was not afraid to work out the consequences of such a policy. Suppose Germany sank into economic and political chaos.

In spite of what one might say, there is no reason to fear that such a state of things should have repercussions in France: the French government is solid enough to resist, and it will then remain for us to use Germany's political situation to prevent her from harming us. In the event Germany is left to herself and the inevitable catastrophe follows, the populations of the Left Bank of the Rhine will accept, with satisfaction even, the assistance which we provide them, and which would not go beyond the occupied territories and ourselves; the customs line created in March of last year must be reestablished along the Rhine and around the occupied part of the Ruhr.

As a tariff wall was gradually raised along this line, the barrier with France would be brought down. The franc would be introduced, and the whole area exploited for purposes of reparation. Belgian cooperation would be essential, but France could do without British or American support if necessary: their occupation zones were just small islands completely surrounded by French and Belgian areas.[147] It is hard to avoid the conclusion that Seydoux had lost his balance here. It might have made sense to argue that the bourgeois order was so well-entrenched in Germany that there was no real danger of a Communist revolution in that country, no matter what France did on the Rhine. But to actually contemplate with relative equanimity the prospect of a Communist Germany—at the time "chaos" and "Communism" were used almost interchangeably in bourgeois political circles—just did not make sense. With both Germany and Russia Communist, Poland, weak and geographically vulnerable, would not be able to hold out for long. Even in 1920, France had been unwilling to provide military support for Poland. If Poland fell, France alone would confront a Communist bloc stretching across Asia to the Rhine. The bulk of Germany would be freed of the Versailles restraints; the Anglo-Saxon powers would have been alienated by France's Rhenish policy. And this was a matter of little interest to France?

Seydoux's willingness to "disinterest ourselves in Germany's fate" and if necessary opt for a Rhenish solution grew from the exasperation that constant frustration produces. It was a sense of powerlessness that had conditioned his willingness to take extreme and dangerous measures. Through threats alone, France had been unable to force Germany to make a serious effort; on the other hand, to go in and reorganize all of Germany, he later wrote, was "beyond our power."[148]

There was, however, a certain amount of ambiguity in Seydoux's position. At the beginning of December he still had not come out in favor of the Rhenish mark, the touchstone of a willingness to opt for a Rhenish solution. "What makes the seizure of 'gages' in Germany like the mines and the forests so very risky," he argued, "is that their yield is in the form of paper marks—that is, in a currency which disappears the moment one wants to get hold of it. Once this currency is stabilized, at whatever rate of stabilization, it will constitute a firm ground on which to build."[149] This point could have been used to support the case for a Rhenish mark. But he only argued the need for a stabilization of the existing German currency.

Moreover, in a long memorandum of February 1923—that is, shortly after the Ruhr occupation had begun—Seydoux outlined a Rhenish solution, including a special currency, but basically as a means of putting pressure on Germany to accept a larger solution. It was only in the event that the German government simply gave up and left the country without a government that he saw a Rhenish solution as a permanent alternative.[150]

As far as the Rhenish mark was concerned, it was not Seydoux but rather Tannery, head of the German section in the Ministry of Finance, who made the really decisive argument. Tannery's analysis of the question was technical in nature. Emergency money—"Notgeld"—could not solve the monetary problems that would arise following the occupation: "Notgeld," Tannery told the Ruhr committee on December 22, was "a palliative whose effectiveness would only be short-lived."[151] A new currency would be necessary, he argued in a note the next day, in the event of an economic rupture with unoccupied Germany. But whether there was a rupture or not, only such monetary measures could allow France to reap sizable advantages from the occupation: "If the present monetary situation in the occupied territories is not modified, the seizure of the 'gage' would only have as a practical immediate result (aside from the pressure exerted on Germany) something important of course, but limited: the execution of the Reparation Commission's coal program, the supply of coke for our industry, and the possibility of exploiting the forests of the Left Bank. If a monetary reform is put into effect, then there is the prospect of very important results from a financial and political point of view."[152]

Tannery was aware that the "unavoidable consequence" of the creation of a new currency would be "the political, economic and financial separation of the occupied territories from the rest of the Reich."[153] The logic of the situation had worked itself out. The exploitation of what Seydoux was to call the "Rhenish compact"— the Left Bank plus the Ruhr—was, as Coste had shown, the only effective measure both for raising money and for putting pressure on Germany. But for such exploitation to be profitable, a Rhenish mark was necessary, and this in turn implied the political separation of the Rhineland from Germany.

What then was the connection between Rhenish policy and the reparation question? An active Rhenish policy was above all a means of exerting "moral pressure" on Germany to make a real effort to pay, as Tirard himself had noted in April 1921.[154] Until Germany gave in, a policy of economic exploitation would at least bring in some money. If Germany never gave in, then a Rhenish solution would be acceptable as an alternative to a settlement with the Reich as a whole. France would get a lot less than she could theoretically get from all of Germany, but at least the payments would actually be made. More important, the gradual emergence of a separate Rhenish entity would provide political compensation for any financial sacrifice being made. Such was the theory. The problem in practice was that the more serious the occupation was, the more permanent it would have to be. The further France went with her Rhenish policy, the harder it would be to turn back, even if Germany began to show signs of giving in. There would be pressure to allow the considerable investment of resources, energy and prestige in a Rhenish policy a chance to pay itself off. There would be a moral commitment to those Rhinelanders who had cooperated with France that could not easily be forgotten when Germany's attitude appeared to change. There was the danger, that is, of the Rhenish policy taking on a life of its own.

Can one go further and say that the Rhenish question was actually more important than reparation, and that France pressed for a default in order to have a pretext for pursuing a Rhenish policy? To my mind, the overwhelming weight of the evidence suggests a negative answer. Reparation, with all it implied about the relation between France and Germany within the structure of power in Europe, was for most of this period the central issue. The Rhenish question was only brought into play as a weapon in the reparation conflict and always (at least down to August 1923) remained the subordinate question. If the French government wanted a Rhenish solution as an end in itself, it would not have been so reluctant to adopt measures like the Rhenish mark, which was finally coming to be accepted only on the basis of economic reasoning.

As for Poincaré himself, he had not directly taken part in the development of Ruhr doctrine that had culminated in the Tannery note of December 23. Nor did he fully share in the evolution of Seydoux's thought. To be sure, he pushed for a declaration of voluntary default in the latter half of 1922. But the real question was what he would do in the event a default were declared. At the London Conference of December 1922, he pressed for action similar to that suggested by the Ruhr committee. But his final proposals were very mild in comparison with the doctrine the Seydoux group had worked out. Poincaré was clearly reluctant to get involved in the enormous political problems that would result from a serious Rhenish policy. If it could be prevented at all, he did not want to break with the British over reparation.

With the failure of the London Conference of August 1922, it was the Reparation Commission that had to decide the question raised by the German note of July 12. Bradbury, even before the conference met, had formally proposed that a moratorium on further cash payments in 1922 be unconditionally granted. The French wanted to reject the German request.

On August 31, the Reparation Commission handed down its decision on the subject. The German government was asked to submit a wide-ranging plan of financial reform, including proposals for an "eventual reduction" of the reparation debt. There was no mention of guarantees or *gages*. The moratorium request would be judged in conjunction with this plan. Poincaré was furious with the text of this decision. He took out his anger on Dubois, who was in effect dismissed. Poincaré's old collaborator Barthou replaced him as French delegate on the Commission.[155]

But the real problem could not be solved so easily. France, it seemed, was becoming increasingly isolated on the Commission. Belgium, concerned above all with the preservation of the Anglo-French entente, in the past had generally tried to straddle the fence on reparation questions; now, it seemed, Belgium was siding with Britain on the moratorium issue. Because of her reparation priority, Belgium was scheduled to receive the bulk of the next cash payments. The Belgians were therefore allowed to take the lead in making arrangements with the German government for these payments.

At the end of September, an agreement was worked out: the Belgians would accept short-term German bonds instead of cash for the rest of the 1922 payments. When Poincaré learned of this agreement, he had his ambassador in Brussels express his "pained astonishment that Belgium had accepted an arrangement which amounted to a moratorium in disguise."[156]

But soon events began to drift the other way. The Belgian government, unwilling to side too clearly with Britain, moved closer to France. It now seemed that when the next payment fell due on January 15, 1923, a voluntary default would be declared. Bradbury, with Treasury support, launched a desperate effort to head off this eventuality.[157] Only a dramatic shift in policy, a clear opting for a policy of trust, had a chance of leading to a solution, he felt. "Until the German Government," he wrote in early November, "—or rather a German Government, for I doubt whether anything can be hoped for from the present combination—really takes the matter in hand, remedial measures are useless and coercive measures would only precipitate the catastrophe."[158]

In his plan, which was presented to the Reparation Commission on October 8, Bradbury called for a full moratorium through 1923 and 1924, possibly extended through 1926, covering all cash payments under the treaty and including even reparation in kind: deliveries under the treaty would be financed by German bonds, guaranteed by the recipient power. To assure that Germany used this period of grace to restore her finances, he proposed a "mixed Commission" with power to fix the price at which the Reichsbank's gold would be sold. If the inflation did not cease, Germany would lose all her gold. There was no more effective guarantee than this, for the Germans would understand that if they lost their gold, the "last barrier" separating them from utter financial ruin would disappear. In general, since the aim was the reestablishment of German credit, he disapproved of even threats of coercion; from the financial point of view, an atmosphere of trust was preferable.[159]

The French reacted bitterly to the Bradbury note. France, Seydoux wrote, might even end up paying for reparation in kind. A straight-out moratorium would be more honest. The whole plan might collapse anyway, since there was nothing that obliged Germany to balance her budget. Lasteyrie argued along the same lines: a loan was the only answer, but this was impossible without a financial control of Germany. The Bradbury note would rule out such measures and all hope of a loan would vanish.[160]

Poincaré shared this point of view. He particularly resented the change of tune on Bradbury's part: the British delegate had long endorsed the idea of a tightening of financial control. Poincaré therefore supported the idea of a French counterproject stressing the importance of control—a reversion to his policy in the early part of the year. The Allies would have to agree to allowing the Committee of Guarantees to interfere in German administration. If they refused, France would act alone.[161]

The French counterproject was prepared and presented to the Commission on October 18.[162] It called for the imposition of a really tight control over German finances: the control authority could veto expenses and dictate increases in taxation. Clearly the British and French schemes were at opposite poles. Poincaré on October 14 asked for Belgian support in the Reparation Commission—the Belgian government had apparently promised to side with France in these matters.[163]

Poincaré's entire position, in fact, was getting stronger at this time. At the end of October Mussolini came to power in Italy. His nationalistic tendencies led him to pursue a more pro-French line on reparation than his predecessors had followed.[164] In Britain as well there had been a welcome change in government in October. Following Poincaré's refusal to stand by Britain at Chanak, it seemed that Lloyd George was willing to allow his country to drift to war with Turkey with only the discredited Greeks as allies. On various grounds discontent had long been growing, but this was the last straw. Lloyd George was replaced by a Conservative government headed by his old collaborator Bonar Law, regarded as more sympathetic to France.

Bonar Law was, in fact, attached to France emotionally. Shortly after he took office, Wickham Steed, the editor of the *Times,* sent the French ambassador Saint-Aulaire a letter declaring the new government's intention to turn over a new leaf in relations with France. The letter, which was "fully approved" by Bonar Law, Curzon (who remained as Foreign Secretary) and others in the new government, amounted to a repudiation of Lloyd George's way of dealing with France. Law and his associates, Steed declared, would honestly seek real collaboration with the French government, especially on the Near Eastern question and on reparation. Their desire was to wipe the slate clean of the mutual distrust and suspicion that had accumulated since the armistice.[165]

There seems little doubt that the new government did change the style of British diplomacy. "We are in the presence," Saint-Aulaire wrote at the end of the year, "of the most honest effort England has made since the armistice to reach agreement with us."[166] But the substantive change in British policy was not nearly so great. Unlike Lloyd George, Bonar Law did not see reparation as the real cause of Britain's economic problems—rather, he blamed the policy of deflation for the sluggish economic situation.[167] He was not disposed therefore to cut the reparation debt as an end in itself. He wanted a reduction because he believed that Germany could not pay the sums required by the Schedule of Payments. In the key area of control, Bonar Law actually took a softer line than Lloyd George had taken in August. Complete power over the German budget, he said in January 1923, would make the Allied control authority the real government of Germany; this in itself would obstruct the restoration of German credit.[168] Other measures rooted in distrust of Germany—the *gages* and threats of sanctions—would also interfere with efforts to restore Germany's finances. But on the other hand, previous experience had indicated that Germany would not pay except if forced to do so; he and other British officials admitted that perhaps the demand for coercive measures was justified: Germany's good faith in itself was certainly no adequate guarantee that a settlement would work.[169] The truth is that Law, whose pessimistic temperament contrasted sharply with the optimism of his predecessor, doubted whether there was any way out. This led to a certain passivity—which did not go unnoticed by the French—a tendency to criticize, but also a willingness ultimately to let events take their course.[170]

The change in the British government was viewed in France as a sign that British policy was evolving favorably, and the rather abrasive French policy, which was in large measure responsible for Lloyd George's fall, was maintained intact. The Near Eastern situation, as the Chanak incident had revealed, was the most effective lever. On November 11 Poincaré proposed what amounted to a deal with the British. He would support them in the Near East if in exchange they backed him on the reparation question. "We have the very sincere intention," he wrote Saint-Aulaire, "of remaining in agreement with the British cabinet in the Near East. We certainly hope that in exchange it will no longer oppose the unanimous desires of France in the reparation question and that it will seek to better understand our interests in the Tunisian and Moroccan affairs. . . . It is we who would speak to England the way Lord Derby spoke to us today: either you march with us or we will be forced to renounce the Entente."[171] Curzon rejected the proposed arrangement: this was "Italian diplomacy" worthy of Signor Schanzer.[172] Poincaré therefore kept up the pressure. On January 5, 1923, for example, he instructed the French delegation at the Lausanne peace talks with Turkey not to cooperate too readily with the British.[173]

The other area in which Poincaré employed abrasive tactics was the question of the proposed Brussels conference on reparations and war debts. He had been pressing for this since the end of the August conference in London. The British had resisted, hoping for a softening of the American attitude on the inter-Allied debt: they did not want to be the only major creditor to be making concessions. But American policy remained unchanged. On October 14 the unofficial American delegate on the Reparation Commission pleaded for a more flexible attitude to make a general settlement of international indebtedness possible. Secretary of State Hughes replied three days later: "To talk about reduction or cancellation is merely a waste of time.

This Government's position has always been that the question of debts is irrelevant to the question of German reparations.'' The same point was made to French officials in October and November, and Hughes proclaimed it publicly in a speech to the American Historical Association on December 29.[174]

Poincaré, anxious for the conference, was irritated at the delay. In the middle of the British political crisis he ordered Saint-Aulaire to tell Curzon that Britain must stop delaying the Brussels conference, or else France would be forced to act alone. These orders were carried out on October 19, the very day the Lloyd George government fell. The use of such tactics is a measure both of Poincaré's distrust of the British and of his eagerness for the conference as the only peaceful way out of the problem. Bonar Law, however, like his predecessor, viewed the conference with distaste, but in order to accommodate the French agreed to hold preliminary talks at an Allied conference in London in December.[175]

By the time this London conference met, the Wirth government had submitted a new moratorium request. The German note of November 14 called for a three- to four-year moratorium on all treaty payments, including payments in kind (except insofar as reconstruction deliveries could be financed without recourse to inflationary measures). A foreign loan would also be granted for the purpose of stabilizing the mark. There were no figures or deadlines setting out a precise program for budgetary equilibrium; no guarantees of any sort were offered to the Allies. This plan had been based on the minority report issued by foreign experts convoked by the German government. (The majority, which included Keynes, did not view a foreign loan as essential to a stabilization operation.)[176]

The Wirth government fell a few days later and was replaced by a new ministry under the businessman Wilhelm Cuno. Supposedly "above parties," the Cuno government was in fact oriented somewhat more to the right than its predecessor had been. On reparation, however, the change in government had little effect on policy. Cuno endorsed the note of November 14 and stressed that he was continuing Wirth's reparation policy.[177]

The German moratorium request was not well-received in France. The French government, Seydoux wrote on November 21, should not "accept any plan for the stabilization of the mark and foreign assistance to Germany, of whatever variety, if this plan is not tied to a reparation system, and above all to a completely strict and clear-cut program of financial and administrative reform in Germany, linked to a very precise system of control.''[178] What Seydoux was aiming at was a wide-ranging solution of the whole problem: a moratorium with appropriate guarantees and a foreign loan would assure both the stabilization of the mark and the payment of some reparations during the moratorium period; a reduction of the reparation debt, made possible by Allied concessions on the war debt question, would facilitate the raising of loans. Poincaré approved Seydoux's ideas on December 3.[179]

Within the British government, there was a certain amount of sympathy for the French point of view. ''The German proposals of the 14th November, 1922,'' a Foreign Office memorandum for example argued, ''contain nothing but vague schemes for the stabilization of the mark exchange. They imply a four year moratorium, but they afford no guarantee of the eventual payment of reparation.'' The author added that it would be ''unjust'' to advise the French to accept these terms because ''in no matter arising out of the execution of the Treaty of Versailles has the conduct of the German Government been such as to inspire any confidence whatever in the good faith of that Government or in their intention or in their desire to fulfil the treaty obligations which they have contracted.''[180]

Bonar Law himself felt that France should in fact be met part way. At the London Conference he was willing to make an important concession on the war debt question if this could be part of a general solution. Britain, he said, would risk having to pay more out to America than she would receive from the Allies and Germany together if this sacrifice would make a final settlement possible.[181] This amounted to the withdrawal of the Balfour Note.

It was on the question of guarantees that the British and French parted ways. At London Poincaré called for the occupation of the Ruhr. It was not his intention to punish Germany for the past and he referred to the ''obvious need for a moratorium.'' But mere promises would no longer suffice. As a guarantee, the Essen and Bochum districts—this is, most of the Ruhr industrial area—would be occupied militarily. He would then ''say to the Germans that for months and months they had promised reforms. 'We shall not fix the date of our departure until you have carried out the financial reorganization on the lines of the note of the Reparation Commission, admitted supervision of the Reichsbank, nor before the definite installation of the Committee of Guarantees at Berlin.' " A customs line would be drawn around the Ruhr and other occupied territories. If this attempt "to obtain the goodwill of Germany by the pressure of the occupation of Essen and Bochum" failed, then the whole occupied area would be exploited economically.[182]

British opinion was overwhelmingly hostile to a move into the Ruhr and Bonar Law had no intention of going along with it. According to Hankey's diary, Law considered a break with France "almost inevitable," but wanted to put it off for a few weeks in order to "give the Lausanne Conference a chance."[183] Bonar Law did in fact play for time. On December 10, the German government submitted a reparation plan embodying certain concessions: the Germans would attempt to stabilize the mark on their own, without waiting for a foreign loan, and offered to try to raise a loan, part of which would go to reparation during the moratorium period.[184] The plan was vague, but Law said that the Allies might make a counterproposal, suggesting that German industry guarantee the loan; if this raised enough money within three or four months, the moratorium could be granted.[185] Poincaré was averse to further delay, but the British Prime Minister did succeed in convincing him to put off the resumption of the conference for a few weeks. It was to meet again in Paris in early January.

In the meantime Poincaré made a strong effort to accommodate British opinion. He had long hesitated on the Ruhr question; as late as December 3 he still had not made up his mind.[186] It was apparently only on December 6 that he had decided to take the plunge.[187] But this decision was not too firm, and Poincaré began to recede from the position he had taken at London as soon as he returned to France. By December 14, the British ambassador in Paris learned that the French government hoped to avoid a military operation in the Ruhr; Poincaré intimated that the exploitation of Rhenish resources would be an adequate guarantee.[188] On December 24, high French officials met to consider the question, and it was decided that the measures to be taken in the Ruhr would not be military in nature—at least not at first. If the Allies approved, Seydoux argued, there would be no need for troops. Poincaré shared this point of view. The control of trade with the Ruhr would be sufficient.[189]

That same day Saint-Aulaire informed Bonar Law of the new

French position. The next conference, the French ambassador said, would consider three issues: the scaling down of the reparations and war debts, the restoration of Germany's finances, and the question of *gages*. On the first two points "he expressed himself in an extraordinarily confident manner on the ease with which such an understanding could be promptly arrived at." The third point was the problem. But here Poincaré no longer proposed a military occupation of the Ruhr. Rather "a number of customs officers and engineers" would be sent in to establish control over the "exports from the Ruhr district"; export duties would be levied, raising 500,000,000 gold marks a year.[190]

Thus French policy had been radically altered in two fundamental areas. The demand for a military occupation was being dropped, and the idea of exploiting the occupied areas economically—or even just threatening to do so—was also ruled out. "Any exploitation of the Left Bank of the Rhine," Poincaré declared at the December 24 meeting of high officials, "will provoke the opposition of the English who will view it as a preparation for a territorial undertaking."[191]

With the existing doctrine thus abandoned, what did Poincaré propose to put in its place? In fact, he had no clear idea of what he wanted, and French doctrine from this point on was weak and confused. The government itself, as the notes of the December 24 meeting show, was hopelessly divided. Lasteyrie vigorously contested the idea that any measures in the Ruhr could be really productive: "You will only raise paper marks, and I do not want them." Le Trocquer took a hard line: selling the coal could raise money—a view which took no account of the more sophisticated line of reasoning developed by Coste, his own Inspector-General of Mines. Poincaré himself failed to coordinate policy by enunciating a clear line himself. He limited himself to insisting that the two ministries, Finance and Public Works, agree on a program by January 4. But with the ministers fundamentally split, was it reasonable to ask for an agreement without giving any general instructions at all?[192]

The Ruhr doctrine Poincaré finally seized upon was artificial in the extreme. The British might refuse to go along even with the reduced French demands. In that case France would have to act alone, and troops would be necessary. But a break with Britain would not mean that British views could be ignored entirely. Because of the British attitude, he said at the December 24 meeting, it was necessary "to prepare an isolated action which cannot appear to be inspired by territorial ambitions. It is therefore necessary to declare a default on deliveries of coal, for then the operation will have a clearly determined goal: to provide us with the coal we need."[193]

The fact was, of course, that France did not need any more coal. Germany was in default, but the default was mild. Throughout 1922 she had supplied about 80 percent of the coal she was supposed to deliver to France under the Reparation Commission schedule.[194] Poincaré was seizing on a pretext for action, and the pretext was allowed to determine the type of action to be undertaken. Against the wishes of General Degoutte, who wanted an encirclement of the Ruhr in order to minimize contact with the miners, the French cabinet opted for a plan, elaborated by Foch, for a partial occupation of the area. Only the Essen district would be occupied. The line of occupation would therefore cut right through the heart of the Ruhr.[195] The idea was to only occupy that portion needed to supply coal to the Allies and to the occupied areas on the Left Bank, but the whole of the occupied territories was not to be exploited as an economic unit. In fact, the whole line of policy developed by Coste, Seydoux and Tannery had been abandoned.

Thus Poincaré, in order to conciliate British opinion (which would be against him in any case) had adopted a plan which even if successful would not have brought France any significant advantage, for the coal default was no longer a problem. The logical structure of French policy had been weakened, but the concessions Poincaré made did not have the desired effect on the British. In the December 24 interview with Saint-Aulaire, Bonar Law stated the British position more forcefully than ever. The French measures, he said, though producing only a "negligible" amount of money, would be enough to sabotage Germany's recovery. The reparations depended on the "restoration of German credit." "But who," he asked, "would lend money to Germany if coercive measires in the Ruhr now taken foreshadowed the continuance of the uncertain conditions and prevented the growth in the measurable future of healthy economic conditions?" This implied that coercion had no place in reparation policy, but later he softened his position on this point: the British government would not try to force Germany to do things which it was "physically impossible" for her to do, but perhaps if the debt were reduced, and if the Germans accepted a "reasonable plan . . . perhaps fortified by pledges,'' the British government would declare that if Germany failed to live up to her promises, then Britain would ''associate herself with France in any coercive measures which would be devised to compel her to do so.''[196]

In itself, this was a reasonable offer, and if Poincaré had trusted Britain it could have been the basis of an agreement. But promises of this sort had been made many times in the past; when the moment for action came, the British government, though admitting that Germany was to blame, had always vetoed really effective action. Faith in such promises had gradually been destroyed. Of course Bonar Law was seen as more honest than Lloyd George. But still, British public opinion had not changed, and whatever the new government's intentions, widespread revulsion at the very thought of a Ruhr occupation would probably be enough to hold the government back.

Moreover, Poincaré had said so often that threats and ultimata would yield only empty promises, and that the time for action and solid results had come, that it was extremely difficult to go back on his policy of ''no moratorium without 'gages.' '' It was not the domestic political situation that locked him into this rigid policy. The fall of Lloyd George, who had come to be detested in France ''not as much as the Kaiser, but perhaps a bit more than Bethmann-Hollweg,'' had helped to arrest the growing disillusionment with Poincaré: his policy in the Chanak affair had after all played an important role in precipitating Lloyd George's downfall.[197] It seems in fact that personal pride played a greater role than domestic politics in shaping Poincaré's policy. He had so often attacked his predecessors for caving in to the British that it was psychologically difficult for him to behave in the same way.

Poincaré may be presumed to have had conflicting feelings on the question of the Ruhr occupation: the vacillating and uncertain policy he pursued on the eve of the occupation can be understood in no other way.[198] Reluctant to break with the British, yet also unwilling to abandon completely the policy he had been pursuing since July, he still sought in January 1923 somehow to reconcile his feelings. The French plan of January 2 was the result.

This plan was presented to the last Allied conference, which met in Paris on January 2. Poincaré in effect formally offered to abandon the military occupation in exchange for economic *gages:* various taxes and levies, raised in the Ruhr and in the occupied territories, plus deliveries in kind, would raise a milliard gold marks a year during a two-year moratorium period. As a guarantee for coal deliveries, a control over the distribution of German coal was demanded similar to that exercised after the Spa conference in 1920. The old proposals about a mutual cancellation of inter-Allied debts and an equivalent amount of "C" bonds, and about measures to facilitate the "mobilization" of the debt, were set out formally. A tight control over Germany's finances—a veto power over spending and authority to increase taxation—were again demanded. If Germany failed to comply with these arrangements, sanctions would be imposed "immediately and automatically": there would be a military occupation of both the Bochum and Essen districts and the establishment of a customs line running around the entire occupied area.[199]

In limiting his demands in this manner, Poincaré felt he had gone as far as he could go, but to Bonar Law this was not nearly far enough. In order to get anything substantial from Germany, the British Prime Minister argued, a restoration of German credit was essential. The French demand for complete financial control would amount to making the Allied control authority the real government of Germany: "that in itself would make the German credit very difficult." The proposals with regard to the Ruhr, setting up a "more or less undefined power," would also "go a long way to prevent the recovery of credit." But the "most vital point" was that the French proposals to raise money were inconsistent with the idea of a moratorium: Germany would have to reimburse those who supplied these funds and resources to France, and this would utterly sabotage the effort to balance Germany's budget.[200]

The British Prime Minister had now decided to stand unequivocally for principle: only a plan based essentially on trust, virtually ruling out force, had a chance of solving the problem. He was opposed to attempts to "patch up some arrangement which would make a pretence of getting money out of Germany which we indeed believe you cannot get." If Britain and France were divided over basics, they might as well face up to that fact.[201]

The British scheme, also presented to the Paris Conference on January 2, called for a radical change in the whole approach to reparation. In effect, a new schedule of payments would be established. For four years Germany would pay nothing for reparation or under other headings of the peace treaty—even deliveries in kind would have to be paid for in cash, unless an agreement to the contrary were reached with Germany. Beginning in the fifth year, Germany would pay a 2 milliard gold mark annuity, gradually rising to a maximum of 3⅓ milliard gold marks. The plan was worked by means of bonds: a provision for gradually diminishing discounts meant that the sooner Germany redeemed the bonds, the less it would cost her in the long run. The idea was to give her a strong incentive to raise money quickly and transform the reparation debt into ordinary private obligations. The present value of the reparation debt would ideally be on the order of 37 milliard gold marks, but would come to more if the German government failed to avail itself of the redemption provisions and the reparations were allowed to drag on indefinitely. In any case, the obligations set out in the Schedule of Payments would be substantially reduced. In exchange for this reduction, the Allied debt to Britain would be canceled, and Germany was to stabilize the mark in accordance with the procedure set out in the majority report of the foreign experts.

As far as control was concerned, the British plan in theory did provide for "a considerable measure of interference with German democratic independence in matters of finance." A "Foreign Finance Council" with "very wide powers" was to be set up, independent of and largely superseding the Reparation Commission and the Committee of Guarantees. The Council would, however, have "wide discretion" as to how and to what extent it would exercise its authority. It would be composed of an Englishman, a Frenchman, a Belgian, an Italian, an American and a neutral European, with the German Minister of Finance, its *ex officio* chairman, entitled to vote in case of a tie. Thus even if France were supported by Belgium and Italy, the other representatives could legally block her moves. In the event the Council found that Germany was not living up to her revised obligations, including her new obligation to restore budgetary equilibrium, the Allied Powers could impose sanctions on her—but only if they unanimously agreed on the measures to be taken.[202]

In France, the British ambassador in Paris reported, this new plan "created the bitterest disappointment, not to say anger."[203] At the Paris Conference on January 3, and again the next day, Poincaré criticized the British scheme at great length. It would overturn the treaty without granting France anything in exchange. The constitution of the Foreign Finance Council, and the provision for unanimity in case of sanctions, would in fact shackle France. Poincaré had finally gotten the Reparation Commission on December 26 to declare a voluntary default (on deliveries of timber); Italy and Belgium sided with France and Bradbury was outvoted three to one. Only now did the British propose to change the procedure. "Poor Reparation Commission!" Poincaré sneered at the January 4 meeting of the conference. "It was rather severely punished because Sir John Bradbury had for once been put in a minority."[204]

Poincaré obviously doubted that the proposed Council would establish an effective control of German finance. Only force would work, and under the British procedure there would never be sanctions. "Today France was told: 'Patience, it is too soon to act, there will always be time to take sanctions tomorrow.' In France there was a shop-sign which was supposed to be displayed at barbers' shops: 'Free shaves tomorrow.' But tomorrow never came and the sanctions would have to be postponed interminably."[205] The British plan was really based on according Germany "entire and unlimited confidence."[206] After all the disappointments on the past few years, after all the evidence of Germany's bad faith, how could such an approach even be considered?

The gap between France and England, both Bonar Law and Poincaré felt, could not be bridged. The two different points of view were "irreconcilable"; the disagreement was "absolutely irremediable." Only if Britain came over "to the side of the ditch on which Belgium, France and Italy stood" could an agreement be reached.[207]

This analysis was in fact correct. Belgium and Italy now sided with France. Bonar Law's principled stand meant that no compomise was possible. Moreover, in the French view nonmilitary measures were contingent on British cooperation. With Britain opposed there was no alternative to a military operation. Nothing Germany did could now prevent it. Beginning in October, Stinnes, backed by the German government, had made repeated overtures for an industrial entente. These belated attempts were turned aside by Poincaré.[208] The German government, which had been in close contact with British officials since early December, had prepared a last offer: a loan guaranteed by the banks and industry would raise significant sums. The plan was never presented, and it would not have made any difference if it had been. Not only were the figures limited, but the scheme provocatively called for freeing Germany from her "economic and political chains," and was contingent on Allied withdrawal from the three towns occupied in March 1921, and on the evacuation of the Rhineland "as soon as possible."[209]

A Ruhr occupation was therefore inevitable. But the timber default was too slight a basis for such a grave move. Poincaré therefore waited until the Reparation Commission, again by a three to one vote, declared a coal default on January 9. Poincaré now had the pretext he had said was necessary. He did not even wait for Germany to default on the January 15 payment, although cash and not coal was the real root of the problem. On the morning on January 11, French and Belgian troops entered the Ruhr. The great test of strength, whose outcome was to determine the structure of European politics right down to 1939, had finally begun.

The Ruhr
Chapter Eight
Occupation
of 1923

THE RUHR occupation was the climax of the reparation dispute. But
the move into the area had not been a goal which the French government had pursued with single-minded devotion. And it is incorrect to
say, as one distinguished historian has claimed, that French policy in
the Ruhr amounted to the application of "a plan which had been
ready since the end of 1919 in the files of various parts of the government."[1] For the key thing to bear in mind about the move into the
Ruhr is that Poincaré had abandoned the plan his officials had worked
out for a serious economic exploitation of the area, and he had not
come up with any plan of his own to replace it with.

With no clear idea of what he wanted to do, it is hardly surprising that Poincaré was reluctant to face up to the full implications of
his decisions. There is no evidence that he sought at last a decisive
test of strength with Germany. He in fact tried to play down the significance of the move. "Prudence" and "moderation" were the
watchwords. "It was decided," Seydoux reported on January 9 to the
interministerial committee set up to consider the occupation, to be
cautious in applying the military measures and "to reduce them to the
minimum." The official notification delivered to the German government on January 10 must be seen in this light: the French government, it said, had for the time being no thought of proceeding to "an

operation of a military nature, nor to an occupation of a political character." The troops were there only to protect the engineers' mission, the MICUM.[2] The MICUM was empowered solely to supervise the distribution of the coal and coke produced in the region. In itself this was no radically new demand: a similar control had been imposed at Spa in mid-1920. There was no reference to the idea of an eventual Allied takeover of the mines, and there was nothing in the formal notification that purported to give any Allied body the right to collect taxes in the occupied areas or in any other way to exploit them economically.[3] Clearly much of the French program had been dropped—or at least was being held in reserve.

The proclamation of General Degoutte, commander of the occupying forces, and an order of his of January 11 outlining the occupation regime, were marked by the same moderation: the normal life of the population would not be disturbed; the administration, including the police, would remain intact; German law would remain in effect; there would be no prior restraint of the press.[4] And Poincaré, in his remarks to the French Chamber of Deputies on January 11, stressed similar themes: France had been forced into the move by the absolute unacceptability of the alternatives proposed; French aims were limited; the government still wanted to negotiate with Germany and help her restore financial stability. (French officials were in fact still working on a moratorium scheme that would provide the basis for these talks.)[5] There was no rousing call for an all-out effort to win, for the move was not portrayed as the beginning of a decisive confrontation. Poincaré did not even claim that the occupation would have a significant effect on reparation payments. If the British had cooperated and nonmilitary measures alone had been put into effect, he said, the economic controls the French had proposed to set up would have been "productive," raising perhaps a milliard gold marks a year (a figure less than half as big as the one prescribed in the Schedule of Payments). But the present arrangements would inevitably be less profitable.[6]

It was hardly likely, however, given the political tensions that had led up to the occupation, that the move into the Ruhr could fail to be a confrontation of the first order. The Germans, who had not seriously prepared for the move, immediately began to resist. The reaction was reflexive—there was no attempt to work out with any care the long-term consequences of various courses of action, or to weigh alternatives against each other. The French wanted to get more coal through force? Then Germany would resist, and no reparation coal— that is, no coal paid for by the German government—would be handed over at all.[7] The French authorities then offered to buy the coal they wanted directly from German industry; the money would come from the coal tax receipts which would be taken over by the occupation authorities.[8] But even the sale of coal was forbidden by the German government on January 14.[9]

The French retaliated by occupying the Bochum area on January 15, and then the Dortmund zone on January 17. (See Map.) These military measures laid the basis for further economic sanctions, which began to be applied the next day, both in the Rhineland and in the Ruhr: the German coal tax, forest profits, and customs receipts in the occupied areas would be taken over—but as yet no duties were to be imposed on trade with unoccupied Germany.[10] At the same time, the French sought to get the coal they wanted through direct pressure. The first requisition orders were issued on January 15. When these orders were resisted, troops were sent in to seize the coal. The presence of troops led only to the cessation of work at the mine, and direct seizures were suspended for a while.[11]

By the time direct seizures were reinstituted in February, the transport problem had come to dominate the whole situation. Beginning January 17, the French tried to extract the coal by rerouting trains and barges destined for Germany.[12] Originally the German government had not intended to resist the French on transport, but by January 16 had changed its mind.[13] Coal trains for France were not allowed to circulate; if the occupying forces tried to reroute trains to France, the German railroad people would redirect them back to unoccupied Germany by a roundabout route. If the French tried to control the trains with military force, the Germans on the spot would go on strike. By early February the entire railroad system on the Left Bank was on strike; the Ruhr trains on the whole, however, were functioning normally.[14] German resistance was so successful that "by January 31 not one ton of fuel had made it to the border."[15] The French were reluctant to use too much force for fear of precipitating a general strike; Gen. Degoutte felt he did not have enough troops to risk setting off such a serious crisis.[16] The reroutings were also suspended until February.[17]

Thus the whole process of German resistance and French retalia-

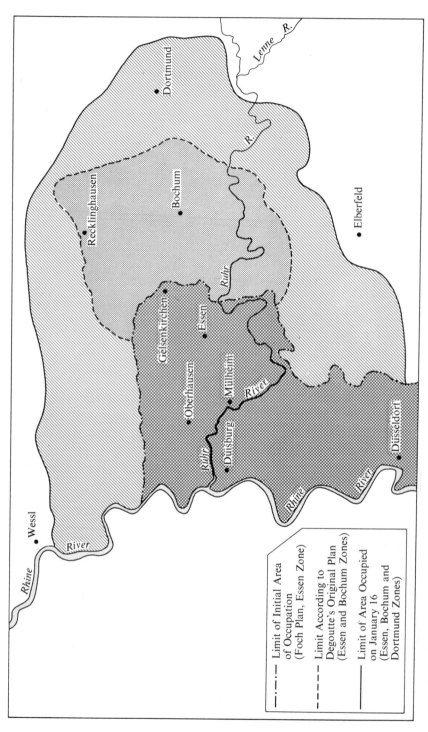

The Ruhr: Stages of Occupation and Occupation Plans. (*Source: Degoutte Report, Folder "Cartes et Graphiques."*)

Lenne R.

Dortmund

R.

Recklinghausen

Bochum

Elberfeld

Ruhr

Gelsenkirchen

Essen

Oberhausen

Mülheim

Ruhr

River

Duisburg

Düsseldorf

Ruhr

Wessl

River

Rhine

Rhine

River

—·—·— Limit of Initial Area
of Occupation
(Foch Plan, Essen Zone)

— — — Limit According to
Degoutte's Original Plan
(Essen and Bochum Zones)

———— Limit of Area Occupied
on January 16
(Essen, Bochum and
Dortmund Zones)

tion had acquired a certain momentum. German officials were instructed to ignore French authority and take orders only from Berlin; all reparation payments, including reparation in kind, were suspended, and Germany refused to pay for occupation costs any more; the Reich began to organize and finance the resistance.[18] Given the German government's unwillingness or inability to introduce adequate monetary and fiscal reforms, the effort in the occupied areas was to be financed by the most famous hyperinflation the world has ever seen.[19] Inflation, which had so far been so advantageous to the Germans in the reparation dispute, was now to turn against her: it was the collapse of the mark which more than anything else lay at the root of the political and economic crisis which would eventually bring the Berlin government to recognize that it would have to come to terms with the French.

But if it is obvious that a process of escalation was taking place, it is also clear that there were limits beyond which this process could not go. Neither side proposed to tear up, or even formally to suspend, the peace treaty—concern for the British reaction was the dominant consideration here. On the German side, there was no general strike, and although Cuno approved a program of sabotage, outright violence (on both sides) was surprisingly limited.[20] On the diplomatic front, Cuno in public took a hard line: there would be no negotiations, he declared on March 22, until the French evacuated the area.[21] But this position was softened when the German government on May 2 proposed a reparation scheme with a nominal value of 30 milliard gold marks as a basis for negotiations; the talks would start from the assumption that the Ruhr would be evacuated swiftly. These terms were totally unacceptable to Poincaré, as was a new German proposal of June 5 (in which Keynes had had a hand) which called for an "impartial, international body" to arbitrate the question; the diplomatic deadlock was to persist for the rest of Cuno's tenure as chancellor.[22]

On the French side as well there was a similar phenomenon: an escalation of the conflict, but within limits. One result of the initially mild action of the French authorities was that the impression took hold in France that the government had not acted forcefully enough. German defiance had in effect been tolerated. One incident was particularly striking. The German industrialist Thyssen had been brought before a French military tribunal for failing to obey a requisition order. He was acquitted of one of the charges and found guilty of another. But because of attenuating circumstances—the court found merit to his argument that as a German citizen he was bound by German law, which the French admitted was still in effect—he was merely fined a sum which he easily paid. This verdict was the signal for large anti-French demonstrations in the occupied areas. All this was seen as evidence of Poincaré's failure to impose French authority.[23]

This problem was, however, recognized even within the government, and new measures were prepared to deal with it. Coal was still the key concern. By the end of January it was decided to impose a coal blockade: no coal would be allowed to move from occupied to unoccupied Germany. The measure took effect in early February.[24] Given the fact that funds from the Reich enabled the miners to continue working in spite of the loss of markets this entailed, this measure was to result in a vast stockpiling of coal at the pithead—apparently a totally unintended but very fortunate consequence from the French point of view.

For the first time, French measures began to reach beyond coal. A general reparation default was declared on January 26, and this provided a kind of legal basis for a broadened occupation policy. The expulsion of German officials—long an aim of Tirard's—had begun by January 23.[25] On February 6, it was decided to extend the blockade to goods manufactured in the occupied areas. The aim was to make the Ruhr magnates suffer.[26] The Ruhr and the Rhineland were to be treated differently. Licenses for sales to unoccupied Germany would be issued freely to Rhenish industry, since the aim was to raise money through a customs duty to be imposed on such shipments; but in the case of the Ruhr, where the aim was political, relatively few licenses would be issued. These measures were put into effect on February 12. They were once again to result in a large stockpiling of manufactured goods in the occupied areas. Trade going the other way—that is, from unoccupied Germany to the Ruhr and the Rhineland—was left untouched until mid-June, when it too was subjected to a regime of licenses. Even so, trade in certain commodities—above all, food—was not affected.[27]

More extreme measures of coercion were considered and rejected. On January 31, Maginot, the Minister of War, asked General Degoutte to prepare a program for paralyzing industry in the occupied territories. Three specific measures were proposed for study: industry could be cut off from its supplies of raw material; water might no longer be pumped out of the mines (so the mines would in effect be flooded); the electric power stations could be occupied and industry threatened with a cutoff in power.[28] But these ideas were abandoned when Degoutte refused to carry out such a program. He stressed moral considerations in his reply to Maginot: the criticism directed against Germany for destroying mines and factories in Belgium and Northern France during the war would apply equally well to France if she now adopted a similar policy.[29] But his real concern was political. A total cutoff in raw material supplies, he wrote on February 4 to Guillaume, a high official in the Ministry of Public Works, "would very quickly stop the entire economic life either just in the Ruhr or in the whole Rhineland, and this, it seems to me, cannot be contemplated. It would reduce the working class to famine, and raise it against us, and it would antagonize the neutral powers." The problem as he saw it was that the Germans as a bloc were resisting French measures, and the key to success was to break up the bloc by winning over the workers; coercion should be directed against the industrialists and bureaucrats who were the backbone of the resistance.[30] This was why he favored the expulsions of German officials and the blockade on industrial exports from the area (which he believed would hit the industrialists more than the workers). With regard to the mass of the population, he—and indeed the government as a whole—opted for a mild policy, and in particular sought to cultivate the workers by assuring their food supply, setting up public soup kitchens, and so on.[31]

Thus by the beginning of February a French policy was finally taking shape. In January the French hardly knew what they wanted. Clearly the government had not prepared for a confrontation—but then again neither had the German government. On both sides measures were hastily improvised, each side acting more to frustrate the perceived, and often misperceived, aims of the other than to execute a plan whose ramifications had been thought out in advance. Thus the initial French concern to maintain the economy in the occupied areas and prevent a general strike derived in large measure from the French conviction that the Reich wanted to precipitate such a crisis as a way of forcing the French to withdraw; it was not the result of an attempt to weigh the disadvantages of an economic crisis against its advantages, for example as a prelude to the economic organization of the occupied areas under French auspices.[32]

This problem of lack of direction was so fundamental that it did not go undetected in France. Widely respected reporters, like Bourget of the *Journal des Débats,* constantly criticized the government's failure to formulate and impose a clear policy.[33] Attacks along these lines by André Tardieu, Poincaré's most important enemy on the right, began in his paper *L'Echo National* on January 22. So Poincaré had a strong political incentive to work out a plan of action.

What aims were to be adopted? In January the only aim had been to win—that is, to get the coal the French had said they were coming in for. But how was this to be done? By making life so intolerable for the population in the occupied areas that either they or the Reich would abandon their resistance and accept French terms? The most significant thing about French policy during this phase of the occupation was that this course of action was not adopted. The defeat of Maginot's proposal for "extreme measures" was the first sign of this. A more explicit decision to exclude a harsh policy was made when the transport question came up. There were two possible choices, according to the February 3 report of Bréaud and du Castel, the French experts sent to the Ruhr to look into the question: either do nothing beyond providing for the transport of coal and coke to France and Belgium and for the supply of the army, or organize and run a rail system to serve the occupied area. In setting up a Régie to run the trains—the decision was made in February and the Régie began operations in March—the French were opting for the second alternative. The meaning of this choice was spelled out in April by Bréaud, by this time head of the Régie: "our aim is to reestablish economic life" in the region.[34]

More generally, it is important to stress the limitations on French occupation policy, which were especially striking in the first half of the year. One might have expected that the French concern for reparation and interest in Rhenish autonomy would have led Poincaré back to the program for a serious economic exploitation of the occupied areas that Coste and Seydoux had developed in the latter half of 1922. Indeed, the very measures of resistance that Germany had adopted gave France a strong incentive for moving in this direction. If the local administration was an important element in German resistance, the French might have tried to bring it into line by getting control over it financially—that is, by setting up a separate administrative budget for the Rhineland, a measure that would also be justified as part of the system for the full economic exploitation of the area. In the legal sphere, as a basis for the introduction of some measure of administrative autonomy in the region, one might have expected some movement toward the idea of a military government for the occupied areas. Similarly the Reich's role in financing the resistance, and the consequent collapse in the value of the mark, gave the French a strong incentive for introducing a new currency in the occupied territories; by December 1922 this had become a crucial element in the plan for the economic exploitation of the occupied areas. If the mark were driven out, it could no longer be used to finance the resistance; full economic and political control, and hence a fully effective exploitation, would be impossible as long as the rapidly deteriorating mark continued to circulate.

Yet the French never really opted for a policy of this sort. What movement they did make in this direction was halfhearted at best. In the area of administration the limited scope of French policy is particularly striking. The local administration was viewed as the backbone of German resistance. Yet there was no attempt to put the local administration under direct French control—no local administrative budget under French supervision, no abrogation of German law, or of the Reich's authority over its officials in the occupied areas. Instead the French chose a policy of expulsion. In increasing numbers, German officials were ejected from the area.[35] But the expulsions failed to shake the Reich's control over the local administration. On August 31 the Rhineland Commission—at this time essentially a tool of the French government—passed an ordinance giving itself the power to fill the posts left vacant by the expulsions.[36] It is unclear how much of an effect this move had, but it certainly did not succeed in giving French control over the local officials. Thus the French government had opted for slow-working, ad hoc measures; a more radical organic solution to the problem of administrative obstruction was in effect ruled out.

The question of the Rhenish mark provides the clearest indication of the self-imposed restraints on French occupation policy. If the French had wanted to separate the Rhineland off from the rest of Germany, either as an end in itself or as a bargaining chip, or if they had wanted to overcome German resistance by preventing the Reich from financing it, or even if they had just wanted a full economic exploitation of the occupied areas solely for the purpose of getting reparations, the introduction of a new Rhenish currency would have been a natural move. The idea had been considered in 1922 and came up again at the beginning of the occupation. But the aim at this point was not an immediate, thoroughgoing monetary reform, with all that implied about the limitations on German sovereignty along the Rhine. Instead the plans for a new currency were developed in response to the fear that the German government had opted for a "politique du pire"—that it wanted to aggravate the economic situation in the occupied areas as a way of forcing a French withdrawal. If the Reichsbank, as part of this policy, stopped supplying the Ruhr and the Rhineland with fresh cash, the occupation authorities would be forced to issue emergency money—"Notgeld"—to head off a monetary famine. But by the end of January it had become clear that the French had been wrong about Germany's intentions—or that the Germans had changed their minds. The Reichsbank continued to supply its branches in the Rhineland with new money. The Notgeld schemes were therefore dropped.[37]

Since a Notgeld under French control could have functioned as a stepping stone to a more basic monetary reform, the defeat of these proposals was a setback for those in the government—Seydoux, Tirard, Minister for the Liberated Regions Reibel—who for various reasons wanted to create a new Rhenish mark.[38] As for Poincaré himself, he blew hot and cold on the issue in the first half of the year. At times he seemed to press energetically for a new Rhenish currency, but in the last analysis he drew back and no Rhenish mark was issued.[39]

It was coal, rather than the whole economy of the occupied territory, that remained the central issue, at least until August. The coal blockade, given the German policy of maintaining employment in the mines, led to a huge build-up of coal stockpiles. This coal was seized and transported to France as soon as the French had solved the railroad problem by setting up the Régie.

But the seizures provided an unstable basis for coal deliveries; Poincaré therefore aimed at setting up a system for the "regular exploitation" of the mines.[40] As the Germans were unwilling to enter into contractual arrangements, he turned toward the idea of a direct French exploitation of some of the mines. This proposal was formally adopted at the end of July. In August a number of coal and lignite mines and cokeries were taken over; by October the "direct exploitations" had come to provide a significant share of total coal deliveries. (See Fig. 2.) The total tonnage delivered rose slowly but inexorably even before new coal arrangements—the famous "MICUM agreements"—were reached with the German mine owners at the end of November; at that point France was receiving about half of the Reparation Commission schedule, or five-eighths of the amount Germany was providing before the occupation.[41] Thus the French were slowly winning the coal battle, but the effort—the creation of the Régie and the direct exploitations—had been great. The French government had been unable, or unwilling, to force a swift German acceptance of French terms on coal. And the exploitation of the economy of the occupied areas did not extend much beyond coal.

Thus the most significant thing about Poincaré's policy in the first half of 1923 is the direction it did not take. Radical measures were not adopted in part because of Poincaré's continuing unwillingness to accept the occupation as a decisive test of strength with Germany.[42] If France's position as a victorious power, if the whole Versailles system, had been at stake, then an all-out effort would have been called for. Yet Poincaré was unwilling to make that kind of an effort. Thus although Degoutte complained constantly about not having enough troops, Poincaré boasted to the Chamber in May that the Ruhr occupation had been carried out without the mobilization of an additional class (in contrast to what Briand had done in the spring of 1921).[43] And although the success of French policy might in some measure be compromised by financial weakness at home, Poincaré was unwilling to impose a tax increase by raising the question of confidence; instead he allowed the Ministry of Finance plan to be defeated by the Chamber.[44]

Beyond that, Poincaré had a certain political incentive to avoid a radical policy. Certainly he wanted to avoid antagonizing moderate opinion, both at home and abroad, if it could at all be prevented. He did not want to alienate the British more than he already had; his Belgian allies resisted measures like the Rhenish mark which tended to indicate that the occupation would be of indefinite duration; he also sought to accommodate the moderate left within France, which though ambivalent about the Ruhr avoided going into open opposition as long as Poincaré pursued relatively limited goals. Yet this kind of and bring about a moderate Germany, and integrate her into a stable European system. But on what terms might this be possible? What territorial and other changes would be needed to satisfy Germany? This was the kind of question that Lloyd George preferred not to deal with directly. But if the vision was to be realized, the immediate needs were obvious. The new republic in Germany had to be allowed to consolidate its authority. To press the new rulers too hard, he felt, would be unwise: such pressure might cause their fall and result in a Communist or militarist government, and then what would the Allies do? It was obviously better to take an indulgent attitude toward Germany, to be flexible regarding the treaty, to be generous in allowing time for compliance.

If the French, however, tried to obstruct this policy, Lloyd George was prepared to force them into line. After all, France was more vulnerable geographically, and, in 1920, more exposed to the danger of isolation than Britain was. France, in other words, was far more dependent on Britain than Britain was on France, and it was natural that the relative political strength of the two countries should condition the nature of the policy they were to pursue toward Germany. Lloyd George was keenly aware of this; in a talk with Loucheur in London at the end of 1919 he barely concealed his view that because France was weak and vulnerable she could not risk opposing Britain:

The Prime Minister pointed out that France was not left in a very easy situation as a result of the war. In Germany, as all the information he received pointed, France was regarded with sullen hostility. A feeling was growing up in Germany akin to that which had existed in France towards Germany in 1871. France could not count on support from the United States. Consequently it was essential that she continue her close relations with Great Britain. If this was to be the case, the press attacks must cease and bitterness must not be allowed to grow up out of political affairs, such as that of Syria, which were not really of vital importance to either nation.[11]

What, however, were the substantive aims of Lloyd George's German policy? In theory, Lloyd George did not repudiate the treaty, and compliance, he said, was his ultimate goal. But because of his great reluctance to use force to uphold the treaty, the ideal of compliance receded into the distance, and eventually many came to suspect that in practice little separated Lloyd George from the revisionists.

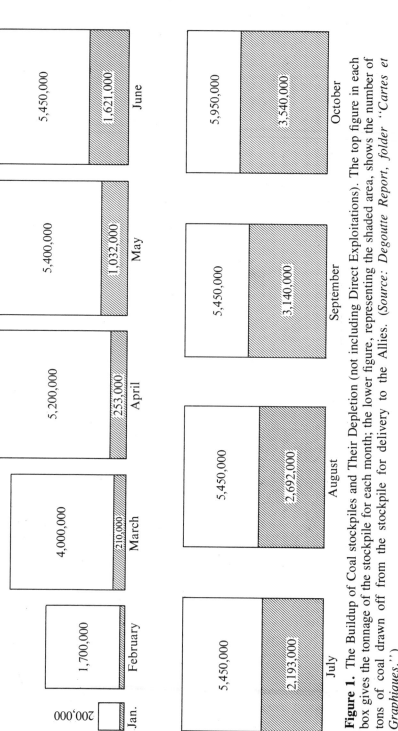

Figure 1. The Buildup of Coal stockpiles and Their Depletion (not including Direct Exploitations). The top figure in each box gives the tonnage of the stockpile for each month; the lower figure, representing the shaded area, shows the number of tons of coal drawn off from the stockpile for delivery to the Allies. (*Source: Degoutte Report, folder "Cartes et Graphiques."*)

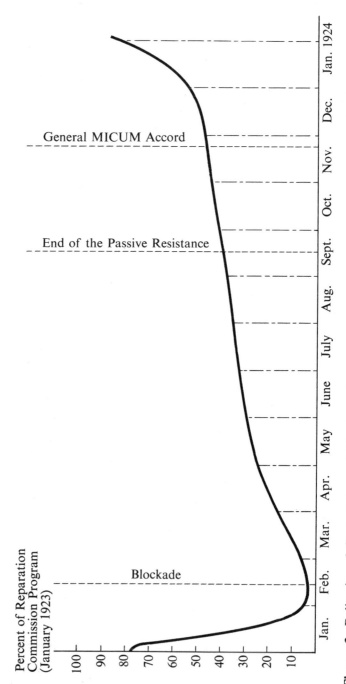

Figure 3. Deliveries of Coal, Coke, and Lignite as Percentage of Original Reparation Commission Schedule. (*Source: Degoutte Report, folder "Cartes et Graphiques."*)

factor should not be overestimated. It was the ineffectiveness of French policy—the fact that the crisis kept dragging on month after month—that was the real root of the alienation of the moderates. The Belgian government in particular was eager for a quick solution, and for that reason pressed for measures at the beginning of the occupation that were actually tougher than the French were willing to accept: for example, it wanted to force the Germans to return to work by threatening to allow the mines to be flooded if they refused.[45] Thus if a radical policy had promised a swift solution, the attitude of the moderates would not have been an important factor.

Was the more radical policy simply unrealistic? The imposition, for example, of a new currency on a hostile population was technically difficult. What if it were boycotted?[46] But this obstacle could in theory be overcome by linking the new currency to a control over the food supplied to the region: in order to buy food, people would have to exchange their German money for the new Rhenish marks. More generally a control over food could have been used to force the strikers back to work, force the reparation deliveries to be renewed, or oblige the population to pay taxes to the occupation authorities. In other words the control of food was the ultimate sanction, the instrument whereby in the final analysis the will of the military authority could be imposed on a hostile population.

But food was a weapon that the French government refused to use in this way. French officials understood the power of this weapon—the German workers, it was said, would go to whoever fed them.[47] But at only one point did Poincaré come close to suggesting that food might be used as a means of control (as a way of forcing the striking railway workers back to work).[48] The more general policy was to treat the food supply as sacrosanct. As Degoutte explained, the reason for this was "political" and not "humanitarian": "all our efforts must tend to set the population against the Government."[49]

How does all this bear on what is perhaps the fundamental problem in the interpretation of French policy in 1923: the relation between the Ruhr occupation and France's ambitions in the Rhineland? The first point to make is that the relatively restrained occupation policy—the refusal to use food as a weapon, the reluctance to impose a full French control on the local administration and economy, the creation of the Régie with all it implied about French concern for the well-being of the local population—was consistent with the whole thrust of French Rhineland policy since the armistice. From the outset the aim had been to wean the Rhenish population away from the Reich and win them over to the French if possible. It followed from this that indirect methods, where the initiative did not rest solely with the French, but was shared fully with the local population, best suited France's purposes.

The Ruhr occupation gave the partisans of a Rhenish policy their chance, and they were determined not to compromise their cause by a hasty, precipitous policy. Thus Tirard, at the start of the occupation, wanted to go slow in introducing the Rhenish mark.[50] The Rhenish separatists were quite often viewed contemptuously in the French documents.[51] Degoutte, moreover, had long advocated a cautious policy. "Any attempt to proceed to an immediate political separation of the Rhineland from the Reich," he had written in June 1922, "seems doomed to a failure whose consequences might be irremediable." A gradual policy was better; in that case, "the Rhineland would separate from Prussia, perhaps from the Reich, like ripe fruit falling from a tree."[52] Actually it was a reorganization of Germany as a whole on a loose federalist basis that Degoutte said should be the aim of French policy. In a report of March 20, 1923, sent to General Serrigny of the Conseil Supérieur de la Défense Nationale, the highest military policy-making body, he set out his views in some detail. He had for a long time stressed "the centrifugal forces which exist in a latent state in Germany and which, in normal periods, do not appear on the surface." But in times of crisis—in late 1918 for example—they become very important. A new crisis of this nature was now developing. In Bavaria the "White Army of Hittler [sic]" was asserting itself; the left was becoming active in Saxony and Thuringia. When the crisis within Germany reached its climax, the population in the occupied areas would turn to France. The strong implication, in this and in Degoutte's other memoranda in 1923, was that it was in France's interest to promote the German crisis.[53]

The advantage of this kind of policy was that the regime that emerged from it would be relatively stable. It was better to let the Rhinelanders take the initiative than for France to impose a measure of separation through military force. A Rhenish political entity created by the local population would be more acceptable internationally, more palatable even to the Germans, than one designed by the French. A new state created in this way would, moreover, be less of a burden on French resources: if for example Rhenish bankers took the lead in setting up a new currency, so much the better for the French treasury.[54]

At the same time as Degoutte and Tirard were promoting the idea of Rhenish autonomy, officials in Paris were developing their own plans for the Rhineland. Seydoux, in a long memorandum of February 16, returned to the policy that he and the Ruhr committee had elaborated in the latter half of 1922: a serious economic exploitation of the occupied areas, including a new currency, would force Germany as a whole to accept France's terms. The Rhenish policy was in essence a bargaining chip; only if Germany completely fell apart would France set up a permanent Rhenish entity. The real goal was an eventual entente with Germany as a whole; with regard to the Rhineland, all he asked for was that the eventual settlement provide for Allied control of the Rhenish railways.[55]

But this was a minimal goal as far as French Rhenish policy was concerned. Immediately the aims began to broaden. On March 6 the Comité restreint, the interministerial committee set up to consider policy in the occupied areas, came out for an "effective neutralization" of the Left Bank. The regime would be similar to that of the Saar: the entire Left Bank would become an autonomous entity, detached from the Reich, under the control of the League of Nations. But all this would be part of a negotiated settlement with Germany: the new Rhenish arrangements would take effect at the same time as the Ruhr was evacuated, following a German payment of 50 milliard gold marks.[56] Seydoux in particular felt that brute force could not be the sole basis for relations with Germany, and that a set of negotiated agreements, focusing in particular on commercial and metallurgical questions, would lay the basis for improved, and even relatively friendly, relations between the two powers in the future.[57]

One can see the difference between Degoutte's Rhenish policy and the kind of approach Seydoux recommended. Degoutte focused on local arrangements while Seydoux's eye was fixed on the international context. To Seydoux an eventual entente with Germany as a whole was the goal; one has the impression that in his eyes the Rhenish arrangements were to function largely as bargaining chips in future negotiations with Germany. To Degoutte, Rhenish autonomy was the aim in itself.

The difference in point of view explains what at first glance might appear bizarre: Seydoux (like Coste before him in 1922), though less committed to the idea of a separate Rhineland, pressed for more radical measures of separation—a full economic exploitation, a Rhenish mark, etc. If the basic aim was to put pressure on the Reich, France had every interest in forcing the pace. But if the French really wanted to create a permanent Rhenish entity, it was important to let the initiative rest basically with the Rhinelanders themselves; and if, as Degoutte proposed, the destruction of the German Reich in its present form was the aim, it was vital to give the German crisis time to develop and really set in.

But what about Poincaré's views on the Rhenish question? Unfortunately the direct evidence in this area is slight. Yet we do know that the Rhenish question was on his mind in early 1923. On the one hand, he sent Louis Loucheur, a deputy and former minister who had played a prominent role in economic diplomacy in 1919 and 1921, over to England in late March and early April to discuss the whole question; Loucheur's scheme, which Poincaré had approved in advance, called for a measure of Rhenish autonomy and international control.[58] And in a despatch to his ambassador in London dated April 14, Poincaré seemed to adopt Seydoux's general approach to the whole question. But his reference to the Rhineland was very vague.[59]

On the other hand Poincaré was at the same time considering a more radical approach to the Rhenish question. The Conseil Supérieur de la Défense Nationale considered the question on March 24, and sent around a "very secret" questionnaire shortly thereafter. This extract from the questionnaire will suffice to convey its tone:

Taking into account the triple necessity:
  (a) of setting up a state able to live on its own resources,
  (b) of establishing as sharp a break as possible between this state and
      the Reich in every area, and
  (c) of assuring an effective League of Nations (and temporarily Allied)
      control in every possible area,
4. Should the Rhenish state possess customs autonomy? In particular,
   should a customs barrier separate it from the Reich?

Poincaré at first felt the matter was urgent and pressed for a swift reply. But on April 5 he turned around and ordered that the studies be suspended.[60]

Why was this inquiry dropped so suddenly? Was the opposition of the Ministry of Finance to a radical Rhenish policy—its obstruction of a new Rhenish currency, for example—responsible to any significant degree? This seems unlikely; the draft of its reply to the questionnaire endorsed the idea of a new currency, and in general it took the line that financial questions were subordinate to political ones. Let the government understand what it was doing: a real monetary reform implied a separate budget for the Rhineland, with the administration and tax collection under French control. This would virtually place the region under French sovereignty. If the government decided that this was what it wanted, the Ministry of Finance would of course carry out the monetary reform—the new currency would be the "consecration" of a political decision.[61]

It is more likely that the study was abandoned because the radical policy appealed to neither of the leading factions. To Seydoux a policy that aimed first and foremost at unilaterally setting up a permanent Rhenish entity had little appeal because it would compromise hopes for an eventual entente with Germany.[62] And Degoutte for reasons discussed above preferred the indirect strategy of letting the initiative rest with the Rhinelanders.

Nevertheless the fact that such a radical policy was considered at all indicates that already in March Poincaré was strongly attracted to the idea of a Rhenish political entity. For the moment he would not choose a particular strategy. He would explore the idea of a negotiated settlement, including special arrangements for the Rhineland, in the elaboration of which the British would play a role. But at the same time events in the occupied areas and in Germany as a whole would be allowed to take their course; perhaps the Rhinelanders themselves would set up a satisfactory regime that all believers in self-determination would have to accept. It was best to keep both irons in the fire; there was no point in ruling anything out prematurely.

In the summer of 1923 the whole situation changed dramatically. French relations with Britain, which were relatively friendly at the start of the occupation, now deteriorated rapidly. The French resented British efforts to work out a compromise settlement, while the British objected to what they viewed as French obstructionism.[63] On July 4 Lord Curzon, the British Foreign Secretary, threatened to break completely with France if an accord on policy were not reached, and in August the affair came to a head with a public exchange of sharply worded notes.[64] But while highly critical of French policy, the British government did not announce any positive action designed to do something about it. The British had played their final card, and the French had easily weathered the storm. As for the Germans, they had all along counted on Britain's ability to force France into line, but now it was evident that these hopes had been misplaced. As Georg Bernhard of the *Vossische Zeitung* put it, the British note amounted to a "final admission of English impotence."[65] This realization paved the way for the new German policy of a direct settlement with France, which Stresemann attempted to carry out when he became Chancellor in August.

The deterioration of French relations with Britain was paralleled within France by Poincaré's break with the Radicals in mid-June, and by a very significant worsening of relations with Belgium, France's ally in the Ruhr, which, although long in the making, began to become especially serious at the end of June.[66] The effect of all this was to weaken Poincaré's ties to relatively moderate elements, and thus free his hand for a more radical policy—a policy which, as will be seen, Poincaré was in fact to embrace in late August.

At virtually the same time as Poincaré turned away from the idea of a negotiated settlement, Germany shifted her course in exactly the opposite direction. The Cuno government fell because of the widespread impression that its policy was too negative, too passive. For Stresemann, Cuno's successor, it was important that German policy be more flexible tactically, that Germany seize the initiative in looking for a way out of the deepening crisis. What this meant was that the passive resistance had to be ended, and that an agreement with the French had to be reached. This was a conclusion that even such superpatriots as Stinnes and Vögler had reached by late August.[67]

Thus, beginning at this time, both personally and through a variety of intermediaries, the new German Chancellor made a series of overtures to the French.[68] On September 1, for example, Baron von Maltzan of the German Foreign Office told the French ambassador of his government's desire to work out an informal understanding with the French government for the termination of the resistance, and on September 4 Stresemann himself made a similar pitch.[69] Poincaré turned a deaf ear to these proposals. He wanted a formal capitulation:

there would be no talks, he insisted repeatedly, until the ordinances ordering resistance were withdrawn.[70]

Margerie, the French ambassador in Berlin, conveyed these terms to the German government; but on September 21 Poincaré ordered him to stop doing even this: "We have the most serious reasons at the present moment not to speed things up."[71] Margerie was upset by his new orders and was perplexed by Poincaré's general policy—if he wanted the resistance to end, did it not make sense to tell the German officials what practical measures they were expected to make and together with them work out arrangements for a transition to a new regime for the occupied areas acceptable to France?[72] But Poincaré had indicated that he wanted to avoid a speedy settlement, and when Stresemann, on September 25, complied with his earlier demand for a withdrawal of the ordinances and called again for direct talks to ease the reestablishment of normal economic life, Poincaré hardened his terms. The revocation of the ordinances was not enough; there would be no talks until the effective end of German resistance—that is, until reparation deliveries were resumed. Arrangements for ending the resistance would have to be worked out locally in the occupied areas. But at the same time he instructed the French authorities in the Ruhr to remain relatively passive if they were approached—if the mine owners wanted to talk, they were to listen, without, however, "taking any initiative."[73]

The German government continued trying to engage the French in talks, but these attempts were unavailing. It was only on December 12, after the MICUM agreements on renewed coal deliveries had been put into effect and an agreement covering the railroad system had been reached, that Poincaré agreed somewhat halfheartedly to talks.[74] But by then the situation had changed radically. The crucial moment had passed.

Why did Poincaré block talks which might have brought about a swift resolution of the crisis? We can immediately rule out his own explanation for his refusal to talk to the Germans, that he had promised that the eventual settlement would be inter-Allied in nature, and that he would not go back on his word.[75] For what was involved here was not a final settlement of the reparation affair, but rather a proposal to work out a kind of *modus vivendi* that would facilitate the restoration of economic life in the occupied areas. Poincaré, more-

over, sought to exclude the British at this point: "English intervention will only obstruct the natural course of events."[76] By the fall of
1923 relations with the British had in fact deteriorated to the point
where Poincaré was ready to threaten a blockade of the British-occupied Cologne zone to force acceptance of French plans for the
Rhenish railway system.[77] Given the general evolution of the French
attitude that this symbolizes, it is unlikely that a concern for Britain
underlay Poincaré's silence.

What then is the answer? Was Poincaré simply being vindictive
in pushing Germany to the wall? Was his policy merely negative?
Perhaps he still had no coherent policy at all, with no clear idea of
what he really wanted. Or did he, as he said at the time, have the
"most serious reaons" for dragging things out, and if so what were
they?

The answer, I think, is that he did have his reasons: he was aiming at a restructuring of Germany along the lines sketched out by
Degoutte, and above all at the creation of a Rhenish entity. But Poincaré was generally a cautious man, and French officials as a whole
were worried about leaks; it is thus not surprising that an explicit
statement of such a policy has not found its way onto paper. For
direct evidence on Poincaré's motives at this point, the best we have
is his secret testimony to a Senate committee on November 26, 1923.
He looked forward with pleasure to the creation of an autonomous, or
even independent, Rhenish entity: "Once the disaggregation begins,
it is certain that local interests will reassert their ancient power."[78]

But Poincaré's testimony is in itself too weak a reed on which to
rest a general analysis of French motives in the second half of 1923.
A broader analysis must rest on indirect reasoning; the circumstantial
evidence supports the view that Poincaré was aiming at a decomposition of the German Reich. Seydoux and others in high places in
France certainly spoke at this time as if this were Poincaré's goal:

Seydoux [wrote President Millerand's assistant Vignon] then spoke to
me of the ideas that Laroche [another high official at the Quai d'Orsay] had
set out:

M. Poincaré is negative—his policy of excluding England makes sense
if he then intends to deal with Germany, but it is not in his temperament to
negotiate. . . .

And then is it wise to destroy German unity? Who knows what will
happen in twenty years. One must not pursue a short-sighted policy. After a

crisis Germany will pick herself back up and a reconstitution of her unity in a spirit of revenge might be the program of a Reich more dangerous to us than that whose ruin we would have sought.[79]

The Socialist ex-minister Albert Thomas analyzed the situation in much the same way. In early October Stresemann had sent Dr. Paul Bonn, the director of the Deutsche Bank, to see Thomas: could he find out if Poincaré would receive a German—the former minister von Raumer was mentioned—for negotiations on the whole affair, "bearing in particular on the organization of the regime in the Ruhr and in the Rhenish territories"? Thomas sent Poincaré a carefully worded letter, arguing that a "decomposition of Germany" was not a condition of lasting French security, and that it would be better—if all precautions against German bad faith were taken—to help those men in Germany who were willing to practice a policy of cooperation with France. Thomas sent Millerand, with whom he was on good terms, a copy of this letter. Millerand replied that he shared Thomas's views "et on ne l'ignore pas."[80] (The "on" in all likelihood refers to Poincaré himself.)

Seydoux, Thomas and Millerand thus structured the problem in much the same way. France could get satisfaction on reparation, and reap additional political benefits, if she entered into talks with Stresemann; or France, by refusing to talk, could try to bring about such chaos in Germany that the Reich would fall apart. By the beginning of November even Seydoux, who earlier had apparently supported the hard-line policy of pushing Germany to the wall, thought the time for negotiations had come: "Seydoux," wrote Vignon on November 5, "thinks that from now it is with the Germans that we must settle our affairs—that the evolution of our policy must be complete, that we can expect nothing from our allies"—Seydoux, that is, had opted for the first alternative.[81]

The interesting thing here is that Degoutte, who lobbied for the second alternative, presented the choice in almost identical fashion. "Two paths," he wrote on August 29, were apparently open. On the one hand, the French could take a "conciliatory attitude" toward the Stresemann government, and get "serious satisfactions" relatively quickly, on both reparation and security. The other choice was to refuse to cooperate at all. Stresemann would be "swept away"; Germany would suffer a "financial and economic catastrophe" and would succumb to "a period of troubles and disorders," ultimately resulting in the "reorganization of Germany" on the loose federal lines that Degoutte had repeatedly called for.[82]

Thus the idea that France had to choose between these two alternatives was shared by some of the highest and most influential officials in the government—by men whose views differed greatly among themselves. In these circumstances it would be very surprising if Poincaré himself did not, at least to a considerable degree, see things in much the same terms. And if he did, that would mean that his refusal to talk was based on a hope of destroying the German Reich, at least in its present form.

But circumstantial evidence of this sort, suggestive though it might be, can only take us so far. Fortunately, there is a good deal more that can be inferred from a close examination of events within the occupied areas. I am not referring here to French dealings with the separatist groups, nor to French support of the separatist coup of October 21. This aspect of French policy is fairly well known. The French had not precipitated the separatists' move, they had not prepared for it, were in fact surprised by it; and although they supported it, their support was far from wholehearted: in the French documents an element of contempt was rarely missing when the Rhenish separatist groups were discussed.[83] Far more significant for our purposes is the less well-known Otto Wolff affair—the French contacts with the important Ruhr industrialist Otto Wolff and his associates Carp and Becker. For it is only in the context of this affair that a major shift in basic French policy can be understood. Indeed the talks with the Wolff group played a key role in bringing this shift about in the first place.

The shift took place in late August on two key questions: who in Germany would the French negotiate with? And how would the German resistance be ended? Since the beginning of the occupation, Poincaré had repeatedly insisted on official talks. When the banker Hjalmar Schacht, for example, in March suggested semi-official negotiations—he proposed that German industrialists come to Paris to work out a solution—Poincaré categorically rejected the idea.[84]

This was still Poincaré's attitude well into the summer. On or just before July 21 a number of German mine directors approached the Belgian occupation authorities at Gladbeck with a proposal to discuss the conditions under which the resistance might end and economic life in the region be restored. The German delegation was headed by a certain Witte, a high official in the Prussian state mines at Recklinghausen. Witte was in contact with Berlin and on August 3 transmitted the views of the German government. (Cuno was still chancellor.) The Reich was willing to end the resistance and resume reparation deliveries, if the French and the Belgians agreed to then withdraw from the mines, give the railroads back to the Germans and return to the idea of an "invisible" occupation. The expelled officials would be allowed to return, and the German authorities would again administer the occupied areas. After the reparation deliveries had resumed on their normal scale, a total military withdrawal would begin.[85]

Evidently the German government was calling for an eventual return to the status quo ante. Frantzen, the French head of the MICUM, returned to Paris to report on the affair. He apparently toned down the German terms considerably, since he gave the impression that the Germans were willing to accept the occupation in its original mild form and that an agreement was within reach. Seydoux was enthusiastic: if these talks resulted in an agreement, "we would arrive at the result that we sought when we went into the Ruhr, that is, that the 'pledges' would be exploited and coal deliveries made under our supervision." The British government, moreover, would be obliged to accept what France was doing, since it was based on collaboration with the German authorities—"this would be, with regard to England and world opinion, the biggest success we could hope for." And Poincaré, in an August 20 telegram to Degoutte, set out in great detail the French position for these talks. He was willing to return to the original idea of an invisible occupation, but eventual withdrawal would take place in stages as the entire reparation bill (or really what was left of it after it had been scaled down by an amount equivalent to an eventual cancellation of at least part of the inter-Allied debt) was gradually paid. This was the standard French position. The Ruhr rail system would be run by the Germans, but the Régie would remain intact on the Left Bank. The expelled officials would be allowed back subject to veto: the minor officials would on the whole be permitted to return, but the important ones would be kept out. He insisted, moreover, that the German negotiator in these talks officially represent the Reich. Nothing came of these talks, due possibly to the governmental crisis in Germany. But for our purposes, the affair deserves attention because of the light it throws on Poincaré's attitude at this point: as late as August 20, he was willing to accept a deescalation, worked out with official representatives of the German government.[86]

But within the space of a few days this whole attitude was to change drastically. This was the change that took place in the context of—and most likely as a result of—the contacts with Otto Wolff and his associates Carp and Becker. The Wolff affair began in July. At the Phoenix firm (an enterprise headed by Carp, who together with Wolff held the majority of its stock) the French authorities in July noticed that the mine officials had become more conciliatory—the MICUM engineers were able to get the information they wanted without a military secort.[87] And at the end of the month, a certain Herr Wulf (or Wulff—the orthography varies), an associate of Becker, approached Gen. Denvignes of the French occupation force to give certain information about the different political tendencies within the German steel industry and suggest direct contacts between a group of medium-sized firms he had organized and the MICUM. According to Denvignes, Wulf seemed to think that German resistance "would end by means of isolated negotiations with private individuals, spreading out bit by bit into tacit agreements on a local scale," rather than by a formal, official capitulation.[88]

On August 5, Carp saw Gen. Denvignes. Carp spoke of the campaign he had long been pursuing for a rapprochement and economic entente with France (Denvignes agreed that this was the case); he was seen, he said, as the leader of the group of industrialists that advocated such a policy. Stinnes was the head of the opposing group, the "English party," hostile to any accommodation with France, and "until now" the predominant group among German industrialists. (Sharp antagonism toward Britain was a leitmotif running through the whole history of attempts at Franco-German rapprochement, from April 1919 on.) Carp insisted on his patriotism: "my role is not to betray my government but to enlighten it." He could not do much more than he was doing, and had no specific proposal to make.

Denvignes, bearing in mind both Wulf's remarks and the Gladbeck talks (in which a representative of the Phoenix group had participated) did have a suggestion to make. He asked Carp "if he did not foresee that the German government would soon agree to more or less semi-official discussions with the aim of reaching a detente and a modus vivendi which would conceal a capitulation and be the signal for a final detente. Will the big industrialists, to avoid total ruin, not take initiatives in this sense?'' Carp answered that the industrialists could do no more than put pressure on their own government to pursue this kind of policy. It is clear from Denvignes's remarks that the end of the resistance was still the French goal, and that the French authorities were willing to facilitate the task of any German government ready to cooperate. As long as the Ruhr industrialists were German patriots and refused to do anything not authorized by the Reich, the French had no choice but to deal with the representative, official or semi-official, of the German government.[89]

But it gradually was to become clear that the attitude of the Wolff group on these matters—its willingness to accept the present structure of the Reich and its constitutional forms—was at the very least somewhat ambivalent. The first sign of this emerged in an interview Becker had with Denvignes on August 6 (that is, the day after Carp had visited him). Becker reiterated much of Carp's analysis of the general situation, but unlike Carp he specifically addressed the issue of Rhenish separatism. ''Neither Dorten nor Smeets''—the chief separatist leaders—''would make the Rhenish Republic.'' He then distinguished between a break with Prussia and a separation from Germany, saying that if the Allies wanted it, a German Land, similar to Bavaria or Wurttemberg, could be created in the occupied areas, and the occupation itself could continue indefinitely: ''You can maintain it until the time of a total pacification, that is, up to the time when French and German interests are completely intertwined.''[90] On the other hand Becker, who had certain ties to Stresemann, sought to facilitate contact between the French and the future chancellor, suggesting a number of possible intermediaries.

The next events took place about a week later. On August 11 the Dusseldorf separatist leader von Metzen saw Denvignes. Von Metzen offered to help break the resistance by trying to get the miners at the Neumühl mine—owned by Phoenix—to return to work. The miners, who had been targeted by his group's propaganda, had, he claimed, been won over to the separatist cause. He asked for French help with the venture: could the miners be paid in hard currency, raised through the sale to France of the coal they mined, and could France guarantee their food supply? Two days later Carp had an interview with Denvignes, saying that most of the Neumühl miners were ready to return to work, but the technical personnel were very hesitant. He would try to convince them to cooperate. Denvignes drew the conclusion that the two visits were not purely coincidental, but that von Metzen and Carp were working together: the moderate industrialists wanted to create a case of "force majeure" which would justify their decision to end the resistance in the eyes of the Berlin authorities.[91]

On August 17, Carp returned to Denvignes together with Otto Wolff. Both men were about to go to Berlin to try to convince Stresemann, by now the new Chancellor, to allow them to reach agreements with the MICUM for a resumption of economic activity. Carp was worried about the danger of communism if the economic disorder continued. Wolff stressed long-term political considerations, echoing views earlier expressed by Becker. He ruled out an independent Rhenish state, a "new Alsace-Lorraine"—to perpetuate Franco-German hostility would only profit England. But then he added: "If you are afraid of an over-unified Germany, let a Rheno-Westphalian state be created within the framework of the German federation. Germany will then include an additional state, similar to Bavaria, Saxony or Wurttemberg, very independent of Berlin, and Prussian power and influence will thus be reduced, which will set your minds at ease." The occupation would continue on "a very effective and very friendly" basis until the interests of the two countries were so intertwined that conflict was utterly out of the question. The new Rhenish state would then be a link tying France and Germany together. This set of ideas corresponded to an important strand in French Rhenish policy from 1919 on.[92]

The previous day von Metzen had seen the French authorities. He no longer needed French financial support for the Neumühl affair—he had managed to obtain hard currency through a prominent Dusseldorf banker, an Alsatian named Griess (or Gries). Griess in turn was closely related to the Otto Wolff group, which, it was assumed, was the real source for the financing of the operation.[93] Griess was also involved with the Wulf consortium of mines. Wulf's plan, according to Denvignes, was to generalize to his whole group the negotiations being carried out with the Neumühl miners.[94]

Exactly what were Otto Wolff and his associates up to? There was no question in the minds of the French officials involved that all these events were part of a coordinated movement. The industrialists involved were determined to end the resistance, since the present chaotic situation threatened their interests. According to Degoutte, in a long report on the affair that he sent Poincaré on August 18, Wolff and the others were approaching the French through two different routes. The first channel was "direct and more or less official": the Gladbeck talks, the industrialists' overtures to Denvignes, their attempt to get Stresemann's blessing for their attempts to work out an accommodation with the French authorities on the spot. The second way was indirect: they were working through von Metzen. The connection was proven by their financial ties with him via Griess, and both von Metzen's and Carp's concentration on the Neumühl mine. All this meant, Degoutte said, that the industrialists were willing to "take the initiative in abandoning passive resistance and in entering into relations with me, with or without Berlin."[95]

Poincaré's reaction to these events was extremely important. On August 24, Carp and Wolff, back from Berlin, asked to see Degoutte, who wired Paris for instructions. A telegram from Poincaré came the next day: "as soon as the talks are authorized by the Chancellor," Degoutte was to pursue them himself.[96] But that very same day Poincaré radically shifted his position. The talks with the industrialists were necessarily unofficial in nature; the industrialists could not represent their government. The German government's proposals could only be made through official channels—through the French embassy in Berlin or the German embassy in Paris. The negotiations with the industrialists, insofar as they dealt with technical matters, were to be conducted by the MICUM engineers. But then he added: "the day that it appears to you that these talks are taking a turn—and you are the sole judge of that—you will summon them [i.e., the industrialists] before you and personally conduct the talks in agreement with M. Tirard and the representatives of the Belgian government.[97]

This document calls for somewhat Talmudic exegesis. The suggestion that the German government make its proposals through official channels must be viewed in the light of the fact that Poincaré had effectively closed these channels off by refusing to engage in official talks. In effect he was saying that no negotiations with representatives of the German government were possible, and that he would only talk with the industrialists in their private capacity. This was a complete switch from the earlier French position that there would be no private talks with the industrialists, and that only official proposals would get a hearing. Similarly the earlier French interest in facilitating the end of the resistance, as manifested in French reaction to the Gladbeck talks and Denvignes's remarks to Carp on August 5—the willingness, that is, to save the face of the German government and work out an informal settlement—now disappeared. For Stresemann, it soon became clear, was willing to accept the ideas of Wolff, Carp and Becker on the gradual and local liquidation of the resistance, and he discreetly encouraged their talks with the French authorities.[98] But Poincaré was no longer willing to explore the possibilities for a settlement with Germany that this new attitude had opened up. The end of the resistance in the occupied areas was no longer his primary goal. He obviously had other things on his mind.

What these were can be inferred from the passage in his August 25 letter where he referred to the talks "taking a turn." What exactly did this mean? If matters came up unrelated to the technical problems of a resumption of work, these matters could only be political in nature. What Poincaré was asking Degoutte to do, therefore, was to conduct political negotiations with private individuals; and talks that were extralegal in form were obviously also to be extralegal in substance, dealing in all probability with the elaboration of a special regime—autonomy or whatever—for the occupied areas. The very vagueness of the passage suggests the correctness of this interpretation: it would be dangerous to be too explicit when talking about these sensitive matters.

Or to make the point another way: why did Poincaré's basic policy shift on August 25? The change must be understood in the context of the Wolff affair. For the first time it seemed that respectable elements in the occupied areas were coming around to the idea that the Rhenish territories should have a special political status, that ties with the Reich should be loosened and links with France strengthened—exactly the attitude the French had long hoped to see take shape. If Wolff and his colleagues were ready, as Degoutte had reported, to act "with or without Berlin," then it was best to try to get them to act on their own initiative. To create a breach with Berlin was to lay the groundwork for a Rhenish political entity, based on the Rhinelanders' right to self-determination, and not on authority granted by the Reich.

Thus it seems that beginning in late August Poincaré was rallying to Degoutte's point of view. That Poincaré was giving the general wide authority to conduct the talks with the industrialists is one measure of the degree to which he shared his views; another is the seriousness with which Poincaré at this time took the documents in which Degoutte made his case for a "reorganization of Germany on a federalist basis."[99] In these documents, Degoutte stressed the significance of the talks with the industrialists—for the first time, he had an important practical argument with which to support his views. This is another reason for thinking that the Wolff affair played a key role in shaping Poincaré's policy.

Now the whole argument can be put together. Objectively, the effect of French policy was to drag out and in some ways to aggravate the German crisis. French moves—especially the blockade of the Ruhr—had, as Denvignes for example had pointed out, played an important part in creating the conditions for a "respectable" Rhenish movement, of which the Wolff affair was the first important sign.[100] As Degoutte commented on these developments: "The policy we have so far been pursuing is thus beginning to bear its fruit."[101]

French support for disreputable separatist movements—the groups led by Dorten, Matthes, etc.—fit into this general policy. The separatist movement, Degoutte wrote on September 9, lacked a significant political base in the area and was incapable of "achieving a decisive success." Its role was "a role of propaganda and not of realization. It is permitted to think that it will act chiefly by reaction. Just as in 1918, when many Rhinelanders came to support a Rhenish Republic through fear of an annexation by France, separatist activities can lead the organized parties, the middle classes, workers and peasants to accept and to demand autonomy within the framework of the Reich." In particular an understanding with the Center Party and the Socialists—these two parties were "the necessary backbone for any political system" in the Rhineland—was to be sought.[102] And Poincaré himself took up the argument toward the end of the month: if the French refused to talk with Stresemann, the Reich would have to let the Rhenish Centrists deal directly with France in order to prevent the Rhineland from "falling into the hands of certain separatists," and this prospect justified his refusal to negotiate with Germany even after the ordinances were withdrawn.[103] The implication of all this is clear: France was trying to aggravate the crisis within Germany—by refusing to deal with Stresemann, by discreetly supporting the separatists, etc.—because the crisis would result in the reordering of German affairs that best suited French interests.

The same set of calculations lay behind French policy on the question of the Rhenish mark, the touchstone of France's Rhenish policy for the whole period. On September 22 and 23, a number of high officials from the Ministry of Finance and in the French administration in the occupied areas met to consider the monetary question. They came up with a "Plan for monetary action in the occupied territory," which was approved by the Minister of Finance on September 28. This document argued that no thorough monetary reform was possible until the occupied region had achieved fiscal and administrative autonmy—i.e., a separate budget. As Germany sunk deeper into political and economic chaos, the local population would turn to the occupation authorities: "At this moment financial and administrative autonomy would be within reach, and the occupying authority can take charge of setting up a bank of issue." In the meantime a system of gold certificates would be created in cooperation with Rhenish interests to tide the area over the transitional period.[104] Again it is hard to avoid the conclusion that the French government was counting on the continuation of the disorder within Germany, and that it in fact sought to aggravate the situation there in order to achieve its own goals.

The problem with this policy is that it presumed that events could take one and only one course: given Poincaré's refusal to negotiate, the crisis within Germany could only deepen—there was little that the Berlin government could do about it. But on October 16 the German government decided on a monetary reform, and the Rentenmark would be issued on November 15. On the whole, French officials were convinced the Rentenmark would fail. Seydoux, for example, said on November 23 that it was "stillborn."[105] But Poincaré took fright, and in a letter to Lasteyrie of November 8 insisted on the great importance of launching the new Rhenish currency before the German monetary reform became effective.[106] If there was to be a race, it was no longer a foregone conclusion that France would win. The situation was slipping out of control. If the Rentenmark was successful, could it be kept out of the Rhineland? What justification would there be for a new Rhenish mark?

Still it seemed to the French government in September and October that its policy was progressing satisfactorily. The crisis in Germany was really setting in. As the currency headed toward total collapse, the central government began to lose its hold on the country. Relations between the Reich and the reactionary government of

Bavaria, which had long been difficult, became particularly tense in mid-October; there was also a dispute with the leftist governments of Saxony and Thuringia, in both of which the Communists participated. After an abortive Communist uprising in Hamburg at the end of October, Stresemann moved against the Saxon government with force. In the Rhineland, the government worried that the separatists (who had conducted their putsch in late October) might get some popular support if the subsidies to the area were cut off—yet they could not be continued indefinitely if a stable currency was to be instituted. The situation, therefore, seemed to be developing along the lines that Degoutte had sketched out.

Within the occupied area, moreover, it seemed that "respectable" elements were now turning toward France. Otto Wolff and his group were moving rapidly toward the idea of an outright separation from the Reich. They wanted a mixed commission—the industrialists and the occupation authorities—formally to supervise the resumption of economic life, and in reality, according to Seydoux, to govern the area.[107] On November 25 Wolff called for "a Rheno-Westphalian Parliament."[108] And in fact Degoutte in mid-November set up a system of joint economic councils in the Ruhr.

Meanwhile, a group of Rhenish leaders—the dominant figure here was Adenauer, then the Mayor of Cologne—had also reached the conclusion that for both economic and political reasons some arrangement had to be worked out with the French. The Reich was about to cut off funds to the unemployed workers in the occupied territories; something therefore had to be done to restore the economic situation if a total catastrophe was to be avoided. Given Poincaré's unwillingness to deal with the Berlin government, it followed that the Rhinelanders had to take matters in their own hands and deal with the occupying authorities directly. This was all the more necessary since if nothing were done the French might impose a regime run by outright separatists like Dorten, Matthes and their followers. Reluctantly, first at a meeting in Hagen on October 25, and then through a series of decisions taken in November, the central government agreed to authorize the Rhinelanders to do whatever they had to to salvage their situation. A committee of Rhinelanders—the Committee of Fifteen, as it was called—did negotiate with Tirard in November. The high point came on November 23 when the Rhenish side proposed the "Moldenhauer Plan," a scheme for a de facto, and in principle temporary, separate government for the occupied areas. Complementing these political discussions were the negotiations for a gold-based Rhenish currency; this would be necessary since the German authorities were initially unwilling to allow the new Rentenmark into the area. Adenauer's friend Louis Hagen was the most important Rhenish personality in these talks.[109]

Yet all these efforts came to naught. In the Ruhr, Degoutte's system of economic councils never really became the de facto government of the area. The main reason was that Poincaré acceded to his Minister of Finance's demand that the chief council have no responsibility in the key area of food supply; Lasteyrie was afraid of involving France financially.[110] In the Rhineland, Tirard simply turned down the Moldenhauer Plan at the same meeting that it was proposed. Exactly why he did so is not clear; the reason he gave to the Rhinelanders was that a purely provisional plan would not be acceptable to French public opinion.[111]

The negotiations for a new Rhenish currency were also to prove fruitless. French policy in this affair was marked by both lethargy and confusion. Thus Poincaré, for example, on November 21 suddenly demanded that the new currency be based on the franc, rather than on gold as had been assumed all along. Although time was at a premium, this new demand threatened to set the talks back to the starting point.[112] And indeed it does not seem that the government had absolutely decided that a new Rhenish currency was preferable to a stable German mark—Poincaré wrote Degoutte on October 8 that the plan for gold certificates was purely provisional in nature, covering the period until either the occupied territories became financially and administratively autonomous, or until the Reich created its own "healthy currency."[113] And when it became clear in January 1924 that the Rentenmark was succeeding, the Ministry of Finance proved very willing to drop the whole gold certificate scheme.[114]

Thus French policy in the Rhineland was characterized neither by vigor nor by clarity of purpose. Poincaré evidently wanted a Rhenish buffer state, but he was unwilling to impose it through sheer force, and was even unwilling to make the commitment of French resources needed to create institutions that might eventually form the framework of a separate political entity. One might understand Poincaré's refusal to settle for half a loaf in the form of a de facto, and in theory temporary, separation of the area, if he were willing to impose a separatist solution as a last resort; but given his unwillingness to do so, the French rejection of the Moldenhaure plan hardly makes sense.

Indeed, Poincaré's failure to work out with any care even the direct implications of his policy seems virtually imcomprehensible. France was deliberately pushing Germany toward the abyss, with the idea that Germany might somehow fall apart, and that a separate regime in the Rhineland would somehow come about. It was as though these developments would take place automatically, without the French government having to take any initiative at all, or make any effort to control the situation directly.

Thus there was little if anything done even in the way of contingency planning to meet the threat of an economic catastrophe. The basic long-term economic problem of markets for the industry of the Ruhr and the Rhineland, should unoccupied Germany sink into chaos, was treated very lightly. Degoutte, for example, in his important memorandum of September 9, blandly asserted that France would help Rhenish industry "find markets to replace those they lack, we will thus decrease its orientation toward the east and direct it instead toward France and her colonies. We can furthermore collaborate with it in the reopening of the Russian market."[115]

Did Poincaré also feel there would be no problem? It is hard to believe that someone with his political experience could possibly think the solution would be so simple: French business was sure to oppose such a large-scale "invasion" of goods from the occupied areas. But whether he was aware of the problem or not, it seems clear that he was unwilling to face it, believing probably that if the larger issues involving the structure of the German Reich were resolved, then these more technical economic problems would somehow take care of themselves.

His failure to work out a careful policy in this area is apparent when we examine the way he dealt with the immediate problem of a resumption of economic activity in the Ruhr. As Poincaré had ordered, this was handled directly in negotiations with the Ruhr industrialists. The Wolff group (Phoenix, Rheinische Stahlwerke) was the first to enter into talks, and a provisional agreement was initialed on October 7: reparation coal would be delivered, and the coal tax—both in the future and for the period since the start of the occupation— would be paid. In exchange the firms would be allowed to conduct business again under the control of the Reparation Commission. It was assumed that the German government would reimburse the firms for what they turned over to the Allies, but the Reich refused to cooperate in this way. The French therefore made certain concessions, especially on the size of the coal tax arrears, and a final text of the "provisional arrangement" was signed on October 21. This agreement covered about 15 percent of the Ruhr's output of coal and coke, and was followed by a similar accord with Krupp on November 1.[116]

The most important talks took place with the Bergbauverein, headed by Stinnes, the mines in which accounted for 80 percent of the Ruhr's output. The talks began in mid-October; the Stinnes group did not want to both pay the coal tax and provide reparation coal free of charge. How could both things be financed? Seydoux suggested that the industrialists could meet these conditions by repatriating the funds they had earlier sent abroad—very sizable sums, as everyone knew. But Stinnes's representative Frick said these funds exceeded the value of the industrialists' German assets, and they would prefer to give up the latter in order to hold onto their foreign fortune. To Seydoux, this meant that Stinnes was threatening mass unemployment, and soon it became clear that the Bergbauverein was willing to contemplate a mass lockout to impose acceptable terms on the French—and on its own workers, for it sought to use the occasion to suppress the eight-hour day. Seydoux urged that the French take a hard line and resist this attempt at "blackmail": he told Frick that if Stinnes carred out his threat, the occupation authorities would feed the workers and take over the mines themselves.[117]

Was this pure bluff? The answer is no: Poincaré intended to carry through on this threat. Although Lasteyrie strongly objected to any further extension of direct exploitation on a major scale, Poincaré ordered that the takeover of Stinnes's property begin if he refused to accept France's terms.[118] The question was no longer whether the industrialists would both pay the coal tax and deliver the reparation coal—this they had conceded on October 26. The bone of contention in early November was Article XVII of the draft agreement—the problem was the German demand that all payments and deliveries should be credited to Germany on the reparation account. Stresemann had made this a condition for eventual reimbursement by the Reich. The idea was to rule out the possibility of Germany having to pay for the Ruhr occupation. As Poincaré was aware, it was the fundamental question of the legitimacy of the occupation that was being raised, and even Seydoux, eager as he was for a quick settlement, was determined to take a firm stand on this question of principle.[119] On November 13, Poincaré ordered Degoutte to arrest Stinnes—to "seize his person"—should he attempt a lockout, either to put pressure on the French or to force his workers to accept a ten-hour day. Stinnes, he added, "had since the Spa Conference personally been the obstacle to any entente for the payment of reparation and to a possible accord between France and Germany. He must therefore be clearly pushed aside and told that his establishments will be operated by means of a sequester if he does not accept our propositions: these should be presented to him as an ultimatum."[120]

The next day the ultimatum was presented to the representatives of the Bergbauverein. Stinnes was absent, but the others rejected Poincaré's terms. The French then broke off the talks. Poincaré ordered the seizure of some of Stinnes's property. Thyssen was also to be hit. A lockout was announced for the end of the month. On November 18, Stinnes's Erin mine was occupied without incident, and two days later the miners decided unanimously to go back to work under French engineers.[121]

Poincaré was overjoyed. Stinnes, he ordered on November 20, was not to be received. "Our whole effort," he said, "must tend on the contrary to push him aside." The workers preferred to work under the French than to accept a ten-hour day. This showed how foolish the French would be to allow Stinnes to "reestablish his situation and maintain his fortune."[122] And the same day he wrote Degoutte that the results at the Erin mine should be headlined, and added:

I think the workers should be told that we are ready to directly run all mines whose current management demands a ten-hour day. With regard to Stinnes, please speed up measures for the direct exploitation of the mines in his group. As I have already told you, there is no question of again allowing him into the negotiations; he is at present setting policy for the German government and the industrialists; he is the worst enemy of German democracy and of ourselves.[123]

Thus Poincaré was announcing his readiness for an indefinite extension of the direct exploitation system. One is stunned by how little thought went into this decision, which so fundamentally contradicted what up to then had been basic assumptions of French policy, for throughout 1923 it was always admitted within the French government that the French engineers could not possibly manage the bulk of the Ruhr mines.[124] Nor is it clear what the larger political implications of this new policy were to be: was it in any way linked to hopes for a Rhenish political entity? If so, the actual connection is unclear; it seems more likely that the connection was not in fact worked out. One has the impression, based for example on the highly emotional nature of Poincaré's references to Stinnes, that this vision of a direct takeover of the Ruhr economy derived from pure impulse. It was, moreover, to be abandoned almost as soon as it was proposed—this vacillation on basics was symptomatic of the incoherence of French policy at this crucial point.

Already on November 19—the day before the Erin miners voted—a compromise on Article XVII had been reached in the talks with the industrialists. Poincaré at first resisted, but Frantzen, the head of the MICUM, came to Paris and convinced him to accept the final agreement. The Germans, he said, needed a face-saving formula; the alternative was mass starvation.[125] On November 23 the final MICUM agreement was signed, and industrial activity quickly recovered.

So Poincaré had decided to stop short of forcing a complete economic catastrophe. The policy he had been pursuing since August had been predicated on the assumption that there would be a very serious economic crisis, and that such a crisis was desirable from the French point of view. Now forced to confront the prospect of a collapse up close, he drew back from pursuing his policy to the bitter end.

Given that Poincaré was willing to allow an economic recovery, one wonders why he did so little to make sure that it occurred in a framework that would in one way or another be advantageous to France. Direct negotiations with the German government might have resulted in a broader settlement, and at the very least in a formal promise to reimburse the industrialists for all the deliveries and payments they made. As it was, Poincaré did not even get that, and the MICUM arrangements would fall apart if the Reich simply refused to pay the industrialists, who could not continue to advance the necessary sums out of their own pockets indefinitely. Or alternatively Poincaré could have sought to set up a Rhenish entity, with its own budget and currency, raising taxes which could go in part toward financing the MICUM deliveries. But here too in the final analysis his efforts were halfhearted; he trusted in the ability of events to take a desirable course on their own, rather than in his ability to control the course of events through an active policy. One wonders if Poincaré had any clear idea of what he was trying to accomplish and how he proposed to go about it. If he did, his strategy must have been very subtle indeed, for no coherent and consistent policy can be inferred from the sources.

The MICUM agreements were considered a French success at the time, but it is clear now that they marked the failure of Poincaré's policy. These arrangements, with the tremendous burden they placed on the industrialists, were obviously unstable and could work only if the Reich cooperated.[126] An alternative, which corresponded to the conception of the occupation that had evolved in late 1922, was to make the occupied region into a self-sufficient economic entity, exploited by means of fiscal measures. If this had been imposed—by pure coercion, through some form of agreement with Stresemann, or in negotiations with prominent representatives of the local population—the situation would have been completely different. Then France would control the situation: she could then allow the special regime for the occupied areas to be dismantled gradually, as acceptable arrangements with Germany were worked out and put into effect. But in the aftermath of the MICUM agreements and with the restoration of economic life in the occupied territories, there was no longer any hope for a Rhenish solution, and Poincaré did not have enough bargaining power left to shape the basic lines of the settlement with Germany.

There is one last matter that has to be discussed: Poincaré's acceptance of the idea of an "international" solution to the affair. At the beginning of the occupation, he had insisted that the British would not be excluded from eventual negotiations with Germany for a settlement of the whole reparation problem.[127] But how much of a role would the British be permitted to play? The French had long wanted, and in 1923 continued to seek, a settlement whereby both the nominal reparation debt and the nominal inter-Allied debt would be scaled down by equivalent amounts.[128] Obviously Britain, and if possible America too, would take part in the elaboration of this general settlement of international indebtedness. But beyond that, how much of a role Poincaré was willing to allow Britain varied with circumstances, although in general he was not willing to go very far. He ruled out in particular anything that would reduce what France was to get under existing arrangements: as far as the French share was concerned, the reparation liability would remain intact, except insofar as reductions resulted from a settlement of inter-Allied indebtedness.[129]

But a new reparation settlement, even apart from a settlement of the inter-Allied debts, was exactly what the British government wanted. In late July, the Foreign Secretary Lord Curzon supported a proposal the German government had made the previous month for an investigation of the question of German capacity to pay by an impartial international body, as a prelude to just such a scaling down of the reparation debt.[130] Poincaré resented these British efforts to pose as mediators and draw the French into new concessions: "We do not want to continue descending the slope that the British have been pulling us down since the Treaty of Versailles."[131] He therefore became increasingly reluctant to accept what now appeared as British intrusion into the Ruhr affair. Britain's refusal to go into the Ruhr with France, he wrote on May 7, meant that she had no right "to intervene in a debate in which she has disinterested herself."[132] This meant that Britain would play no role in negotiating an end to the occupation or a deescalation of the affair; the terms for a resolution of the crisis—and this, rather than the form of the ultimate reparation settlement, was the key issue at the time—would be dictated by France.

Thus the French categorically rejected the British proposal for an "impartial" international committee. Their argument was that the question was political and not economic in nature; there was no point examining Germany's capacity to pay—at the present moment nonexistent in the eyes of the bankers—when the real problem was how to make Germany willing to pay. This was the aim of the French action in the Ruhr.[133] And when the idea of a committee of experts was revived in the fall, Poincaré took the same line. On October 15 he wrote to his ambassador in Washington:

It is pointless to try to evaluate Germany's capacity to pay, which is null since the Reich has voluntarily gone bankrupt. . . . It is equally useless to have third parties, however qualified they might be, examine Germany's financial situation. Everyone is familiar with it. What is needed now is for the German people to grasp their present situation and finally make the effort needed to balance the Reich's budget, which will enable a stable currency to be created. It does not seem that things have reached that point yet in Germany, since they are continuing to conceive artificial schemes to create currencies which will have no real basis and will not be able to last.[134]

But just four days later this policy was to be totally abandoned. The British had just approached the Americans with a plan for an experts' group which could either be an independent body or could report to the Reparation Commission. The Americans agreed to participate (although in the event the second option was chosen, the American on the committee would be a private citizen rather than a representative of the government). Secretary of State Hughes was worried that if nothing were done and events continued along their present course, Germany would fall apart.[135] The British then informed Poincaré of this "American offer," and Poincaré, without waiting for details, immediately accepted the idea of a committee of experts to advise the Reparation Commission.[136] It is clear that at this point the idea was to consider a general settlement of the reparation problem.

But soon Poincaré began to backtrack and sought to limit the scope of the inquiry. The actual reparation debt, he insisted, could not be questioned, nor could the experts examine the Ruhr occupation itself. The idea was to see how Germany could restore her finances, and the aim was to set reparation payments for the relatively brief transitional period until budgetary stability was reached. In no case could this period go beyond 1930, he said on November 6; four days later he wrote that the plan was to reach only through 1926.[137]

These terms angered Hughes, but Poincaré went ahead anyway and the Reparation Commission issued invitations for two committees. The first committee was to consider budgetary and monetary questions, and the second was to study the problem of repatriating the massive foreign holdings that had resulted from the great post-war exodus of German capital. The terms of reference were very general. Soon the Dawes and McKenna committees—each took the name of its chairman—were to begin work.

Thus Poincaré's decision to accept an international committee of experts, whatever his subsequent attempts to qualify the terms of his acceptance, marked an important break with existing policy. To allow a committee to come up with a payment plan, even for a limited number of years, was virtually equivalent to a scaling down of the total debt, for at the end of the period covered by the plan it would be most unlikely that a French government would be able to insist on a return to the full Schedule of Payments. Belgium and Italy took a much softer line than France on the question of the size of the debt, and were more likely in the future to side with Britain than with France when problems of enforcement came up. The alternative was to insist on the continued validity of the Schedule of Payments, thereby ruling out the need for inter-Allied negotiations for a new payment plan in which France would be virtually isolated. The German default, which was the legal basis for the sanctions, would thus continue; France would be in a stronger position to extract favorable terms, both from Germany and from her allies. In its extreme form this would amount to the exclusion of the British until they too had accepted France's terms—a cancellation of the inter-Allied debt in exchange for an equivalent scaling down of the theoretical reparation debt and the resolution of the conflict through purely bilateral negotiations with Germany. It seems in fact that Seydoux was inclined to pursue this kind of policy. He told Vignon on November 5 that "it is henceforth with the Germans that we must settle our affairs—the evolution of our policy must be complete, we can no longer expect anything from our allies." [138]

Of course a policy of this sort contradicted Poincaré's policy of forcing Germany to the precipice as a prelude to a complete reorganization of the Reich. But then the question is: if he was serious about his German policy, why then did he adopt a policy whose fundamental purpose was to restore German finances? Perhaps he calculated that the work of the experts would be slow to bear fruit, and by then events in Germany would have taken their course. But the very fact that the experts were meeting would give the Berlin authorities hope, and would induce them to hold on; and there was no reason to think that the Allies, when the financial plan was eventually put into effect, would use their financial power to reorganize Germany along the lines dear to Poincaré.

One is therefore left wondering why Poincaré opted for an international solution at that particular time. Did his allies offer any special inducement? Did they, for example, show a new willingness to meet French views on the war debt question? Britain made no new concession on the inter-Allied debt problem. Hughes, on the other hand, in a talk with the French chargé on October 22, took a sympathetic line on this matter, but made no firm promises. In any case, he made his remarks several days after Poincaré had decided to accept a committee of experts, so this could not have been a factor.[139] Or perhaps Poincaré was even at this point so committed to the alliance with Britain that he did not dare pursue the policy Seydoux proposed. It is true that his attitude toward the British was ambivalent. Sometimes he wanted to bring them in, but could be easily talked out of it, and at other times he wanted to keep them out, but could readily be convinced to change his mind.[140]

And the British attitude itself was by no means monolithic. Curzon and Crowe in the Foreign Office were very hostile to France, but the Prime Ministers—first Bonar Law and then Baldwin—tended to be much more sympathetic, and there were even signs that the British were willing to accommodate the French on the Rhenish question.[141] Given all this it is not surprising that Poincaré did not want to break all ties with Britain. But this still does not explain his sudden willingness to accept an international committee. For if France had sought a solution through direct talks with Germany, that would by no means have prevented an eventual restoration of good Anglo-French relations; it is in any case hard to argue that the risk of alienating Britain that this policy would have entailed was any greater than the similar risk Poincaré took on when he went into the Ruhr and then supported Rhenish separatism. The United States for its part positively welcomed Franco-German talks.[142]

One can therefore question whether a compelling explanation for Poincaré's decision to accept a committee of experts exists at all. Perhaps the decision was impulsive—perhaps there was no clear and consistent logic underlying the various moves Poincaré was making. We are therefore, in other words, led back to the problem of the coherence of French policy in 1923. The chronology provides some clues to an answer.

Suppose Poincaré had agreed to an experts' committee *after* the main MICUM accords were signed. Then the explanation would be easy: when directly faced with the actual prospect of economic chaos, famine and revolt both along the Rhine and in unoccupied Germany, he drew back from his policy of aggravating the German crisis and chose instead to permit economic recovery. This was the meaning of the MICUM accords. But given the seriousness of the situation, the presumed incapacity of the German government to restore stable conditions by itself, and the limited amount the French could or would do to help, the only way out was to turn to the Anglo-Saxons for financial assistance.

But the problem here is that Poincaré's decision to accept the experts' committee was made on October 19, just a few days before he decided on impulse to support the separatist Putsch in the Rhineland. The main MICUM accord was signed over a month later. Thus in late October he was still seeking to aggravate the German crisis. Why then had he reversed previous policy by agreeing to the experts' committee? Or, looking at it from the other side, if agreeing to the experts' committee meant that Poincaré had in the final analysis decided that a German collapse was not in France's interest, why then did he continue to pursue a policy that tended to aggravate the crisis in Germany?

One has the impression that again the different aspects of French policy were working at cross purposes—that Poincaré had no firm conception of where he wanted to go and what it would take to get there, but rather proceeded on impulse, never able to integrate the moves he was making into a clear and consistent policy. France was to pay a heavy price for this. As in the case of his refusal to organize the occupied territories economically under French auspices, Poincaré had failed to set up a situation which he could in very large measure control—a situation, that is, where France would virtually set her own terms. He allowed the chance to create such a position to slip through his fingers. The result was that France more or less had to accept the terms others would set, terms which ultimately were to condemn the Treaty of Versailles and open way for the resurgence of Germany as the dominant power on the European continent.

It is clear, I think, that there was nothing inevitable about what happened in 1923. The story might have had a very different ending if French policy had had a firmer conceptual foundation. Poincaré failed in 1923 not because success was impossible, but because he had no clear idea of what his aims were and what it would take to achieve them. And given the importance of this great test of strength in the history of international politics in the interwar period, if France had succeeded in the Ruhr, events after 1923 might well have taken a completely different course.

But by the end of the year, the eventual collapse of the Versailles system was predictable with a high degree of confidence. The cards had been dealt; all that remained was for the hand to be played out. Seydoux, as usual the most perceptive of the French policy makers, already understood by this time that the Europe of Versailles was a thing of the past. France, he said on December 27, was unavoidably entering along the path of a "financial reconstruction" of Europe, and could no longer deal with Germany as "victor to vanquished." Once France had set out on this path there would be no turning back.[143] But little did he suspect just how far that path would go, or how swiftly it would be traveled.

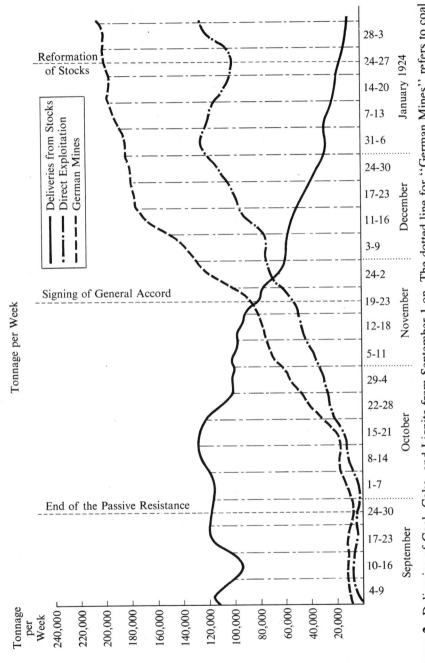

Figure 2. Deliveries of Coal, Coke, and Lignite from September 1 on. The dotted line for "German Mines" refers to coal deliveries arising from the MICUM agreements. (*Source: Degoutte Report, folder "Cartes et Graphiques."*)

Appendix

A Note on the Transfer Problem in Economic Theory

The reparation dispute stimulated a considerable amount of work by economists on the problem of unilateral transfers. On the early development of this field of economic theory, see Lloyd Metzler, "The Theory of International Trade," in Howard Ellis, ed., *A Survey of Contemporary Economics* (Philadelphia: Blakiston, 1948); on the question of a presumed shift in the terms of trade, see two articles by Paul Samuelson: "The Transfer Problem and Transport Costs," reprinted in American Economic Association, *Readings in International Economics* (Homewood, Ill.: R. D. Irwin, 1968), and "On the Trail of Conventional Beliefs about the Transfer Problem," (MIT Economics Department Working Papers, No. 54, 1970).

Perhaps the most famous episode in the development of this area of economic theory was the exchange Keynes had with Bertil Ohlin in the *Economic Journal* in 1929. Ohlin argued that shifts of "purchasing power" facilitated the transfer; Keynes disputed the point.[1] Ohlin was in fact arguing that money transfers influenced what Keynes was later to call "effective demand," and thereby helped bring about the real transfer. Economists now view Ohlin's analysis as the more "Keynesian" of the two, and it is not surprising, given the way Keynes's general economic views were evolving, that he was (without any fanfare to be sure) to come around to Ohlin's point of view. He conceded the key point in a letter to Ohlin in January 1931:

"As to your point that reparations cause a shift in the demand curve of the receiving country irrespective of any rise in the price level of that country, I do not think I disagree with you."[2] But the problem with income-oriented analysis in general is that it is based on assumptions about institutional behavior—in particular, the behavior of the banking system—that do not necessarily hold. Ohlin, incidentally, recently admitted this point, and regretted that he had not been more explicit about these matters in his original articles.[3]

All this has a direct bearing on the economics of reparation for the period studied here, since an optimistic attitude toward the transfer problem is often based on assumptions about income effects. I want to show, however, that this kind of optimism is not justified for the period in question. Because the issue is a little complicated, the problems with the income approach can best be brought out by means of a simple two-equation model; since the point of the model is to bring the problem of income effects into sharp focus, price and exchange rate effects are deliberately neglected, and there is no equation representing a mechanism for balance-of-payments equilibrium. Assume then that the only capital movement is the payment of reparation R (counted as positive for the creditor and as negative for the debtor), and that the only other foreign transactions are imports and exports of goods and services, N and X respectively. Then the balance of payments surplus (or, if negative, deficit) b would be the difference between R plus earnings from exports, on the one hand, and expenditures on imports on the other: $b = R + X - N$. Assume also that G, government spending on goods and services, depends to some extent on the amount of reparation received or paid out, and that in particular when reparation receipts increase (or, for the debtor, when payments diminish) G also expands, but by no more than the change in the amount of reparation:

$$G = G(R), \quad 1 \geqslant G'(R) > 0.$$

(This analysis, of course, applies to both the creditor and the debtor, the only difference being that in the case of the latter the value of R is negative. For the debtor, therefore, an increase in the absolute value of R would *reduce* both G and b.) The government deficit d would then in each case be equal to total spending minus net receipts. Letting T represent taxation:

$$d = G - (T + R).$$

Now assume that the monetary authorities do not set the money supply completely arbitrarily, but that the supply of money M depends on both the payments surplus (reserves of foreign money and their equivalents being used as a basis for credit) and the government deficit (the central bank creating money to help the government cover it), i.e.:

$$M = M(b,d), \frac{\delta M}{\delta b} > 0, \frac{\delta M}{\delta d} > 0.$$

Assuming the usual Keynesian analysis of the demand for money L, with Y representing money income and r the rate of interest, we have:

$$L = L(Y,r), \frac{\delta L}{\delta Y} > 0, \frac{\delta L}{\delta r} < 0.$$

Then equilibrium in the money market would yield:

$$(1) \ M(b,d) = L(Y,r), \frac{\delta M}{\delta b} > 0, \frac{\delta M}{\delta d} > 0, \frac{\delta L}{\delta Y} > 0, \frac{\delta L}{\delta r} < 0.$$

Assuming in the usual fashion that consumer spending C depends on disposable income $Y - T$, in such a way that when disposable income increases, so does consumer spending, but by not as much, and that investment or business spending I depends inversely on the rate of interest, the equation for equilibrium in the market for goods and services would be:

$$(2) \ Y = C(Y - T) + I(r) + X - N + G, \ 1 > C'(Y - T) > 0, \ I'(r) < 0.$$

Finally, for simplicity we take taxes and exports as both being determined exogenously; imports N are assumed to be an increasing function of income, with the proviso that not all of an increase in income is spent on imports:

$$T = \bar{T}, \ X = \bar{X}, \ N = N(Y), \ 1 > N'(Y) > 0.$$

The question of the significance of income effects then boils down to the problem of how much the change in income resulting from the payment of reparation increases imports, and thus shifts the balance of trade in such a way as to effect the transfer of the real wealth the payment ultimately represents. In other words, we are concerned with the net effect of the payment of reparation on the balance of payments: for income effects to increase the stability of the payments mechanism, the increase in the payments surplus must be less than the amount of reparation, the difference being due to the countervailing influence of increased income: $\frac{db}{dR}$ should be less than one.

Indeed, the closer $\frac{db}{dR}$ is to zero, the more powerful income effects are, and the less need there is to rely on the price and exchange rate mechanism to effect the real transfer. Since

$$b = R + X - N, \frac{db}{dR} = 1 - N'(Y)\frac{dY}{dR};$$

it follows immediately that $\frac{db}{dR}$ is less than one if and only if $\frac{dY}{dR}$ is positive.

The whole question thus turns on the size of $\frac{dY}{dR}$; we are especially interested in the sign of this derivative.

To find it, simply differentiate equations (1) and (2) with respect to R via the chain rule, and solve for $\frac{dY}{dR}$ bearing in mind that

$$b'(R) = 1 - N'(Y)\frac{dY}{dR}$$

and

$$d'(R) = G'(R) - 1$$

(these last two results following from the definitions of b and d and the assumptions about the exogeneity of X and T). The calculation of $\frac{dY}{dR}$ is then straightforward, and only the result is presented here:

$$(3) \quad \frac{dY}{dR} = \frac{\dfrac{\delta L}{\delta r}\dfrac{G'(R)}{I'(r)} + \dfrac{\delta M}{\delta b} + \dfrac{\delta M}{\delta d}(G'(R) - 1)}{\dfrac{\delta L}{\delta Y} + N'(Y)\dfrac{\delta M}{\delta b} + \dfrac{\dfrac{\delta L}{\delta r}}{I'(r)}(1 - C'(Y - T) + N'(Y))}$$

It follows from previous assumptions that all three terms in the denominator of this equation are positive, so the whole denominator is positive. Therefore the sign of $\frac{dY}{dR}$ depends on the sign of the numerator; but of the three terms in the numerator, the first two are positive, and the last one is negative. This implies that if government spending depends in no significant way on reparation receipts, and if the supply of money is essentially uninfluenced by the payments surplus—that is, both $G'(R)$ and $\frac{\delta M}{\delta b}$ are negligible—then the income effect can actually be destabilizing: $\frac{dY}{dR}$ would be negative, and $\frac{db}{dR}$ would be greater than one. For in that case, the chief effect of reparation receipts on the creditor nation would be to reduce the government deficit, and thus to reduce the pressure on the central bank to create new money to cover the deficit. On the other hand, the more tightly reparation receipts or payments were linked to actual government spending, and the more the money supply was influenced by the payments surplus or deficit, the more powerful income effects would be.

How does this analysis apply to France and Germany in the period after World War I? In the case of both countries, it appears that $G'(R)$ was not very great. The rate of government spending in France, most notably on reconstruction, did not depend essentially on the receipt of reparation money, nor did the need to pay reparations have a significant dampening effect on government spending in Germany: the willingness of both nations to use inflationary methods of finance meant that the flow of reparation money did not significantly control the rate of government spending in either country. And because this was a period of great inflation on both sides, the direct monetary effect of the payments deficit or surplus—that is, $\frac{\delta M}{\delta b}$ —is difficult to gauge: the effect of changes in holdings of foreign currencies and their equivalents was certainly swamped by domestic inflationary forces. On the other hand, in both cases monetary policy was very sensitive to the government deficit; since the two governments were unable to fully cover the deficits through normal borrowing, they were forced during this period to seek advances from the central banks. Thus the actual payment of reparation, if it had taken place, might well have been on balance inflationary for Germany and deflationary for France. The effect in that case would have been to expand Germany's imports and thus "worsen" her balance of trade; the effect on France would have been the opposite. Thus, insofar as one can abstract from changes in prices and exchange rates and gauge the impact of income effects taken by themselves, this simple model leads to the conclusion that for the period in question there is no reason for assuming that income effects would have been a powerful stabilizing force, and thus the income-oriented analysis of the payments mechanism by no means warrants an optimistic approach to the transfer problem as it existed in the early 1920s.

But this in turn implies that for the analysis of the transfer problem, the price and exchange rate mechanism stressed in the traditional theory remains indispensable. In this approach, the problem of stability turned on the empirical question of the various price elasticities involved: the system is stable if a small decline in a country's exchange rate tends to improve its balance of payments.[4] Again, if the system is stable, an optimistic attitude toward transfer is justified, for in that case the exchange rate depreciation caused by the transfer will result in suitable changes in the balance of payments. Keynes's view, however, was that the elasticities were such that a fall in the exchange rate would not increase the earnings from foreign trade—the fall in prices would more than counterbalance the increase in the physical quantity sold. Keynes first asserted (correctly) that this was possible, but then simply assumed (without evidence or argument) that this possibility was a fact.[5] His pessimism was at first, however, borne out by estimates of price elasticities made in the 1940s. But these findings were soon shown by G. H. Orcutt in an important article to have been based on faulty statistical method. More recent estimates have yielded more optimistic conclusions about the stability of the price and exchange rate mechanism in general, and thus about the possibility of transfer, even without taking income effects into account.[6] Whether such conclusions apply to the early 1920s is a question that no one, to my knowledge, has yet answered.

The question of the ease with which the market mechanism at that time would have been able, if at all, to effect the payment of reparation must, therefore, be left unanswered. But, as noted in the text, such a question is of essentially academic interest anyway. For to the extent that the market mechanism proved inadequate, alternative channels could have been created to permit the payment of reparation. This in fact was the whole point of the Seydoux Plan. And this in turn implies that the problem of reparation was in no sense a technical economic problem whose "answer" depends on the estimation of a whole complex of elasticities and various other parameters; if the will had existed, the technical problems of an inadequate market mechanism could certainly have been overcome. And it was the question of will—of willingness to pay, willingness to receive, willingness to work out ways of overcoming both technical and political problems—that ultimately was decisive: reparation was always far more a political than an economic problem.

Abbreviations
Used in Notes

AE, Allemagne, 269

Archives of the French Ministry of Foreign Affairs, Series "Europe 1918–1929," Subseries "Allemagne," vol. 269.

AJ⁵ 320

Archives of the French Delegation to the Reparation Commission, carton 320.

AJ⁶

Archives of the Reparation Commission

Akten: Cuno

Akten der Reichskanzlei Weimarer Republik: Das Kabinett Cuno.

Baruch Diary

Bernard M. Baruch, "American Delegation to Negotiate Peace. Memoranda, Comments and Notes in Diary Form," Baruch Papers, Princeton University.

Cab 24/108/CP 1560

Great Britain, Cabinet Office. Memoranda and Documents (class Cab 24), vol. 108, Cabinet Paper 1560.

Chambre, *Débats*

Journal officiel de la République française, Débats parlementaires, Chambre des Députés.

Chambre, *Documents*

Journal officiel de la République française, Documents parlementaires, Chambre des Députés.

Clémentel

Etienne Clémentel, *La France et la politique économique interalliée* (Paris: Presses Universitaires de France, 1931).

Cmd. 2169 of 1924	Great Britain, Parliament. *Accounts and Papers.* 1924 session, paper "Cmd. 2169."
DBFP	Great Britain, Foreign Office. *Documents on British Foreign Policy, 1919–1939,* First Series.
Degoutte Report	General Degoutte, *L'Occupation de la Ruhr.* A great number of documents are appended to this secret report; they are identified by their PA—Pièce Annexe—number.
Demande de moratorium	France, Ministère des Affaires Etrangères, *Documents Diplomatiques, Demande de moratorium du gouvernement allemand à la Commission des Réparations (14 novembre 1922).* (Paris, 1923).
Doc. rel. aux rep.	France, Ministère des Affaires Etrangères. *Documents relatifs aux réparations.*
F^{12}	Archives of the French Ministry of Commerce.
F^{30}	Archives of the French Ministry of Finance.
FO 371/7479/C89981G	Great Britain, Foreign Office, Political Correspondence, vol. 7479, paper C89981G.
FO 408/7/C7546	Great Britain, Foreign Office, Confidential Print (Germany), vol. 7, paper C7546.
FRUS	United States, Department of State, *Papers Relating to the Foreign Relations of the United States*
FRUS, PPC	United States, Department of State, *Papers Relating to the Foreign Relations of the United States: The Paris Peace Conference*
Lapradelle	Albert Geouffre de Lapradelle, ed., *La Paix de Versailles.*
Mantoux	*Les Déliberations du Conseil des Quatre (24 mars—28 juin 1919): Notes de l'officier interprète Paul Mantoux*
Munitions Committee	United States Congress, Senate, Special Committee Investigating the Munitions Industry, Seventy-Fourth Congress, Second Session
OAR	Suda L. Bane and Ralph H. Lutz, eds., *Organization of American Relief in Europe, 1918–1919*
Parl. Deb., Commons	Great Britain, *Parliamentary Debates,* House of Commons

Recueil	Conférence de la Paix, *Recueil des Actes de la Conférence*
Sénat, *Débats*	*Journal officiel de la République française, Débats parlementaires, Sénat*
T-120/2403/E212806	United States National Archives Microfilm publication T-120, reel 2403, frame E212806

Notes

1. A New Economic Order

1. This impression derives from an examination of various sources, including the Ministry of Commerce, Ministry of Finance and Foreign Ministry archives in Paris and parliamentary debates and documents. There is in fact little evidence that other French leaders gave much attention during the war to the economic problems of the peace. Clemenceau in particular seems to have deliberately avoided postwar questions during the war: the war itself, he proclaimed in his ministerial declaration, would be his sole concern (*Journal officiel de la République française, Débats parlementaires, Chambre des Députés,* November 20, 1917, pp. 2962–63—this source will henceforth be cited as "Chambre, *Débats,*" and its Senate equivalent will be similarly cited as "Sénat, *Débats*"). There was a Bureau d'Etudes Economiques attached to the Prime Minister's office, but its importance is open to question. One of its members, the deputy and economist Adolphe Landry, even complained publicly in March 1918 that this body was being ignored by the government (Chambre, *Débats,* March 15, 1918, p. 945). Clemenceau's close associate Louis Loucheur, the Minister of Armament, also seems to have neglected postwar questions at the time: it was only after the armistice that the Ministry of Armament was converted into the Ministry of Industrial Reconstitution and Loucheur began to play a leading role in formulating broad economic policy. Given their preoccupation with the war, Clemenceau's and Loucheur's attitude toward postwar problems makes sense; what is surprising is that these questions were apparently neglected even by the Ministry of Finance. There is nothing in this ministry's archives, nor in the papers of L. L. Klotz, Clemenceau's Minister of Finance, to indicate that this normally preeminent ministry was concerned with these problems at the time. Nor in the pertinent files of the Ministry of Commerce and the Foreign Ministry is there any reference to the attitude of the Ministry of Finance, or any correspondence with it on these issues. Indeed, Klotz did not even attend the September 1918 meeting at which Clémentel's views were adopted as government policy, even though financial questions figured prominently in the latter's plans. On the Finance Ministry's neglect of the

question see also Klotz's brief colloquy in the Chamber with his former collaborator Charles de Lasteyrie: his silence, when Lasteyrie charged him with failing to prepare a policy on postwar questions, strikes me in the context of the colloquy as an implicit admission that this criticism was well-founded (Chambre, *Débats,* February 9, 1921, p. 406).

2. On Clémentel see the *Dictionnaire des parlementaires français,* ed. Jean Jolly, (Paris: Presses Universitaires de France, 1963), 3:1071–73, and especially J. F. Godfrey, "Bureaucracy, Industry and Politics in France during the First World War: A Study of Some Interrelationships," (Ph.D. diss., St. Antony's College, Oxford, 1974). My account of Clémentel's general policy is based on his parliamentary speeches, his book *La France et la politique économique interalliée*—hereafter cited as "Clémentel"—and relevant material in the Ministry of Commerce archives, fonds F^{12} at the Archives Nationales in Paris, especially cartons F^{12}7798, 7988, 8039, 8104 and 8106.

3. *L'Europe nouvelle,* (14 December, 1918), 4:2340. See also n. 57 below.

4. Jean-Baptiste Duroselle stressed this link in two recent articles: "Bilan et perspectives économiques de l'Europe," *Revue d'histoire moderne et contemporaine* (Jan.-March 1969) and "Strategic and Economic Relations During the First World War," in *Troubled Neighbours: Franco-British Relations in the Twentieth Century,* ed. Neville Waites (London: Weidenfeld, 1971). The book on Franco-American relations in this period by his student André Kaspi, *Le Temps des Américains, 1917–1918* (Paris; Publications de la Sorbonne, 1976), contains more information on this whole question and in particular on Monnet's role. According to Duroselle, Monnet's ideas were the principal inspiration behind Clémentel's policy, but this view seems unlikely: the impression I got from the evidence, especially from F^{12}7797, is that Monnet was more an executor than a creator of this system, and in particular it seems quite clear that Monnet's plan for the pooling of Allied shipping marked no "revolutionary" change in French policy as elaborated by Clémentel, which had long favored the pooling of Allied resources (see also n. 16 below).

5. The plan is set out in its fullest form in Clémentel's long letter to Clemenceau of 19 September 1918 (F^{12}8104, folder "Propositions des Ministères"; published in Clémentel, pp. 337–48).

6. "There can be no question," Clémentel declared to the Senate, "of creating an aggressive, exclusive League which would eternally perpetuate the conflict. We only claim to remain masters of our own markets, and—faced with a scarcity of raw materials during the period in which the world is going to try to repair the ruins piled up by the premeditated will of German militarism—to reserve these raw materials by preference for our own friends, and for the neutrals who are also the innocent victims of Prussian terrorism. But the organization that we would like to see take shape, if necessary—and its formation will be swift and easy thanks to our efforts and to Allied cooperation—will not be closed to our enemies, except if they themselves close the door by refusing to accept the Entente's conditions, the conditions of a just and humane peace" (Sénat, *Débats,* February 7, 1918, p. 73). Daniel Serruys, a philologist who had become a high Ministry of Commerce official, made a similar point in a July 1918 speech to the Comité National d'Etudes Sociales et Politiques (F^{12}7985, PF XI-8): "Control must be conceived of as a *defensive* weapon, designed to assure the economic life of the Allies after the war, much more than as a weapon of *offensive* war, designed to annihilate Germany economically. The Allies would themselves be the losers if they forbade themselves from selling to Germany what they did not need themselves" [Emphasis his]. See also Henri Hauser, *Germany's Commercial Grip on the World,* trans. M. Emanuel (New York: Scribner, 1918), pp. 182–83.

7. A remark by Blazeix, a high Ministry of Commerce official, typifies this attitude: "Pour permettre aux alliés de concurrencer une semblable organisation, il faut avoir des méthodes semblables à celles qui ont permis aux sociètès allemandes d'acquérir leur puissance considérable" (Entretien de M. Runciman et de M. Clémentel," August 16, 1916, F^{12}7797). "In the economic battle that we must engage in after the war," Clémentel himself wrote in

1918, "we will defeat Pan-Germanism only by taking up some of the weapons used by Germany, above all, that of organisation" (preface to Henri Hauser, *Les Régions économiques* [Paris: Grasset, 1918], p. 3). See also the account of Hauser's lecture "L'adaptation à la France des méthodes économiques allemands," *Journée Industrielle*, February 7, 1919. The theme of emulating German methods is also evident in the files of the Comité Consultatif des Arts et Manufactures (CCAM) (see n. 9). In June 1917, for example, the eminent metallurgical chemist Henry Le Chatelier, president of the heavy industry section of the CCAM, called for "technical collaboration, such as exists in all German industrial groups" ($F^{12}7995$, folder "Comité consultatif des arts et manufactures"). See also Clémentel's remarks during the debate on the consortiums (Chambre, *Débats*, June 28, 1918, p. 1835).

8. See the sources noted in n. 2 and the following material in the archives of the French Foreign Ministry: Series "Guerre 1914–1918," vols. 1216–19, 1276–77. For the public discussion of an Allied economic bloc, see the articles listed in Camille Bloch, *Bibliographie methodique*, pp. 381–82, and Bernd Bonwetsch, *Kriegsallianz und Wirtschaftsinteressen: Russland in den Wirtschaftsplänen Englands und Frankreichs 1914–1917* (Dusseldorf: Bertelsmann Universitätsverlag, 1973). Bonwetsch showed how the hope for an economic bloc focused on the question of Russia: both Britain and France wanted to exclude German trade from Russia and through a system of preferential tariffs secure the Russian market for themselves. The thrust of this policy was clearly anti-German, but Bonwetsch says (e.g., p. 10) that in a less obvious way it was directed against America as well. The attempt, he says, was bound to fail, if only because the Russians had no intention of allowing Britain and France to seize the dominant economic position held by Germany before the war: Russia wanted to liberate herself from all foreign economic domination, and not just change masters. Bonwetsch is certainly right in arguing that the question of the Russian market played a central role in shaping plans for an Allied economic bloc in Britain and France, and he is clearly justified in stressing Russian Resistance. (See the documents in Boris Nolde, *Russia in the Economic War* [New Haven: Yale University Press, 1928], esp. pp. 158–70.) But the French sources just cited give the very clear impression that the question of preferential tariffs was just one element in the plan for an Allied economic union—and from the standpoint of the French government, a subordinate one at that. The control of raw materials was Clémentel's prime concern; the tariff question was essentially secondary. An agreement with both Britain and America on raw materials thus became the central aim of his policy: for this reason Clémentel had no trouble adapting his ideas to the new situation created in 1917 by America's entry into the war and Russia's "defection." So far from being the end of the story, the Paris Economic Conference really marks its beginning.

9. An organ of the Ministry of Commerce, the Comité Consultatif des Arts et Manufactures was charged by law in April 1917 with studying the problems of the postwar economy. The CCAM made many suggestions along these general lines; its records are preserved in the Ministry of Commerce archives, fonds F^{12} at the Archives Nationales, Paris (esp. cartons $F^{12}7995$, $F^{12}8045–62$, $F^{12}8105$). See also the May 1918 report of its president on the "organization of production after the war" in $F^{12}8038$, folder "Après-guerre, concessions minières," and the CCAM's *Rapport général sur l'industrie française* (Paris: Imprimerie Nationale, 1919). For the views of Clémentel's close associate Henri Hauser, see Société d'Ingénieurs Civils, *Travaux préparatoires du Congrès du Génie Civil, Session nationale, Mars 1918*, section 8 ("Organisation rationnelle du travail industriel"), pp. 3–11. Clémentel gave some indication of his own views on the subject of postwar industrial organization in his remarks to the Chamber during the debate on the consortiums (Chambre, *Débats*, June 28, 1918, pp. 1841–42).

10. See in the archives of the French Ministry of Foreign Affairs, Paris, Series "Guerre 1914–1918," vol. 1216—Foreign Ministry sources will henceforth be cited in the form "AE, Guerre, 1216." This volume is a collection of Clémentel's papers donated to the Foreign Ministry in 1954.

11. This discussion of the Paris Economic Conference is based on the printed minutes,

Conférence économique des gouvernements alliés tenue à Paris les 14, 15, 16 et 17 juin 1916.
Programme, procès-verbaux des séances et acte de la conférence in F¹²8104, and on pertinent
Ministry of Commerce files, esp. F¹²7988, folder "La Conférence économique de Paris. Les
négociations." For the text of the resolutions adopted by the conference, see United States,
Department of State, *Papers Relating to the Foreign Relations of the United States, 1916, Sup-
plement,* pp. 975–977—this series will henceforth be cited by the abbreviation "FRUS." For a
Soviet view of the Conference, see D. S. Babichev, "Rossiia na Parizkskoi soiuznicheskoi
Konfertsii 1916g., po ekonomicheskim voprosam," *Istoricheskie Zapiski* (1969), 83:38–51. I
am grateful to Harley Balzer for help with the translation of this article.

    12. *Conférence économique,* p. 42.

    13. *Conférence économique,* pp. 42–43.

    14. This discussion of the inter-Allied economic machinery is based mainly on the follow-
in sources: J. Arthur Salter, *Allied Shipping Control;* Salter, *Slave of the Lamp,* esp. pp.
80ff.; Daniel Serruys, "La structure économique de la coalition," *Revue de Paris* (July 15,
1918), 25:326–45; FRUS 1917, Supp. 2, 1:334–445 and 516–666; FRUS 1918, Supp. 1,
1:498–617; Edwin Gay Papers, Hoover Institution, Stanford, California; R. H. Tawney, "The
Abolition of Economic Controls, 1918–1921," *Economic History Review* (1943), 13:1–30; and
Pierre Larigaldie, *La Politique économique interalliée: Les organismes interalliés de contrôle
économique* (Paris: Longin, 1926).

    15. This phrase is quoted in Suda L. Bane and Ralph H. Lutz, eds., *The Blockade of Ger-
many after the Armistice, 1918–1919,* p. 831, and had earlier been used by Dwight Morrow in
a letter to Edward Stettinius, quoted in Harold Nicolson, *Dwight Morrow* (New York: Harcourt,
Brace and Co., 1935), p. 215.

    16. The idea that the system was to a considerable degree deliberately shaped contradicts
certain accepted views on the subject. Tawney, for example, wrote that the systems of wartime
controls—both the British and the inter-Allied systems—were "only to a small extent the result
of design" (Tawney, "Abolition of Economic Controls," p. 6). Clémentel, however, insisted
that he had been consciously seeking to bring about a system for the pooling of Allied resources
during the war—a policy, he said, that was rooted in the principles of the Paris Economic Conference (Clémentel, pp. 150, 158, 166). The archival evidence bears out these claims. See in
particular Fleuriau's despatches of September 3 and 5, 1917, F¹²7797, dossier "Mission de M.
Clémentel à Londres, 15–27 août 1917"; Cambon to Ribot, September 3, 1917, (AE, Paix,
218;) and Clementel's reports of August 5 and 27, 1917, AE, Guerre, 1276.

    17. Cambon to Ribot, September 3, 1917, AE, Paix, 218; Clémentel reports of August 5
and 27, 1917, AE, Guerre, 1276; Clémentel to Painlevé, October 18, 1917, AE, Guerre, 1277;
Clémentel, pp. 150–95.

    18. Clémentel, pp. 158, 166, 194. For a contemporary source, see, for example, Fleuriau
to the Prime Minister, September 3, 1917, F¹²7797.

    19. See Clémentel, pp. 150–95, and in general AE, Guerre, 1276–77.

    20. Salter, *Slave of the Lamp,* esp. pp. 80ff.; Duroselle, "Strategic and Economic Rela-
tions," p. 60 and p. 69, n. 61.

    21. See the sources in n. 14, esp. Salter, *Allied Shipping Control.*

    22. Salter, *Allied Shipping Control,* pp. 243–44.

    23. The evidence on both points is abundant. For evidence that the Americans on these
bodies favored the continuation of the inter-Allied system, see Summers to Baruch, November
5, 1918, in United States Congress, Senate, Special Committee Investigating the Munitions Industry, Seventy-Fourth Congress, Second Session, Part 30, Exhibit 3361—henceforth cited as
"Munitions Committee." The retention of the system was linked in their minds to the League;
see, for example, Field to Gay, November 14, 1918, Gay Papers, box 3. Leading European officials associated with the inter-Allied bodies, such as Lord Robert Cecil, Salter and Monnet,
also shared these hopes.

24. See for example, Chambre, *Débats*, June 28, 1918, pp. 1841–42; Sénat, *Débats*, February 7, 1918, pp. 70–73.

25. Chambre, *Débats*, June 28, 1918, pp. 1836, 1842–44.

26. This account of the consortium system is based primarily on a series of critical articles published by the economist Léon Polier in *L'Europe nouvelle* (issues of May 4, 8 and 25, July 6 and December 14, 1918), and on Clémentel's reply to this criticism (Chambre, *Débats*, June 28, 1918, pp. 1833–44, 1849–51). See also F. Bassetti, *Les Consortiums étudiés spécialement au point de vue de leur développement en France pendant la guerre* (Paris : E. Sagot, 1919), and Raymond Guilhon, *Les consortiums en France pendant la guerre* (Paris: Librairie générale de droit et de jurisprudence, 1924).

27. *Journal officiel*, 27 November 1918, p. 10232.

28. See the sources in n. 26 and articles on the consortium question in the following issues of the *Journée Industrielle:* April 16, June 21, August 6, 1918; January 10 and 17–24, 1919.

29. On British policy on these matters there is some material in V. H. Rothwell, *British War Aims and Peace Diplomacy, 1914–1918;* by far the best account, however, is Robert Bunselmeyer's 1969 Yale doctoral dissertation, "The Cost of the War: British Plans for Postwar Economic Treatment of Germany, 1914–1918," a version of which has recently been published.

30. Great Britain, *Parliamentary Debates, House of Commons*, Fifth Series, LXXXV (August 2, 1916), cols. 331–42, 389–98—henceforth cited as *"Parl. Deb.,* Commons"; FRUS 1916, Supp., p. 983.

31. Great Britain, Cabinet Office, Minutes, April 3, 1917, in Cab 23, vol. 2, minute 112, item 4, Public Record Office, London—Cabinet records will henceforth be cited in the standard short form, in this case, Cab 23/2/112/4; Thomas Jones, *Whitehall Diary,* ed. Keith Middlemas, 1:30; W. A. S. Hewins, *Apologia of an Imperialist* (London: Constable, 1927), 2:132–33; 153–55. The papers of the Milner Committee, which was officially called the Cabinet Committee on "Terms of Peace (economic and other non-territorial desiderata)," are in Cab 21/71 and 78.

32. Cab 23/4/247/8, October 9, 1917; Cab 24/4/G156, Carson memorandum, September 20, 1917. The minutes and papers of the Economic Offensive Committee are in Cab 27/15 and 16.

33. Cab 24/4/6175, November 16, 1917.

34. Cab 23/4/283/17, November 27, 1917.

35. Cab 23/5/312/6, January 3, 1918; Cab 24/4/G177 is the report in question. One such pledge, approved by the War Cabinet the next day, was embodied in Lloyd George's important war aims speech of January 5: "The economic conditions at the end of the war will be in the highest degree difficult. Owing to the diversion of human effort to warlike pursuits, there must follow a world-shortage of raw materials, which will increase the longer the war lasts, and it is inevitable that those countries which have control of raw materials will desire to help themselves and their friends first" (Cab 23/5/314/2 and Appendix, January 4, 1918). On May 28 the British government privately made another pledge of this sort, promising to "give full recognition to the principle that the more fortunately situated members of the Alliance should do their utmost to aid in repairing the sufferings and losses which the less fortunate have incurred in the common cause" (Derby to Pichon, AE, Guerre, 1219).

36. Cab 23/5/312/6, January 3, 1918.

37. *Ibid.*

38. See for example Cab 24/4/G190, January 21, 1918, and the *Times* (London), July 24, 1918, p. 8. Nor was this the only pressure: see the letters from the Conservative minister Walter Long to Lloyd George, October 3, 1918 (with enclosures) and to Bonar Law, October 3 and 4, 1918, Bonar Law Papers, 84/2/3–5, Beaverbrook Foundation, now housed at the House of Lords Record Office, London. See also the account of a deputation to the Prime Minister from

the National Union of Manufacturers on July 31, 1918, Lloyd George Papers, F/215/5, Beaver-brook Foundation, now housed also in the House of Lords Record Office, London.

39. Cab 27/44/EDDC 37.

40. Cab 27/44/EDDC 50, October 21, 1918.

41. Keynes to Chamberlain, April 19, 1918, Cab 27/45, p. 27. The letter is printed in *The Collected Writings of John Maynard Keynes,* vol. 16 (ed. Elizabeth Johnson), pp. 289–90. See also Keynes to Chalmers, April 18, 1918, *ibid.,* p. 288.

42. Cab 27/44/EDDC 51.

43. *Ibid.*

44. Cab 27/44/EDDC 55 and minutes 15/2; Cab 23/8/501/7, November 13, 1918. With minor changes this plan is reproduced in Salter, *Allied Shipping Control,* pp. 329–30. For the text of the Foreign Office memorandum as received by the Allies, see Allied Maritime Trans-port Council, *Minutes and Documents,* ed. J. A. Salter (London, 1919), part 2, pp. 6–15, a copy of which is in the Gay Papers, box 6.

45. Suda L. Bane and Ralph H. Lutz, eds., *Organization of American Relief in Europe, 1918–1919,* p. 48. This collection of documents, drawn primarily from papers in the Hoover Institution, will henceforth be cited as "OAR."

46. Crawford to Polk, October 15, 1918, FRUS 1918, Supp. 1, 1:613.

47. See the note of Lord Reading of December 31, 1918, quoted at length by Clémentel in Chambre, *Débats,* July 22, 1919, p. 3627.

48. FRUS, *The Lansing Papers,* 1:311–12.

49. In August 1917 Clémentel had proposed to the British a scheme for inter-Allied con-trol of food and raw material. Lord Robert Cecil outlined the scheme to the War Cabinet on August 20. Clémentel, he said, "Proposed that this economic weapon, when fully organized, might be utilized after the war as a means of keeping the peace, and he rather relied on this aspect of the question to secure the adhesion of President Wilson to the scheme" (Cab 23/3/220/3). Extracts from an October 6 letter to Wilson are quoted in Clémentel, pp. 220–21. On November 22 Clémentel reiterated the point in another letter to Wilson (F¹²7988, folder "Question des matières premières"). Clemenceau himself evidently made the same argument in a December 6 letter to the American President (see Clémentel's report to Clemenceau on his London conferences of August 1918, p. 16, in F¹²7798, folder "10A. GB4").

50. Charles Seymour, *The Intimate Papers of Colonel House,* entry of January 27, 1918, 3:366–67; see also Seymour, 3:268, and on Wilson's intentions in this regard, Wiseman to Reading, August 16, 1918, in Seymour, 4:62–63. For the French account of these contacts, see Tardieu to Clémentel, January 25 and 27, 1918, AE, Guerre, 1217.

51. In a speech to the Congress on December 4, Wilson declared that if Germany after the war continues "to live under ambitious and intriguing masters interested to disturb the peace of the world," she might be excluded from "free economic intercourse" with the nations who had come together to secure world peace (Woodrow Wilson, *War and Peace,* 1:133). Clémentel frequently alluded to this speech; see, for example, Sénat, *Débats,* February 7, 1918, pp. 71–72, and Chambre, *Débats,* June 28, 1918, p. 1841.

52. In October 1918, House's official commentary on this point stressed that it only applied among League members and noted in particular that "this clause naturally contemplates fair and equitable understanding as to the distribution of raw materials" (Seymour, *Papers of Colonel House,* 4:193–94).

53. Sénat, *Débats,* February 7, 1918, pp. 70–73; Daniel Serruys, "La Structure écono-mique de la coalition," *Revue de Paris,* (July 15, 1918), 25:326–45; Serruys's speech to the Comité National d'Études Sociales et Politiques, July 1918 (F¹²7985, PF XI–8); Henri Hauser, "De Naumann à Kuhlmann, Mitteleuropa et la clause de la nation la plus favorisée," *Action nationale* (1918). On Serruys, one of the most important permanent officials in the Commerce

Ministry, see Jean Serruys, *De Colbert au Marché Commun* (Paris: Emile-Paul, 1970), pp. 278ff.

54. *L'Europe nouvelle* (February 16, 1918), 1:276.

55. *Ibid.*, pp. 276–77.

56. For example, Pertinax articles, *L'Echo de Paris*, May 19 and 28, 1918; C. Bouglé, *L'Evènement*, June 23, 1918; G. Doumergue, *Le Petit Parisien*, July 13, 1918. See also the clippings in AE, Guerre, 1217–19. On Lebon: *L'Economie Nouvelle*, August 1919. On the CGT: "Memorandum du Mouvement Ouvrier Français," Feb. 1918, in *Rapport sur l'action générale de la CGT depuis août 1914* (Paris, 1918), pp. 84–85.

57. In response to a July 1918 request from Clémentel, Hauser drafted a memorandum entitled "Principales questions d'ordre économique dont le ministère de Commerce aura à se préoccuper lors de la conclusion du Traité de Paix" ($F^{12}8106$). Earlier he had written a "Note sur l'Union économique de l'Europe occidentale" ($F^{12}7985$, PF XIV–110) and some time in mid-1918 he drafted a third memorandum, "Esquisse d'une politique économique de l'Europe occidentale" (unsigned copy in $F^{12}7985$, PF XIV–9; the original, in Hauser's handwriting, is in $F^{12}8106$). Judging from the reiteration of ideas and the reappearance of phrases from these memoranda in the September 19 letter, as well as the existence of notes for this letter in Hauser's handwriting ($F^{12}8106$), it seems evident that it was Hauser who drafted this important document. The text of the September 19 letter and the minutes of the meeting at which it was adopted as government policy in $F^{12}8104$, folder "Propositions des ministères." The letter is also printed in Clémentel, pp. 337–48. In this printed version, the letter is addressed to Wilson as well as to Clemenceau, but this is hardly credible. The letter alludes to the Paris resolutions, but in the meeting that adopted the program outlined in the letter as government policy, it was agreed that in dealing with the Americans, no reference would be made to the Paris program. Moreover Clemenceau declared at this meeting "qu'il est nécessaire de préparer très fortement les négociations avec le gouvernement américain et le Président Wilson, en se gardant, dans ces préparations, de la remise d'un document quelconque. . . . ." Otherwise, the printed version is an exact reproduction of the draft preserved in the archives.

58. "It is through the economic organization of the world," Clémentel wrote, "that we will prevent the return of Prussian militarism." Later he alluded to the "rational and systematic utilization of the raw materials weapon as a means of making German industry collaborate peacefully with the other nations." (Clémentel, pp. 343, 348).

59. "Esquisse" (see n. 57), pp. 5–6.

60. Clémentel, p. 338.

61. Clémentel, p. 341.

62. Clémentel, pp. 338, 344–345. Hauser had also referred to the danger of French isolation. If no economic union were formed on the lines he suggested, France would be exposed, he said, "soit à consentir à un rapprochement forcé avec l'Allemagne, soit à être reçue, mais par grâce et comme un associé de deuxième rang, dans un consortium anglo-saxon" (Hauser, "Esquisse," $F^{12}7985$).

63. A certain preoccupation with prestige was in fact a striking feature of official French thought on these questions: "assistance" was demeaning, Anglo-American tutelage was a real danger, and only a scheme of "cooperation," based on equality, was consistent with French honor and dignity. See, for example, Clémentel's report of August 5, 1917, AE, Guerre, 1276, and Fleuriau to Pichon, March 6, 1918, AE, Guerre, 1218.

64. Clémentel, pp. 338–39.

65. Clémentel, p. 339.

66. Clémentel, p. 347.

67. Notes of this meeting are in $F^{12}8104$, folder "Propositions des ministères."

68. *Ibid.*

69. *Ibid.*

70. Clémentel, pp. 341, 342.

71. F[127]7985, PF VIII–19b.

72. Clémentel, p. 342.

73. Clémentel, p. 343.

74. See especially Hauser, "Principales questions" (F[128]106), pp. 1, 2, 5; Clémentel, p. 343.

75. Clémentel, p. 343.

76. The published American documents show how the War Purchase and Finance Council evolved out of an American desire to limit and coordinate European requests for assistance (FRUS 1917, Supp. 2, 1:546–76). Secretary of the Treasury McAdoo explicitly noted that the work of this inter-Allied council was "of such vital importance and of such urgent necessity in order to relieve the Treasury of some of the stupendous and unbearable demands now being made upon it. . . ." (McAdoo to Wilson, January 14, 1918, Munitions Committee, Part 32, Exhibit 4019). For further evidence, see Munitions Committee, Part 29, Exhibits 2994, 2997 and 2998.

77. FRUS 1918, Supp. 1, 1:532–33. Documents in the Gay Papers, box 3, show that Philip Franklin, the chairman of the United States Shipping Control Committee, blocked efforts at cooperation. He was quoted in a memorandum of December 4, 1918, as having said in June that sharing detailed information on the use of American vessels with the AMTC would be "equivalent to giving information to the enemy."

78. Clémentel to Tardieu, January 23, 1918, and Tardieu to Clémentel, January 25, 1918, AE, Guerre, 1217; Tardieu to Pichon, March 7, 1918, AE, Guerre, 1218.

79. Clémentel and Pichon to Tardieu, April 16, 1918, AE, Guerre, 1218; Clémentel and Pichon to Tardieu, May 10 and 19, 1918, and Tardieu to Clémentel and Pichon, May 13, 1918, AE, Guerre, 1219.

80. Pichon to Billy, September 26, 1918, Tardieu Papers, dossier "Après-Guerre," Ministry of Foreign Affairs, Paris; Billy to Pichon, n.d., *ibid.;* Wilson, *War and Peace,* pp. 257–58.

81. William Diamond, *The Economic Thought of Woodrow Wilson* (Baltimore: Johns Hopkins University Press, 1943), pp. 169, 182–84, 187—the phrase "new world order" is Diamond's; Ray Stannard Baker, *Woodrow Wilson and World Settlement,* 2:282, 326, quoted in Diamond, p. 187.

82. There was a serious effort to "make these negotiations extend to post-war conditions, but we are dodging that in every way, but it can not be dodged, *it is too important,* and you might as well begin to figure on it" (Summers to Baruch, August 18, 1918, Munitions Committee, Part 30, Exhibit 3342; emphasis his).

83. Hoover to Wilson, November 7, 1918, and Hoover to Cotton, November 7, 1918, OAR, p. 32.

84. Hoover to Wilson, November 4, 1918, OAR, p. 29, and Hoover to Wilson, October 24, 1918, OAR, p. 27.

85. Hoover to Wilson, October 24, 1918, OAR, p. 27.

86. Hoover to Cotton, November 7, 1918, OAR, p. 33.

87. Hoover to Wilson, November 11, 1918, OAR, p. 38.

88. C. S. Duncan to Gay, January 1, 1919, Gay Papers, box 3. See also House to Wilson, November 27, 1918, in United States, Department of State, *Papers Relating to the Foreign Relations of the United States. The Paris Peace Conference,* 13 vols. (Washington, 1942–47), 2:640—henceforth cited as "FRUS, PPC."

89. House to Wilson, July 20, 1919, House Papers, box 121a, House Collection, Sterling Memorial Library, Yale University, New Haven.

90. Jones, *Diary*, 1:70–71. This quotation is the editor's paraphrase of Astor's note.

91. *Ibid*. Reading was in fact appointed to represent the British government in inter-Allied negotiations on these matters.

92. Billy to Klotz, September 18, 1918, Tardieu Papers, dossier "Après-Guerre," Ministry of Foreign Affairs, Paris.

93. McAdoo to Wilson, October 26, 1918, United States Treasury, Bureau of Accounts, Record Group 39, box 51, National Archives, Washington.

94. Rathbone Memorandum, October 22, 1918, *ibid*.

95. Billy to Pichon and Tardieu, n.d., Tardieu Papers, dossier "Après-Guerre," Ministry of Foreign Affairs, Paris; *L'Illustration*, October 20, 1920—a partial translation was printed in 67th Congress, 2nd Session (1921–22), Senate Document 86, *Loans to Foreign Governments*, p. 263. This latter source will henceforth be cited as "Senate Document 86 of 1921."

96. Baker, *Wilson and World Settlement*, 3:320; Senate Document 86 of 1921, pp. 3–10; Tardieu to Leffingwell, November 4, 1918, *ibid.*, pp. 27–28; Tardieu to Klotz and Tardieu to Lebrun and Loucheur, both of November 11, 1918, Tardieu Papers, dossier "Après-Guerre," Ministry of Foreign Affairs, Paris.

97. Senate Document 86 of 1921, pp. 3–10.

98. For example, Bernard Baruch, one of Wilson's closest economic advisors, argued a few months later that the United States should aid Europe not "with a free and open hand, but with a stinted hand" in order to force the Europeans to help themselves. (Baruch Diary, April 21, 1919, Baruch Papers, Princeton University Library). For the Hoover reference, see Treasury memorandum, October 21, 1918, Munitions Committee, Part 32, Exhibit 4143; for Crosby, Crosby to McAdoo, November 21, 1918, Munitions Committee, Part 32, Exhibit 4144.

99. McAdoo to Crosby, November 21, and Crosby to McAdoo, November 13, 1918, FRUS, PPC, 2:533–36.

100. *Ibid.*, p. 538.

101. McAdoo to Crosby, December 7, 1918, *ibid.*, p. 537; for McAdoo's earlier view, see McAdoo to Wilson, October 26, 1918, McAdoo Papers, box 525, Library of Congress, Washington.

2. Reparation at the Peace Conference

1. Chambre, *Débats*, November 20, 1917, p. 2973.

2. *Ibid.*, p. 2972.

3. Chambre, *Débats*, December 29, 1918, p. 3733.

4. *Ibid.*

5. *Ibid.*

6. See Chapter 7 for a discussion of the whole Rhenish issue.

7. Box 6N137, dossier 3, Fonds Clemenceau, War Ministry Archives, Vincennes.

8. Clemenceau to Lloyd George, 15 November 1918, and notes of the meeting, "Conférence de Londres (10 Downing Street) (2 Décembre 1918— 11 heures matin)," 6N72, Fonds Clemenceau.

9. "Conférence de Londres (3 Décembre 1918 à 4 heures)," 6N72, Fonds Clemenceau.

10. Louis Loucheur, *Carnets secrets, 1908–1932*, p. 71.

11. Woodrow Wilson, *War and Peace*, I 1:313.

12. Hoover to House, December 10, 1918, OAR, p. 78.

13. *Ibid.*, p. 79.

14. OAR, pp. 81–84.

15. $F^{12}8104$; two parts of this document, the "Note introductive" and the "Avant-projet établi par la conférence des directeurs du Ministère," were evidently drafted by Hauser—earlier drafts in his handwriting can be found in $F^{12}8106$.

16. Clémentel wrote that Clemenceau "s'est déclaré d'accord avec les principes et la méthode de travail que je crois nécessaire d'adopter pour mener à bien les négociations d'ordre économique à la Conférence de la Paix" (Clémentel to Pichon, n.d., but probably written between January 20 and 22, $F^{12}8039$, folder "Problèmes d'après-guerre'"); Puech report, *Journal officiel de la République française, Documents parlementaires, Chambre des Députés,* 1919, Annexe 6670, p. 445—henceforth cited as "Chambre, *Documents.*"

17. "Avant-project" (see n. 15), pp. 18, 20.

18. "Note introductive" (see n. 15), p. 4.

19. Conférence de la Paix, *Recueil des Actes de la Conférence,* 28 vols. in 8 parts (Paris, 1922–34), part I, *Actes du Conseil Suprème, Recueil des Résolutions* (Paris, 1934), no. 52. This source will henceforth be cited as *"Recueil."*

20. FRUS, PPC, 3:730–31.

21. *Recueil,* part IV (Commissions de la Conférence—Procès-verbaux, Rapports et Documents), B (Questions générales), 7 (Commission Economique), p. 11; and Puech report, p. 445.

22. *Recueil,* IV, B, 7, p. 12.

23. *Recueil,* IV, B, 7, minutes of meeting of February 8, with annexes, pp. 16ff.

24. *Ibid.*

25. *Ibid.,* p. 21.

26. FRUS, PPC, 4:68.

27. Oscar P. Fitzgerald IV, "The Supreme Economic Council and Germany: A Study of Inter-Allied Cooperation after World War I" (Ph.D. diss., Georgetown University, 1971) is the most complete study of this body.

28. FRUS, PPC, 3:934.

29. FRUS, PPC, 10:1–2, 4–5.

30. Clémentel to other French ministers, November 6, 1919, p. 4, in $F^{12}8066$, folder, "C.S.E. (General No. 4)." See also FRUS, PPC, 10:418–24; Clémentel's remarks in Parliament, Chambre, *Débats,* July 22, 1919, pp. 3627–29, and September 16, 1919, pp. 4352–53; and Clémentel, pp. 313–17.

31. Leffingwell to Davis, May 7, 1919, in Baker, *Woodrow Wilson and World Settlement,* 3:373–75.

32. OAR, pp. 591–97.

33. *Ibid.,* p. 595.

34. See in particular for the United States, Chapter 9 of Robert D. Cuff, *The War Industries Board: Business-Government Relations during World War I* (Baltimore: Johns Hopkins University Press, 1973), and for Germany the important article by Gerald Feldman, "Economic and Social Problems of the German Demobilization, 1918–19," *Journal of Modern History* (1975), 47(1):1–23. For Britain, see R. H. Tawney, "The Abolition of Economic Controls, 1918–1921," *Economic History Review* (1943), 13(1–2):1–30.

35. See for example Davis to Rathbone, March 10, 1919, Munitions Committee, Part 32, Exhibit 4154. On French awareness of American hostility to the consortiums, see Tardieu to Billy, December 14, 1918 and Billy to Tardieu, January 8, 1919; Tardieu Papers, French Foreign Ministry Archives, dossier "Après-Guerre."

36. McFadden to War Trade Board, Oct. 30, Nov. 10, Nov. 16 and Nov. 27, 1918, and McFadden to Norman Davis, November 27, 1918, Record Group 39 (U.S. Treasury Department, Bureau of Accounts), box 51, United States National Archives, Washington.

37. Tardieu to Billy, December 14, 1918, and Billy to Tardieu, January 8, 1919, Tardieu Papers, dossier "Après-Guerre," Foreign Ministry Archives, Paris.

38. *Journée Industrielle,* Jan. 10, and Jan. 17, 1919; Chambre, *Débats,* Feb. 14, 1919, p. 638.

39. *Journée Industrielle,* January 17, 1919; Charles Maier, *Recasting Bouregois Europe,* pp. 74–76.

40. See Henry Ehrmann, *Organized Business in France* (Princeton: Princeton University Press, 1957), pp. 15–32.

41. *Journée Industrielle,* Jan. 23, 1919.

42. *Journal officiel,* November 27, 1918, p. 10232.

43. Philip Mason Burnett, *Reparation at the Paris Peace Conference from the Standpoint of the American Delegation,* 1:632; Philip Kerr minute, February 25, 1919, Lloyd George Papers, F/89/2/32, Beaverbrook Library, London.

44. Lord Riddell (George A. Riddell), *Intimate Diary of the Peace Conference and After, 1918–1923,* p. 38. Material in Poincaré's recently published diary for 1919 confirms that Klotz was kept ignorant of the reparation negotiations conducted by Loucheur (Poincaré, *A la recherche de la paix, 1919,* pp. 279, 285–86).

45. Weill-Raynal searched in vain for evidence that this phrase had been uttered (Etienne Weill-Raynal, *Les Réparations allemandes et la France,* 1:19, n. 2). Klotz himself denied having made the remark when he was accused of it in 1921, and he was probably right since during the peace conference period, all he was criticized for was for not refuting posters that had demanded that Germany pay—it is hard to understand why his opponents should have attacked him in such an indirect way if grounds for a more direct attack had been available. See Chambre, *Débats,* March 7, 1919, p. 1065, September 5, 1919, p. 4192, and February 9, 1921, p. 424.

46. Chambre, *Débats,* December 3, 1918, p. 3236, and March 13, 1919, pp. 1165–66; Senat, *Débats,* December 3, 1918, p. 813.

47. Sénat, *Débats,* December 19, 1918, p. 845.

48. Chambre, *Débats,* March 13, 1919, p. 1162.

49. It is difficult to prove the negative point that French demands were not as extravagant as is generally assumed. But there is an additional piece of evidence that should be noted. In the Chamber's Foreign Affairs Commission on August 13, 1919, Klotz was asked why the debt did not include war costs. He replied that total payments of principal and interest on such a debt, amortized over a one hundred-year period, would amount to about 5000 milliard francs (4000 milliard gold marks), a "somme impossible que même la fantaisie la plus invraisemblable des écrivains et des littérateurs ne prétendrait écrire" (minutes, p. 8). Why then did the French government not declare at the outset that the inclusion of war costs was out of the question? Klotz pointed out that on December 11 in Bristol, Lloyd George had called for their inclusion in the bill. "Quel eut été l'émoi de l'opinion publique," he asked, "si nous avions tenu un pareil langage? si nous avions dit 'non' alors que la Grande Bretagne disait 'oui'?" (minutes, p. 5). So the French government, he said, made no public declaration at all. Of course, Klotz expressed these views after the fact, and they are therefore not necessarily to be taken at face value. But it is interesting that Klotz took this line when he could have easily defended the omission of war costs by alluding to American opposition. A copy of the minutes of this hearing are in the archives of the French Delegation to the Reparation Commission (fonds AJ[5] at the Archives Nationales, Paris), carton AJ[5]54, folder "Bons. Discussions à la Chambre et au Sénat."

50. See Pierre Miquel, *La Paix de Versailles et l'opinion publique française,* pp. 431–32.

51. Chambre, *Débats,* March 7, 1919, p. 1065.

52. See Burnett, *Reparation,* 1:109n.; there are extracts from this document in André Tardieu, *The Truth about the Treaty,* pp. 280–84, and in L. L. Klotz, *De la guerre à la paix. souvenirs et documents,* pp. 155–93. On February 10, Klotz read extracts from this document to the Supreme Council (FRUS, PPC, 3:955). Note Loucheur's contempt for Klotz in his descrip-

tion of the incident: "Klotz veut faire son petit effet en lisant la traduction du rapport allemand sur les industries des régions envahies. Pendant cette lecture, Wilson se lève, je le sens agacé, il se met derrière la chaise de Mantoux; une fois la séance levée Baruch vient me parler: il est le confident du Président, celui-ci n'est pas content! il a notamment été froissé de la lecture faite par Klotz parce qu'il semblerait qu'on le considère comme trop favorable aux allemands et qu'il a la prétention de ne pas l'être; il veut simplement être juste" (Loucheur, *Carnets secrets*, p. 70).

53. See, for example, Miquel, *Paix de Versailles*, pp. 426–27; and *Le Temps*, March 6, 1919, p. 2.

54. Burnett, *Reparation*, 1:3–8, 411–12. See also Peter Krüger, *Deutschland und die Reparationen 1918/19*, p. 41.

55. Miquel, *Paix de Versailles*, pp. 13–19, 532–53; the phrase quoted is on p. 453.

56. Charles Rist, "Indemnité de Guerre et Commerce Internationale," *L'Action Nationale*, April 1919; Charles Gide, "L'Indemnité de Guerre" *La Paix par le Droit*, May-June 1919; André Lebon, *Les Conditions économiques de la paix* (Paris, n.d.—text of a lecture he gave on December 12, 1918); Lebon, "La solution interalliée de la question des dommages de guerre," *Revue politique et parlementaire*, October-December 1918.

57. *Journée Industrielle*, May 11–12, 1919; *L'Humanité*, May 22, 1919.

58. "Memorandum du Mouvement ouvrier français," *Rapport sur l'action générale de la CGT depuis août 1914*, p. 84.

59. Miquel, *Paix de Versailles*, pp. 461–70.

60. Chambre, *Débats*, March 7, 1919, p. 1060; for Stern's views, see Chambre, *Débats*, December 28, 1918, pp. 3679ff., and Chambre, *Documents*, 1918, Annexe 5344, p. 2015.

61. Chambre, *Débats*, March 7, 1919, p. 1060.

62. Robert Bunselmeyer, "The Cost of the War" (diss.), chaps. 8 and 9, and especially pp. 169–71, 192, 265–66, 318, 322, and 399–400.

63. Riddell, *Intimate Diary*, pp. 2–3; see also David Lloyd George, *Memoirs of the Peace Conference*, 1:300.

64. See, for example, his Bristol speech of December 1918, quoted in Lloyd George, *Memoirs*, 1:307.

65. "Conférence de Londres (10 Downing Street) (2 Decembre 1918—11 h. matin)," carton 6N72, Fonds Clemenceau, French War Ministry Archives, Vincennes.

66. Inga Floto, *Colonel House in Paris: A Study of American Policy at the Paris Peace Conference 1919* (Aarhus: Universitetsforlaget i Aarhus, 1973), p. 152.

67. Cab 23/7/459/9, August 15, 1918. See also Harold Nelson, *Land and Power: British and Allied Policy on Germany's Frontiers, 1916–19*, pp. 16, 47.

68. Cab 23/14/491B (an especially secret series of Cabinet minutes was numbered "A" or "B"), October 26, 1918.

69. Cab 23/14/541A, March 4, 1919.

70. For an extract from the speech, see Lloyd George, *Memoirs*, 1:309. Cunliffe and Hughes were leading members of the Cabinet Committee on Indemnity, which issued a report in December 1918 asserting that Germany could pay the entire cost of the war. The papers of this committee are in Cab 27/43, and its report is in Cab 29/2, paper P. 38.

71. Thus Lloyd George and other leaders of the moderate left in Britain stressed the link between punishing the war criminals, from the Kaiser on down, and establishing the League as a meaningful institution. (Bunselmeyer, "Cost of the War" [diss.], pp. 154, 263; Nelson, *Land and Power*, p. 16). Lloyd George dealt directly with the question of the responsibility of the German people in Parliament on July 3, 1919: since the whole nation had wholeheartedly backed this war of aggression, the whole nation must be punished for it (*Parl. Deb.* Commons, July 3, 1919, cols. 1221–22).

72. Speech of June 14, 1917, in Wilson, *War and Peace*, p. 62.

73. *Ibid.*, speech of December 4, 1917, p. 129. This view was implicit in Wilson's policy

2. **Reparation at the Peace Conference**

at the outset of American belligerency. In his address to the Congress asking for a declaration of war, he implied that the destruction of the present German regime was essential to peace: "In the presence of its organized power, always lying in wait to accomplish we know not what purpose, there can be no assumed security for the democratic Governments of the world" (*ibid.*, p. 14). By mid-1918, this aspect of American policy had become clear-cut and explicit. In his "Four-Point Speech" of July 4, 1918, Wilson demanded "The destruction of every arbitrary power anywhere that can be separately, secretly, and of its single choice disturb the peace of the world; or, if it cannot be presently destroyed, at the least its reduction to virtual impotence." (*ibid.*, p. 233)

74. *Ibid.*, speeches of December 4, 1917, February 11, July 4, and September 27, 1918; pp. 129, 133, 182–83, 233–34, 255.

75. *Ibid.*, speech of June 14, 1917, pp. 64–66; speech of December 4, 1917, p. 129.

76. *Ibid.*, speech of April 2, 1917, p. 11.

77. *Ibid.*, speeches of September, 2, 1917 and June 19, 1917, pp. 11, 61–62.

78. See the speech of June 14, 1917, *ibid.*, pp. 62–63.

79. *Ibid.*, speech of December 4, 1917, p. 131.

80. Woodrow Wilson, *Messages and Papers*, p. 807.

81. See Wilson to Smuts, May 1919, in Sarah G. Millin, *General Smuts*, (Boston: Little, Brown, 1936), 2:232–33.

82. Wilson, *War and Peace*, speech of December 4, 1917, p. 131.

83. "For Germany will have to redeem her character, not by what happens at the peace table, but by what follows" (*ibid.*, speech of September 27, 1918, p. 256).

84. *Ibid.*, p. 301.

85. Klaus Schwabe, "Woodrow Wilson and Germany's Membership in the League of Nations, 1918–19," *Central European History* (March 1975), 8(1):12–13.

86. See Burnett, *Reparation*, 1:17–30.

87. Cab 23/9/534/1, February 19, 1919.

88. *Recueil*, IV, B, 6, p. 25; Albert Geouffre de Lapradelle, ed., *La Paix de Versailles*, 7:352—this important series, henceforth cited as "Lapradelle," contains stenographic transcripts of many commission meetings. In addition, at the start of the conference, Klotz proposed a plan for a Financial Section of the League of Nations, which he said would be particularly useful in solving problems relating to the "reapportionment of war costs among the Allies" (transcript of February 4 meeting of Financial Commission, Lapradelle, 7:332; the text of this project is in Klotz, *De la guerre à la paix*, pp. 196–200).

89. French ideas were presented to Wilson through Monnet and Vance McCormick (Vance McCormick Diary, entries for January 16, 17 and 21, Hoover Institution).

90. Norman Davis Papers, box 11, Library of Congress, Washington.

91. Senate Document 86 of 1921, p. 270.

92. Davis to Rathbone, March 10, 1919, Munitions Committee, Part 32, Exhibit 4154.

93. *Ibid.*, and Davis to Rathbone, March 14, 1919, Munitions Committee, Part 32, Exhibit 4158.

94. See the extract from Norman Davis's unpublished "Peace Conference Notes" of July 5, 1919, quoted in Burnett, *Reparation*, 1:50, n. 15.

95. SEC Appendix 82, FRUS, PPC, 10:165.

96. On the drafting of the "war-guilt" clause, see Burnett, 1:26–27, 66–70; Fritz Dickmann, *Die Kriegsschuldfrage auf der Friedenskonferenz von Paris 1919* (Munich: R. Oldenbourg, 1964). For the Davis quotation, see Burnett, 1:826.

97. On this, see Lord Beaverbrook (William Maxwell Aitken), *Men and Power, 1917–1918*, pp. 91–112.

98. Lapradelle, 4(2):735–36, gives the French translation of Cunliffe's speech; it is this that is now retranslated back into English.

99. *Ibid.*, p. 737.

100. *Ibid.*, p. 736, 737–38. The gold mark was defined in the treaty as the quantity of gold that could be exchanged for a mark before the war. After the war, the dollar was the only major currency still on the gold standard; therefore the value of the gold mark has a function of the purchasing power of the dollar. For convenience, four gold marks were reckoned to be worth a dollar. A hundred millard gold marks thus meant 25 milliard dollars (a "milliard" is the European word for "billion" and will be used here). The pound sterling was then worth about five dollars, and was therefore reckoned at twenty gold marks; there were supposed to be five francs to the dollar, and hence the franc was calculated as equivalent to four-fifths of a gold mark.

101. *Ibid.*, p. 740.

102. *Ibid.*

103. *Ibid.*, pp. 740–41.

104. The transcript of this February 22 meeting of the second subcommission is not in Lapradelle, but there is a copy in the Klotz Papers, foΔ94, Bibliothèque de documentation internationale contemporaine, Nanterre; the quotation is on pp. 11–13.

105. *Ibid.*

106. *Ibid.* Emphasis added.

107. Burnett, *Reparation* 1:50; the inner quotations are from a June 25, 1934 letter from Lamont to Burnett.

108. Cunliffe to Lloyd George, March 2, 1919, Lloyd George Papers, F/89/2/37.

109. Kerr to Lloyd George, February 28, 1919, Lloyd George Papers, F/89/2/35.

110. Cab 23/15/541A, March 4, 1919.

111. House, who felt that the British financial representatives were "largely incompetent," had met Montagu over dinner a few nights earlier; House Diary, entry for March 10, 1919, 15:88, Edward House Collection, Sterling Memorial Library, Yale University, New Haven.

112. Burnett, *Reparation* 1:55–56, based on conversations with Davis in 1938; Loucheur, *Carnets secrets*, p. 71. There is no record of this meeting in FRUS, PPC.

113. Burnett, 1:56.

114. Montagu, in fact, was bitter about his replacement. At the beginning of June, when Lloyd George had second thoughts and proposed drastic changes in the reparation settlement, he (Lloyd George) suggested to Baruch that Baruch and Montagu get together with Loucheur to work out some arrangement. Montagu refused. Baruch noted in his diary that Montagu told him "that he regretted that he could not go in the matter with me, that he was sure that he would not be given the authority and backed up in case he came to an agreement; that he had tried that once already, and that he would not do so again" (Bernard M. Baruch, "American Delegation to Negotiate Peace. Memoranda, Comments and Notes in Diary Form," entry for June 2, 1919, p. 61, Baruch Papers, Firestone Library, Princeton University—henceforth cited as "Baruch Diary").

115. See especially Arno Mayer, *Politics and Diplomacy of Peacemaking*, pp. 624–32.

116. Baker, *Wilson and World Settlement*, 3:454.

117. *Les Délibérations du Conseil des Quatre (24 mars–28 juin 1919), Notes de l' officier interprète Paul Mantoux*, 1:47—this source will henceforth be cited as "Mantoux."

118. Baker, *Wilson and World Settlement*, 3:450.

119. *Ibid.*, p. 454.

120. Burnett, *Reparation*, 1:710.

121. See the account of the morning meeting of the Council of Four on March 26 in Mantoux, 1:24–31, and Loucheur, *Carnets secrets*, pp. 73–74.

122. Davis to Wilson, March 25, 1919, in Baker, Wilson and World Settlement, 3:383 and in Burnett, *Reparation*, 1:711.

123. Mantoux, 1:31.

124. Burnett, *Reparation,* 1:59, 718–19.

125. Mantoux, 1:24–25, meeting of March 26 (11 A.M.).

126. Mantoux, 1:29, 30.

127. Loucheur, *Carnets secrets,* pp. 74–75.

128. "Règlement des Réparations," April 5, 1919, Fonds Clemenceau, carton 6N74, War Ministry Archives, Vincennes.

129. Mantoux, 1:32–36.

130. *Ibid.,* p. 37.

131. *Ibid.*

132. *Ibid.,* p. 39.

133. *Ibid.*

134. *Ibid.,* p. 40.

135. *Ibid.,* and Loucheur, *Carnets secrets,* p. 74. For confirmation of these figures, see Keynes to Lloyd George, March 28, 1919, in *The Collected Writings of John Maynard Keynes,* vol. 16 (ed. E. Johnson), pp. 449–50.

136. See Stephen A. Schuker, *The End of French Predominance in Europe,* p. 15.

137. The calculation is simple. 120 milliards less an immediate 20 milliard payment of liquid resources—in 1919 the Allied experts agreed that this was a reasonable figure—left 100 milliards to be amortized. At 5 percent interest plus an additional 1 percent for amortization, the annuity would be exactly 6 milliard gold marks. Part of this annuity might be paid in the form of paper marks. But that would not affect its value in terms of gold.

138. The question of the present value of the May 1921 Schedule of Payments is the subject of some debate. It is sometimes contended that its real value was much less than 100 milliards—say only 50 or 60 milliards. For present purposes it is sufficient to point out that the annuity called for by the Schedule of Payments—2 milliard gold marks plus 26 percent of the value of German exports—would have been about 4 and one half milliard gold marks for the period 1925–1928 on the basis of actual exports for those years. If Germany had complied with the Schedule, exports presumably would have been higher, boosting the annuity, thus further increasing exports, and so on, to a point where the 6 milliard·figure might well have been reached. For an analysis of the present value of the Schedule of Payments, see chapter 5, n. 85.

139. Brian R. Mitchell, *European Historical Statistics* (New York: Columbia University Press, 1975), p. 785, summarizing W. G. Hoffman, *Das Wachstum der deutschen Wirtschaft seit der Mitte des 19. Jahrhunderts* (Berlin: Springer, 1965). The figures are for current marks, but because of the stabilization these are the same as gold marks for this period.

140. United States Department of Commerce, Bureau of the Census, *Historical Statistics of the United States* (Washington: U.S. Government Printing Office, 1975), Tables F1, U1—U25.

141. Figures derived from *ibid.,* Tables F1 and U1—U25.

142. C. H. Feinstein, *National Income, Expenditure and Output of the United Kingdom, 1855–1965* (Cambridge: Cambridge University Press, 1972), Tables 3 and 37. I am grateful to C. Knick Harley for pointing out this example to me.

143. John Foster Dulles, "Memorandum of Conference had at President Wilson's Hotel, Paris, April 1, 1919, at 2 P.M.," Burnett, *Reparation,* 1:776; Thomas W. Lamont, "Reparations," in *What Really Happened at Paris,* edited by Edward M. House and Charles Seymour, p. 272, quoted in Burnett, 1:777.

144. Statement quoted in Sarah G. Mullin, *General Smuts,* 2:207.

145. Burnett, *Reparation,* 1:829.

146. Memorandum to the Prime Minister, March 29, 1919, William K. Hancock and Jean van den Poel, eds., *Selections from the Smuts Papers,* (Cambridge: Cambridge University Press, 1966), 4:93–94. In this scheme, the Reparation Commission could set the annuity by modifying "up or down," in accordance with German capacity, a scale of payments to be set

by the Treaty. Thus the plan Smuts outlined was similar to the regime set up by the Treaty of Versailles; the Versailles system in one regard was in fact more lenient, in that it only allowed downward alterations of the annuity, which also was to be set in accordance with German capacity.

147. Bonar Law Papers, 97/1/17, Beaverbrook Foundation, House of Lords Record Office, London.

148. Burnett, *Reparation,* 1:829.

149. *Ibid.,* pp. 794–95, 803.

150. Mantoux, 1:153–62; Burnett, 1:832, 836, 842.

151. Burnett, 1:625.

152. *Ibid.,* p. 689.

153. *Ibid.,* p. 690.

154. *Ibid.,* p. 691.

155. Mantoux, 1:29.

156. Burnett, *Reparation,* 1:873.

157. John Foster Dulles, "The Reparation Problem," *The New Republic* (March 30, 1921), 26:134.

158. Burnett, *Reparation,* 1:502.

159. See Loucheur's remarks in the second subcommission, February 18, Lapradelle 4(2):714.

160. See for example the Loucheur-Tatsumi Colloquy, February 17 meeting, a printed stenographic transcript of which is in the Klotz Papers, foΔ94.

161. "Il est bien entendu," Loucheur declared in this connection, "qu'il est formellement convenu que les moyens de paiement que nous trouverons pour nos ennemis ne doivent jamais en aucune façon, troubler l'équilibre de nos différentes commerces" (in February 18 meeting of the second subcommission of the CRD, Lapradelle 4(2):709).

162. See Loucheur's comments in the second subcommission, February 20, Lapradelle 4(2):728–29.

163. Stenographic transcript of March 4 meeting of the second subcommission, Klotz Papers, foΔ94.

164. Dulles, "Reparation Problem," p. 134.

165. Burnett, *Reparation,* 2:711. Minutes of the March 24 meeting of the second subcommission.

166. To put the matter more rigorously, it is apparent that different strategies of investment, consumption and borrowing yield different "streams" of surplus real wealth, the present value of each of which can be calculated only with respect to a given rate of interest (or set of rates of interest, if this factor is allowed to change over time). Which stream has the greatest capital value—and can therefore be said to represent German "capacity"—thus depends on the particular rate of interest (or set of rates) chosen. A large surplus at the outset, for example, would cut down on initial investment and consumption. With a restricted industrial plant and a population weakened by reduced consumption, the future surplus available would be smaller than the corresponding amount that might result from a more generous policy at the outset. The relative value of the "stream" of surpluses generated by a particular strategy obviously depends on how the factor of time is weighted, and thus on the interest rate used to compute the capitalized value of each "stream."

167. Mitchell memorandum, "The Payment of Indemnities by the Central Powers," February 22, 1919, Gay Papers, Box 4. On Mitchell, see the memorial volume, Arthur Burns, ed., *Wesley C. Mitchell, The Economic Scientist,* (New York: National Bureau of Economic Research, 1952).

168. André Poisson, "L'Excédent de revenu annuel de l'Allemagne après la guerre," *Travaux accomplis par la Commission des Réparations jusqu'au mois de juin 1920* (Paris,

1920), Document 22. Poisson's memorandum was written in April, 1919. This source can be consulted at the Hoover Institution and at the Bibliothèque de Ducumentation Internationale Contemporaine in Nanterre.

169. See especially F. W. Taussig, "Germany's Reparation Payments," *American Economic Review* (March 1920), Supp., 10(1):33–49, and Jacob Viner's remarks in the Round Table discussion of "Economic Problems Involved in the Payment of International Debts," *American Economic Review* (March 1926), Supp., 16(1):91–97.

170. For a more detailed discussion of the theory of transfer, see the appendix.

171. Dulles, "Reparation Problem," p. 135.

172. The mid-March report of the Committee of Three, which epitomized the point of view that the payment of reparation would injure the creditors' economies by making them "a dumping ground for Germany's surplus products" is praised by the two scholars whose views on reparation have carried the most weight. Weill-Raynal declares that the report "was based on purely economic considerations" (*Les Reparations*, 1:51); and Philip Mason Burnett praised the report in similar terms in his lengthy and widely cited "Introduction" (*Reparation*, 1:55, 56).

173. Burnett, l:xiii.

174. On these contacts see Krüger, *Deutschland und die Reparationen*, pp. 131–37, 176–81; M. J. Bonn, *Wandering Scholar* (New York: J. Day, 1948) pp. 235–36; and in general German Foreign Ministry, Political Archive, *Akten betreffend geheime Vermittlungsaktionen und Agententätigkeit* (26 April 1919–22 June 1919), Band 1, U.S. National Archives microfilm publication T-120, reels 2403–04, frames E212806–694—henceforth the following abbreviated form will generally be used: "T-120/2403–04/E212806–964."

175. For example Krüger, *Deutschland und die Reparationen*, p. 137; Redlich memo, May 26, 1919, T-120/2404/E212921; Redlich account of his talk with Massigli, May 2, 1919, T-120/2403/E212806ff.; Redlich memo, n.d., T-120/2404/E212906; Aufzeichnung, May 12, 1919, T-120/2403/E212856; Redlich memo of May 26, 1919 on his talks with Massigli of May 22, T-120/2404/E212918–921.

176. The whole question of the implications of France's overture to Germany is considered in greater detail in chapter 4.

177. Redlich memo, May 2, 1919, T-120/2403/E212808; Aufzeichnung (n.a.), May 12, 1919, T-120/2403/E212851ff.; Redlich memo (n.d.), T-120/2404/E212915—916; Redlich memo, May 26, 1919, T-120/2404/E212921.

178. Krüger, *Deutschland und die Reparationen*, pp. 136, 177.

179. *Ibid.*, pp. 134–38; Harry Kessler, *The Diaries of a Cosmopolitan*, trans. and ed. Charles Kessler (London: Weidenfeld and Nicolson, 1971), pp. 98–99.

180. Krüger, *Deutschland und die Reparationen*, pp. 131–32, 135, 176.

181. *Ibid.*, p. 134.

182. See FRUS, PPC, vols. 4 and 5, *passim;* for example, 5:546, 738–40.

183. FRUS, PPC, 5:740.

184. *Ibid.*, 6:796.

185. *Ibid.*

186. *Ibid.*, pp. 902–17.

187. Krüger, *Deutschland und die Reparationen*, pp. 176–79. On the later negotiations, see chapters 3 and 4.

188. FRUS, PPC, 6:855–56.

189. *Ibid.*, pp. 852, 856.

190. These were the estimates of Keynes and Dulles (Burnett, *Reparation*, 1:135); Lamont also estimated the current value of the German offer at 40 milliard gold marks (FRUS, PPC, 11:202).

191. FRUS, PPC, 6:856.

192. *Ibid.*, p. 854.

193. *Ibid.*

194. *Ibid.*, pp. 853–54.

195. *Ibid.*, p. 861.

196. Mantoux, 2:273, Council of Four, June 2.

197. Burnett, *Reparation*, 2:26, 118, 105.

198. *Ibid.*, pp. 130–31, 145ff.

199. Mantoux, 2:270–71. Council of Four, June.

200. Barnes to Lloyd George and Lloyd George to Barnes, both June 2, 1919, Lloyd George Papers, F/4/3/17–18; Cecil to Lloyd George, May 5, 8 and 27, 1919, Lloyd George Papers, F/6/6/41, 43, 47; Curzon to Lloyd George and Lloyd George to Curzon, July 7 and 8, 1919, F/12/1/21–22.

201. British Empire Delegation, minutes (Cab 29/28), 32nd meeting, May 30, 1919.

202. Cab 29/28, 33rd meeting, June 1, p. 9.

203. Cab 29/28, 34th meeting, June 1, p. 6.

204. *Ibid.*, p. 7.

205. Mantoux, 2:266.

206. *Ibid.*, p. 267.

207. *Ibid.*, p. 273.

208. House Diary, vol. 14, entries for August 22 and October 26.

209. House Diary, vol. 15, entry for March 31, 1919.

210. Baruch Diary, entry for June 2, p. 60. For evidence of Wilson's personal disgust at Lloyd George, see also Burnett, *Reparation*, 1:136n.

211. FRUS, PPC, 11:197–222; Baker, *Wilson and World Settlement*, 3:469–504.

212. FRUS, PPC, 11:198, 203.

213. This was the opinion of L. L. Summers, *ibid.*, p. 200.

214. FRUS, PPC, 11:200.

215. *Ibid.*, pp. 199, 202–203.

216. *Ibid.*, p. 202.

217. *Ibid.*, p. 222.

218. Baruch Diary, entry for May 20.

219. *Ibid.*, entries for May 20 and May 21.

220. "France," Lloyd George told the British Empire Delegation on June 10, "was in favour of the two alternatives which he had placed before the Council, but the United States was not" (Cab 29/28, 35th meeting, June 10).

221. Mantoux, 2:269.

222. Mantoux, 2:277–83 and 382–86 on Silesia, 246, 346–48 and 392 on the League.

223. *Ibid.*, pp. 267–68, 270–71.

224. *Ibid.*, pp. 270, 272, 393–94.

225. *Ibid.*, pp. 338–39, 354–57.

226. *Ibid.*, pp. 339, 355.

227. Burnett, *Reparation*, 2:124, 160.

228. *Ibid.*, p. 124.

229. Riddell, *Intimate Diary*, p. 87; Cab 29/28, 33rd meeting June 1; Bonar Law to Lloyd George, May 31, 1919, Bonar Law Papers, 10/3/93, Beaverbrook Foundation, House of Lords Record Office, London.

230. Mantoux, 2:355–56.

231. Burnett, *Reparation*, 2:201.

232. *Ibid.*, p. 199.

233. *Ibid.*, p. 201.

234. FRUS, PPC, 6:522.

3. Indulgence

1. Mantoux, 1:43. Count Ulrich von Brockdorff-Rantzau was Foreign Minister of Germany and head of the German delegation at the peace conference.

2. Sénat, *Débats,* October 11, 1919, p. 1623.

3. Chambre, *Débats,* September 25, 1919, pp. 4578–80.

4. *Ibid.,* p. 4580.

5. *Ibid.,* p. 4578.

6. *Ibid.,* p. 4573.

7. Compare, for example, the remarks of the Liberal leader Maclean in July 1919 with his comments in February 1920 (*Parl. Deb.,* Commons, July 21, 1919, cols. 953–54, and February 12, 1920, cols. 269, 275); similarly see the *Economist,* April 5, 1919, p. 556, May 10, 1919, p. 767, and July 17, 1920, p. 91. For examples of "advanced" Liberal opinion, see Trevor Wilson, ed., *The Political Diaries of C. P. Scott,* (Ithaca: Cornell University Press, 1970), pp. 374, 378, 380. On Labour, compare the mild allusions to reparation in the *Report of the Nineteenth Annual Conference of the Labour Party* (held June 1919; pp. 216–17) with the discussion in the *Report of the Twentieth Annual Conference* which took place a year later (pp. 112, 132ff.). See also Carl Brand, *The British Labour Party* (Stanford: Hoover Institution Press, 1974), pp. 60–67.

8. "Militaristic ambitions and imperialistic policies are by no means dead," he wrote "even in counsels of the nations whom we most trust and with whom we most desire to be associated in the task of peace. Throughout the sessions of the conference in Paris, it was evident that a militaristic party, under the most influential leadership, was seeking to gain ascendancy in the counsels of France. They were defeated then but are in control now." (Wilson to Senator Hitchcock, March 8, 1920, *New York Times,* March 9, 1920, p. 1).

9. Tardieu's articles appeared in *L'Illustration;* see especially the issues of May 1, May 22 and July 24, 1920. Baker, in *Woodrow Wilson and World Settlement,* epitomizes the Wilsonian view.

10. See, for example, the Hankey memornadum, "Towards a National Policy," July 1919, Cab 21/159. On this, see Stephen Roskill, *Hankey: Man of Secrets,* 2:111–13.

11. Conversation of December 3, 1919, Cab 23/35/2.

12. See John Maynard Keynes, *A Revision of the Treaty,* pp. 3–5.

13. On the ratification debate, see E. Beau de Loménie, *Le Débat de ratification du traité de Versailles* (Paris: Denoël. 1945), pp. 82–131, and Etienne Weill-Raynal, *Les Réparations allemandes,* 1:129–36; or see the transcript in Chambre, *Débats,* September 1919.

14. Chambre, *Débats,* September 11, 1919, p. 4277, and September 5, 1919, p. 4192.

15. *Ibid.,* September 5, 1919, pp. 4196–97.

16. *Ibid.,* September 11, 1919, pp. 4282, and Sénat, *Débats,* October 11, 1919, p. 1624.

17. John Maynard Keynes, *The Economic Consequences of the Peace* pp. 187–88.

18. In a recent article François Crouzet wrote that the French press more or less ignored Keynes, and "the name of Keynes was never pronounced in the parliamentary debates of this period" ("Réactions françaises devant *Les Conséquences économiques de la paix* de Keynes," *Revue d'histoire moderne et contemporaine* (January-March 1972), 19:7). Crouzet is certainly mistaken in this matter. There were frequent references to Keynes in articles and in the parliamentary debates on reparation in this period; and he was referred to in a way that clearly supposed that the reader or the audience knew very well what he stood for. See, for example, Chambre, *Débats,* July 20, 1920, the remarks of Tardieu (p. 2981), Léon Daudet (p. 2985), and Loucheur (p. 2991); Poincaré in the *Revue des Deux Mondes* (March 15, April 1, August 15, 1920—pp. 475, 711, 892) and in *Le Temps* of January 24, 1921. See also *Le Matin* of

January 28, 1920, and the important articles devoted to Keynes in *L'Europe nouvelle*, January 10, 1920 (pp. 3–4) and January 31, 1920 (pp. 170–71) and again on April 24, 1920.

19. "Moved by insane delusion and reckless self-regard, the German people overturned the foundations on which we all lived and built" (Keynes, *Economic Consequences*, p. 1).

20. See especially Henri Hauser, "Un Avocat de l'Allemagne: John Maynard Keynes," *Action nationale* (April 1920), 11:26–51, esp. pp. 30, 36, 41, 43.

21. Thus the French government in early March 1920 succeeded in having a paragraph containing this phrase deleted from an Economic Memorandum to be adopted by the Supreme Council. It was evidently for this reason that the French objected to this paragraph, because everything else in it duplicated other provisions of the memorandum. See Great Britain, Foreign Office, *Documents on British Foreign Policy 1919–1939*, First Series, (London, 1947–   ), 7:392n.—henceforth cited as "DBFP"—and Cmd. 646 of 1920.

22. The leading economists thought along these lines. See, for example, Charles Rist, "Indemnité de guerre et commerce international," *Action nationale* (April 1919), 7:26–37; Charles Gide, "L'Indemnité de guerre," *La Paix par le droit* (May–June 1919), pp. 201–212; Gaston Jèze, "La Liquidation financière de le guerre," *Action nationale* (January–March 1919), 6:esp. 248–51. Statesmen like Loucheur were fully aware that the payment of reparation was related to the creation of a German trade surplus; see, for example, Chambre, *Débats*, September 11, 1919, p. 4282.

23. *Journal of Modern History* (March 1947), 19(1):69.

24. Keynes had long felt that France intended to use reparation as a means of dismembering Germany—see his comments of December 5, 1918, in Burnett, *Reparation at the Paris Peace Conference from the Standpoint of the American Delegation*, 11:436. See also the remarks of the banker Walter Leaf in the *Economist*, February 7, 1920, p. 279, and the *Economist's* own editorial of February 5, 1921, p. 215. Lloyd George himself had similar suspicions; see Jones, *Whitehall Diary* (entry for March 7, 1921), 1:131.

25. Georges Soutou, "Der Einfluss der Schwerindustrie auf die Gestaltung der Frankreichpolitik Deutschlands 1919–1921," p. 544, and Soutou, "Problèmes concernant le rétablissement des relations économiques franco-allemandes," 582. Soutou's underestimation of Loucheur's importance prevented him from grasping the real significance of these French moves.

26. The figures in this section are drawn from the following sources: G. Tochon, "Nos besoins en charbon et le Traité de Paix," *Action nationale* (December 1918), 5:418–21; France, Ministère de l'Economie et des Finances, Institut National de la Statistique et des Etudes Economiques, *Annuaire statistique de la France*, 1966 ed., p. 229; and Sergent (Under-Secretary of State in the Ministry of Finance) to the Foreign Minister, December 13, 1918, $F^{12}8039$, folder "Exploitation des mines."

27. Georges Soutou, "La France et les Marches de l'Est, 1914–1919," *Revue historique* (1978), 260(2): 341–88, esp. pp. 360, 382. See also Pierre Renouvin, "Les Buts de guerre du gouvernment français," *Revue historique* (1966), 235:36, and Walter McDougall, "French Rhineland Policy and the Struggle for European Stabilization," p. 16.

28. Raymond Poincaré, *A la recherche de la paix*, pp. 82, 105, 122, 310.

29. Réponse de Monsieur Cavallier," Oct. 15, 1916, $F^{12}7985$ folder "PF-XI." For Foch's reluctance to occupy the Ruhr area, see "Conversation entre M. Lloyd George et le Maréchal Foch," December 1, 1918, Fonds Clemenceau, 6N72.

30. Jean-Noël Jeanneney, *François de Wendel en République: 'L'Argent et le Pouvoir 1914–1940*, pp. 37–38. For a contrary view see Charles Maier, *Recasting Bourgeois Europe*, p. 71. Actually it does not seem that either Jeanneney or Maier presents enough evidence to fully settle the question of the Comité des Forges's war aims.

31. AJ^5233, folder "Réparations et restitutions. Domaine industriel en général," subfolder "Mines et métallurgie"; Note Pinot, May 8, 1920, complaining about the way these

demands were ignored, Millerand Papers, carton 72, folder "Comité des Forges de France," Bibliothèque Nationale, Paris; Jeanneney, *François de Wendel*, pp. 121–22. On Loucheur's attitude, see chapter 2.

32. Maier, *Recasting Bourgeois Europe*, pp. 200–201; Soutou, "Der Einfluss," p. 544; Soutou, "Rétablissement," pp. 585–86; Jacques Bariéty, "Le Rôle de la minette dans la sidérurgie allemande," esp. pp. 251–52; Jeanneney, *François de Wendel*, pp. 116–131, 151–54.

33. *Akten der Reichskanzlei Weimarer Republik: Das Kabinett Müller*, 1:169—henceforth the following form will be used to cite books in this series: "Akten: Müller 1." On Pinot's plan see Maier, p. 387, and Jeanneney, p. 124.

34. For a typical argument about iron ore as a weapon to compel coal deliveries, see the conclusions of the July 1, 1918 meeting of the Bureau de'études économiques, AJ^5233, folder "Réparations et restitutions. Domaine industriel en général," subfolder "Mines et Méitallurgie"; for criticisms of this policy, see an unsigned memo from the Ministry of Armament's Direction des Mines of Oct. 29, 1918, in $F^{12}8035$, folder "D.673. Métallurgie," and the "Réponse de Monsieur Cavallier" of October 15, 1916, in $F^{12}7985$, folder "PF-XI." On the episode of the cutting off of minette, see the Coste memorandum of June 15, 1922, in the Ministry of Foreign Affairs Archives, Paris, Series "B. Relations Commerciales 1920–1929," volume 69—henceforth an abbreviated form will be used: AE, Rel. Com., 69. On these matters in general and in particular on the German response see Bariéity, "Rôle de la minette," pp. 266–67, Maier, *Recasting Bourgeois Europe* pp. 198–99, Soutou, "Der Einfluss," pp. 544–46, Stephen Schuker, *The End of French Predominance in Europe,* p. 222ff., esp. p. 227.

35. Norman J. G. Pounds, *The Ruhr: A Study in Historical and Economic Geography* (London: Faber & Faber, 1952) p. 172.

36. See Soutou, "Der Einfluss", pp. 544–45; "Aufzeichnung über die gegenwärtige Sachlage in den Fragen der Witschaft-Verhandlungen mit der Entente," July 30, 1919, T-120/2412/E219692; Bergmann's report to the Cabinet, Oct. 30, 1919, T-120/1667/743293. Loucheur's "compromising spirit", the German delegates recognized, carried over to noneconomic areas such as the Rhineland question: see Lersner to Auswärtiges Amt, (AA), August 7, 1919, T-120/2069/D933266. For a report on the negotiations up to the German coal offer, see Lersner to AA, August 265, 1919, T-120/2069/D933297.

37. T-120/2070/D933503; see also Soutou, "Der Einfluss," pp. 544–45.

38. See Soutou, "Der Einfluss," *passim;* Soutou, "Rétablissement," *passim;* Bariéty, pp. 273–74, for the 1922 affair.

39. Akten: Müller 1:171 n. 7. For the full document, see T-120/1642/D715933ff.

40. Memorandum of January 22, 1921, in T-120/5561/Serial K2125.

41. See Krüger, *Deutschland und die Reparationen,* esp. pp. 161, 175, 195ff., 211.

42. *Ibid.,* pp. 147–51; Akten: Scheidemann, pp. 88–90, 146.

43. Krüger, pp. 11–12, 19–20, 66, 74.

44. Krüger, e.g. pp. 71, 115; Akten: Scheidemann, p. 352.

45. Krüger, pp. 35–40; Akten: Scheidemann, pp. 78–80, 159–60. Erzberger, a leading member of the new government, wanted to go even further and try to escape liability for damages suffered by northern France after the German "peace offer" of December 1916 (Akten: Scheidemann, p. 78).

46. This was not entirely to the liking of the British government, nor for that matter was it to the taste of other elements in the French government. "I hear that Loucheur is extremely active in forcing on the organisation work of the Reparations Commission," Philip Kerr wrote Lloyd George on August 16. "Peel is hanging things up as much as he can, but with an active and able man like Loucheur pressing things forward with all his might and supported by a very active Belgian delegate it is not at all easy" (Lloyd Gorge Papers, F/89/4/11). Kerr was very close to Lloyd George at this time. For Loucheur's aloofness from the established ministries

and their resentment, see Serruys, "Note pour Monsieur le Ministre" on "Négociation avec les Allemands," (n.d.), in F^{12}8115, folder "Traité de Paix 1919. Office de compensation (1920)." On these negotiations in general, see the minutes of the CORC, in the archives of the Reparation Commission (fonds AJ^6 in the Archives Nationales, Paris), cartons AJ^{6}7, AJ^{6}82.

47. Archives of the French Delegation to the Reparation Commission (fonds AJ^5 at the Archives Nationales, Paris), carton 312, folder "Main d'oeuvre allemande. Grands travaux." There is another copy in AJ^{5}313, folder "Main d'oeuvre allemande. Dossier complet."

48. CORC minutes, July 11, 1919, AJ^{6}7. A November 12, 1919 letter from the German delegate Von de Suire recognized that German workers "will be, in all probability, kept strictly isolated" (AJ^{5}312, folder cited in n.47).

49. See, for example, M. Harmel, "Le syndicalisme français et la main d'oeuvre étrangère," *L'Information ouvrière et sociale,* June 27, 1920. For the material on the building trades union (Fédération du Bâtiment), see the report of the meeting of its Comité National, Sept. 13–14, 1919, in *Travailleur de Bâtiment,* no. 201, Oct. 1919, p. 8ff.; the report of the Comité National to the seventh national congress, pp. 26, 81–86; and the stenographic transcript of this congress (held November 19–24, 1919 in Tours), pp. 560–603. All this material is in the Institut Français d'Histoire Sociale in Paris.

50. See the German union's declaration at the Amsterdam conference of July 1919, *Voix du Peuple* 2nd series, No. 7, July 1919; Paeplow to the French and Belgian building trades unions, Dec. 17, 1918, Federation du Bâtiment, *Rapport du Comité National au 7e Congrès National,* p. 81.

51. For the discussion among German officials and labor representatives on French proposals for the use of German labor, see T-120/5461/K439694, Jan. 19, 1921.

52. On the January talks: minutes of a German cabinet meeting of January 16, 1920, with appended documents, T-120/1668/743873–899. On Millerand's policy, see Soutou, "Rétablissment," p. 582ff., and discussion to follow in chapter 3.

53. See Edouard Bonnefous, *Histoire politique de la Troisième République,* 3:102–11.

54. Chambre, *Débats,* March 26, 1920, p. 746.

55. DBFP, 7:286; Archives of the French Ministry of Finance, (fonds F^{30}, consulted at the Ministry of Finance, Paris), carton 1359, folder "Emprunt international," minutes of a February 13, 1920, meeting of Allied Minister of Finance in London.

56. See especially the "Bankers' Memorial" of January 15, 1920, in Germain Calmette, *Recueil de documents sur l'histoire de la question des réparations, 1919–5 mai 1921,* pp. 191–96.

57. See Seydoux's "Note au suject de la situation économique de l'Europe," May 1, 1920, Millerand Papers, unclassified, Bibliothèque Nationale, Paris.

58. Celier to Keynes, June 30, 1920, Keynes Papers, Marshall Library of Economics, Cambridge, England.

59. Celier to Keynes, June 13 and November 10, 1919, Keynes Papers.

60. Avenol to Klotz, April 26, 1919, F^{30}1359, folder "Emprunt international."

61. Guionic Diary, entry for March 2, 1920, in Raymond Poincaré Papers, Biliothèque National, Paris. François Guionic was Poincaré's secretary at the time.

62. Haguenin to Foreign Ministry, March 10 and 19, 1919, Ministry of Foreign Affairs archives, series "Europe 1918–1929," subseries "Allemagne," vol. 6.

63. Haguenin to Petit, Feb. 27, March 8, and April 23, 1920, Millerand Papers, carton 59, folder "Allemagne," Bibliothèque Nationale, Paris.

64. Haguenin to Foreign Ministry, April 16, 1920, *Ibid.;* Seydoux "Note pour le Président du Conseil," May 12, 1920, Millerand Papers, carton 57, folder "Hythe," Bibliothèque Nationale, Paris. See also chapter 4.

65. The best short analysis of the coal question is in Maier, *Recasting Bourgeois Europe,*

pp. 194ff. See also Henri Marcesche, *Le Charbon: Elément de réparations et de négociations dans le Traité de Versailles et les accords qui l'ont suivi* (Lorient: Imprimerie le Bayon-Rogers et Henrio, 1933); Maurice Olivier, *La Politique du charbon, 1914*–1921 (Paris: F. Alcan, 1922); and Robert Lafitte-Laplace, *L'économie charbonnière de la France* (Paris: Jouve, 1933).

66. Treaty of Versailles, Part VIII, Annex V, Paragraph 10.

67. DBFP, 5, no. 99, annex 2.

68. DBFP, 2:749; Reparation Commission annex 77, February 17, 1920, in AJ^{6}203; Reparation Commission, *Travaux accomplis,* pp. 17–19.

69. Akten: Müller 1:335. For arguments of a similar nature, see Akten: Fehrenbach, p. 64.

70. Reparation Commission, minutes no. 9, February 9, 1920, and minutes no. 15, February 20, 1920, in AJ^{6}203. "Needs" were determined on the basis of 1913 consumption.

71. See the Reparation Commission sources in n. 68.

72. DBFP, 7:26, 32–37. The quotation is on p. 33.

73. See for example, Mantoux, 1:27, and DBFP, 15:455.

74. See DBFP, 15:477, 483; Jacques Seydoux, "La Question des réparations depuis la paix," *Revue d'économie politique* (1921), 35:709. This article was originally published anonymously, but Seydoux is identified as the author in Jacques Seydoux, *De Versailles au Plan Young.*

75. DBFP, 7:33–36; 10:204.

76. "Conversation entre M. Lloyd George et le Maréchal Foch," Dec. 1, 1918, Fonds Clemenceau, 6N72.

77. Cab 24/105/CP 1222; Cab 23/21/25/5. For the French view, see Loucheur, "Note sur la question des matières premières," November 23, 1920, in the Loucheur Papers, box 11, folder "U,V," Hoover Institution; A. Merrheim, "Le probleme du charbon et la Conférence de Spa," *L'Information ouvriére et sociale,* August 12, 1920, last paragraph; Lafitte-Laplace, *L'économie charbonnière, pp.* 22–26; and in general F^{12}8075.

78. See the Sauerwein article in *Le Matin,* February 25, 1920, and a February 23 article in the same journal, the subheadline of which was "Nos alliés vont-ils, en empêchant notre reconstitution maritime, nous mettre en état de vassalité économique?" For the views of some rightwing political leaders, see Poincaré in the *Revue des Deux Mondes,* 57:233; Tardieu in *L'Illustration,* February 21, 1920, pp. 132–33; and a sensational speech by Barthou in Chambre, *Débats,* March 25, 1920, esp. pp. 714–16.

79. *L'Europe nouvelle,* which a month earlier had received Keynes's book sympathetically (calling it "un grand acte de courage civique") now expressed concern about the shift of British opinion: "Les dispositions de l'opinion publique anglaise à l'égard du Traité de Paix et la facilité avec laquelle nos alliés ont adopté les suggestions en concernant la révision ont etonné l'opinion française" (February 21, 1920, p. 297). Even the very moderate economist Charles Rist felt that the tendency of British liberals to sympathize with Germany had been carried a bit too far (*Revue d'économie politique,* January-February 1920, p. 142).

80. DBFP, 9:163. The literature on this episode from the standpoint of German domestic politics is extensive. See especially Johannes Erger, *Der Kapp-Luttwitz Putsch: Ein Beitrag zur deutschen Innenpolitik 1919/20* (Dusseldorf: Droste, 1967); George Eliasberg, *Der Ruhrkrieg von 1920* (Bonn: Verlag Neue Gesellschaft, 1974) and Erhard Lucas, *Märzrevolution im Ruhrgebiet* (Frankfurt: März Verlag, 1970).

81. DBFP, 9:158–60, 170–80.

82. Millerand to Cambon, March 19, 1920, Millerand Papers, carton 59, folder "L'int^{on} des 25–27/3," Bibliothèque Nationale, Paris.

83. DBFP, 7:544–45, and 9:184–85.

84. DBFP, 9:205–06, Derby to Curzon, March 20, 1920.

85. *Ibid.*, p. 215, Derby to Curzon, March 21, 1920.

86. *Ibid.*, pp. 273, 278–79, 290, and 7:585. This information is confirmed by the French documents in the Millerand Papers, carton 59, folders "Notes" and "Président du Conseil. La Ruhr. mars-avril 1920." Bibliothèque Nationale, Paris.

87. DBFP, 9:276–78, Curzon to Derby, April 1, 1920.

88. *Ibid.*, p. 282. The British representative in the Rhineland had been reporting that the Ruhr insurrection was mainly antimilitarist rather than Bolshevik in orientation, that orderly conditions prevailed, and that work and life were "proceeding much as usual" (DBFP, 9:220, 231, 231n., 248, 256, Stuart to Curzon, March 22, 24, and 26).

89. DBFP, 9:303; Cmd. 1325 of 1921, pp. 70–71.

90. DBFP, 9:303, 306, Kilmarnock to Curzon, April 3, 1920.

91. DBFP, 9:311.

92. *Ibid.*, pp. 283–84, 302.

93. *Ibid.*, pp. 317–22.

94. Jones, *Diary,* 1:108–11. This outburst of racism was by no means a personal quirk of the prime minister's; for a survey of British attitudes on the subject see Keith Nelson, "The 'Black Horror' on the Rhine," *Journal of Modern History,* December 1970.

95. DBFP, 9:346–47, Curzon to Derby, April 8, 1920.

96. *Ibid.*, p. 379, April 11, 1920.

97. *Ibid.*, p. 382, Derby to Curzon, April 11, 1920.

98. *Ibid.*, p. 288, April 1, 1920.

99. *Ibid.*, pp. 296n, 307–08, 342, 321.

100. *Ibid.*, pp. 198, 204–5.

101. *Ibid.*, 7:41 (February 13) and 286 (February 28). See also the French notes of the February 13 meeting in $F^{30}1359$, folder "Emprunt international."

102. Cmd. 646 of 1920, pp. 6, 8.

103. AJ^51322, folder 134.

104. *Ibid.*, for notes of this meeting and the April 7 letter from Millerand to Poincaré confirming the decision taken.

105. *Ibid.*

106. Parallel to this conflict over the substance of policy was a struggle over where power to formulate policy would reside. Poincaré claimed that it was the responsibility of the Delegate to the Reparation Commission to make French reparation policy. He might consult with other organs of government, but would not take orders from them. On April 6, for example, he flatly refused to share the minutes of the Commission with the government; as justification for this, he cited paragraph 8 of Annex II which provided that "all proceedings of the Commission shall be private"! This was a point of view that Millerand and Marsal could not tolerate indefinitely. But instead of confronting the issue directly, they circumvented Poincaré's opposition by agreeing directly with the British on the principle of the fixed sum at San Remo. Poincaré thereupon resigned his post at the Reparation Commission; his successor, Louis Dubois, agreed to recognize the authority of the government in these matters. See AJ^5319, folder 148, subfolder "Decret du 2 mars et ses modifications."

107. DBFP, 8:193.

108. *Ibid.*

109. *Ibid.*, pp. 7, 8.

110. *Ibid.*

111. *Ibid.*

112. Cab 23/21/33, appendix I, Conference of Ministers, May 28, 1920. On Nitti's "pronounced pro-Germanism," see, for example, Roskill, *Hankey,* 2:161–62.

113. DBFP, 8:18.

114. *Ibid.*, p. 204.

115. *Ibid.*, p. 193.

116. *Ibid.*, pp. 11, 193.

117. *Ibid.*, pp. 11, 12.

118. *Ibid.*, pp. 149–50.

119. *Ibid.*, p. 13.

120. *Ibid.*, p. 150.

121. *Ibid.*, p. 151.

122. *Ibid.*, p. 152.

123. *Ibid.*

124. Originally the European Allies, including Great Britain, contended that the Reparation Commission had the right under this article to demand, for example, specific shares of stock. The "unofficial" American delegate refused to accept this interpretation, and as a result the question was left unresolved. No one, however, proposed setting down a less rigidly defined schedule of payments—calling for so many million gold marks worth of securities, for example, but leaving the choice of securities up to the Germans. In all likelihood, this neglect resulted from the Commission's belief that the neutral securities available to the German government were not sufficient even to finance German needs for food and raw material, as provided in Article 235 (AJ⁶203, minutes no. 12 and no. 16, February 13 and 23, 1920). But there were other forms of payment besides securities; by paragraph 19 of Annex II of the treaty, the Commission was authorized to accept payment in virtually any form. These, however, were neglected, and the difficulties involving securities were allowed to obstruct the execution of this article. Instead of dictating, or even proposing, a plan for the payment of the twenty milliards, the Commission on March 5 asked the Germans how they intended to execute it (AJ⁶203, minutes no. 20). But this proved fruitless: by the end of June, the Germans had still not proposed anything. At Spa in mid-July the German delegation made the totally unacceptable claim that the twenty milliards had already been paid. This threw the problem back to the Reparation Commission, which, however, on July 26 adjourned consideration of the question *sine die*. As a French memorandum of March 5, 1921, pointed out, although Article 235 gave the Commission the right to set the manner and timing of the payment of the 20 milliards, "up to the present the Commission has fixed nothing" (AJ⁶102, Annex 726a). See the historical note z157, circulated May 8, 1920, in AJ⁶1245, and file 13/96 in AJ⁶1941.

125. See T-120/2069/D933148 and the minutes of the CORC, July 3 and 11, 1919, for the original interpretation (AJ⁶7 and AJ⁶370); for the situation in mid-1920, see Theunis to Salter, June 19, 1920, Annex 316, in AJ⁶98.

126. On Article 248, see AJ⁶1944, file 13/108a; AJ⁶1960, file 13/173; AJ⁶1973, file 13/210. For evidence of French moderation in this matter, see AJ⁵417, folder "Renseignements financiers," extract from the minutes of the November 30, 1920 meeting of the Reparation Commission's Financial Service Managing Board. This body carried on talks with the Germans on this question, the record of which reveals the great reluctance of the Allies to give effect to Article 248; see AJ⁶101, Annex 662, AJ⁶1311, minutes 79, 93, 94, 105, 126, 127 (September 14, 1920 to February 15, 1921), and AJ⁶1248, z727. A basic legal problem compounded the difficulty of giving meaning to Article 248, since in their "Reply" to the German "Observations" on the treaty, the Allies had declared that they would not interfere in German internal affairs, and in particular would not dictate to the Germans on matters related to their budget. See Weill-Raynal, *Les Reparations allemandes et la France*, 1:120–22.

127. See, for example, Mantoux, 1:27ff.

128. DBFP, 8:192, 201.

129. In fact, in early May, the Germans submitted a memorandum evaluating, in accordance with the protocol, French material damages. The figure—7 milliard marks—struck the French as absurdly low. See Weill-Raynal, *Les Reparations*, 1:166–70, and Calmette, *Recueil de documents*, pp. 261–63.

130. Marsal to Millerand, May 12, 1920, F^{30}1275, folder "Zone Sterling," subfolder "Divers."

131. *Ibid.*

132. Minutes of the morning meeting of May 15, p. 17. AJ^{5}319, folder 137, "Conféerences de Hythe et de Boulogne," subfolder "Conférence de Hythe (May 1920)." These are the British secretary Hankey's notes, amended by those of the French interpreter Camerlynck. Hankey's version of Millerand's remarks is in DBFP, 8:259.

133. DBFP, 8:265.

134. *Ibid.*, pp. 263–66.

135. *Ibid.*, p. 268.

136. *Ibid.*

137. *Ibid.*, p. 269.

138. *Ibid.*, p. 273.

139. *Ibid.*, pp. 317–18, 330, 333.

140. *Ibid.*, pp. 263, 278.

141. "Extrait d'un compte-rendu par M. de Fleuriau," May 18, 1920, F^{30}1304, folder "Notes et documents sur les réparations, 1920–1924"; Cab 24/107/CP 1495 Annex 1, p. 379.

142. DBFP, 8:315.

143. *Ibid.*

144. Speaking of the reference at Hythe to the "parallel liquidation" of reparation and the inter-Allied debt, Chamberlain remarked in the Cabinet on May 21 that "one advantage of this arrangement was that if the French showed themselves unreasonable towards the Germans, we should be in a position to adopt a similar attitude towards them, and, consequently, to check them" (Cab 23/31/30, p. 162). On May 15 Churchill argued for the utilization of the French debt as a means of pressuring the French to adopt a moderate stance on reparation. To remit the debt now, he stated, would be to "deprive ourselves of one of the means of effecting a good arrangement for Germany" (Cab 24/105/CP 1316).

145. Cab 24/105/CP 1259; and Cab 23/21/30, May 21, 1920, p. 161ff.

146. Cab 24/97/CP 584, February 6, 1920, note by Basil Blackett on inter-Allied indebtedness; Cab 24/105/CP 1259, May 12, 1920, wherein Blackett reiterated his views and was endorsed by the Chancellor of the Exchequer, Austen Chamberlain; Cab 24/103/CP 1093, April 17, 1920, for Curzon's support of the scheme; Derby to Lloyd George, June 4, 1920, Lloyd George Papers, F/53/1/38. The Treasury proposal for canceling the French debt was an integral part of a larger plan that proposed that Great Britain pay in full its debt to the United States. Lloyd George and other cabinet ministers simply did not want to pay this debt, and wanted to use the French debt to Britain as a weapon with which to force American concessions, leading ideally to a general cancellation of indebtedness. See Cab 23/31/30, May 21, 1920, p. 149. Chamberlain brought up the question again in November (Cab 24/116/CP 2214), but the Treasury proposal was again turned down by the cabinet (Cab 23/23/72, December 17, 1920).

147. "Arrangements to be made as between the Allies," F^{30}1304, folder "Notes et documents."

148. On May 25 Celier wrote Norman Davis, now an Assistant Secretary of State, to ask whether the United States could in any way take part in a general settlement of "the international charges left by the war," involving "perhaps even annulment" of war debts (Senate Document 86 of 1921, pp. 271–72). Davis, however, felt it was absurd for the French to go on thinking that the United States, by forgiving part of the inter-Allied debt, should "pay such part" of the indemnity "as Germany cannot pay." The French, he wrote on May 22, "still have the idea that the United States is a Santa Claus" (FRUS, 1920, 2:391). Davis's reply to Celier marked no change in the rigid American attitude: the idea of trying the repayment of the inter-Allied debt to the payment of reparation was bluntly rejected (Davis to Celier, July 23,

1920, Senate Document 86 of 1921, pp. 272–73). The United States Treasury fully shared this point of view (Rathbone to Houston, Leffingwell and Davis, May 25, 1920, *ibid.*, pp. 80–81). Lloyd George on August 5 again attempted to get the United States to make some concession, but President Wilson's reply of November 3 shows that the American attitude was as unyielding as ever (*Combined Annual Reports of the World War Foreign Debt Commission* [Washington, 1927], pp. 72–74).

149. See Lord Riddell, *Intimate Diary*, p. 195.

150. DBFP, 8:262, 268–71.

151. *Ibid.*, p. 273.

152. *Ibid.*, pp. 275–77.

153. *Ibid.*, pp. 277–78.

154. See *Le Temps*, May 18, 1920, p. 1; Chambre, *Débats*, May 28, 1920, esp. pp. 1694, 1702, 1709, 1713.

155. See esp. *Le Matin*, May 3, 1920, and the *Revue des Deux Mondes*, June 1, 1920.

156. *L'Illustration*, May 22, 1920, esp. pp. 304–5.

157. *L'Illustration*, July 24, 1920, p. 57.

158. See chapter 2.

159. *L'Illustration*, July 24, 1920, p. 57.

160. Chambre, *Débats*, May 28, 1920, p. 1702. In fact Tardieu in 1919 had also advocated a figure of this sort: see chapter 2, n. 128.

161. Chambre, *Débats*, May 28, 1920, p. 1700.

162. As *L'Europe nouvelle* pointed out in its June 6 issue, p. 765.

163. Chambre, *Débats*, May 28, 1920, pp. 1698, 1700, 1703, 1709–10, 1713, 1715, 1721–22.

164. *Ibid.*, p. 1707. The best study of Socialist policy on reparation and related questions is the first part of Richard Gombin, *Les Socialistes et la guerre* (Paris: Mouton, 1970).

165. Chambre, *Débats*, May 28, 1920, p. 1703.

166. *Ibid.*, p. 1705.

167. *Ibid.*

168. *Ibid.*, pp. 1703, 1708.

169. Cab 23/21/37, Appendix II, Conference of Ministers, June 14, 1920, p. 285.

170. For the text, see Calmette, *Recueil de documents*, pp. 244–49.

171. See, for example, Sally Marks, "Reparations Reconsidered: A Reminder," *Central European History* (December 1969), 2:356.

172. The small but highly paid American army on the Rhine was costing as much as the entire French army of occupation (DBFP, 8:313).

173. DBFP, 8:309–10.

174. In particular, the Foreign Office was often kept ignorant of the important negotiations on reparation (see DBFP, 8:267, 16:581–84). For an example of Lloyd George's increasingly autocratic temper, see the story of his quarrel with Riddell in late 1920 in A. J. P. Taylor, ed., *Lloyd George: A Diary by Frances Stevenson* (New York: Harper and Row, 1971), pp. 294–95.

175. Cab 24/107/CP 1495, p. 370.

176. DBFP, 10:221, Kilmarnock to Curzon, May 5, 1920.

177. DBFP, 8:311.

178. *Ibid.*, pp. 441, 540.

179. *Ibid.*, p. 440.

180. *Ibid.*, p. 451.

181. *Ibid.*, pp. 449–51.

182. *Ibid.*, p. 540.

183. The text is in Calmette, *Recueil de documents*, pp. 263–69.

184. Akten: Müller 1:159–60, 171.

185. Wiedfeldt to Müller (Reconstruction Ministry), April 27, 1920, and Stinnes proposal, April 29, 1920, T-120/1642/D715924–934. There are excerpts in Akten: Müller 1:170–71, ns. 6 and 7.

186. Akten: Müller 1:126–27, 170.

187. Akten: Müller 1:319ff.; Akten: Fehrenbach, pp. xxxv, 1–5, 20.

188. Akten: Fehrenbach, p. 18.

189. *Ibid.*, pp. 71–72.

190. DBFP, 8:569–70.

191. *Ibid.*, p. 570.

192. *Ibid.*, p. 567.

193. *Ibid.*, pp. 586–90.

194. *Ibid.*, pp. 585–86, Wirth to Jaspar, July 13, 1920.

195. *Ibid.*, p. 641.

196. This was the conclusion that followed from figures collected not just by the French, but also by British and American coal experts on the Reparation Commission, who certainly had no interest in proving a German default (see n. 68). As Millerand pointed out, the accuracy of these figures was not challenged by the German delegation at Spa (DBFP, 8:572).

197. DBFP, 8:397–99.

198. *Ibid.*, p. 402.

199. *Ibid.*, pp. 414–18, 511–13.

200. Stinnes to Simons, July 4, 1920, T-120/1634/D716223.

201. DBFP, 7:510–11.

202. Hankey's description, quoted in Roskill, *Hankey*, 2:178–79; DBFP, 8:532.

203. DBFP, 8:531.

204. *Ibid.*, pp. 531, 533, 536–38.

205. *Ibid.*, pp. 570–73.

206. *Ibid.*, pp. 576–81.

207. *Ibid.*, pp. 590–92.

208. *Ibid.*, pp. 580, 582.

209. *Ibid.*, pp. 582–83.

210. *Ibid.*, pp. 597–605.

211. *Ibid.*, p. 602.

212. *Ibid.*, pp. 602–3.

213. *Ibid.*, pp. 603–4; see also *ibid.*, p. 626, where Millerand imputes this motive to the British.

214. *Ibid.*, pp. 607, 609; Roskill, *Hankey*, 2:179. Marsal's account of the incident in a secret meeting of the French Senate in March 1922 is even more extreme than the one related in the published British documents. According to Marsal, when Millerand proved at first relucatnt to accept Lloyd George's conditions, the latter threatened to break the conference and then declare before Parliament that the French government "has sent its niggers with their bayonettes and machine guns against the women and children of the Ruhr miners and has broken the Alliance in order to assure French heavy industry its coal supplies at £2 below the market rate" ("Séance Secrète du Sénat, 28 Mars 1922," Millerand Papers, unclassified material: correspondence with François-Marsal, folder "Sénat. 28 Mars 1922," Bibliothèque Nationale, Paris. On this incident see the *Times* (London), July 16 and August 4, 1920, and esp. March 30, 1922, p. 12d.

215. DBFP, 8:614–16, 620, 628.

216. "Note pour le Président du Conseil," Millerand Papers, Vol. 42, Foreign Ministry Archives.

217. *Ibid.*, p. 635. The Agreement was in terms of 92nds because only the four major

creditors, France, the British Empire, Italy and Belgium, who together accounted for 92 percent of the reparations, agreed to finance the advances.

218. For the text of the arrangements adopted at Spa, see Calmette, *Recueil de documents,* pp. 274–77, and France, Ministère des Affaires Etrangeres, *Documents relatifs aux reparations,* 1:50–60.

219. Chambre, *Débats,* July 20, 1920, pp. 2976–3005, and July 30, 1920, pp. 3300–27.

220. Chambre, *Débats,* July 30, 1920, p. 3309.

221. "Notre solution," Auriol noted, "c'est l'emprunt international, gagé par les reconnaissances de dette de l'Allemagne, garantie par l'aval solidiare des alliés" (*ibid.,* p. 3313).

222. On the July 20 vote of confidence, of the 212 deputies who belonged to either the extreme right-wing Independent group or to the much larger Entente Républicaine Démocritique, only 11 voted against the government, and only 12 abstained. The figures were twice as large proportionately for the more moderate right-center groups, the Gauche Républicaine et Sociale, and the Républicains de Gauche. Together these groups comprised 199 deputies, of whom 26 voted against the government and a further 31 abstained. Among the 115 members of left-center groups, Radicals and Républicans Socialistes, opposition to the government was proportionately still greater: 19 negative votes and 24 abstentions. But on the whole, all the bourgeois parties supported Millerand's reparation policy. The real opposition came from the Socialists. Of the 130 hostile votes, the 68 Socialist deputies provided 64 of them. The same trends are evident in the July 30 vote on credits for the advances, although at this point opposition to the government's reparation policy had increased somewhat: whereas on July 20, the vote was 384 to 130 with 71 abstentions, on July 30, it was 338 to 145 with 95 abstentions. This is based on the lists of members of parliamentary groups, as printed in Chambre, *Débats,* March 18, 1920, p. 634.

223. Chambre, *Débats,* July 30, 1920, p. 3310, and articles by Doumergue and Fribourg in *Le Matin,* August 1, 1920.

224. Richard Ullman, *The Anglo-Soviet Accord,* pp. 142–43, 149, 152, 210.

225. See Ullman, chaps. 5 and 6. The affair can be followed in some detail in DBFP, 11:chap. 2, and AE, Grande Bretagne, 45.

4. The Seydoux Plan

1. See the memorandum from the Reparation Commission's Berlin Information Bureau, "Attitude de la presse et l'opinion publique vis-à-vis de la Conférence de Spa," in AJ⁵318, folder "Conférence de Spa," subfolder "Conférence de Spa."

2. Boris, Ferry, Prangey, Sonolet and Weill-Raynal, note of July 12, 1920, F¹²8122, folder "Spa, 1920," subfolder "Documents allemands du sujet des réparations et observations des administrations françaises (Conférence de Spa)." There are other copies in the Millerand Papers, 42, Foreign Ministry Archives, Paris.

3. Document no. 7, *ibid.;* AJ⁵340, folder "Prestations en nature"; Aron note, November 5, 1920, "Exécution du Traité de Versailles, Note sur les paiements en nature," esp. pp. 40ff., AJ⁵301, folder "Notes de M. Aron"; Annex 444, October 9, 1920, AJ⁶98.

4. See the Aron note cited in n. 3, p. 40; Etienne Weill-Raynal, "La Réparation des dommages de guerre et la paix du monde," *L'Information ouvrière et sociale,* September 3, October 3 and October 7, 1920, esp. October 7, p. 7.

5. Literally "victims," but in this context Frenchmen entitled to compensation for war damages.

6. Document no. 7, cited in n. 3; AJ⁵417, folder 3, subfolder "Exportations . . . ".

7. Not just between the Allies and Germany, but also between the German government and the German firms producing the reparation goods; see document no. 10 in the subfolder cited in n. 2.

8. Document no. 7, cited in n. 3.

9. Celier to Clemenceau, October 28, 1919, F³⁰701.

10. Celier note for the Minister, December 8, 1919, and memorandum by Sergent of December 11, 1919, in F³⁰1504, folder "Signature du Ministre . . .".

11. Chambre, *Débats*, July 20, 1920, p. 2977.

12. Issue of July 1, 1920.

13. Chambre, *Débats*, July 20, 1920, p. 2985.

14. Soutou's articles provide the best account of the affair: "Der Einfluss der Schwerindustrie auf die Gestaltung der Frankreichpolitik Deutschlands," pp. 546–47, and especially "Problèmes concernant le rétablissment des relations économiques franco-allemandes," pp. 582–89. See also Mayer to Muller, March 28, 1920, T-120/4509/K439576–577, and Mayer to Simson, September 20, 1920, T-120/3485/H248700–704, for German perceptions of Millerand's policy, and Boyé to Mayer, June 24, 1920, T-120/5352/L436849, for proof that the Ruhr magnates were unwilling at the time to discuss these matters with the French.

15. Minutes of a meeting of Oct. 23, 1920, quoted in Georges Soutou, "Die deutschen Reparationen und das Seydoux-Projekt 1920/21," *Vierteljahrshefte für Zeitgeschichte* (1975), 23(3):247.

16. Laurent's formal instructions of June 26, 1920, characterized the goal of French policy in this way: "Lier le relèvement économique de l'Allemagne au nôtre, dans la mesure qui nous semblera le plus convenable, de façon à l'empêcher de se dresser contre nous et d'en tirer tous les avantages qu'il peut nous procurer" (quoted on p. 3 of the Aron note cited in n. 3).

17. H. A. Marx to Simons, August 26, 1920, T-120/1328/500789–791.

18. Laurent to Millerand, September 12, 1920, and Millerand to Laurent, September 22, 1920, in F³⁰1275, folder "Zone Sterling," subfolder "Négociations préalables, 1920."

19. *Ibid.*, Laurent to Leygues, October 1, 1920.

20. *Ibid.*, Leygues to Laurent, October 4, 1920.

21. *Ibid.*

22. When Lloyd George received a telegram from Derby informing him that the French government refused to go to Geneva, he "stormed away at the bad faith of the French in trying to break one agreement after another. 'They were worse than the Bolsheviks; we must take a firm stand; we must let the French know that rather than break our word in this matter we will stand by the Germans and let the world know' " (Thomas Jones, *Whitehall Diary*, 1:121).

23. DBFP, 8:762.

24. DBFP, 10:513, Derby to Curzon, September 10, 1920.

25. *Ibid.*, p. 531, September 20, 1920.

26. *Ibid.*, p. 529, Curzon to Derby, September 15, 1920.

27. DBPF, 8:759, 761, 762; Sauerwein article in *Le Matin*, October 14, 1920.

28. French reply of October 8 to British note of October 5, F.O. 371/4727/C8400, in Public Record Office, London; Note for the British Embassy in Paris of October 20, AJ⁵320, folder "Conférences de Bruxelles et de Paris."

29. DBFP, 10:537, 549–50, 520, 525, and 8:792–94.

30. DBFP, 10:557, Derby to Curzon, November 10, 1920; *Documents relatifs aux réparations*, 1:69–70.

31. Laurent to Foreign Minister, October 21, 1920, AJ⁵320, folder "Conférences de Bruxelles et de Paris."

32. On Seydoux see the introduction to Seydoux, *De Versailles au Plan Young*, and François Seydoux, "Hier au Quai d'Orsay—Jacques Seydoux, Mon Père," *Revue des Deux Mondes*, January 19, 1964.

33. Göppert to Simson, June 30, 1920, T-120/1642/D715938.

34. Dresel to Secretary of State, May 3, 1920, memorandum of interview with M. Seydoux on April 17, 1920, 751.62/7, in United States National Archives Microfilm Publication

M569, Records of the Department of State Relating to Political Relations Between France and Other States, 1910–1929, reel 3. See also Seydoux's "Note au sujet de la situation économique de l'Europe," March 5, 1920, "Dossier personnel rapporté par M. Millerand à Boulogne et Bruxelles," Millerand Papers, Bibliothèque Nationale, Paris.

35. "Note pour le Président du Conseil," May 12, 1920, Millerand Papers, "Dossier personnel, rapporté par M. Millerand à Boulogne et Bruxelles," Bibliothèque Nationale, Paris; "Note pour le Président du Conseil," June 5, 1920, AE, Paix, 92.

36. "Note pour le Président du Conseil," July 12, 1920, AE, Millerand Papers, 42.

37. Seydoux to Serruys, July 16, 1920, quoted in Soutou, "Rétablissement," p. 594.

38. Seydoux to Vignon, Oct. 25, 1920, AE, Millerand Papers, 15.

39. See, for example, A. Poisson, "Note sur la situation financière de l'Allemagne," December 18, 1920, esp. pp. 36ff., in AJ^{5}76.

40. De Fleuriau to Leygues, October 10, 1920, F^{30}1275, folder "Zone Sterling," subfolder "Négociations préalables, 1920."

41. Seydoux to Dubois, November 18, 1920, AJ^{5}321, folder 145. Seydoux's opinion of England, implicit here, was more bluntly stated in a letter to Dubois of November 16, 1920: A "mercantile" nation, England "as always has sought only her own immediate advantage . . ." (AJ^{5}321, folder 145).

42. Seydoux to Dubois, November 16, 1920, cited in n. 41.

43. "Le Rôle de la minette," pp. 244–58, esp. pp. 249–250, republished in his book *Les Relations franco-allemandes après la première guerre mondiale,* pp. 134–49.

44. See chapter 3.

45. Thomas Boyle, author of a detailed study of Allied policy on German disarmament, summarized his findings as follows: as opposed to Britain, "France evinced a consistent distrust of disarmament as a reliable guarantee of European security, regardless of any success in enforcement of the treaty clauses" ("France, Great Britain, and German Disarmament, 1919–1927," Ph.D. diss., SUNY Stony Brook, 1972, abstract).

46. Gen. Serrigny (Secretary of the CSDN), "La Forme de mobilisation à adopter pour la préparation des prochains plans de mobilisation," Nov. 10, 1922, p. 12, in carton CSDN Q20-Q23, folder "No. 19, CSDN. Séance du 13 Novembre 1922," War Ministry Archives, Vincennes.

47. Cited in Soutou, "Seydoux-Projekt," p. 247.

48. See chapter 3, and discussion to follow in chapter 4. See also the extracts from the industrialists' 1922 discussion in Bariéty, "Le role de la minette," pp. 273–74.

49. Because the Rhenish question became closely linked with reparation only in mid-1922, a detailed discussion of the development of French Rhineland policy will be put off to chapter 7. The sources for this brief description are basically the same as those cited in that chapter. On the Bavarian side of the affair, there is some material in Walter McDougall's, "French Rhineland Policy and the Struggle for European Stabilization." But much work remains to be done in this area. Haguenin's correspondence with the Quai d'Orsay in 1919 (Ministry of Foreign Affairs archives, series "Europe 1918–11929," subseries "Allemagne," vols. 6 and 8) and with Millerand's *chef de cabinet* Albert Petit in 1920 (Millerand Papers, carton 59, folder "Allemagne," Bibliothèque Nationale) is very important in this connection. In this latter source, his letter of April 16, 1920, is worth quoting at length. Speaking of Bavaria, he writes: "Note importante: pour la politique secrète à faire là, éviter avec le plus grand soin l'entremise des militaires, et aussi l'intrusion . . . d'agents provocateurs ou de dilettantes indiscrets. La Bavière est fort excitée contre la Prusse. Eviter de découvrir le jeu de la France. Il est possible qu'une politique séparatiste, ou tout au moins *fédéraliste se dessine bientôt en Bavière*—à condition qu'on n'y voie pas notre main" [emphasis in original].

50. See Seydoux's article "La Question des réparations depuis la paix," *Revue d'economie politique* (1921), 35:673–712, esp. p. 709.

51. See, for example, A. Poisson, "Note sur la situation économique de l'Allemagne," July-October 1920 and "Note sur la situation financière de l'Allemagne," December 18, 1920, both in AJ⁵76. Cf. Léon Polier, "La Faillite allemande et les réparations," *L'Europe nouvelle* (December 26, 1920), pp. 1934–35. The British shared this point of view. See, for example, a July 6, 1920 note of Lord D'Abernon, who can hardly be accused of anti-German bias, in DBFP, 9:593. See also Cmd. 1114 of 1921.

52. Draft note by Leith Ross, British representative on the Managing Board of the Reparation Commission's Financial Service, AJ⁶1983, file 13/210, Z820, p. 3. The British Delegate on the Reparation Commission, Sir John Bradbury, also saw things in this way. He told Bergmann and Melchior, a German financial expert, "that the problem of tapping taxable wealth, if such wealth existed, was a purely mechanical problem which, given time was capable of solution" (Bradbury to Chamberlain, June 9, 1920, Lloyd George Papers, F/7/3/13).

53. For example, see Tardieu in *L'Illustration*, January 22, 1921, p. 60. See also the report of the Brussels experts on the German financial question, which comments on a frank admission by the German Minister of Finance on October 27, 1920, that the budgetary deficit was an excellent means of propaganda (*Documents relatifs aux reparations*, 1:79); and the Poisson note on Germany's financial situation, pp. 36ff., cited in n. 51.

54. See his "Note pour le Président du Conseil," July 12, 1920, AE, Millerand Papers, vol. 42, and, for example, his note of October 15, 1920, elaborating the scheme; Aron, in his November 5 study of reparation in kind, took this note as his point of departure and quotes from it extensively (see n. 3).

55. Göppert to Auswärtiges Amt, August 9, 1920, T-120/4509/K241891.

56. Page 8, col. 3. Weill-Raynal was then a junior member of the French Delegation to the Reparation Commission.

57. Pages 1829, 1831.

58. Issue of December 12, 1920, p. 1827.

59. *L'Europe nouvelle*, December 19, 1920, p. 1885; *L'Illustration*, December 25, 1920, p. 492 and January 15, 1921, p. 41; *Revue des Deux Mondes*, January 1, 1921, p. 221; and *Le Temps*, January 24, 1921.

60. Bergmann to Simons, December 17, 1920, T-120/4512/K243959; Mayer to Auswärtiges Amt, December 16, 1920, T-120/5585/K603475ff.

61. Raymond Poincaré, *A la recherche de la paix*, p. 35; Cheysson, "Conversation avec M. Poincaré, le 8 janvier 1921," AE, Millerand Papers, vol. 46.

62. The text of the instructions, dated December 11, 1920, is in AJ⁵321, folder 143. The Brussels Conference is the only important reparation conference held during this period whose minutes are not included in the published British documents. In accordance, however, with the procedural notes of November 11 and 12, the minutes were forwarded to the Reparation Commission, and can still be found in the Commission's archives: AJ⁶362, folder 14/160 (1).

63. See the "Instructions," cited in n. 62. On the attitude of certain elements within Germany, see Saint Quentin to Briand, March 6, 1921, which comments on a *Berliner Tageblatt* article of that date, in the Archives of the French Ministry of Foreign Affairs, Paris, Series "Z Europe 1918–1929," subseries "Allemagne," vol. 460—henceforth cited as "AE, Allemagne, 460—and especially the notes of Bresciani-Turroni, then an observer with the Reparation Commission in Berlin, in AJ⁶353, folder 14/15.

64. See the "Instructions," cited in n. 62.

65. Marsal to Millerand, September 11, 1920, AE, Millerand Papers, 15.

66. See, for example, State Secretary Hirsch's comments in a January 8, 1921, meeting with German industrialists, T-120/5160/K440167ff.

67. Seydoux to Leygues, December 17, 1920, AJ⁵320, folder "Conférences de Bruxelles et de Paris"; Germain Calmette, ed., *Recueil de documents sur l'histoire de la question des reparations*, p. 358.

68. Seydoux to Leygues, December 17, 1920, cited in n.67. Even the most conciliatory German officials accepted the idea that agreement on any workable reparation plan should be predicated on the retention of Upper Silesia, and this principle was formally laid down in the "Instructions" to the delegates to the Brussels Conference. But the arguments about reparation in the interministerial committee, for example, turned on other points—the idea that a conciliatory attitude on economic matters was the way to retain Upper Silesia was not stressed—and since the Brussels "Instructions" were not treated as a sacred text by the delegates in any case, there is some room for doubt as to how firmly the German government was committed to insisting on these preconditions. See T-120/1634/D735052 and *passim*, and Akten: Fehrenbach, pp. 330ff.

69. Seydoux to Leygues, December 21, 1920, in folder cited in n. 67.

70. See Soutou, "Seydoux-Projekt," p. 254.

71. See Soutou, 'Seydoux-Projekt," pp. 238, 252, 256.

72. T-120/4512/K243961; another copy: T-120/5585/K603488.

73. Simons to Bergmann, December 18, 1920, T-120/5585/K603490. On the desire to slow down the talks see Soutou, "Seydoux-Projekt," pp. 252–56; Martius to Auswärtiges Amt, December 21, 1920, T-120/3483/H24739ff.; Auswärtiges Amt to Bergmann, December 31, 1920, T-120/5160/K439996.

74. Cuntze memorandum, July 29, 1920, T-120/1634/D735139ff.

75. Reichswirtschaftsminister Scholz memorandum, September 2, 1920, T-120/1634/D735227ff.

76. Minutes of August 14 and September 21 meetings, T-120/1634/D735086, D735212ff.

77. Müller to Simons, October 21, 1920, T-120/3485/H248903.

78. T-120/1634/D735270ff.; Müller to Simons, Oct. 21, 1920, T-120/3485/H248903; Reconstruction Ministry Memo, October 14, 1920, T-120/3485/H248915–926.

79. Simons memo, September 30, 1920, T-120/3485/H248742-744; Akten: Fehrenbach, pp. 330–33; Bergmann to Simons, December 17, 1920, T-120/5585/K603488. According to Soutou, the issue was settled in favor of the Economics Ministry at a ministerial council on November 12, but the notes of a November 19 meeting of the KLK show that a final cabinet decision had still not been rendered ("Seydoux-Projekt," p. 250; T-120/5160/K439866).

80. Seydoux to Leygues, December 22, 1920, in folder cited in n. 67; "Compte-rendu sommaire des travaux de la Conference de Bruxelles," AJ⁵321, folder 143.

81. Laroche to Dubois, December 27, 1920, in the folder cited in n. 67.

82. Aron note cited in n. 3.

83. See the notes of the January 7 meeting attended by Seydoux, Cheysson, D'Abernon, Bradbury and Delacroix, in the folder cited in n. 67. In fact, it seems from this document that the British delegates actually supported Seydoux's proposals at this time, but the notes are somewhat ambiguous on this point. For the note handed Bergmann, see Calmette, *Recueil de documents*, pp. 372–76.

84. *Doc. rel. aux rép.*, 1:71–114.

85. For the text of the questionnaire and the German replies, see Cab 29/33/AJ230 or AJ⁶362.

86. *Doc. rel. aux rép.*, 1:77–91.

87. *Ibid.*, and see chapter 4 below.

88. "Note pour le Président du Conseil," January 19, 1921, AE, Allemagne, 457.

89. Joseph Addison to Sydney Waterlow, December 13, 1920, F.O. 371/4730/C14119, in the Public Record Office.

90. Viscount D'Abernon, *The Diary of an Ambassador*, 1:77–78, 124; D'Abernon to Curzon, December 9, 1920, DBFP, 10:561. Cf. Carl Schulkin, "Lost Opportunity: The Reparation Question and the Failure of the European Recovery Effort" pp. 305–6. Schulkin is mistaken in contending (p. 305) that D'Abernon received no instructions; they are in F.O. 371/4730/13331,

dated December 8, 1920, and were approved by the Cabinet on December 6 (Cab 23/23/66/1). But these instructions were very vague, and his main point holds: D'Abernon at Brussels acted on the orders not of the cabinet as a whole but of Lloyd George personally.

91. D'Abernon, *Diary of an Ambassador,* entry for December 13, 1920, p. 107.

92. Schulkin, "Lost Opportunity," pp. 308–11; Soutou, "Seydoux-Projekt,"p. 253; Bergmann memorandum on meetings of December 1921, T-120/1635/D735572ff.

93. D'Abernon, *Diary of an Ambassador,* entry for December 28, 1920, p. 113, and D'Abernon to Curzon, Dec. 29, 1920, FO 371/4730/C14940.

94. Seydoux note of December 29 and notes of January 7 meeting in the folder cited in n. 67.

95. See the notes of the January 7 meeting, AJ⁵320, folder "Conférences de Bruxelles et de Paris."

96. *Ibid.*

97. *Ibid.*

98. Bergmann "Vermerk," n.d., T-120/5585/K603511.

99. Simons to Bergmann, January 1, 1921, T-120/1635/D735589ff.

100. "Niederschrift über die Besprechung des Reichswirtschaftsministeriums mit Vertretern des Reichsverbandes der deutschen Industrie und der Grosseisenindustrie am 8 Januär 1921 in Essen über Fragen der Brüsseler Verhandlungen," T-120/5160/K440167ff.

101. Kilmarnock to Curzon, January 13 and 14, 1921, DBFP, 16:445; Laurent to Leygues, January 12 and 15, 1921, in the folder cited in n. 67.

102. Leygues to Laurent, and Seydoux to Haguenin, both January 8, 1921, AE, Relations Commerciales, 28. For the members of the group, see "Commission pour l'étude des questions Franco-allemandes," January 4, 1921, AE, Laurent Papers. See also Seydoux to Poincaré, February 1, 1922, AE, Millerand Papers, 20, for a description of this body.

103. T-120/1635/D735687ff.

104. Laurent to Leygues, January 15, 1921, AJ⁵320, folder "Conférences de Bruxelles et de Paris."

105. *Ibid.*

106. T-120/1328/500871ff.

107. D'Abernon to Curzon, January 19, 1921, DBFP, 16:447–48, and F.O. 371/5916/C1532; the unpublished version is more complete.

108. D'Abernon to Curzon, January 26, 1921, DBFP, 16:451; Seydoux "Note pour le Président du Conseil," January 19, 1921, AE, Allemagne, 457. There is some question regarding Bergmann's feelings on these figures: see Soutou, "Seydoux-Projekt," pp. 259–60. In this context, it is interesting to note that a few months later he proposed a scheme of annuities of this order of magnitude: see T-120/1642/D716407.

109. See AJ⁵320, folder "Conférences de Bruxelles et de Paris."

110. Bergmann to Auswärtiges Amt, January 21, 1921, T-120/5160/K440151.

111. T-120/5160/K440151ff.

112. Soutou, "Seydoux-Projekt," pp. 260, 268; Bücher to Simons, February 24, 1921, T-120/1642/D716332ff.

113. Memorandum of January 22, 1921, T-120/5561/Ser. K2125.

114. Calmette, *Recueil de documents,* pp. 376–77.

115. DBFP, 15:70–71 (meeting of January 27); Jones, *Diary,* 1:129; cf. also Briand's remark a month later, when the idea of a provisional settlement again came up: "He had proposed this at Paris, but Mr. Lloyd George had given him such a smack in the eye that he had to abandon it" (DBFP, 15:291). This was all clear at the time; see the *Times* (London) January 28, 1921, p. 10, col. a. Thus Keynes's thesis in *A Revision of the Treaty* (pp. 24–28) that the Paris scheme was a concession to the French designed to assure Briand's continuance in office is untenable.

116. For the text see Calmette, *Recueil de documents*, pp. 378–81; for a calculation of present value, based on rather optimistic projections of the development of the German export trade, see Etienne Weill-Raynal, *Les Reparations allemandes et la France*, 1:680–82.

117. DBFP, 15:117–18; *Le Temps*, February 2, 1921, p. 1; *Times* (London), January 31, 1921, p. 10, and February 3, 1921, p. 9.

118. *Times* (London), February 7, 1921, p.15c,d.

119. *Ibid.*, January 31, 1921, p. 10d.

120. AE, Allemagne, 458, Laurent to Briand, February 1, 1921.

121. DBFP, 16:458, D'Abernon to Curzon, February 4, 1921.

122. "Paiement des réparations. Question des sanctions," March 26, 1921, AE, Allemagne, 461. The idea that Great Britain deliberately blocked the consummation of a Franco-German industrial entente appears to have gained a certain currency, for it was repeated in a number of accounts written by men who had been connected with the Reparation Commission—Weill-Raynal in *Les Réparations*, (1:591), the Belgian Gaston Furst, in *De Versailles aux Experts*, p. 115, and the Italian A. Antonucci, in *Le Bilan des réparations et la crise mondiale* (Paris: Berger-Levrault, 1935), pp. 32–35. Some elements in the German press also interpreted the "abandonment of the Seydoux program" in this manner (Kilmarnock to Curzon, February 1, 1921, DBFP, 16:454). There is, however, little evidence that the British deliberately sabotaged the Brussels arrangement for the reasons suggested by Seydoux. British officials, it is true, often opposed schemes for reparation in kind on the ground that such arrangements favored the French (e.g., Llewellyn Smith notes on the Brussels Experts' report, Cab 29/33/AJ233, p. 305; Lord D'Abernon in Cab 23/23/80/4, December 30, 1920, p. 351); and there is some evidence that the British Board of Trade did not look with favor upon French economic revival (A. Geddes memorandum, February 12, 1920, Cab 24/98/CP 621). But there is little to indicate that the British saw any danger to themselves in the cultivation of Franco-German economic ties. I came across but one British official who even alluded to this "danger"— and in a most tentative way at that, indicating that such a view was far from common in official circles in Britain (Kilmarnock to Curzon, January 22, 1921, F.O. 371/5961/C2011; cf. his despatches of March 13 and March 19, 1921, DBFP, 16:475 and 508).

123. Roskill, *Hankey*, 2:209. On September 20, 1920, Kerr had written Lloyd George a letter very much in this vein, arguing that "Great Britain must deliberately draw in its horns in the matter of foreign policy" (Lloyd George Papers, F/90/1/18).

5. Impatience

1. *Times* (London), February 7, 1921, p. 15 (Lloyd George speech of February 5); Thomas Jones, *Whitehall Diary*, 1:130–31; Cab23/25/24/21, p. 140.

2. See, for example, leading articles in the *Economist* (December 11, 1920), 91:1025, and (January 29, 1921), 92:159–60; the chairmen of the big banks were arguing along similar lines at the time (*Economist* [January 29 and February 12, 1921], 92:179–80, 290). Labour made the same argument in February: the Parliamentary Committee of the Trades Union Congress and the Executive Committee of the Labour Party jointly declared that "our present crisis of unemployment is the direct outcome of a suicidal foreign policy"; the attempt to extract reparation was condemned in particularly forceful language (*Times* [London], February 18, 1921, p. 10).

3. *Economist*, 91:580, and 92:80.

4. Austen Chamberlain memorandum, February 25, 1920, Cab 24/99/CP 728; Basil Blackett memorandum, July 2, 1920, Cab 24/108/CP 1560.

5. CAB 24/108/CP 1560.

6. *Ibid.* Leading bankers argued along similar lines. Lord Inchcape, chairman of the Na-

tional Provincial Bank, for example, declared at the beginning of 1920: "I cannot help thinking that we should do better to stick to the 'high road' of economy and work, which, though arduous and unpleasant must eventually lead to strength and prosperity" (*Economist*, February 7, 1920, p. 271). A year later when some of his colleagues had turned against deflation, Inchcape hailed the "rough but salutary" process by which prices had been brought down as ushering in "a return to more normal conditions" (*Economist*, February 12, 1921, pp. 289–90).

7. See A. C. Pigou, *Aspects of British Economic History, 1918–1925* (London: Macmillan, 1947), p. 184. For the similar American experience, see Milton Friedman and Anna Jacobson Schwartz, *A Monetary History of the United States* (Princeton, N.J.: Princeton University Press, 1963), pp. 229–37.

8. In a memorandum of December 29, 1920, on the "Safeguarding of Industries Bill," Sir Robert Horne, President of the Board of Trade, referred to "the widespread uneasiness and disorganisation produced by the importation of cheap goods from collapsed exchange countries." To avoid this problem would raise a "storm of protest" from industry. For political reasons, the measure to be enacted (a heavy duty) would be directed only against Germany. This, he hoped, would "check the flood of German goods produced and marketed under the present collapsed exchange condition." (Cab 24/117/CP 2374). It was of course not the decline in the foreign exchange value of the mark as such, but rather the gap between the internal and external values of the mark, which gave German exports a competitive advantage in world trade.

9. *Times* (London), February 8, 1921, p. 12.

10. DBFP, 15:82, 77, 94; Briand to Jusserand, February 2, 1921, AE, Allemagne, 458.

11. The text is in Great Britain, *British and Foreign State Papers*, 1921, 114:26–29.

12. DBFP, 15:330; cf. Cab 23/25/29, p. 173.

13. Lord D'Abernon later wrote that "all the English experts, except perhaps some unknown person behind the scenes" had opposed the idea of an export tax at the time (D'Abernon, *Diary of an Ambassador*, 1:330); his own diary shows, however, that Sir Robert Horne, who had earlier opposed the scheme, now seemed to think the idea practicable (Cab 24/108/CP 1537; D'Abernon, 1:134). Lloyd George, incidentally, who prided himself on his neglect of "expert" opinion in all matters of state, was so impressed with Horne's relative indifference "to financial and economic theory" that he soon chose him to replace Chamberlain as Chancellor of the Exchequer (D'Abernon, 1:147, entry for March 22, 1921; Horne was appointed to this post a few days later; see D'Abernon, 1:137, for another example of Lloyd George's contempt for the "experts," and for Loucheur's initial reaction to the export tax scheme).

14. Pigou, *Aspects of British Economic History*, p. 142; R. K. Snyder, *The Tariff Problem in Great Britain, 1918–1923* (Stanford: Stanford University Press, 1944), p. 78.

15. *L'Illustration*, December 25, 1920, p. 492; *Revue des Deux Mondes*, February 1, 1921, p. 661. For an excellent discussion of the circumstances surrounding the fall of the Leygues government, see Sen. François Albert's "Chroniques politiques" in the January and February 1921 issues of the *Revue politique et parlementaire*.

16. The best theoretical analysis of the relation between political pressure and economic interest to my mind remains Elmer E. Schattschneider's *Politics, Pressures and the Tariff* (New York: Prentice-Hall, 1935), chap. 3, esp. pp. 122–23 and pp. 285–88.

17. This striking difference in government-industry relations between France and Germany has been noted by a number of the historians who have examined this period in detail. The most interesting attempt at explanation is in Maier, *Recasting Bourgeois Europe*, pp. 70–85, 409–10. See also Soutou, "Die deutschen Reparationen und das Seydoux-Projekt," p. 257. On the role of business in making German policy, see also Peter Krüger, *Deutschland und die Reparationen*, pp. 11–12, 74, and especially the Schmitt memorandum of November 25, 1919, describing the system of continuous contact between business and government in policy formulation, T-120/3679/H284982ff. The affair of a participation of French capital in Upper

Silesian industry provides the best case study of the role of business in foreign policy making at this time: deferring to the wishes of the government, French industry reluctantly entered into negotiations with the Silesian industrialists in late 1920. Pressure had to be applied continually, since the industrialists, "from the point of view of the development of their own businesses" had little interest in the affair. For example, Millerand, Seydoux and Loucheur, meeting in November 1921 with Robert Pinot (the leading figure at the Comité des Forges), insisted on the vital political importance of a successful negotiation; the industrialists, Pinot wrote, therefore "had to give in." (Pinot to Laurent, November 14, 1921, AE, Laurent Papers, folder "Haute-Silésie"). Documentation on this can be found in AE, Pologne, 212 and 216, and AE, Millerand Papers, 57; two articles by Georges Soutou provide an excellent analysis of the affair: "La politique économique de la France en Pologne (1920–1924)" *Revue historique* (1974), 251: esp. 94–116, and "Les mines de Silésie et la rivalité franco-allemande (1920–1923): arme économique on bonne affaire?" *Relations internationales* (May 1974), no. 1, pp. 135–54. Jeanneney's study of Wendel reinforces this view of the limited role of industry in foreign policy making during this period.

18. On Lloyd George's policy, see chapters 3 and 4 above.

19. See AE, Allemagne, 457, *passim,* especially Jacques Seydoux, "Note pour le Président du Conseil. I. Réparations. Décisions à prendre," January 21, 1921, and "Réunion du 23 Janvier chez le Président de la République," January 24, 1921.

20. *Ibid.*

21. See the Seydoux note cited in n.19.

22. "Réunion du 23 Janvier chez le Président de la République," January 24, 1921, AE, Allemagne, 457. The following officials attended this meeting: Millerand, Briand, Doumer, Loucheur, Dubois, Berthelot, Seydoux and Cheysson.

23. *Ibid.*

24. *Ibid.*

25. DBFP, 15:220.

26. D'Abernon to Curzon, February 17, 1921, DBFP, 16:466; Laurent to Leygues, February 23, 1921, AE Allemagne 459.

27. DBFP, 15:224–25.

28. *Ibid.,* pp. 225–27.

29. *Ibid.,* p. 223.

30. *Ibid.,* pp. 250–51. The Germans had resisted Allied demands to turn over Germans accused of war crimes, pursuant to the provisions of the treaty.

31. *Ibid.,* p. 118.

32. *Ibid.,* pp. 228–30, 236, 253.

33. *Ibid.,* p. 229.

34. *Ibid.,* pp. 232, 234.

35. *Ibid.,* p. 236.

36. *Ibid.,* pp. 234, 243–44.

37. *Ibid.,* p. 234.

38. *Ibid.*

39. *Ibid.,* pp. 243, 253, 257.

40. D'Abernon, *Diary of an Ambassador,* 1:134. See also DBFP, 15:253.

41. DBFP, 15:252, 257.

42. *Ibid.,* pp. 257, 265.

43. *Ibid.,* pp. 286–95.

44. *Times* (London), February 14, 1921 (p. 9), February 17, 1921 (p. 10), and February 18, 1921 (p. 10); Carl Schulkin, "Lost Opportunity," p. 364.

45. See, for example, Loucheur's remarks of March 6, 1921, DBFP, 15:299.

46. DBFP, 15:302.

47. *Ibid.*, p. 301.

48. *Ibid.*, pp. 305–31; D'Abernon, *Diary of an Ambassador*, 1:140–41.

49. Thus one of the leading German experts, Dr. Melchior, declared in a speech to the Hamburg Chamber of Commerce on July 20, 1920, that Germany's only tactic was to play for time (Seydoux to Celier, July 26, 1920, F^{30}1274, folder 1, subfolder "Accord de Spa"). Seydoux was keenly aware that at the same time that the German government was proclaiming its inability to make foreign payments, German industrialists like Stinnes were exporting considerable amounts of capital—and the German government refused to do anything about it (notes of Seydoux-Von le Suire conversation of March 2, 1921, AE, Allemagne, 460, p. 37ff.).

50. Etienne Weill-Raynal, *Les Réparations allemandes et la France*, 1:493–535, especially tables pp. 498, 522–23, 528.

51. See Laurent to Briand, April 9 and 14, AE, Allemagne, 461; Laurent to Berthelot, April 26, AE, Alemagne, 463.

52. See "Paiement des réparations. Question des sanctions," March 26, 1921, AE, Allemagne, 461.

53. Millerand to Briand, March 6, 1921, AE, Allemagne, 460.

54. Briand to major embassies, April 7, 1921, AE, Allemagne, 461.

55. AE, Allemagne, 461, p. 247ff.

56. Sénat, *Débats*, April 5, 1921, p. 582.

57. Chambre, *Débats*, April 12, 1921, p. 1574.

58. François André Paoli, *L'Arme française de 1919 à 1939*, 2:256bis.

59. See Laurent to Briand, April 12, 1921, AE, Allemagne, 461.

60. Laurent to Briand, April 11, 1921, AE, Allemagne, 461.

61. Briand to Laurent, April 13, 1921, AE, Allemagne, 461.

62. Briand to Laurent, April 15, 1921, AE, Allemagne, 462.

63. FRUS 1921, 2:41.

64. *Ibid.*, pp. 44–45.

65. *Ibid.*, pp. 46ff.

66. See Schulkin, "Lost Opportunity," pp. 413–14, esp. n. 33.

67. Laurent to Briand, April 28, 1921, AE, Allemagne, 463.

68. Briand to major embassies, April 7, 1921, AE, Allemagne, 461.

69. Briand to Saint-Aulaire, April 16, 1921, AE, Allemagne, 462.

70. DBFP, 15:470, 471–73.

71. *Ibid.*, p. 472.

72. This is based on the text of the plan (DBFP, 15:471–73) and on a Wigram memorandum on the plan (DBFP, 16:578–79)—Wigram was an official in the British Foreign Office. As written, the two features of the French plan—the coal tax and the scheme for control of foreign trade—might be taken as separate and unconnected. The first would raise "3 to 4 milliards of gold marks a year," and the German government was to reimburse exporters in paper marks for foreign bills turned over to the Control Office. Is one to assume then that the total annuity would be the sum of what the two "means of payment" would raise, i.e., 5 to 8 milliard gold marks annually? This is hardly credible, for clearly the French intended to have the sums raised by the coal tax transferred into foreign currencies, and no money could be exchanged other than through the Control Office. Thus, as written, the scheme to a certain degree does not make sense—the confusion in all probability resulting from the haste in which it was drawn up. To make sense out of it, the two aspects of the scheme must be seen as complementary, and it is in this sense therefore that it is interpreted here.

73. Cab 23/25/29, p. 172; Cab 24/122/CP 2855; Thomas Jones, *Whitehall Diary*, 1:155–56.

74. Cab 23/25/31, pp. 195–204.

75. DBFP, 15:470–71.
76. *Ibid.*, p. 475; Cab 23/25/32, p. 206.
77. DBFP, 15:481, see also pp. 482, 484.
78. *Ibid.*, p. 503.
79. *Ibid.*, pp. 289, 297.
80. *Ibid.*, p. 520; see also p. 526.
81. See *ibid.*, pp. 528, 560.
82. *Ibid.*, pp. 561–62.
83. *Ibid.*, pp. 554, 575.
84. The formal figure for the debt would be adjusted later to take account of various secondary factors: the Belgian war debt, for which Germany was liable, and various credits to Germany on reparation account, such as credit for German state property in some of the ceded territories.
85. This is the figure Weill-Raynal arrived at after an extremely detailed calculation based on purely arbitrary projected German export figures (*Les Réparations*, 1:681, 682–702). Other scholars are inclined to virtually dismiss the "C" bonds as a hoax designed to fool the public and set the present value of the Schedule of Payments at 50 milliards, the value of the "A" and "B" bonds (Sally Marks, "Reparations Reconsidered: A Reminder," *Central European History* (December 1969), 2:356–65) or at most at 64 milliards (Steven A Schuker, *The End of French Predominance in Europe*, pp. 14–15). But this argument is based on the false assumption that because all of the "C" bonds could not be issued in the near future none of them could. In fact, for some of the "C" bonds to be issued, the level of German exports only had to be 4 milliard gold marks a year. Even in 1922, the best sources put German exports much higher than that: 6.3 milliards at 1913 prices, and because the gold mark in 1922 was worth a lot less than the 1913 mark, the gold mark figure would be perhaps 50 percent higher or about 9 milliard gold marks (B. R. Mitchell, *European Historical Statistics*, p. 494). (There are much lower estimates based on notoriously unreliable German figures for the period—see Chapter VI, n. 24). The export figures for 1925 are even more relevant: 12½ milliard marks, equal to the same number of gold marks, because of the stabilization at prewar parity (Mitchell, p. 494). This corresponded under the Schedule to an annuity of over 5 milliards, equivalent to over 87 milliard gold marks worth of bonds—i.e., to 37 milliards worth of "C" bonds. There is one final point in this regard that should be mentioned. German exports were not autonomously determined; their size depended on the whole balance of payments and in particular on reparation payments actually effected. It follows that if Germany had complied with the Schedule of Payments, her exports would have expanded, thereby increasing the annuity in the next period; this would have led to a further increase in both exports and the level of payment, and the positive feedback process would continue year after year. Thus if it were taken seriously, the value of the Schedule of Payments might have been substantially higher than even Weill-Raynal thought; if it were not taken seriously, no calculation based on the formal terms of this document would have much meaning in any case.
86. D'Abernon, *Diary of an Ambassador*, 1:169, 171; DBFP, 15:585.
87. *Revue d'économie politique*, 1921, p. 415; *Revue des Deux Mondes*, May 15, 1921, p. 474.

6. A New Beginning?

1. Akten: Fehrenbach, pp. lxviii–lxx, 662, 666–72.
2. See Ernst Laubach, *Die Politik der Kabinette Wirth*, pp. 5, 7, 32, 36–37, 40. The Cabinet had directed as early as June 1919 that policy would be based on two points: "The Treaty should be carried out as far as this is physically possible, but our interests should be vigorously

defended''; "at the same time, the revision of the Treaty must be sought. Both go inseparably hand in hand" (T-120/3679/H284897). For a discussion of German reparation policy in this period, see also David Felix, *Walther Rathenau and the Weimar Republic: The Politics of Reparations*. Rathenau was Minister of Reconstruction in the first Wirth government and then Foreign Minister in the second Wirth government until his assassination in June 1922.

3. Akten: Wirth, pp. 630, 637.

4. Laubach, *Kabinette Wirth*, pp. 21. 55ff.; Felix, *Walther Rathenau*, p. 78; Louis Loucheur, *Carnets secrets*, pp. 87–89.

5. See Laubach, pp. 61–66; Felix, pp. 91–94; Akten: Wirth, pp. 3–4, 7–13, 118; "Aufzeichnung des Staatssekretärs Dr. Hirsch," T-120/1643/D716913ff.; "Die Belastung der Sachwerte als Teil des Reparationsprogramms," June 27, 1921, T-120/1643/D716979ff., published in Julius Hirsch, *Die deutsche Währungsfrage* (Jena: Kommissionsverlag von G. Fischer, 1924), p. 58ff.

6. See Hirsch's remarks in a cabinet discussion of August 1, 1921, Akten: Wirth, pp. 174ff., and the Economics Ministry memorandum "Die Belastung der Sachwerte als Teil des Reparationsprogramms," T-120/1643/D716996.

7. Laubach, *Kabinette Wirth*, pp. 145ff.; Felix, *Walter Rathenau*, p. 94.

8. Gaston Furst, *De Versailles aux Experts*, p. 137.

9. D'Abernon to Curzon, DBFP, 16:787; Felix, Walther Rathenau, pp. 94–98; Weill-Raynal, *Les Réparations*, 2:80–82; Wirth to Dubois, Dec. 14, 1921, *Doc. Rel. aux rep.*, 1:206; minutes of the British Cabinet Finance Committee, Dec. 6, 1921, Cab 27/71/37.

10. Loucheur, *Carnets secrets*, pp. 84–92; Walther Rathenau, *Tagebuch 1907–1922* (Dusseldorf, 1967), pp. 243–56; Laurent to Briand, June 4, 1921, and "Réparations en Nature, Négociations de Paris, 28 juin-1 juillet," July 7, 1921, AE, Alemagne, 465; Weill-Raynal, *Les Reparations*, 2:29.

11. Loucheur, *Carnets secrets*, p. 90; *Doc. rel. aux rep.*, 1:253–61 for the text of the accord.

12. DBFP, 16:707–723; Cmd. 1547 of 1921.

13. DBFP, 16:713–115, Bradbury to Blackett, July 13, 1921.

14. *Ibid.*, pp. 804–5, Curzon to Harding, Nov. 10, 1921.

15. See for example Weill-Raynal, 2:13–23; *Doc. rel. aux rep.*, 1:187–93.

16. Laubach, *Kabinette Wirth*, pp. 75–76.

17. Akten: Wirth, pp. 303–9; Laubach, pp. 77–78, 115, 119; Felix, *Walther Rathenau*, p. 78; D'Abernon to Curzon, Oct. 11, 1921, DBFP, 16:784–85. On French attempts to put the Wiesbaden agreement into effect, see, for example, Poincaré to Laurent, July 12, 1922, AE, Allemagne, 473, Poincaré to Margerie, Sept. 7, 1922, AE, Allemagne, 474, and Poincaré to Margerie, Dec. 21, 1922, AE, Allemagne, 477.

18. See for example, Seydoux, "Réparations en nature," June 9, 1921, AE, Allemagne, 465.

19. Most particularly in his important Saint-Nazaire speech of October 9: see Georges Suarez, *Briand: sa vie, son oeuvre*, 5:210–13. See also Chambre, *Débats*, October 21, 1921, pp. 3631–32.

20. See in general Suarez, *Briand*, 5:199–287, and Sen. François Albert's "Chroniques politiques" for the period in the *Revue politique et parlementaire*, vols. 108–110 (July 1921–Feb. 1922). For Curzon's speech and the French reaction, see the *Times* (London), Nov. 25 and 26, 1921. On Anglo-French relations in this period see in general AE, Grande-Bretagne, 47.

21. Louis Loucheur, "La Faillite de l'Allemagne," Sept. 10, 1921, and Jacques Seydoux, "Question des réparations, situation générale," Oct. 29, 1921 AE, Millerand Papers, 18; Seydoux note of Nov. 5, 1921, AE, Millerand Papers, 19. See also Laurent's despatches to Briand, Oct. 3 and 4, 1921, AE, Allemagne, 467, for a similar condemnation of Wirth's "passivity." The politics of the German inflation, one of the most fascinating topics in the history of

the interwar period, has not been adequately explored in the scholarly literature, nor can it be analyzed here. Constantino Bresciani-Turroni's *The Economics of Inflation: A Study of Currency Depreciation in Post-War Germany* is primarily a statistical analysis, woefully inadequate on the political side of the question, especially given all the material that is currently available There are, however, certain indications that the French analysis outlined in the text was not far off the mark: a Schubert memorandum of January 22, for example, assumed that if it were not for reparation, the German government would have found the energy to solve its financial problems (see chapter 3, n. 40). See also Bresciani, pp. 46, 105, for evidence on the proinflation position of the industrialists Stinnes and Klöckner.

22. Loucheur, "La Faillite de l'Allemagne," Sept. 10, 1921, and Seydoux, "Question des réparations, situation générale," Oct. 29, 1921, AE, Millerand Papers, 18; Seydoux note, Nov. 5, 1921, and Loucheur note, Nov. 9, 1921, AE, Millerand Papers, 19.

23. See Bresciani, *Economics of Inflation,* pp. 43–46. In private, Reichsbank officials at the time knew better: see Carl-Ludwig Holtfrerich's unpublished article, "Reichsbankpolitik 1918–1923 zwischen Zahlungsbilanz- und Inflationstheorie."

24. Germany had a double interest in falsifying these statistics: the variable part of the annuity was a function of the value of her exports; and portraying a large trade deficit was useful for propaganda purposes. On the basis of a comparative study of German and foreign statistics, French officials occasionally complained about the German figures: see, for example, Laurent to Briand, Dec. 2, 1921, AE, Allemagne, 469. See also Bresciani, *Economics of Inflation,* pp. 242–44.

25. In fact the enormous purchases of paper marks by foreign speculators were payments of this sort. With the collapse of the currency these mark holdings became relatively worthless, and these foreign purchases amounted to a unilateral transfer—in effect a gift—to Germany of 15 milliard gold marks, a figure which (even after deducting what Germany paid out under the treaty in this period) exceeds in real terms what West Germany received in Marshall Plan aid after World War II! See Carl-Ludwig Holtfrerich, "Internationale Verteilungsfolgen der deutschen Inflation, 1918–1923," to be published in Gerald Feldman, ed., *Historische Prozesse der deutschen inflation 1914–1923,* and also Holtfrerich's, "Amerikanische Kapitalexport und Wiederaufbau der deutschen Wirtschaft 1919–23 im Vergleich zu 1924–29," *Vierteljahrschrift für Sozial- und Wirtschaftsgeschichte,* 64:2 (1977), 497–529.

26. For a fuller argument on this point, see Bresciani, *Economics of Inflation,* pp. 83–84, 90–92.

27. A licensing system could be used to secure the valorization of marks used in foreign trade; since marks unaccompanied by licenses could not be used by foreigners to purchase German goods, they would become valueless abroad, and the illegal export of capital could thereby be suppressed.

28. Millerand to Vignon, Nov. 5, 1921, AE, Millerand Papers, 19, and "Réunion chez le Président de la République," Oct. 27, 1921, AE, Allemagne, 467. For his views at the time of the London Conference, see Millerand to Briand, May 1, 1921, AE, Millerand Papers, 48. For Loucheur's and Seydoux's advocacy of a system of controls, see the sources cited in n. 21 above.

29. Seydoux note, Nov. 29, 1921, AE, Millerand Papers, 19.

30. See, for example, Donald Blaisdell, *European Financial Control in the Ottoman Empire* (New York: Columbia University Press, 1929) and John A. Levandis, *The Greek Foreign Debt and the Great Powers, 1821–1898* (New York: Columbia University Press, 1944).

31. Minutes of the London Conference of April and May 1921, DBFP, 15:chap 4, *passim,* esp. 528, 530, 559–60, and minutes of experts' meetings at the conference in AE, Relations Commerciales, 71.

32. Worthington Evans, War Secretary, in a meeting of reparation experts, May 1, 1921, 10 PM, in AE, Relations Commerciales, 71.

33. *Doc. rel. aux rep.,* 1:156, 161–62.

34. "Plan général du paiement des réparations," April 19, 1921, p. 20, AE, Allemagne, 462; Seydoux note, May 13, 1921, in AE, Allemagne, 512, published as an unsigned article in *L'Europe nouvelle,* May 14, 1921, pp. 621ff. and reprinted in Jacques Seydoux, *De Versailles au Plan Young* pp. 49–57.

35. DBFP, 15:535.

36. See chapter 3, n. 126.

37. On its work, see AJ⁵266, document "CGFa 657bis," "Note resumée sur les travaux du Comité des Garanties depuis sa création en mai 1921 jusqu'à la fin de l'année 1922," AJ⁵413, folder "Echéances des 15 janvier et 15 février 1922," and AJ⁶452, 454, 581ff. The most important documents are published in Reparation Commission, *Official Documents relative to the Amount of Payments to be Effected by Germany under Reparation Account,* vol. 2 (London: H.M. Stationery Office, 1922): see in particular Committee of Guarantees to Wirth, June 28, 1921, p. 15. Note also the absence of pressure in the committee's discussion of the budget question with German officials on Sept. 26 and 27, 1921, in AJ⁶583, Annexes CG 78, 78bis and 79.

38. Committee of Guarantees minutes, Sept. 14, 1921, AJ⁶454.

39. *L'Europe nouvelle,* June 11, 1921, reprinted in Seydoux, *De Versailles au Plan Young,* pp. 57ff.

40. Loucheur, "La Faillite de l'Allemagne," Sept. 10, 1921, AE, Millerand Papers, 18.

41. *Ibid.*

42. Seydoux note, "La politique de la France à l'égard de l'Allemagne et de l'Angleterre," Aug. 1, 1931, AE, Allemagne, 466.

43. December 5 note, AE, Millerand Papers, 19; December 17 note, AE, Allemagne, 470.

44. Blackett to Crowe, Nov. 22, 1921, DBFP, 16:817. See also Wigram memorandum, November 25, 1921, DBFP, 16:824, and the discussions in the Cabinet Finance Committee of December 1 and December 6, 1921, Cab 27/71/36 and 37.

45. Crowe to Blackett, Nov. 30, 1921; Waterlow memo, Nov. 30, 1921, and Fass reports of Dec. 2, 3, 7, 8 and 9, DBFP, 16:825–44. See also the Chancellor of the Exchequer's remarks in the Dec. 1, 1921, meeting of the Cabinet Finance Committee, Cab 27/71/36, and his memorandum of Nov. 28, Cab 24/131/CP3512.

46. "Réunion du 7 décembre chez le Président du Conseil," AE, Allemagne, 469; Fass report, Dec. 2, 1921, DBFP, 16:829.

47. Fass reports of Dec. 2, 3, 7, 8 and 9, DBFP, 16:829–46; Curzon to Hardinge, Dec. 5, 1921, DBFP, 16:838.

48. See Bradbury to Horne, Nov. 7, 1921, Cab 24/131/CP3554. More generally, see Bresciani, *Economics of Inflation,* pp. 46–47; for particular examples, see the report of Leith Ross, British representative on the Committee of Guarantees, of July 2, 1921, in FO 408/5, and studies by H.C.F. Finlayson, British representative on the Reparation Commission's Berlin secretariat, of Dec. 12, 1921 and Jan. 31, 1922, AJ ⁶ 585, Annexes CG163 and 196b.

49. See especially D'Abernon's memorandum on "The Supposed Effect of Reparation on Trade and Exchange," Dec. 24, 1921, DBFP, 16:855–57, and his dispatches to Curzon of Oct. 25, 1921, Cab 24/131/CP2528, of Dec. 26, 1921, FO 408/6, and of March 29 and 31, 1922, FO 408/7. The quotation is from his "Memorandum respecting the German Financial Position," Nov. 15, 1921, DBFP, 16:808–9.

50. Horne memorandum, Nov. 28, 1921, Cab 24/131/CP3512, and his remarks in the Dec. 1, 1921, meeting of the Cabinet Finance Committee, Cab 27/71/36.

51. Horne memo of Nov. 28, 1921, Cab 24/131/CP3512.

52. DBFP, 16:817–19, Bradbury to Blackett, Nov. 21, 1921.

53. See, for example, Briand's comments in a meeting with Lloyd George on Dec. 22, 1921, DBFP, 15:795.

54. Horne's remarks, Cab 27/71/36, Dec. 1, 1921.

55. See Briand's declarations in the *Petit Parisien,* May 6, 1921; Cheetham to Curzon, May 18, 1921, FO 371/6029/C10197; Hardinge to Curzon, May 26, 1921, FO 371/6029/C10197; Hardinge to Curzon, May 26, 1921, FO 371/6030/C10905.

56. Wigram memorandum, Nov. 3, 1921, DBFP, 16:799. The text of the Committee of Guarantees report of October 29, 1921 was published in Reparation Commission, *Official Documents,* 2:25ff.

57. Leith Ross report, July 2, 1921, FO 408/5/C13788; Blackett to Crowe, Nov. 22, 1921, DBPF, 16:817.

58. Loucheur to Briand, Dec. 8, 1921, AE, Allemagne, 469; DBFP, 15:767.

59. "Conversation 'Aux Chequers' Entre Mr. Lloyd George, Sir Robert Horne et Mr. Loucheur," Dec. 8, 1921, Loucheur, *Carnets secrets,* pp. 185–88; notes of meetings of Dec. 19–22, 1921, DBFP, 15:767, 770–72, 794–96.

60. DBFP, 15:800–5.

61. *Ibid.,* 15:790, 792, 794; 19:3 and 15n.

62. "Réunion du 6 janvier," AE, Relations commerciales, 81; DBFP, 19:38–39.

63. DBFP, 19:62–63.

64. *Ibid.,* 15:801, 786.

65. *Ibid.,* p. 786.

66. Saint-Aulaire to Briand, Dec. 14, 1921, Ministère des Affaires Etrangères, *Documents relatifs aux négociations concernant les garanties de securité contre une aggression de l'Allemagne* (Paris, 1924), pp. 90–93; DBFP, 15:785, 787; DBFP, 19:3–5.

67. Loucheur, *Carnets secrets,* pp. 185–88; DBFP, 15:760–61, 764–65, 773.

68. Loucheur, *Carnets secrets,* pp. 186–87; DBFP, 15:761–63.

69. See DBFP, 15:780, and also Ullman, *The Anglo-Soviet Accord,* p. 449; Jones, *Diary,* 1:196.

70. DBFP, 15:799; 19:32, 36.

71. *Ibid.,* 15:773; 19:12, 36.

72. *Ibid.,* 19:91, 161.

73. Lloyd George memorandum, Jan. 4, 1922, Cmd. 2169 of 1924, p. 119; DBFP, 19:36.

74. *Ibid.,* 19:24; 15:786–87.

75. DBFP, 19:57–58; French memorandum of Jan. 8, 1922, Cmd. 2169 of 1924, p. 123; see also DBFP, 19:13.

76. DBFP, 19:2–7; British memorandum, Jan. 4, 1922, Cmd. 2169 of 1924, pp. 118–22.

77. See for example Curzon's allusion to "the eastern frontier of France, which is also the external frontier of Britain," memorandum of Dec. 28, 1921, DBFP, 16:863; and in general Arnold Wolfers, *Britain and France between Two Wars* (New York: Norton, 1966), chap. 14.

78. DBFP, 17:*passim,* esp. Nos. 76 and 432; C. J. Lowe and M. L. Dockrill, *The Mirage of Power* (London: Routledge and Kegan Paul, 1972), 2:364–74.

79. See Curzon to Hardinge, June 13, 1921, DBFP, 17:240–41; and Lowe and Dockrill, 2:367.

80. Jones, *Diary,* 1:196.

81. See for example the second and third paragraphs of the memorandum of Jan. 4, 1922, Cmd. 2169 of 1924, p. 114. On Lloyd George's shifting political fortunes, Lord Beaverbrook's *The Decline and Fall of Lloyd George* (London: Collins, 1963) is still to my mind the best and most exciting account. See also Michael Kinnear, *The Fall of Lloyd George: The Political Crisis of 1922* (Toronto: University of Toronto Press, 1973).

82. Millerand to Briand, Jan. 7, 8 and 19, 1922, and Briand to Millerand, Jan. 8 and 9, 1922, in Suarez, *Briand,* 5:365–68, 371–73, 382–83, 388–90.

83. *Ibid.,* Millerand to Briand, Jan. 11, 1922, pp. 396–97. The "piece of paper" remark

is a characteristic allusion to Bethmann Hollweg's famous comment about the treaty guaranteeing Belgian neutrality.

84. Suarez, *Briand*, 5:392; Sen. François Albert, "Chronique politique," *Revue Politique et Parlementaire* (Feb. 10, 1920), 110:277–87.

7. Poincaré in Power

1. Poincaré to Laurent, Jan. 19, 1922, and Laurent to Poincaré, Jan. 21, 1922, AE, Allemagne, 385.

2. Poincaré to Saint-Aulaire, Jan. 23, 1922, AE, Millerand Papers, 58. See also Jay Kaplan, "France's Road to Genoa: Strategic, Economic and Ideological Factors in French Foreign Policy, 1921–1922," (Ph.D. diss., Columbia University, 1974), pp. 134–50.

3. On Feb. 2, 1922, for example, he instructed Dubois, the French delegate on the Reparation Commission, to "study the possibility of a large-scale operation based on external loans, which would provide a positive and practical solution to the reparation problem" (AE, Millerand Papers, 20). A loan scheme was also a key feature of the French reparation plan of January 2, 1923: France, Ministère des Affaires Etrangères, *Documents Diplomatiques, Demande de moratorium du gouvernement allemand à la Commission des Réparations (14 novembre 1922). Conférence de Londres (9–11 décembre 1922). Conférence de Paris (2–4 janvier 1923)* (Paris, 1923)—henceforth cited *"Demande de moratorium"*—p. 90ff. In the archival sources there are continued references to the loan scheme throughout 1922. The Minister of Finance, Charles de Lasteyrie, was a particularly ardent advocate of such a solution, in his opinion "the only practical solution of the reparation problem" (Lasteyrie to Seydoux, March 23, 1922, AE, Relations Commerciales, 82).

4. Poincaré to Dubois, Feb. 2, 1922, AE, Millerand Papers, 82. On the linkage between control and "mobilization," see Poincaré to Dubois, Jan. 19, 1922, AE, Allemagne, 473, and Lasteyrie's remarks in the "Réunion tenue chez M. le Président du Conseil, le 13 octobre 1922" (AE, Millerand Papers, 23): "He is still convinced that one can only get out of the present situation by means of a loan; for this loan to succeed, however, it is first necessary that Germany's finances be restored and controlled."

5. Minutes of meeting with British leaders, June 19, 1922, AE, Millerand Papers, 50.

6. See his "Note au sujet des accords de Wiesbaden," Feb. 6, 1922, $F^{30}1360$, in which he argued that whatever the objections of French industry, substantial payment in kind was essential, and also Chambre, *Débats*, Feb. 7, 1922, p. 306.

7. Seydoux to Poincaré, Feb. 1, 1922, and "Réunion au Ministère des Finances," Feb. 6, 1922, AE, Millerand Papers, 20.

8. *Doc. rel. aux rep.*, 1:281–312. This shift incidentally is one measure of the resurgence of Seydoux, who in 1921 had been somewhat overshadowed by Loucheur. Another indication is the leading role played in 1922 by the Inspecteur Général des Mines Coste, a friend of Seydoux's since childhood, in the elaboration of plans for the occupation of the Ruhr. Coste, who had headed the Allied commission set up in 1920 to supervise the distribution of German coal, had not been allowed by Loucheur to participate in the meetings that had considered a Ruhr occupation in 1921. See Seydoux, "Note pour M. de Peretti," May 20, 1922, AE, Relations Commerciales, 69.

9. *Le Temps*, June 28, 1922.

10. For example, Poincaré to Saint-Quentin, Sept. 2, 1922, and Poincaré to Laurent, Oct. 24, 1922, AE, Allemagne, 475–76.

11. Poincaré to Laurent, July 12, 1922, AE, Allemagne, 473; Poincaré to Laurent, Sept. 7, 1922, and Poincaré to Saint-Quentin, Sept. 24, 1922, AE, Allemagne, 475; Poincaré to Laurent, Oct. 24, 1922, Laurent to Poincaré, Oct. 28, 1922, AE, Allemagne, 476; Poincaré to

Margerie, Dec. 14 and Dec. 21, 1922, and Margerie to Poincaré, Dec. 22, 1922, AE, Allemagne, 477. See also *Demande de moratorium,* pp. 84–85.

12. See chapter 5, n.17.

13. See Jacques Bariéty, "Le rôle de la minette," pp. 273–74.

14. Le Trocquer to Poincaré, July 26, 1922, AE, Millerand Papers, 22.

15. Seydoux note, Aug. 17, 1922, AE, Millerand Papers, 22.

16. Hermann-Josef Rupieper, "Politics and Economics: The Cuno Government and Reparations, 1922–1923," pp. 124–27, 139–43.

17. See, for example, Poincaré to Millerand, Aug. 13, 1922, AE, Millerand Papers, 51, and his remarks in the Senate on June 29, 1922, quoted in *Le Temps,* July 1, 1922. Lasteyrie had long been a strong critic of the idea that a Ruhr occupation could be profitable; see his talk to the Comité Nationale d'Etudes Sociales et Politiques of Dec. 12, 1921 on "Les Accords de Wiesbaden" (copy at the Bibliothèque de Documentation Internationale Contemporaine, Nanterre) and his letter to Poincaré of Aug. 22, 1922, AE, Relations Commerciales, 69.

18. Minutes of meeting of Feb. 5, 1922, AE, Millerand Papers, 20.

19. Chambre, *Documents* (Session Extraordinaire de 1921), Annex 3537, pp. 432ff.; Chambre, *Débats,* Feb. 16, 1922, p. 418.

20. DBFP, 19:135.

21. For the text of the German project, see Reparation Commission, *Official Documents,* 3:97–202; for Poincaré's reaction, see his dispatch to principal French ambassadors, Jan. 31, 1922, AE, Allemagne, 471.

22. Poincaré to Dubois, Feb. 2, 1922, AE, Relations Commerciales, 82. Emphasis in original.

23. See his remarks in the "Réunion chez le Ministre des Finances," Feb. 5, 1922, AE, Millerand Papers, 20.

24. Notes of Feb. 25 meeting, AE, Millerand Papers, 20.

25. "Réunion tenue dans le cabinet de M. le Président du Conseil," March 4, 1922, AE, Millerand Papers, 20.

26. AE, Millerand Papers, 20.

27. *Ibid.* The text, dated March 15, was published in Reparation Commission, *Official Documents,* vol. 6.

28. *Doc. rel. aux rep.,* 1:208–15.

29. Bradbury to Blackett, March 22, 1922, Cab 24/136/CP 3915. British opposition to foreign exchange controls was deep-seated; see their official comments on this question in DBFP, 19:212.

30. Bradbury to Treasury, March 24, 1922, FO 408/7/C4819.

31. *Doc. rel. aux rep.,* 1:216–18; Akten: Wirth, pp. 630, 635, 659.

32. AE, Relations Commerciales, 69.

33. *Le Temps,* April 25, 1922.

34. See especially Renata Bournazel, *Rapallo: Naissance d'un mythe,* chap. 5.

35. DBFP, 19:77–78, 100–1, 159–70, 174.

36. See Bournazel, *Rapallo,* pp. 22, 28, and DBFP, 19:77–78, 100–1, 159, 170, 174.

37. See, for example, Bournazel, p. 175.

38. *Ibid.,* p. 199.

39. Cab 23/36/29.

40. Carl Bergmann, *The History of Reparations,* p. 123.

41. On the Hermes-Rathenau split, see Akten: Wirth, pp. 661–62, 671–74, 710; Addison to Balfour, May 27, 1922, FO 408/7/C7888; and David Felix, *Walther Rathenau and the Weimar Republic,* pp. 151–53. On the negotiations in Paris, see Akten: Wirth, p. 797 n.5, pp. 808ff. For the text of the final agreement, see Wirth to Reparation Commission, May 28, 1922, and Reparation Commission to Wirth, May 31, 1922, *Doc. rel. aux rep.,* 1:223–35.

42. Akten: Wirth, pp. 808–9, 817–18.

43. Cabinet meeting of May 23, 1922, Cab 23/30/29.

44. FO 371/7481/C11157.

45. Akten: Wirth, pp. 806–7.

46. FO 408/7/C7546.

47. Poincaré to Dubois, May 26, May 28, and May 31, 1922, AJ⁵387, "Dossier A."

48. Poincaré to Dubois, May 28, 1922, AJ⁵387, "Dossier A."

49. *Doc. rel. aux rep.*, 1:223–35.

50. See especially Poincaré's correspondence with Dubois, AJ⁵387, "Dossier A."

51. See discussion to follow in chapter 7.

52. See n. 50 above.

53. Loan committee report of June 10, 1922, *Doc. rel. aux rep.*, 243–50.

54. Poincaré to Margerie, June 11, 1922, and Margerie to Poincaré, June 12, 1922, AE, Allemagne, 473.

55. Seydoux memorandum, June 23, 1922, AE, Millerand Papers, 21. That a certain community of interest existed between Germany and British banks is clear. Horne on several occasions stressed that the London banks, which had been doing a big business financing German imports, would lose a lot of money in the event of a default. See for example his remarks in the Cabinet Finance Committee, Dec. 1 and Dec. 6, 1921, Cab 24/131/CP 3551.

56. The French minutes of this meeting are in AE, Millerand Papers, 50; an extract from the British notes is in FO 371/7479/C89981G.

57. *Ibid.*

58. Blackett to Crowe, Nov. 22, 1921, DBFP, 16:817.

59. "Note of Interviews between Sir B. Blackett and Dr. von Simson . . .," July 3, 1922, FO 408/8/C9523. Also in FO 371/7479.

60. *Doc. rel. aux rep.*, 2:111.

61. "Note sur la demande de moratorium de l'Allemagne," July 15, 1922, AE, Millerand Papers, 22.

62. Poincaré to Saint-Aulaire, July 28, 1922, AE, Millerand Papers, 50.

63. Cmd. 2258 of 1924, p. 10.

64. *Ibid.*, compare pp. 10–11 with pp. 85–90.

65. For the text, see *Le Temps*, Aug. 22, 1922.

66. Jaunez to Poincaré, Sept. 16, 1922, AE, Allemagne, 475.

67. Minutes of Franco-Belgian talks, Nov. 23, 1922, AE, Relations Commerciales, 138.

68. For example, Réunion tenue chez M. le Président du Conseil, le 13 octobre 1922," AE, Millerand Papers, 23.

69. In the discussions at London, Poincaré characterized him as even more important than the Minister of Finance: Cmd. 2258 of 1924, p. 27.

70. Note of Aug. 17, 1922, AE, Millerand Papers, 22.

71. AE, Millerand Papers, 22.

72. AE, Allemagne, 473.

73. Millerand to Poincaré, Aug. 10, 1922, AE, Millerand Papers, 51; Poincaré to Dubois, Aug. 3, 1922, AE, Allemagne, 474.

74. Cmd. 2258 of 1924, esp. pp. 10, 77.

75. *Ibid.*, pp. 10–11, 31–35.

76. *Ibid.*, p. 22.

77. See especially his remarks on "Les Accords de Wiesbaden" cited in n.17 above, and Lasteyrie to Poincaré, Aug. 24, 1922, AE, Relations Commerciales, 69.

78. Cmd. 2258 of 1924, p. 32.

79. *Ibid.*, pp. 11, 31.

80. *Ibid.*, pp. 62, 64.

81. *Ibid.*, p. 88.

82. Cab 27/71/40.

83. Cab 23/30/44, Aug. 10, 1922.

84. *Ibid.*, pp. 84–88.

85. *Ibid.*, p. 26.

86. *Ibid., passim,* esp. pp. 65, 77.

87. Poincaré in fact was aware of this, at least at the end of the year: "Réunion chez le Président du Conseil, le 17 décembre 1922," AE, Millerand Papers, 24.

88. Cmd. 2258 of 1924, pp. 9, 10, 53, 54, 60, 71.

89. For the text of the agreement, see *Le Temps,* July 23, 1922, p. 6.

90. "Note sur la demande de moratorium de l'Allemagne," AE, Millerand Papers, 22.

91. See, for example, Aron note "Au sujet de la demande de moratorium de l'Allemagne du 12 juillet 1922," July 28, 1922, AJ^{5}387, "Dossier A."

92. See *The Times* (London), July 14, 1922, p. 6. The problem was compounded by the fact that the French translation of his remarks was stronger than the English original: see *Le Temps,* July 15, 1922. French officials frequently objected to Lloyd George's actions: see for example the "Note de M. de Lasteyrie," Aug. 13, 1922, AE, Relations Commerciales, 136, and Poincaré's Bar-le-Duc speech of Aug. 21, 1922, *Le Temps,* Aug. 22, 1922, p. 2.

93. Cab 23/40/42, July 25, 1922. He reiterated the point in the cabinet on August 12: "If we made it clear to the United States that the action of America was responsible for the chaos in Europe, it would be a negotiating pawn when our representative went to Washington" (Cab 23/30/45).

94. Cab 23/30/42, July 25, 1922.

95. *Ibid.*

96. Bar-le-Duc speech, *Le Temps,* Aug. 22, 1922, p. 2.

97. Cmd. 2258 of 1924, p. 6; Bar-le-Duc speech, *Le Temps,* Aug. 22, 1922, p. 2. See also "Note de M. de Lasteyrie," Aug. 13, 1922, AE, Relations Commerciales, 136, and Lasteyrie's speech of August 20 blaming the Balfour Note for having "paralyzed" the conference, reported in *Le Matin,* Aug. 21, 1922. The text of the French plan dated July 25, 1922 was published in *Le Temps* on Aug. 27, 1922; a translation appeared in the *Manchester Guardian Commercial Supplement,* Sept. 28, 1922, p. 464.

98. Cab 23/30/46.

99. Cab 23/30/45.

100. Cab 23/30/44.

101. Poincaré to Millerand, Aug. 13, 1922, AE, Millerand Papers, 51.

102. See *Le Temps,* July 1, 1922, and Sen. François-Albert's "Chronique politique" in the *Revue politique et parlementaire,* July 1922, esp. pp. 129–30.

103. See especially Poincaré, *A la recherche de la paix,* pp. 246, 261, 287, 310–11, 316, 319, 321, 375, 378.

104. Tardieu to Poincaré, May 16, 1920, 324 AP 118, National Archives, Paris. The whole correspondence in this folder extended from May 9 to May 20, 1920.

105. Sen. François-Albert, "Chronique politique," *Revue politique et parlementaire,* Feb. 1922, p. 283.

106. This is based on François-Albert's "Chroniques politiques" for 1922 in the *Revue politique et parlementaire.*

107. FO 371/7481/C11430. See also another Foreign Office memorandum of Aug. 8, 1922, FO 371/7482/C11669.

108. See Jacques Bariéty, "Les réparations allemandes, 1919–1924: objet ou prétexte à une politique rhénane de la France," *Bulletin de la Société d'histoire moderne* (1973), 15th series, no. 6, pp. 21–23, and chap. 2 of his thesis, "De l' exécution à la négociation," which has now been published as a book: *Les Relations franco-allemandes après la première guerre*

mondiale. See also the excellent study by Walter McDougall, "French Rhineland Policy and the Struggle for European Stabilization," and the book based on this dissertation: *France's Rhineland Diplomacy, 1914–1924.* See also Robert McCrum, "French Rhineland Policy at the Paris Peace Conference, 1919," *Historical Journal* (1978), 21(3):623–48, and the important new study by Georges Soutou, "La France et les Marches de l'Est, 1914–1919," *Revue historique* (1978), 260:2, 341–388. For the British role, see Robert E. Hood, "Sanction Diplomacy: Britain and French Rhine Policy, 1920–24," Ph.D. diss., Georgetown University, 1976. See also the collection of papers presented at a 1974 Franco-German colloquium on the subject: University of Metz, Centre de Recherches, Relations Internationales, *Problèms de la Rhénanie* (Metz: The Centre, 1975).

109. Box 6N72, Fonds Clemenceau, War Ministry Archives, Vincennes. See also McDougall, "French Rhineland Policy," p. 44, for the Foreign Ministry's similar attitude.

110. Foreign Ministry to principal embassies, Nov. 26, 1918, Box 6N72, Fonds Clemenceau, War Ministry Archives, Vincennes.

111. Foch to Clemenceau, Jan. 3, 1919, Pichon to Foch, Jan. 11, 1919, Tirard report of Jan. 31, Foch to Clemenceau, Feb. 8, 1919, Jeanneney to Foch, March 15, 1919, and Pichon to Foch, March 11, 1919; lengthy extracts from these documents are quoted in Bariéty, "De l'exécution," pp. 47–59.

112. Bariéty, "De l'exécution," pp. 56, 60–81.

113. *Ibid.,* p. 64.

114. Tirard to Briand, Aug. 31, 1921, quoting a letter of Tirard's of Oct. 29, 1919, AE, Rive Gauche du Rhin, 4.

115. Tirard to Pétain, Jan. 2, 1919, Series "Armée du Rhin," Box 30, War Ministry archives, Vincennes (Provisional classification); Tirard report for 1920, Jan. 12, 1921, AE, Rive Gauche du Rhin, 3; Tirard, "Note sur la question rhénane," Tirard to Briand, Aug. 24, 1921 and Aug. 31, 1921, AE, Rive Gauche du Rhin, 4; Tirard to Briand, Dec. 20, 1921, and Jan. 2, 1922, and Tirard report for 1921, Jan. 19, 1922, AE, Rive Gauche du Rhin, 5.

116. Bariéty. "De l'execution," pp. 64–65: Georges Wormser, *La République de Clemenceau* (Paris: Presses Universitaires de France, 1961), pp. 343–45, 504–7 (for the minutes of Jeanneney's interview with Mangin).

117. Testimony of July 17, 1919, pp. 50, 113–14, box C7773, Archives Nationales, Paris.

118. See Degoutte's memorandum of February 1920, quoted in François André Paoli, *L'Armée française de 1919 à 1939,* 2:220.

119. Degoutte to Weygand (Foch's chief of staff), Feb. 24, 1921, in Gen Degouette, *L'Occupation de la Ruhr* (Dusseldorf, 1924), Annex no. 3. A limited number of copies of this secret 633-page report were published; over 3000 pages of annexed documents provide extremely valuable material. It is available in the library of the War Ministry archives at Vincennes. Henceforth it will be cited as "Degoutte report."

120. Degoutte to Maginot (War Minister), May 2, 1922, AE, Ruhr, 3.

121. Degoutte to Foch and Maginot, "Note au sujet de l'occupation de la Ruhr," June 1, 1922, Degoutte report, Pièces annexes, p. 106. Emphasis in original.

122. McDougall, "French Rhineland Policy," esp. p. 114.

123. The quotation is from Tirard's report on April 24, 1919, cited in Bariéty, "De l'execution," p. 63.

124. Tirard, "Note sur les conditions d'application de l'accord de Paris en ce qui concerne la sanction intéressant les territoires occupés" and his "Note personnel pour M. le Président du Conseil," both of Feb. 10, 1921, AE, Ruhr, 1.

125. Tirard annual report for 1921, Jan. 19, 1922, AE, Rive Gauche du Rhin, 5.

126. Tirard to Briand, Aug. 31, 1921, p. 10, AE, Rive Gauche du Rhin, 4.

127. Tirard report of 1921, Jan. 19, 1922, p. 5, AE, Rive Gauche du Rhin, 5; Lasteyrie, "Les accords de Wiesbaden" (see n.17 above).

128. Tirard to Briand, April 4, 1921, and Foch note of April 12, 1921, AE, Ruhr, 1; Tirard note "relative aux nouvelles mésures à prévoir," April 18, 1921, AE, Relations Commerciales, 68.

129. "Projet de l'occupation de la région industriel de la Ruhr," April 22, 1921, AE, Relations Commerciales, 68.

130. AE, Relations Commerciales, 68, *passim.*

131. Poincaré, *A la recherche de la paix 1919*, pp. 184, 294–95, 319.

132. Chambre, *Documents*, Session extraordinaire de 1921, p. 442.

133. Degoutte report, p. 25.

134. Degoutte to Maginot, May 2, 1922, and Degoutte's "Rapport sur les modalitiés d'exploitation de la Ruhr," AE, Relations Commerciales, 69; Degoutte's "Note au sujet de l'occupation de la Ruhr," June 1, 1922, Degoutte report, Pièces annexes, pp. 98–106.

135. "Conversation entre M. Lloyd George et le Maréchal Foch," Dec. 1, 1918, 6N72, Fonds Clemenceau, War Ministry Archives, Vincennes.

136. Degoutte to Foch et al., May 19, 1922, AE, Relations Commerciales, 69.

137. Le Trocquer to Poincaré, July 26, 1922, AE, Relations Commerciales, 69.

138. Coste memorandum, "Etudes entreprises en mai 1922 en vue de l'occupation éventuelle de la Ruhr," June 15, 1922, AE, Relations Commerciales, 69; notes of August 9 interministerial committee, *ibid.,* for quotation about the Saar coal.

139. Coste to Degoutte, March 5, 1923, AE, Relations Commerciales, 147.

140. Coste memorandum cited in n. 138 above, pp. 1, 14.

141. Bariéty, "De l'exécution," pp. 87, 137, 148–51.

142. Poincaré to Foch, July 12, 1922, AE, Relations Commerciales, 69.

143. Minutes of August 9 meeting, AE, Relations Commerciales, 69.

144. Lasteyrie, "Les Accords de Wiesbaden" (see n.17 above), p. 32.

145. Lasteyrie to Poincaré, Aug. 24, 1922, AE, Relations Commerciales, 69.

146. "Opération de la Ruhr," Dec. 24, 1922 (notes of discussions among high officials), AE, Millerand Papers, 24.

147. Seydoux note, Nov. 21, 1922, AE, Millerand Papers, 24.

148. Seydoux note, Feb. 16, 1923, AE, Millerand Papers, 25.

149. Seydoux note, Dec. 2, 1922, AE, Millerand Papers, 24.

150. Note of Feb. 16, 1923, AE, Millerand Papers, 25.

151. AE, Relations Commerciales, 141.

152. Note of Dec. 23, 1922, AE, Relations Commerciales, 141.

153. *Ibid.*

154. Tirard to Briand, April 4, 1921, AE, Millerand Papers, 17. His representative on the Ruhr committee made a similar point about the Rhenish mark in December 1922: see Ruhr committee minutes, Dec. 22, 1922, AE, Relations Commerciales, 141.

155. *Doc. rel. aux rep.,* 2:116–17; Etienne Weill-Raynal, *Les Réparations allemandes et la France,* 2:239.

156. Weill-Raynal, 2:233–38; Poincairé to Margerie, Sept. 14, 1922, Jaunez to Poincaré, Sept. 16, 1922, Margerie to Poincaré, Sept. 19 and Sept. 20, 1922, Poincaré to Margerie, Sept. 20, 1922, AE, Allemagne, 475.

157. Niemeyer to Bradbury, Sept. 27, 1922, FO 371/7485/C14129.

158. Bradbury to Baldwin (Chancellor of the Exchequer), Nov. 11, 1922, FO 408/8/C16250.

159. *Doc. rel. aux rep.,* 2:120–29.

160. Seydoux note of October 12, 1922, and "Réunion tenue chez M. le Président du Conseil, le 13 octobre 1922," AE, Millerand Papers, 23.

161. "Réunion tenue chez M. le Président du Conseil, le 17 octobre 1922" AE, Millerand Papers, 23. Poincaré was right that Bradbury's position had shifted. Bradbury's view, according to the minutes of an August 28 meeting of British ministers, was that the "only

chance of keeping Germany going was an unconditional moratorium with control of her finances by foreign advisors appointed by the Reparation Commission from impartial sources'' (FO 371/7984/C12866).

162. *Doc. rel. aux rep.*, 2:145–49.

163. Poincaré to Margerie, Oct. 14, 1922, AE, Millerand Papers, 23.

164. Barrère to Poincaré, Jan. 8, 1923, AE, Millerand Papers, 25.

165. Steed to Saint-Aulaire, Oct. 20, 1922, and Saint-Aulaire to Poincaré, October 21, 1922, AE, Millerand Papers, 23.

166. Saint-Aulaire to Poincaré, Dec. 27, 1922, AE, Allemagne, 477.

167. Cmd. 1812 of 1923, pp. 34, 35, 77.

168. Cmd. 1812 of 1923, p. 141.

169. Foreign Office memorandum, Nov. 23, 1922, FO 408/8/C16157; Saint-Aulaire to Poincaré, Dec. 24, 1922, AE, Allemagne, 477, reporting the ambassador's interview with Bonar Law, and Crowe memorandum of the same meeting, Dec. 22, 1922, enclosed in Curzon to Phipps, Dec. 27, 1922, FO 371/7491/C17594.

170. See Saint-Aulaire to Poincaré, Nov. 1, 1922, AE, Allemagne, 476.

171. Poincaré to Saint-Aulaire, Nov. 11, 1922, AE, Allemagne, 476.

172. Saint-Aulaire to Poincaré, Nov. 12, 1922, AE, Grande-Bretagne, 50. Although Saint-Aulaire had actually toned down Poincaré's instructions in his interview with Curzon, Poincaré reprimanded his ambassador for being unduly provocative—one indication among many of a streak of pettiness and irritability in Poincaré's personality. See *ibid.*, Poincaré to Saint-Aulaire, Nov. 15, 1922.

173. *Ibid.*, Poincaré to French delegation, Lausanne, Jan. 5, 1923.

174. Boyden to Hughes, Oct. 14, 1922, Hughes to Boyden, Oct. 17, 1922, Herrick to Hughes, Oct. 23, 1922, Hughes memorandum on interview with Jusserand, Nov. 7, 1922, AHA speech, FRUS, 1922, 1:168ff., 175, 200.

175. See, for example, Cab 23/32/69, Dec. 7, 1922.

176. Weill-Raynal, *Les Réparations*, 2:256–60; *Demande de moratorium*, pp. 7–22.

177. The best study of Cuno's policy is Hermann-Josef Rupieper's dissertation, "Cuno Government and Reparations." See also Alfred Cornebise, "Cuno, Germany and the Coming of the Ruhr Occupation," pp. 502–31, and the introduction to the volume on Cuno in the Akten der Reichskanzlei series. On the continuity of policy, see Rupieper, pp. 74, 78.

178. Note of Nov. 21, 1922, AE, Millerand Papers, 24.

179. Seydoux project of Dec. 2, 1922, "Reparations," Dec. 4, 1922 (notes of Dec. 3 meeting), and "réunion tenue le 3 décembre 1922," AE, Millerand Papers, 24.

180. "Memorandum on British Policy in Germany," n.a., Nov. 23, 1922, FO 408/8/C16157.

181. Cmd. 1812 of 1923, pp. 35, 38.

182. Cmd. 1812 of 1923, pp. 51–52, 55–56.

183. Diary entry for Dec. 12, 1922, quoted in Stephen Roskill, *Hankey:Man of Secrets*, 2:326–27.

184. Cmd. 1812 of 1923, pp. 57–59.

185. *Ibid.*, pp. 48–49.

186. "Réparations," Dec. 4, 1922 (notes of Dec. 3 meeting), AE, Millerand Papers, 24.

187. "Réparations," Dec. 7, 1922, AE, Millerand Papers, 24.

188. Hardinge to Curzon, Dec. 14, 1922, FO 408/8/C17198.

189. "Opération de la Ruhr," Dec. 24, 1922, AE, Millerand Papers, 24.

190. Memorandum by Crowe, Dec. 24, 1922, enclosed in Curzon to Phipps, Dec. 27, 1922, FO 408/8/C17594.

191. "Opération de la Ruhr," Dec. 24, 1922, AE, Millerand Papers, 24.

192. *Ibid.* Note also the handwritten document entitled "Réparations," Dec. 25, 1922,

apparently written by Millerand's assistant Vignon (AE, Millerand Papers, 24). The author had asked Peretti, a high Foreign Ministry official, what the result of the December 24 meeting had been. Peretti had complained that the proposals of the finance and public works ministries were "deplorably vague—they do not know what they want." They had been given eight days to get things in order. "I then asked," the author wrote, "what instructions they were given. Peretti appeared astonished. I said, 'but what exactly is wanted? He answered, 'but M. Poincaré has constantly repeated it in Parliament.' I objected: 'but he said he could not be precise in Parliament.' Peretti continued by saying that it was up to appropriate administrations to make their proposals."

193. "Opération de la Ruhr," Dec. 24, 1922, AE, Millerand Papers, 24.

194. See Reparation Commission Annex 1718a.

195. Degoutte report, pp. 52–53; Degoutte to Foch and Maginot, Nov. 26, 1922, and War Ministry to Dogoutte, Jan. 3, 1923, in Degoutte, report, Pièces annexes. For a map showing the Degoutte and Foch lines, see Armée du Rhin, box 82 (provisional classification), folder "Cartes et Graphiques," corquis no. 2, "Différents projets d'opérations sur le bassin."

196. Crowe memorandum, Dec. 24, 1922, enclosed in Curzon to Phipps, Dec. 27, 1922, FO 408/8/C17594.

197. Sen. François-Albert, "Chronique politique," *Revue politique et parlementaire,* Nov. 10, 1922, p. 325.

198. On Poincaré's hesitations, see Stephen A. Schuker, *The End of French Predominance in Europe,* p. 21.

199. Cmd. 1812 of 1923, pp. 95–101.

200. *Ibid.,* pp. 140–42.

201. *Ibid.,* p. 140.

202. *Ibid.,* pp. 114–19.

203. Crewe to Curzon, Jan. 3, 1923, FO 408/8/C238.

204. Cmd. 1812 of 1923, pp. 120–32, 188–93. The quotation is from p. 191.

205. *Ibid.,* pp. 191–92.

206. *Ibid.,* p. 122.

207. *Ibid.,* pp. 121, 140, 161, 193.

208. Seydoux note, Nov. 2, 1922, AE, Millerand Papers, 23; "Visite de l'Ambassadeur de l'Allemagne à M. de Peretti," Dec. 7, 1922, AE, Millerand Papers, 24; Cmd. 1812 of 1923, pp. 51–52; Rupieper, "Cuno Government and Reparations," pp. 124–26, 139–43.

209. The original version of the plan had been drafted by Stinnes (see Rupieper, p. 167). On these matters in general, see Rupieper, pp. 85–102, 150–75; Akten: Cuno, pp. 113–16; Cornebise, "Cuno, Germany, and the Coming of the Ruhr Occupation, p. 516; and Charles S. Maier, *Recasting Bourgeois Europe,* pp. 303–4.

8. The Ruhr Occupation of 1923

1. Jacques Bariéty, *Les Relations franco-allemandes,* p. 120.

2. In fact the engineers, at least at first, had to travel around the basin unarmed, with German drivers, and without military escort.

3. The text of the notification was published in *Le Temps* on Jan. 12, 1923.

4. For the texts, see *Le Temps,* Jan. 12 and 13, 1923.

5. "Note soumise à M. Poincaré," Jan. 18, 1923, and "Projet de lettre d'envoi de la Decision de la Commission des Reparations," n.d., AE, Millerand Papers, 25. The text of the plan was published in *Le Temps,* Jan. 27, 1923.

6. Chambre, *Débats,* Jan. 11, 1923, pp. 14–20.

7. Jean-Claude Favez, *Le Reich devant l'occupation franco-belge de la Ruhr en 1923*, p. 72.

8. Poincaré to Herbette (French ambassador in Belgium), Jan. 15, 1923, AE, Ruhr, 5.

9. Favez, *Le Reich*, pp. 72–75; *Le Temps*, Jan. 14, 15, 1923.

10. Poincaré to French ambassadors, Jan. 18, 1923, AE, Relations Commerciales, 142; Rhineland Commission ordinance 136, AE, Relations Commerciales, 143, f. 14. An extension of the occupation to Bochum was needed to provide enough coal tax revenue to pay for the coal the French wanted to buy; the occupation of the Dortmund zone would make possible an effective control of trade with unoccupied Germany, and thus prevent evasion of the payment of customs, since imports and exports could easily be diverted through the unoccupied area.

11. Degoutte to Maginot (War Minister), Jan. 22, 1923, Degoutte Report, PA 139; Degoutte Report, pp. 158, 206; Degoutte to Maginot, Jan. 19, 1922, AE, Relations Commerciales, 142.

12. Degoutte to Maginot, Jan. 19, 1923, AE, Relations Commerciales, 142.

13. Akten: Cuno, pp. 130–49; Rupieper "Politics and Economics: The Cuno Government and Reparations," p. 214.

14. Degoutte Report, p. 218.

15. *Ibid.*, pp. 143–45.

16. Degoutte to Maginot, Jan. 22, 1923, Degoutte Report, PA 139 and p. 159; Degoutte to Poincaré, Jan. 23, 1923, AE, Relations Commerciales, 143.

17. Degoutte Report, pp. 158, 206.

18. Jean-Claude Favez, *Le Reich devant l'occupation franco-belge de la Ruhr*, chaps. 6, 8 and 9; Rupieper, "Cuno Government and Reparations," pp. 210ff; Tirard to Poincaré, Jan. 25, 1923, AE, Relations Commerciales, 143; Degoutte Report, pp. 135ff.

19. On German monetary policy, see Kenneth Paul Jones, "Stresemann and the Diplomacy of the Ruhr Crisis, 1923–1924"; Charles S. Maier, *Recasting Bourgeois Europe*, pp. 367, 376–81; and Gerald Feldman, *Iron and Steel in the German Inflation, 1916–1923, passim,* esp. p. 390.

20. Akten: Cuno, Jan. 9, 1923, pp. 124, 126n.; Rupieper, "Cuno Government and Reparation," p. 210; Favez, *Le Reich, passim;* see Jones, "Stresemann," p. 42, for Cuno's approval of a sabotage program.

21. Jones, "Stresemann," p. 47.

22. See Etienne Weill-Raynal, *Les Réparations allemandes et la France,* 2:chap. 36. For the texts, see France, Ministère des Affaires Etrangères, *Documents diplomatiques. Documents relatifs aux notes allemandes des 2 mai et 5 juin sur les réparations* (Paris, 1923). On Keynes's role, see *The Collected Writings of John Maynard Keynes,* 18: *Activities 1922–1932. The End of Reparations,* chap. 3.

23. Favez, *Le Reich,* pp. 77–78; *Journal des Débats,* Jan. 26 and 27, 1923. See Marin to Poincaré, Jan. 29, 1923, AE, Relations Commerciales, 144, for the sharp protest of an important leader of the moderate right against the outcome of Thyssen's trial.

24. *Le Temps,* Feb. 2, 1923; Poincaré to Herbette, Jan. 29, 1923, AE, Relations Commerciales, f. 240.

25. Tirard to Poincaré, Jan. 23, 1923, AE, Relations Commerciales, 143.

26. Degoutte Report, p. 194, and Degoutte to Guillaume, Feb. 4, 1923, Degoutte Report, PA 247.

27. Degoutte Report, p. 196, p. 193; "Décisions prises au cours de la visite de M. Le Trocquer et du Général Weygand le 6 Février 1923," Degoutte Report, PA 267; Arrêté 48 of June 19, 1923, Degoutte Report, PA 674bis.

28. Maginot to Degoutte, Jan. 31, 1923, quoted at length in the Degoutte Report, p. 185. The idea of a threat to in effect flood the mines had been proposed by the Belgians a few days

earlier: "Visite de l'Ambassadeur de Belgique à M. de Peretti," Jan. 22, 1923, AE, Relations Commerciales, 143.

29. Degoutte to Maginot, Feb. 2, 1923, Degoutte Report, PA 238.

30. The quotation is from Degoutte to Guillaume, Feb. 4, 1923, Degoutte Report, PA 247. The policy of breaking German resistance by winning over the workers through a moderate policy had been laid down by Degoutte on the eve of the occupation, and had been reiterated frequently. See Armée du Rhin, "Instruction sur la conduite à tenir par les troupes en cas d'occupation de la RUHR," Jan. 10, 1923, Degoutte Report, PA 48: "En cas de mauvaise volonté ou de résistance de la part de la population, il faut dans toute la mesure du possible ne pas s'en prendre à la masse, mais à ses chefs ou meneurs; fonctionnaires, bourgmestres, présidents de syndicats, etc." See also Degoutte to Maginot, Jan. 30, 1923, AE, Relations Commerciales, 144: "Nous cherchons à briser la grève par mesures de rigueur contre les gros, de bienveillance vis à vis des petits."

31. Degoutte to Maginot, Feb. 2, 1923, Degoutte Report, PA 238, esp. p. 674; "Séance du 26 janvier," AE, Relations Commerciales, 143, esp. folio 182.

32. One key piece of evidence supporting this initial French view of German tactics was the *Deutsche Allgemeine Zeitung*'s call for "systematic sabotage" to drive the French "from one act of violence to another, never attaining her aims, getting poorer and increasingly hated in Germany and in the whole world" (quoted in Margerie to Poincaré, Jan. 15, 1923, AE, Relations Commerciales, 142, and in Favez, *Le Reich,* p. 109). This was viewed as important since this paper was controlled by Stinnes, and French officials generally viewed Stinnes as the dominant figure in Germany. There was other evidence: Ambassador Margerie's report from Berlin of January 11 ("la politique du pire visent à nous faire reculer devant la necessité de ruiner l'industrie allemande"; Margerie to Poincaré, Jan. 11, 1923, AE, Ruhr, 4), and the apparent attempt of the Reichsbank to create monetary chaos in the occupied areas by cutting off fresh supplies of money to its branches there (*Le Temps,* Jan. 20, 1923; *Journal des Débats,* Jan. 21, 1923). The assumption that Germany was deliberately trying to aggravate the economic situation in the occupied areas was reflected in reports in *Le Temps* and the *Journal des Débats,* the two most influential papers in France at the time, particularly on Jan. 20 and 21; it was only on Jan. 24 that the *Journal des Débats*'s correspondent reported that the Germans no longer seemed to be pursuing such a policy.

33. Especially on Jan. 21, 22 and 27, 1923.

34. Réunion au Quai d'Orsay, 13 Avril 1923," AE, Relations Commerciales, 148, f. 200, for the Bréaud quotation; Degoutte Report, pp. 228ff.; Poincaré to Tirard Feb. 11, 1923, AE, Relations Commerciales, 145.

35. The expulsions began in late January. At first only high officials were "evicted," but the numbers rapidly increased after the mass expulsion of ordinary railroad workers began on April 14. By April 4, Tirard reported, there had been 2,970 expulsions; by May 15, there were 8,532; by June 20, the figure was 16,368; by October 1, over 36,000 expulsions had been pronounced. Since whole families were expelled, the actual number of people forced to leave was much higher—about 135,000 by October 1. See Tirard to Poincaré, April 4, May 23, June 20 and Oct. 9, 1923, in AE, Relations Commerciales, 148, 149, 150.

36. Ordinance 205, AE, Rive Gauche du Rhin, 8.

37. On the fear that Germany was pursuing a "politique de pire," see n. 32 above. On the monetary question at this point, see in general the archives of the French High Commission in the Rhineland, fonds AJ⁹ at the Archives Nationales, Paris, carton AJ⁹3231, and especially in this carton Tirard to Lasteyrie (Minister of Finance), Jan. 20, 1923: "Vous voudrez bien remarquer qu'il s'agit là uniquement de monnaie allemande à répandre dans la proportion ou le marché local l'exige et qu'il ne s'agit en rien de la réforme monétaire qui reste le but de notre politique financière mais qu'on ne saurait, sans le compromettre, tenter à une epoque où le mark

subit lui-même de si importantes variations." See also Tirard to Poincaré, Jan. 26, 1923, and Coste to Seydoux, Jan. 28, 1923, AE, Relations Commerciales, 143; Tirard to Poincaré, Nov. 27, 1923, AE, Relations Commerciales, 268, for a retrospective history of the monetary affair; Tirard to Lasteyrie, Jan. 20, 1923, Tirard to Poincaré, Jan. 11, 1923, Tannery (of the Ministry of Finance) to Lasteyrie, Jan. 26, 1923, in Ministry of Finance Archives, fonds F^{30}, carton F^{30}1360, in the Ministry of Finance, Paris.

38. Seydoux memorandum, Feb. 16, 1923, AE, Millerand Papers, 25; Poincaré to Reibel, Feb. 12, 1923, *ibid.;* Tirard to Lasteyrie, Jan. 20, 1923, AJ^{9}3231.

39. Thus activity in this area lacked real direction. See "Compte-rendu pour Monsieur Tirard," n.s. (Giscard?), Feb. 1, 1923: "En ce qui concerne la question monétaire, on continue de tourner en rond sans aboutir à aucun résultat" (AJ^{9}3231). At the end of March, the Ministry of Finance was asked to study economic and financial aspects of the creation of a new Rhenish state. This of course included the monetary question. Poincaré was at first very eager for its response; the terms of the questionnaire addressed to the Ministry of Finance leave little doubt that he favored an active policy in this area. But then on April 5 he suddenly ordered the studies suspended. See Serrigny to Moreau-Néret, March 26, 1923, enclosing the questionnaire and stressing Poincaré's great interest, and Serrigny to Moreau-Néret, April 5, 1923, in F^{30}1276, dossier "Rhénanie. Constitution de l'état rhénan." See further discussion in chapter 8.

40. See the Degoutte Report, pp. 207–8, quoting Poincaré to Degoutte, March 4, 1923, and citing Le Trocquer to Deguotte, Feb. 25, 1923.

41. Degoutte Report, pp. 326, 387–93.

42. See esp. his speech of May 24, Chambre, *Débats,* May 24, 1923, esp. p. 2102. Cf. Tardieu's speech of May 29, Chambre, *Débats,* May 29, 1923, pp. 2185ff.

43. Degoutte Report, pp. 327, 333–39; Chambre,*Débats,* May 24, 1923, p. 2101.

44. Sen. François-Albert, "Chronique politique," *Revue politique et parlementaire* (April 10, 1923), 115:129–30.

45. Herbette to Poincaré, Jan. 18, 1923, and "Visite de l'Ambassadeur de Belgique à M. de Peretti," Jan. 22, 1923, AE, Relations Commerciales, 142, 143.

46. On fears of a boycott, see the report of a Franco-Belgian commission on the monetary question, issued early in the occupation (no date, no title, but printed), p. 11, and the draft of the Ministry of Finance's reply to the questionnaire mentioned in n.39, both in F^{30}1276, dossier "Rhénanie. Constitution de l'état rhénan."

47. Seydoux, "Note pour le Président du Conseil," Aug. 6, 1923, AE, Relations Commerciales, 150; Vignon, "Conversation avec Seydoux," May 13, 1923, AE, Millerand Papers, 26.

48. Poincaré to Degoutte, June 18, 1923, Millerand Papers, 27. The idea was also in the air at the beginning of the occupation. See the *Journal des Débats,* Jan. 29, 1923.

49. Degoutte to Maginot, July 4, 1923, quoted in Degoutte Report, p. 298.

50. Tirard to Lasteyrie, Jan. 20, 1923, F^{30}1360.

51. See, for example, Degoutte's report of September 9, 1923, in Degoutte Report, *Rapports politiques.*

52. Degoutte to Foch and Maginot, June 1, 1922, Degoutte Report, Pièces Annexes, p. 106.

53. Degoutte Report, Pièces Annexes, *Rapports politiques,* reports of March 20, July 5, July 11, Aug. 29 and Sept. 9, 1923.

54. Thus the emphasis on bringing in local bankers: see AE, Relations Commerciales, 268 (Banque d'Emission en Rhénanie), *passim;* "Plan d'action monétaire en pays occupe," n.s., Sept. 24, 1923, F^{30}1276, dossier "Rhénanie. Constitution de l'état rhénan."

55. Millerand Papers, 25. Seydoux is identified as the author on f. 156. See also his project of April 12, 1923, *ibid.* The idea about the Rhenish railroads had wide appeal in the French government. Le Trocquer, Minister of Public Works, endorsed it on March 31, saying: "He

who controls the railroads controls the whole area.'' The notion had an important effect on the decision to create the Régie, and Poincaré endorsed it as a French aim on June 10. See Poincaré to Saint-Aulaire, June 10, 1923, published in France, Ministère des Affaires Etrangères, *Documents Diplomatiques. Documents relatifs aux notes allemandes des 2 mai at 5 juin sur les réparations* (Paris, 1923), p. 36. On the link with the Régie, see for example Seydoux's note of June 1, 1923, AE, Millerand Papers, 26.

56. ''Réunion du comité interministeriel du 6 mars 1923,'' AE, Millerand Papers, 25; ''Négociations éventuelles avec l'Allemagne,'' n.s., March 10, 1923, *ibid.* For a further elaboration of these ideas, see Seydoux's ''Projet d'accord'' of April 12, 1923, *ibid.*

57. Seydoux note of Feb. 16, 1923, esp. ff. 148, 151–155; Seydoux, ''Note pour le Président du Conseil,'' March 26, 1923, f. 211 Seydoux, ''Projet d'accord,'' April 12, 1923, esp. ff. 260, 265. All in AE, Millerand Papers, 25.

58. Loucheur, ''Note,'' April 10, 1923, AE, Relations Commerciales, 335. For an account of the Loucheur affair, see Rupieper, ''Cuno Government and Reparations,'' p. 268; McDougall, ''French Rhineland Policy,'' p. 274ff.; and Jones, ''Stresemann,'' p. 56.

59. Poincaré to Saint-Aulaire, April 14, 1923, AE, Millerand Papers, 25.

60. Serrigny to Moreau-Néret, March 26 and April 5, 1923, and draft of answer (n.d.), F^{30}1276, dossier ''Rhénanie. Constitution de l'état rhénan.'' The minutes of the March 24 meeting of the Conseil Supérieur de la Défense Nationale are not preserved in the War Ministry archives in Vincennes, or so it appears. The CSDN minutes for the period are in the box CSDN Q20-Q23, but the series jumps from December 1922 to June 1923. On the questionnaire see also Rupieper, ''Cuno Government and Reparations,'' pp. 251–52, and Ludwig Zimmermann, *Frankreichs Ruhrpolitik von Versailles bis zum Dawesplan* p. 165.

61. Draft reply in F^{30}1276, dossier ''Rhénanie, Constitution de l'état rhénan''; Lasteyrie to Poincaré, June 1, 1923, F^{30}1428; Giscard (?), ''Compte-Rendu pour M. Tirard,'' Aug. 29, 1923, AJ^{9}3231.

62. Seydoux of course incorporated plans for a Rhenish entity into his memoranda, but my impression is that he had adopted these proposals essentially for reasons of bureaucratic politics, and that he attached greater weight to broader diplomatic considerations. A private letter to Margerie cited by the latter's biographer shows Seydoux's alienation from the real partisans of a Rhenish policy in Paris: Bernard Auffray, *Pierre de Margerie (1861–1942) et la vie diplomatique de son temps,* p. 428.

63. Saint-Aulaire to Poincaré, Jan. 17, 1923, AE, Relations Commerciales, 142; and in general AE, Millerand Papers, 26–29, *passim,* and AE, Grande-Bretagne, 50–51, *passim.* Many of the principal documents were published at the time: France, Ministère des Affaires Etrangères, *Documents diplomatiques. Documents relatifs aux notes allemandes des 2 mai et 5 juin sur les reparations (2 mai-3 août 1923)* (Paris, 1923).

64. France, Ministère des Affaires Etrangères, *Documents diplomatiques. Réponse du Gouvernement Français à la lettre du Gouvernement Britannique du 11 août 1923 sur les réparations (20 août 1923)* (Paris, 1923).

65. Quoted in Margerie to Poincaré, Aug. 13, 1923, AE, Relations Commerciales, 343.

66. On domestic developments, see Sen. François-Albert's Chronique politique in the *Revue politique et parlementaire,* July 10, 1923, and Edouard Bonnefous, *Histoire politique de la Troisième Republique,* 3:371-6. For an early sign of a developing split with Belgium, see ''Conversation de M. de Peretti avec l'Ambassadeur de Belgique,'' June 29, 1923, AE, Millerand Papers, 27. The emerging conflict with Belgium can be followed in subsequent volumes of the Millerand Papers. The situation became particularly critical in September when the Belgians tried to engage in talks with the German government. Poincaré had his ambassador in Brussels make the following sharp declaration: ''Nous demandons catégoriquement à la Belgique de cesser elle-même toute conversation. C'est à nos yeux une question d'alliance et de loyauté. Voilà trois semaines qu'on nous promet d'en finir et qu'on revient perpetuellement à la

charge. Nous *refusons de la façon la plus formelle* la proposition belge et ne voulons accepter *aucune* entente avec l'Allemagne sur la cessation de la résistance. . . . Si la Belgique persiste dans ses prétentions—contraires aux récentes déclarations de M. Theunis—nous serons forcés de la désavouer expressément. La question est vitale pur nous et aucune transaction n'est possible'' (Poincaré to Herbette, Sept. 24, 1923, AE, Ruhr, 29; emphasis in original).

67. Jones, "Stresemann," p. 93; Favez, *Le Reich,* p. 321; Feldman, *Iron and Steel,* p. 396.

68. Margerie to Poincaré, Aug. 17 and Aug. 24, 1923; Tirard to Poincaré, Aug. 31, 1923, relaying Stresemann's offer to send Schacht to Paris for talks, AE, Ruhr, 27; L'Aumonier Inspecteur, Armée du Rhin, "Entretien avec M. et Mme. Krupp von Bohlen à la prison de Dusseldorf, le 30 août 1923,'' Sept. 1, 1923, AE, Allemagne, 387.

69. Margerie to Poincaré, Sept. 1 and Sept. 5, 1923, AE, Ruhr, 28.

70. "Nous ne pourrons pas nous entendre avec le Gouvernment allemand tant que les ordonnances n'auront pas ete rapportées'' (Poincaré to Margerie, Sept. 1, 1923, AE, Ruhr, 28); "Précisez nettement à M. Stresemann que nous ne pouvons ouvrir ces négociations que lorsque les ordonnances et decrets auront été retirés'' (Poincaré to Margerie, Sept. 6, 1923, *ibid.*). It is hard to imagine how Poincaré could have been more explicit on this point.

71. Margerie to Poincaré, Sept. 20, 1923 (tel. 1235), and Poincaré to Margerie, Sept. 21, 1923 (tel. 742), AE, Rohr, 29.

72. See Margerie to Hermite, September 29, 1923, AE, Relations Commerciales, 347; Auffray, *Pierre de Margerie,* pp. 431–32.

73. Margerie to Poincaré, Sept. 27, 1923, Poincaré to Herbette, Sept. 27, 1923, Poincaré to Margerie, Sept. 27, 1923, Poincaré to Degoutte et al., Sept. 28, 1923, AE, Ruhr, 29; Poincaré to Saint-Aulaire, October 6, 1923, AE, Millerand Papers, 31; Poincaré to Herbette, October 10, 1923, AE, Ruhr, 30. That this was a shift from the earlier French position is clear also from Poincaré to Herbette, April 30, 1923, AE, Relations Commerciales, 336: "La cessation de la résistance ne doit pas être confondue d'ailleurs avec la reprise des prestations, qui decoulera des négociations et ne saurait les précéder.''

74. Margerie to Poincaré, Dec. 11, 1923, Poincaré to Margerie, Dec. 12, 1923, Poincaré to Herbette, Dec. 16, 1923, AE, Relations Commerciales, 348.

75. R. Poincaré, "Récit historique,'' in Georges Suarez, *Une Nuit chez Cromwell* (Paris: Editions de France, 1930), lxxiv-lxxv.

76. Poincaré to Herbette, Sept. 5, 1923, AE, Ruhr, 28.

77. Poincaré to Saint-Aulaire, October 18, 1923, AE, Ruhr, 31.

78. See in this connection "Conversation avec Peretti,'' June 15, 1923, AE, Millerand Papers, 27: to avoid leaks, Peretti, the Political Director at the Quai d'Orsay, urged that as much business as possible should be transacted verbally, "sans remise de papiers.'' See also the document quoted in Bariéty, *Les Relations franco-allemandes,* p. 254. Poincaré's remark about "disaggregation'' is quoted in Denise Artaud, "A propos de l'occupation de la Ruhr,'' *Revue d'histoire moderne et contemporaine* (Jan.-Mar. 1970), 17:19.

79. "Conversation avec Seydoux et avec Laroche,'' n.s. but almost certainly by Vignon, Nov. 7, 1923, Millerand Papers, Bibliotheque Nationale, carton 71. See also Seydoux to Margerie, Sept. 1, 1923: "On est ici assez influencé dans le sens de la République rhénane. Je crois que c'est une illusion; mais je me trompe peut-ètre . . .'' (quoted in Auffray, *Pierre de Margerie,* p. 428).

80. Thomas to Poincaré and Thomas to Millerand, both October 12, 1923, and Millerand to Thomas, October 15, 1923, Millerand Papers, Bibliothèque Nationale, carton 69.

81. "Conversation avec Seydoux,'' Vignon, Nov. 5, 1923, AE, Millerand Papers, 32. The underlying idea was the "Il faut que l'Allemagne passe par une crise pour etre mâtée et être préte à traiter'' (Vignon's paraphrase of Seydoux, in Vignon, "Conversation avec Seydoux et avec Laroche,'' Nov. 7, 1923, Millerand Papers, Bibliotheque Nationale, carton 71).

82. Extract from Degoutte "Note," Aug. 29, 1923, Degoutte Report, *Rapports politiques,* p. 47. Some of the passages quoted were underlined in the original.

83. On these events, see Bariéty, *Les Relations franco-allemandes,* p. 254 and McDougall, "French Rhineland Policy," pp. 320–26. For an example of official contempt for the separatists, see Degoutte's notes of Sept. 9 and Nov. 20, 1923, Degoutte Report, *Rapports politiques.*

84. "Note pour le président du conseil," n.s., Feb. 5, 1923, AE, Relations Commerciales, 144; Margerie to Poincaré, Feb. 22, 1923, AE, Relations Commerciales, 146; Seydoux, "Note pour le président du conseil, " March 15, 1923, and Genoyer to AE, March 16, 1923, and Poincaré to Genoyer, 18 III, AE, Relations Commerciales, 334 (for Schacht and Wolff overtures and Poincaré's response); Poincaré to Tirard, March 18, 1923, AJ⁹ 3296, for Poincaré's refusal to engage in talks with the industrialists.

85. On the Gladbeck talks see Degoutte Report, pp. 409–14, summarizing PA's 727, 738, 748; 780 and 810.

86. Degoutte Report, pp. 409–14; Poincaré's instructions of Aug. 20 are quoted extensively on pp. 412–14; "Note au sujet de la réunion qui eut lieu le 30 juillet au cantonnement de Gladbeck," n.a., n.d., Degoutte Report, PA 738; "Compte Rendu spécial des renseignements," n.d., Aug. 4, 1923, Degoutte Report, PA 748; (Seydoux), "Note pour le président du conseil," Aug. 6, 1923, AE, Relations Commerciales, 150.

87. Degoutte Report, p. 294.

88. Denvignes to Degoutte, Aug. 1, 1923, Degoutte Report, PA 741.

89. Denvignes to Degoutte, Aug. 6, 1923, Degoutte Report, PA 752.

90. *Ibid.*

91. Denvignes to Degoutte, Aug. 13, 1923, Degoutte Report, PA 768; Compte-rendu du chef du 2ᵉ Bureau, Aug. 14, 1923, Degoutte Report, PA 772; Degoutte to Poincaré, Aug. 15, 1923, Degoutte Report, PA 778.

92. Denvignes to Degoutte, Aug. 17, 1923, Degoutte Report, PA 786. There is a different account of the meeting in Stresemann's papers: Wolff told the Chancellor that he had taken a fairly hard line with Denvignes. But Wolff had an obvious interest in establishing his patriotism, especially since he was about to recommend to Stresemann that the German government take the lead in setting up a Rhenish state. No similar motive for distorting what had actually been said can be attributed to Denvignes, and it is Denvignes's account which best corresponds to the rest of the evidence on the affair in French sources, much of which will be summarized here. See Gustav Stresemann, *Vermächtnis: der Nachlass in drei Bänden,* ed. H. Bernhard (Berlin: Ullstein 1932), 1:94–95, summarized in Feldman, *Iron and Steel* pp. 395–96.

93. Chef du 2ᵉ Bureau (Lt. Col. Dumont), "Compte-Rendu N. 4 d'un entretien ayant lieu le 16 Août 1923 avec Monsieur von Metzen," Aug. 17, 1923, Degoutte Report, PA 767. In this document, the banker is called "Monsieur X." He is identified as Griess in Dumont's "Compte-Rendu No. 6," Aug. 24, 1923, Degoutte Report, PA 806, and in the Degoutte Report, p. 417.

94. Denvignes to Degoutte, Aug. 17, 1923, Degoutte Report, PA 786.

95. Degoutte to Poincaré, Aug. 18, 1923, quoted in Degoutte Report, pp. 420–23.

96. Poincaré to Degoutte, Aug. 25, 1923, Degoutte Report, p. 423.

97. Poincaré to Degoutte, Aug. 25, 1923, Degoutte Report, p. 424 and PA 811; also in AE, Relations Commerciales, 344.

98. Margerie to Poincaré, Sept. 1 and Sept. 5, 1923, AE, Ruhr, 28.

99. Degoutte to Poincaré, Sept. 21, 1923, and Poincaré to major embassies and Tirard, Sept. 21, 1923, AE, Ruhr, 29; Margerie to Poincaré, Sept. 23, 1923, AE, Relations Commerciales, 346, for Margerie's skeptical reaction to Degoutte's ideas.

100. Denvignes to Degoutte, Aug. 13, 1923, Degoutte Report, PA 768, p. 1974.

101. Degoutte Report, p. 422.

102. Degoutte, "Note," Sept. 9, 1923, Degoutte Report, *Rapports politiques,* p. 57.

103. Poincaré to Herbette, Sept. 24, 1923, AE, Ruhr, 29.

104. "Plan d'action monétaire en pays occupé," n.s., Sept. 24, 1923, and Lasteyrie to Poincaré, Sept. 28, 1923, F³⁰1276, dossier "Rhénanie. Constitution de l'état rhénan." Attending the meeting (among others) were: de Moüy (director of the Mouvement Général des Fonds and thus the highest permanent official at the Ministry of Finance), Tirard, and Bréaud.

105. (Vignon), "Conversation avec Seydoux," 23 November 1923, AE, Millerand Papers, 32.

106. AE, Relations Commerciales, 268.

107. "Note Seydoux," Sept. 29, 1923, AE, Relations Commerciales, 353; (Seydoux) "Note," Oct. 9, 1923, AE, Millerand Papers, 31; Hoschiller, "Note pour la présidence du conseil," Oct. 29, 1923, AE, Relations Commerciales, 352.

108. Hoschiller, "Note pour la présidence du conseil," Nov. 25, 1923, AE, Millerand Papers, 32.

109. The best account of this whole affair is found in Karl Dietrich Erdmann, *Adenauer in der Rheinlandpolitik nach dem Ersten Weltkrieg,* pp. 79–106, 121–35, esp. pp. 128, 132, 138–39. On the Moldenhauer plan, see *ibid.,* pp. 145, 314. See also Charles S. Maier, *Recasting Bourgeois Europe,* pp. 394–395, Bariéty, *Les Relations franco-allemande,* pp. 240, 255–61, 278–81, and K. P. Jones, "Stresemann, the Ruhr Crisis and Rhenish Separatism: A Case Study of *Westpolitik,*" *European Studies Review* (1977), 7:311–40.

110. On the economic councils: Degoutte to Poincaré, Nov. 11, 1923, Degoutte Report, PA 1068, and Degoutte "Note," Dec. 22, 1923, Degoutte Report, *Rapports politiques.* See also (Seydoux), "Note pour le président du conseil," Nov. 6, 1923, AE, Relations Commerciales, 151. For Lasteyrie's opposition: Lasteyrie to Poincaré, Nov. 12, 1923, AE, Relations Commerciales, 157 (f. 168).

111. Erdmann, *Adenauer in der Rheinlandpolitik,* pp. 145, 314.

112. Poincaré to Tirard, Nov. 21, 1923, and Tirard to Poincaré, Nov. 27, 1923, AE, Relations Commerciales, 268.

113. Poincaré to Degoutte, Oct. 8, 1923, Degoutte Report, PA 918; Seydoux in Sept. 27 minutes of the Comité restreint, AE, Relations Commerciales, 157.

114. Lasteyrie to Poincaré, Jan. 30, 1924, AE, Relations Commerciales, 268.

115. Degoutte Report, *Rapports politiques.*

116. Degoutte Report, pp. 455–470.

117. (Seydoux), "Visite de M. Frick à M. Seydoux," Oct. 15, 1923, AE, Millerand Papers, 31.

118. Lasteyrie to Poincaré, Oct. 23, 1923, AE, Relations Commerciales, 209; Poincaré to Degoutte, Nov. 20, 1923, AE, Millerand Papers, 32.

119. (Seydoux), "Note pour le président du conseil," Nov. 9, 1923, and Poincaré to Degoutte, Nov. 13, 1923, AE, Millerand Papers, 32. On Seydoux's earlier haste to conclude, see, for example, (Degoutte) "Note," Nov. 7, 1923, Degoutte Report, PA 1044.

120. Poincaré to Degoutte, Nov. 13, 1923, AE, Millerand Papers, 32; Degoutte Report, p. 488.

121. Poincaré to Degoutte, Nov. 15, 1923, Degoutte Report, PA 1086. See also Degoutte Report, pp. 494–98, and PA 1095, 1098 and 1078.

122. Poincaré to Tirard, Nov. 20, 1923, AE, Millerand Papers, 32.

123. *Ibid.* Poincaré to Degoutte, Nov. 20, 1923.

124. AE, Relations Commerciales, 209; *passim.*

125. Degoutte Report, pp. 499–501; (Seydoux) "Note pour le président du conseil," Nov. 21, 1923, AE, Millerand Papers, 32.

126. Already on November 25 Wolff, whose good intentions toward France were not in question, said that he was at the end of his tether, and his books were open if the French

authorities wanted to verify this (Hoschiller, "Note pour la présidence du conseil," Nov. 25, 1923, AE, Millerand Papers, 32). For a scathing Ministry of Finance critique of the MICUM agreements, see Mouvement Général des Fonds, Section d'Allemagne, "Note pour le Ministre," Dec. 14, 1923, F^{30}1428. One quotation suffices to convey the tone of this document: the MICUM system "n'a d'autre mérite que d'être une improvisation; elle ne paraît soutenable ni en logique ni en fait."

127. For example, Poincaré to Saint-Aulaire, March 21, 1923, AE, Relations Commerciales, 334.

128. Seydoux Note, Feb. 16, 1923, AE, Millerand Papers, 25; Loucheur Note, April 10, 1923, AE, Relations Commerciales, 335; Lasteyrie to Poincaré, May 31, 1923, AE, Millerand Papers, 26. There are many other examples.

129. Poincaré to Saint-Aulaire, May 1, 1923, AE, Millerand Papers, vol. 26; Poincaré to Saint-Aulaire, May 4, 1923, in *Documents relatifs aux notes allemandes*, p. 14.

130. *Documents relatifs aux notes allemandes*, pp. 31, 65.

131. Poincaré to Saint-Aulaire, May 5, 1923, AE, Millerand Papers, 26. The most striking example of this British attitude was reported by the French ambassador in London at the end of July. Even if the British could get Germany to capitulate unconditionally, Lord Curzon said, she would not do it because "it would not be fair" (English in original; Saint-Aulaire to Poincaré, July 31, 1923, AE, Millerand Papers, 29).

132. Poincaré to Saint-Aulaire, May 6, 1923, AE, Millerand Papers, 25.

133. Seydoux note, June 4, 1923, AE, Millerand Papers, 26; Poincaré to Saint-Aulaire, July 9, 1923, *Documents relatifs aux notes allemandes*, p. 63.

134. Poincaré to Jusserand, Oct. 15, 1923, AE, Millerand Papers, 31.

135. Hughes to Whitehouse, Oct. 25, 1923, FRUS 1923, 2:83–84.

136. E. Weill-Raynal, *Les Réparations allemandes* 2:493ff.; Curzon to Crewe, Oct. 19, 1923, with Poincaré's attached comments, AE, Millerand Papers, 31, ff. 190–191.

137. Poincaré to major posts, Oct. 27, Oct. 31 and Nov. 3, 1923, Poincaré to Laboulaye, Nov. 2, 1923, Poincaré to Jusserand, Nov. 6, 1923, Poincaré to Barthou, Nov. 6 and Nov. 10, 1923, AE, Millerand Papers, 32.

138. (Vignon), "Conversation avec Seydoux," Nov. 5, 1923, AE, Millerand Papers, 32.

139. Laboulaye to Poincaré, Oct. 23, 1923, AE, Millerand Papers, 31; Hughes to Whitehouse, Oct. 24, 1923, FRUS, 1923, 2:79–83.

140. Thus, for example, he asked Degoutte not to conclude any agreements with the industrialists without Reparation Commission approval, but when Degoutte pointed out that these were just provisional accords he allowed him to go ahead. Poincaré to Degoutte, Oct. 9, 1923, and Degoutte to Poincaré, Oct. 12, 1923, Degoutte Report, PA 919 and 936. On the other hand, he was initially opposed to allowing the British to participate in a committee governing the sale of seized metallurgical products: "Il est tout à fait inutile d'y mêler les Britanniques qui n'ont fait que nous gêner dans notre action depuis 9 mois." But Saint-Aulaire convinced him that letting the British take part would be a good idea, and he changed his mind a few days later. Poincaré to Herbette, Oct. 19 and 24, 1923, AE, Ruhr, 31.

141. For Curzon's hostility to France, see the passage from his speech to the Imperial Conference in October 1923 quoted in Thomas Jones, *Whitehall Diary*, 1:247–48. On Bonar Law's attitude, see, for example, Saint-Aulaire to Poincaré, Jan. 17, 1923, AE, Grande-Bretagne, 50. On Baldwin, see the minutes of his meeting with Poincaré in September 1923: "Notes prises au cours d'une conversation privée entre M. Poincaré, Président du Conseil, et M. Baldwin, Premier Ministre de la Grande-Bretagne, à l'ambassade d'Angleterre à Paris, le 19 septembre 1923," AE, Millerand Papers, 31. On the Rhenish question, Tirard reported that Lord Kilmarnock, his British counterpart, had indicated that his government wanted to be represented in the Régie; another French official claimed that Kilmarnock was in contact with a separatist group, and that the British were willing to do what they could to help it. Tirard to

Poincaré, Oct. 13, 1923, AE, Ruhr, 30; Paul Valot to Poincaré, Aug. 21, 1923, AE, Relations Commerciales, 353.

142. Hughes memoranda of May 3 and June 7, 1923, FRUS, 1923, 2:60–65.

143. (Vignon), "Emprunt en Amérique. Premières Réflexions de Seydoux," December 27, 1923, AE, Millerand Papers, 33.

Appendix

1. There is an excellent analysis of this dispute in Jacob Viner, *Studies in the Theory of International Trade* (New York: Harper, 1937), pp. 307–11.

2. Quoted in Bertil Ohlin, "On the Slow Development of the 'Total Demand' Idea in Economic Theory: Reflections in Connection with Dr. Oppenheimer's Note," *Journal of Economic Literature* (September 1974), 12(3):891.

3. *Ibid.*, p. 890.

4. The conditions for stability in terms of supply and demand elasticities are worked out in Robert M. Stern, *The Balance of Payments: Theory and Economic Policy* (Chicago: Aldine, 1973), pp. 62–67.

5. This was stressed by Fritz Machlup in his *International Payments, Debts and Gold* (New York: Scribner, 1964), e.g., p. 430. This assumption about elasticity was made explicitly by Keynes in his 1929 *Economic Journal* article.

6. G. H. Orcutt, "Measurement of Price Elasticities in International Trade," *Review of Economics and Statistics* (May 1950), 32:117–32. For a discussion of the literature on this point, see Stern, *Balance of Payments,* pp. 148–49.

Sources
and Bibliography

Archival Sources

The French archives were the most important source for this study. But it is only for the period after the beginning of 1921 that the French sources seem to be relatively complete. For the earlier period, it was apparently largely a matter of chance whether or not even important files were preserved. Clemenceau had his own private papers destroyed, and the archives of such important ministries for my purposes as Industrial Reconsitituion and Liberated Regions are nowhere to be found. Part of the Loucheur Papers have also been lost. It was necessary to piece together the elements of the story from a variety of spotty sources, and even so certain questions had to be left unresolved—the question, for example, of the industrial talks scheduled with the Germans at the very end of Clemenceau's tenure in office. Finally, in France there were no official minutes of cabinet meetings, and it was considered bad form for ministers to keep even their own personal records of what took place in the cabinet. The following were the principal sources used:

Archives of the French Ministry of Commerce, fonds F^{12}, Archives Nationales, Paris. Valuable primarily for the period before the armistice.

Archives of the French Ministry of Finance, fonds F^{30}, consulted at the Ministry of Finance, Paris.

Archives of the French Delegation to the Reparation Commision, fonds AJ^5, Archives Nationales, Paris.

Archives of the French Ministry of Foreign Affairs, Ministry of Foreign Affairs, Paris.
   (a) Series "Guerre 1914–1918."
   (b) Series "Paix." This covered up to the end of 1920, but most of it was lost during World War II.
   (c) Series "Europe 1918–1929," subseries "Allemagne," "Grande-Bretagne," "Ruhr" and "Rive Gauche du Rhin."
   (d) Series "Relations Commerciales."
   (e) Papiers d'Agents: Millerand Papers, Laurent Papers, Tardieu Papers (for the period of his mission to America).

Archives of the French Ministry of War, Service Historique de l'Armée, Vincennes.
   (a) Fonds Clemenceau. A detailed inventory has been published: France, Ministère d'état chargé de la Défense Nationale, Etat-Major de l'Armée de Terre, Service Historique, *Inventaire sommaire des archives de la Guerre. Serie N, 1872–1919,* by Jean-Claude Devos et al. (Troyes: La Renaissance, 1974).
   (b) Armée du Rhin archives. This collection was still being classified when I used it. The chief item of interest is the Degoutte Report; there is also a copy in the library of the War Ministry archives at Vincennes:
      General Degoutte, *L'Occupation de la Ruhr* (Dusseldrof, 1924). Only a hundred copies of this secret, 633-page report were published; over 3,000 pages of annexed documents—the Pièces Annexes, or PA—provide fundamental source material.

Louis Lucien Klotz Papers, Bibliothèque de Documentation Internationale Contemporaine, Nanterre. Little of interest for my purposes; useful mainly for its collection of transcripts of peace conference commission meetings, which fill certain important gaps in Lapradelle.

Louis Loucheur Papers, Hoover Institution, Stanford University. The main item of interest, Loucheur's diary, has been published.

Raymond Poincaré Papers, Bibliothèque Nationale, Paris. Poincaré's diary for 1919, the most interesting part of this collection, has also been published recently.

André Tardieu Papers, 324 AP, Archives Nationales, Paris. Valuable mainly for Tardieu's unpublished correspondence with Poincaré in 1920.

Alexandre Millerand Papers, Bibliothèque Nationale, Paris. A more personal collection than the one in the Foreign Ministry archives.

   The British archives were also exceptionally rich. Many of the most important collection for this study have either been published or microfilmed and are readily accessible to American readers.

Records of the Cabinet Office, Public Record Office, London. The cabinet minutes (Cab 23) for this period are available on microfilm at a number of locations; I used the collection at the University of California Library in Berkeley. I was also able to consult cabinet memoranda (Cab 24) and certain other cabinet sources at the Stanford University Library—records, including minutes, of international conferences (Cab 29) and records of cabinet committees (Cab 21, Cab 27). The Public Record Office has published a brief but useful survey of this source: *The Records of the Cabinet Office to 1922* (London: Her Majesty's Stationery Office, 1966), PRO Handbook No. 11. More detailed guides to the Cabinet Office papers covering the Lloyd George period have also appeared: List and Index Society *Lists,* volumes 40, 51, 61, 62, 92 and 100 for the cabinet minutes, and volumes 29, 41 and 52 for the cabinet memoranda from 1919 (London: Swift for the Society, 1967–1974).

Records of the Foreign Office, Public Record Office, London: Political Correspondence (FO 371). Most of the important documents have been published in *Documents on British Foreign Policy*. In addition, many of the relevant volumes of FO 371 have been microfilmed and are available at the Widener Library at Harvard University. The Widener Library also has microfilms of FO 408, the "Confidential Print" for Germany, a selection of the most important documents. Fortunately, a very detailed index to FO 371 has been published: Great Britain, Foreign Office, *Index to the Political Correspondence of the Foreign Office* (Nendeln, Liechtenstein: Kraus-Thomson, 1969). This index, however, only gives the file number for each document. To find the volume in FO 371 in which a particular document is located, it is necessary to consult a book which gives the concordance between file and volume numbers: Public Record Office, *Lists and Indexes:* Supplementary Series, no. 13, *List of Foreign Office Records,* vol. 10: *General Correspondence (Political) 1914–1929* (New York: Kraus Reprint Co., 1970). For convenience, in citations I have omitted the file number and have given the volume number in FO 371 directly. There is also a valuable guide to the whole Foreign Office collection: Public Record Office, *The Records of the Foreign Office, 1782–1939* (London: HMSO, 1969), PRO Handbook no. 13.

David Lloyd George Papers and Andrew Bonar Law Papers, Beaverbrook Foundation, House of Lords Record Office, London. A catalogue with abstracts of the Lloyd George Papers can be consulted in the Library of Congress Manuscript Room.

Compared to the British and French collections, the official American sources at the National Archives in Washington were something of a disappointment. The really significant American material was in the private collections, and much of this has been published: Burnett drew his documents mainly from the John Foster Dulles papers (now at the Firestone Library in Princeton), and much of the interesting material in the Hoover Papers at the Hoover Institution was published by Bane and Lutz in their two documentary collections, cited below in the bibliography. But the following archival collections were also useful:

Edward House Papers, Sterling Library, Yale University. Includes the multivolume House Diary, portions of which have been published in Seymour's *Intimate Papers of Colonel House.*

Bernard Baruch Papers, Firestone Library, Princeton University.

Edwin Gay Papers, Hoover Institutions, Stanford University.

Vance McCormick Diary, Hoover Institution, Stanford University.

Norman Davis Papers, Library of Congress, Washington.

The German sources are very extensive, and I made no attempt to exploit them exhaustively. The most important sources have been microfilmed and are available in the United States.

Records of the German Chancellery and Foreign Office, United States National Archives Microfilm Publication T-120. There are complete copies at the National Archives in Washington and at the Center for Research Libraries in Chicago; the Center lends out its microfilm to member institutions through interlibrary loan. A relatively complete list of holdings in U.S. libraries has been published in J.S. Conway, *German Historical Source Material in United States Universities* (Pittsburgh: Council for European Studies, 1973). There are two essential guides to this source: American Historical Association, Committee for the Study of War Documents, *A Catalogue of Files and Microfilms of the German Foreign Ministry Archives, 1867–1920* (Oxford: Oxford University Press, 1959) and George O. Kent, *A Catalogue of Files and Microfilms of the German Foreign Ministry Archives, 1920–1945*, 4 vols. (Stanford: Hoover Institutions, 1962–72). These give the "serial numbers" corresponding to each volume of documents; a "National Archives Supplement" at the end of the Kent volumes tells which reels in T-120 correspond to the different serials. For the convenience of American readers, I used T-120 reel numbers in the notes. Unfortunately, reel numbers were assigned arbitrarily, and only the serial and frame numbers are the same in different depositories. For those working in the original archives now in Bonn, the "Aktenzeichen" and volume number would be the most convenient reference. Here therefore is a table establishing the concordance between reel, serial and archival references, limited to those sources actually used:

Reel No.	Serial	Aktenzeichen	Contents
1. Auswärtiges Amt, 1919			
2069–70	4121	WK Nr. 31, vols. 9–11	Die Friedenskonferenz in Versailles
2403–04	4662	Deutsche Friedensdelegation in Versailles, Pol. 4	Geheime Vermittlungsaktionen und Agententätigkeit
2. Auswärtiges Amt, 1920 and after			
1309	2368	RM6, vol. 1	England
1328	2406	RM7, vol. 1	Frankreich
1634–35	3375	RM5a, vols. 1–2	Genf-Brüssel
1642–43	3243	RM5, vols. 1, 2, 4; RM4a	Reparationsfragen; Spa—Allgemeines
4512	K945	Abt. II, Geheim Akten, vol. 1	Geheim Akten

5352	L1492	Abt. Wirt. II, Frankreich, Industrie 3, vol. 1	Industrielle Beziehungen Frankreich zu Deutschland
3483	9155	W Rep 3, vols. 1, 2, 5	Die Konferenz in Brüssel . . .
3485	9156	W Rep 2, vols. 1, 3, 5, 8	Die Vorbereitung der Konferenzen in Genf und Brüssel
4509	K938	W Rep 8 Nr 10, vol. 1	Wiederaufbau: Frankreich
5160	K1780	W Rep 8 Nr 3A, vols. 1, 2	Organisation der Sachleistungen— Vorschläge Seydoux
5461	K1779	W Rep Nr 10, vol. 1	Wiederaufbau: Allgemeine
5585	K2196	W Rep 2, vol. 8	Vorbereitungen der Konferenzen in Genf
	K2198	W Rep 3, vols. 2, 6	und Brüssel; Die Konferenz in Brüssel
5561	K2125	Handakten 16	Handakten Simson

3. Alte Reichskanzlei

1666–68	3438	R Min 2b, vols. 3–5, 16	Sitzungen des Reichsministeriums (Protokolle)
3679	9523	AA 4	Ausführung des Friedensvertrags

Finally, there are the records of the Reparation Commission itself; this was mildly useful at certain points in the study:

Archives of the Reparation Commission, fonds AJ[6], Archives Nationales, Paris. The Commission's minutes and annexes are at the Hoover Institution, in the Baruch Papers at Princeton, and at various other locations.

Published Collections of Documents, Books, Articles, Dissertations

There is an enormous literature on the reparation question, much of it of rather limited value. For the older literature, the interested reader can turn to the bibliographies by Curth, Sveistrup and Bloch; the bibliographic footnotes in Weill-Raynal's massive study may also be useful. For the more recent literature, see the bibliographies in the works by Maier, Schuker, Krüger and McDougall. All these books are cited in the list that follows.

There seemed little point in including here a lengthy list of works on the subject. Instead this bibliography is essentially limited to material cited more than once in the text; the basic aim is to help the reader locate the work in question.

Akten der Reichskanzlei Weimarer Republik. Karl Dietrich Erdmann; W. Mommsen; H. Booms; and W. Vogel; gen. eds.

  Das Kabinett Scheidemann, ed. Hagen Schultze. Boppard am Rhein: Boldt, 1971.

  Das Kabinett Müller I, ed. Martin Vogt. Boppard am Rhein: Boldt, 1971.

  Das Kabinett Fehrenbach, ed. Peter Wulf. Boppard am Rhein: Boldt, 1972.

Das Kabinett Wirth I und II, ed. Ingrid Schulze-Bidlingmaier. Boppard am Rhein: Boldt, 1973.

Das Kabinett Cuno, ed. Karl-Heinz Harbeck. Boppard am Rhein: Boldt, 1968.

Das Kabinett Stresemann I und II, ed. Karl Dietrich Erdmann and Martin Vogt. Boppard am Rhein: Boldt, 1978.

Auffray, Bernard. *Pierre de Margerie (1861–1942) et la vie diplomatique de son temps.* Paris: C. Klincksieck, 1976.

Baker, Ray Stannard. *Woodrow Wilson and World Settlement.* 3 vols. Garden City, N.Y.: Doubleday, 1922.

Bane, Suda L., and Ralph H. Lutz, eds. *The Blockade of Germany after the Armistice, 1918–1919.* Stanford: Stanford University Press, 1942.

Bane, Suda L. and Ralph H. Lutz, eds. *Organization of American Relief in Europe, 1918–1919.* Stanford: Stanford University Press, 1943.

Bariéty, Jacques. "Le rôle de la minette dans la sidérurgie allemande et la restructuration de la sidérurgie allemande après le traité de Versailles." Centre de Recherches Relations Internationales de l'Université de Metz, *Travaux et Recherches* (1972): 233–77.

Bariéty, Jacques. "De l'exécution à la négociation: l'évolution des relations franco-allemandes après la première guerre mondiale." Doctorat d'état thesis, University of Paris, 1975.

Bariéty, Jacques. *Les Relations franco-allemandes après la première guerre mondiale.* Paris: Editions Pedone, 1977.

Beaverbrook, William Maxwell Aitken, Lord. *Men and Power, 1917–1918.* New York: Duell, Sloan & Pearce, 1957.

Bergmann, Carl. *The History of Reparations.* London: Benn, 1927.

Bloch, Camille. *Bibliographie méthodique de l'histoire économique et sociale de la France pendant la guerre.* Paris: Presses Universitaires de France, 1925.

Bonnefous, Edouard. *Histoire politique de la Troisieme Republique.* vol. 3. Paris: Presses Universitaires de France, 1959.

Bournazel, Renata. *Rapallo, naissance d'un mythe: la politique de la peur dans la France du Bloc National.* Paris: Fondation nationale des science politiques, 1974.

Bresciani-Turroni, Costantino. *The Economics of Inflation: A Study of Currency Depreciation in Post-War Germany.* London: Allen & Unwin, 1937.

Bunselmeyer, Robert. "The Cost of the War: British Plans for Postwar Economic Treatment of Germany, 1914–1918." Ph.D. dissertation, Yale University, 1969.

Bunselmeyer, Robert, *The Cost of the War, 1914–1919: British Economic War Aims and the Origins of Reparation.* Hamden, Conn.: Archon Books, 1975.

Burnett, Philip Mason, ed. *Reparation at the Paris Peace Conference from the Standpoint of the American Delegation.* 2 vols. New York: Columbia University Press, 1940.

Calmette, Germain, ed. *Recueil de documents sur l'histoire de la question des réparations, 1919–5 mai 1921*. Paris: Costes, 1924.

Clémentel, Etienne. *La France et la politique économique interalliée*. Paris: Presses Universitaires de France, 1931.

Combined Annual Reports of the World War Foreign Debt Commission. Washington: Government Printing Office, 1927.

Conférence de la Paix. *Recueil des Actes de la Conférence*. 28 vols. in 8 parts. Paris: Imprimerie Nationale, 1922–35. Copies exist at the Bibliothèque de Documentation Internationale Contemporaine and at the Hoover Institution, which has also published a microfilm edition.

Cornebise, Alfred. "Cuno, Germany and the Coming of the Ruhr Occupation: A Study in German-West European Relations." *Proceedings of the American Philosophical Society* (1972): 502–31.

Curth, Hermann. *Bibliographie zum wirtschaftlichen Problem der deutschen Reparationen*. Jena, 1925–26.

D'Abernon, Edgar Vincent, Lord. *The Diary of an Ambassador*. 2 vols. Garden City, N.Y.: Doubleday, Doran, 1929–30.

Les Déliberations du Conseil des Quatre (24 mars–28 juin 1919): notes de l'officier interprète Paul Mantoux. 2 vols. Paris: Editions du Centre National de la Recherche Scientifique, 1955.

Erdmann, Karl Dietrich. *Adenauer in der Rheinlandpolitik nach dem Ersten Weltkrieg*. Stuttgart: Ernst Klett Verlag, 1966.

Favez, Jean-Claude. *Le Reich devant l'occupation franco-belge de la Ruhr en 1923*. Geneva: Librairie Droz, 1969.

Feldman, Gerald. *Iron and Steel in the German Inflation, 1916–1923*. Princeton: Princeton University Press, 1977.

Felix, David. *Walther Rathenau and the Weimar Republic: The Politics of Reparations*. Baltimore: Johns Hopkins Press, 1971.

France. *Journal officiel de la République française*. Includes parliamentary documents, transcripts of parliamentary debates, records of votes, and other official documents.

France, Ministère des Affaires Etrangères. *Documents relatifs aux négociations concernant les garanties de securité contre une agression de l'Allemagne*. Paris: Imprimerie Nationale, 1924.

France, Ministère des Affaires Etrangères. *Documents relatifs aux réparations*. 2 vols. Paris: Imprimerie Nationale, 1922–24.

France. Ministère des Affaires Etrangères. *Documents diplomatiques: Demande de moratorium du gouvernement allemand à la Commission des Réparations (14 Novembre 1922). Conférence de Londres (9–11 Décembre 1922). Conférence de Paris (2–4 Janvier 1923)*. Paris: Imprimerie Nationale, 1923.

Furst, Gaston, *De Versailles aux Experts*. Nancy, Paris, Strasbourg: Berger, 1927.

Great Britain, Foreign Office. *Documents on British Foreign Policy 1919–1939*. First Series. London: Her Majesty's Stationery Office, 1947–

Great Britain, Parliament. *Accounts and Papers.*
> 1921 Session, vol. 43, "Protocols and correspondence between the Supreme Council and the Conference of Ambassadors and the German Government and the German Peace Delegation between January 10, 1920, and July 17, 1920, respecting the Execution of the Treaty of Versailles of June 28, 1919" (Cmd. 1325).
> 1923 Session, vol. 24, "Inter-Allied Conferences on Reparations and Inter-Allied Debts, held in London and Paris, December 1922 and January 1923. Reports and Secretaries' Notes of Conversations" (Cmd. 1812).
> 1924 Session, vol. 26, "Papers respecting Negotiations for an Anglo-French Pact" (Cmd. 2169).
> 1924 Session, vol. 27, "Minutes of the London Conference on Reparations, August 1922" (Cmd. 2258).

Great Britain. *Parliamentary Debates* (House of Commons).

House, Edward M., and Charles Seymour, eds. *What Really Happened at Paris.* New York: Scribner, 1921.

Jeanneney, Jean-Noel. *François de Wendel en république: l'argent et le pouvoir, 1914–1940.* Paris: Seuil, 1976.

Johnson, Elizabeth, ed. *The Collected Writings of John Maynard Keynes.* London and New York: Cambridge University Press and Macmillan, 1971–
> Vol. 16. *Activities 1914–1919: The Treasury and Versailles.*
> Vol. 17. *Activities 1920–1922: Treaty Revision and Reconstruction.*
> Vol. 18. *Activities 1922–32: The End of Reparations.*

Jones, Kenneth Paul. "Stresemann and the Diplomacy of the Ruhr Crisis, 1923–1924." Ph.D. dissertation, University of Wisconsin, 1970.

Jones, Thomas. *Whitehall Diary.* Edited by Keith Middlemas. 3 vols. London and New York: Oxford University Press, 1969–1971.

Keynes, John Maynard. *The Economic Consequences of the Peace.* London: Macmillan, 1920.

Keynes, John Maynard. *A Revision of the Treaty.* New York: Harcourt, Brace, 1922.

Klotz, Louis Lucien. *De la guerre à la paix: souvenirs et documents.* Paris: Payot, 1924.

Krüger, Peter. *Deutschland und die Reparationen 1918/19.* Stuttgart: Verlags-Anstalt, 1973.

Lapradelle, Albert Geouffre de, ed. *La Paix de Versailles.* La Documentation internationale, vol. 4: "La Commission de réparations des dommages." Paris: Les Editions internationales, 1932.

Laubach, Ernst. *Die Politik der Kabinette Wirth 1921/22.* Lubeck and Hamburg: Mathiesen, 1968.

Lloyd George, David. *Memoirs of the Peace Conference.* 2 vols. New Haven: Yale University Press, 1939.

Loucheur, Louis. *Carnets secrets, 1908–1932.* Edited by Jacques de Launay. Brussels and Paris: Brepola, 1962.

McDougall, Walter. "French Rhineland Policy and the Struggle for European Stabilization: Reparations, Security and Rhenish Separatism, 1918–1924." Ph.D. dissertation, University of Chicago, 1974.

McDougall, Walter. *France's Rhineland Diplomacy, 1914–1924: The Last Bid for a Balance of Power in Europe.* Princeton: Princeton University Press, 1978.

Maier, Charles S. *Recasting Bourgeois Europe: Stabilization in France, Germany and Italy in the Decade after World War I.* Princeton: Princeton University Press, 1975.

Mantoux, Etienne. *The Carthaginian Peace, or the Economic Consequences of Mr. Keynes.* Pittsburgh: University of Pittsburgh Press, 1965.

Marks, Sally. *The Illusion of Peace: International Relations in Europe, 1918–1933.* New York: St. Martin's Press, 1976.

Mayer, Arno. *Politics and Diplomacy of Peacemaking: Containment and Counterrevolution at Versailles, 1918–1919.* New York: Knopf, 1967.

Miquel, Pierre. *La Paix de Versailles et l'opinion publique française.* Paris: Flammarion, 1972.

Mitchell, Brian R. *European Historical Statistics, 1750–1970.* New York: Columbia University Press, 1975.

Mommsen, Hans; Dietmar Petzina; and Bernd Weisbrod, eds. *Industrielles System und politische Entwicklung in der Weimarer Republik.* Dusseldorf: Droste, 1974.

Nelson, Harold. *Land and Power: British and Allied Policy on Germany's Frontiers, 1916–19.* London: Routledge & Kegan Paul, 1963.

Paoli, François André. *L'Armée française de 1919 à 1939.* Paris: Service historique de l'armée, 1969.

Poincaré, Raymond. *A la recherche de la paix, 1919.* Paris: Plon, 1974.

Reparation Commission. *Official Documents.* Vols. 2, 3, 4, 5. London: His Majesty's Stationery Office, 1922–23.

Riddell, George A. Riddell, baron. *Lord Riddell's Intimate Diary of the Peace Conference and After, 1918–1923.* New York: Reynal & Hitchcock, 1934.

Roskill, Stephen. *Hankey: Man of Secrets.* 3 vols. London: Collins, 1970–74.

Rothwell, Victor H. *British War Aims and Peace Diplomacy, 1914–1918.* Oxford: Clarendon Press, 1971.

Rupieper, Hermann-Josef. "Politics and Economics: The Cuno Government and Reparations, 1922–1923." Ph.D. dissertation, Stanford University, 1974.

Salter, James Arthur. *Allied Shipping Control: An Experiment in International Administration.* Oxford: Clarendon Press, 1921.

Salter, James Arthur. *Slave of the Lamp: A Public Servant's Notebook.* London: Weidenfeld and Nicolson, 1967.

Schuker, Stephen A. *The End of French Predominance in Europe: The Financial Crisis of 1924 and the Adoption of the Dawes Plan.* Chapel Hill: University of North Carolina Press, 1976.

Schulkin, Carl. "Lost Opportunity: The Reparation Question and the Failure of the European Recovery Effort." Ph.D. dissertation, University of California, Berkeley, 1973.

Seydoux, Jacques. *De Versailles au Plan Young: réparations, dettes in-teralliées, reconstruction européenne.* Paris: Plon, 1932.

Seymour, Charles, ed. *The Intimate Papers of Colonel House.* 4 vols. Boston and New York: Houghton, 1926–28.

Soutou, Georges. "Der Einfluss der Schwerindustrie auf die Gestaltung der Frankreichpolitik Deutschlands 1919–1921." In *Industrielles System,* edited by H. Mommsen et al., pp. 543–63.

Soutou, Georges. "Problèmes concernant le rétablissement des relations écono-miques franco-allemandes aprés la premiére guerre mondiale." *Francia* (1974), 2:580–96.

Soutou, Georges. "Die deutschen Reparationen und das Seydoux-Projekt 1920/21," *Vierteljahrshefte für Zeitgeschichte* (1975), 23:237–70.

Suarez, Georges. *Briand: sa vie, son oeuvre, avec son journal et de nombreux documents inédits.* Paris: Plon, 1938ff.

Sveistrup, Hans. *Die Schuldenlast des Weltkrieges: Quellen- und Literatur-nachweis zu den Interalliierten Kriegsschulden, den Reparationen und dem Dawes-Plan.* Vol. 1. Berlin: Struppe und Winckler, 1929.

Tardieu, André. *La Paix.* Paris: Payot, 1921. English translation: *The Truth about the Treaty.* Indianapolis: Bobbs, 1921.

Tirard, Paul. *La France sur le Rhin: douze années d'occupation rhénane.* Paris: Plon, 1930.

Ullman, Richard. *The Anglo-Soviet Accord.* Vol. 3 of his *Anglo-Soviet Rela-tions, 1917–1921.* Princeton, N.J.,: Princeton University Press, 1972.

United States, Congress, Senate. *Loans to Foreign Governments.* 67th Con-gress, 2nd Session (1921–22), Sen. Doc. 86.

United States, Congress, Senate, Special Committee Investigating the Munitions Industry. *Hearings and Exhibits.* 74th Congress, 2nd Session.

United States, Department of State. *Papers Relating to the Foreign Relations of the United States* (for 1916–1923). Washington: Government Printing Of-fice, 1925–1938.

United States, Department of State. *Papers Relating to the Foreign Relations of the United States: The Paris Peace Conference.* 13 volumes. Washington: Government Printing Office, 1942–47.

Weill-Raynal, Etienne. *Les Réparations allemandes et la France.* 3 vols. Paris: Nouvelles Editions Latines, 1947.

Wilson, Woodrow. *Messages and Papers.* 2 vols. New York: Doran, 1924.

Wilson, Woodrow. *War and Peace: Presidential Messages, Addresses and Public Papers, 1917–1924.* Edited by Ray Stannard Baker and W. E. Dodd. 2 vols. New York: Harper, 1927.

Zimmermann, Ludwig. *Frankreichs Ruhrpolitik von Versailles bis zum Dawes-plan.* Edited by W. P. Fuchs. Göttingen: Musterschmidt, 1971.

Index